THE SECRET ROOMS

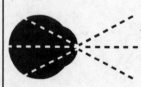

THE SECRET ROOMS

A TRUE STORY OF A HAUNTED CASTLE, A PLOTTING DUCHESS, AND A FAMILY SECRET

CATHERINE BAILEY

THORNDIKE PRESS

A part of Gale, Cengage Learning

GALE
CENGAGE Learning

Farmington Hills, Mich • San Francisco • New York • Waterville, Maine
Meriden, Conn • Mason, Ohio • Chicago

Copyright © 2012 by Catherine Bailey.
All the photographs are reproduced courtesy of His Grace, the Duke of Rutland with the following exceptions: 4, 15, 47, Konrad Gabriel; 48, Mrs. Robin Ravilious; 22, Bridgeman Art Library; 26, 37, Imperial War Museum; 27, 28, 33, Library of Congress; 30, Getty Images; 31, Julian F. Graham/Loon Hill Studios; 32, 34, from Richard Holmes, *The Little Field Marshal*; 36 from "The Long, Long Trail; www.1914-1918.net; 38, from Robert Franklin, *The Fringes of History: The Life and Times of Edward Stuart Worthley*; 39, from Rothesay Stuart Wortley, *Letters from a Flying Officer*.
Thorndike Press, a part of Gale, Cengage Learning.

LIBRARY OF CONGRESS CATALOGING-IN-PUBLICATION DATA

Bailey, Catherine, 1960–
    The secret rooms : a true story of a haunted castle, a plotting duchess, and a family secret / by Catherine Bailey. — Large print edition.
        pages cm. — (Thorndike Press large print peer picks)
    Originally published : New York, New York : Penguin Books, 2013.
    ISBN-13: 978-1-4104-6862-8 (hardcover)
    ISBN-10: 1-4104-6862-3 (hardcover)
    1. Rutland, John Henry Montagu Manners, Duke of, 1886–1940.
    2. Rutland, John Henry Montagu Manners, Duke of, 1886–1940—Family.
    3. Belvoir Castle (England)—History—20th century. 4. Nobility—Great Britain—Biography. 5. Great Britain. Army—Officers—Biography. 6. World War, 1914–1918—Great Britain—Biography. I. Title.
    DA574.R87B35 2014
    941.082092—dc23
    [B]   2013051112

Published in 2014 by arrangement with Penguin Books, a member of Penguin Group (USA) LLC, a Penguin Random House Company

Printed in the United States of America
1 2 3 4 5 6 7 18 17 16 15 14

For my mother

CONTENTS

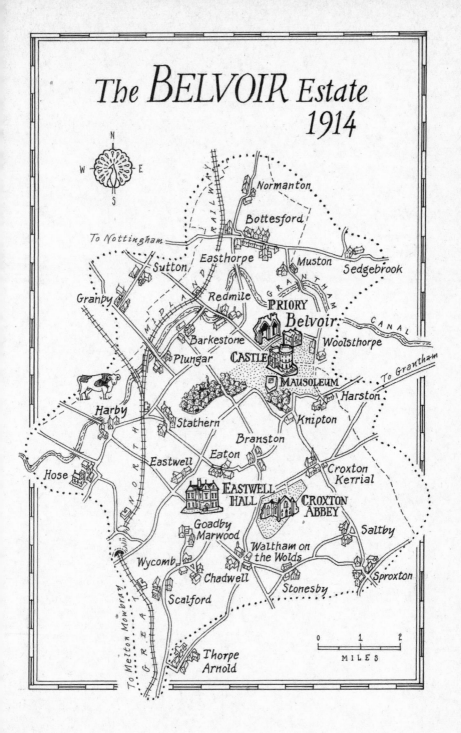

The BELVOIR Estate 1914

N
W — E
S

To Nottingham

Normanton
Bottesford
Easthorpe
Muston
Sedgebrook
Sutton
Granby
Redmile
PRIORY
Belvoir
Barkestone
CASTLE
Woolsthorpe
Plungar
MAUSOLEUM
Harston
Stathern
Knipton
Harby
Branston
Eastwell
Eaton
Croxton Kerrial
Hose
EASTWELL HALL
CROXTON ABBEY
Saltby
Goadby Marwood
Waltham on the Wolds
Wycomb
Sproxton
Chadwell
Stonesby
Scalford

To Melton Mowbray

Thorpe Arnold

RAILWAY
MIDLAND
GRANTHAM
CANAL
To Grantham
NORTH
GREAT

0   1   2
MILES

Belvoir Castle Layouts

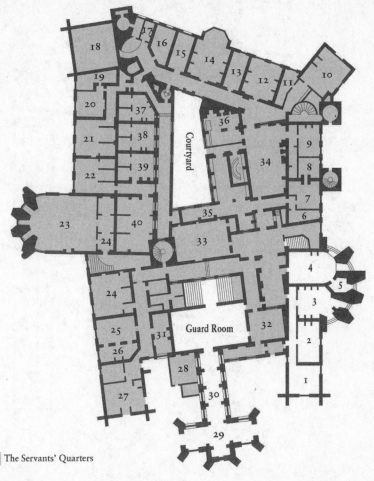

The Servants' Quarters

Fig 1. Belvoir Castle, Ground Floor

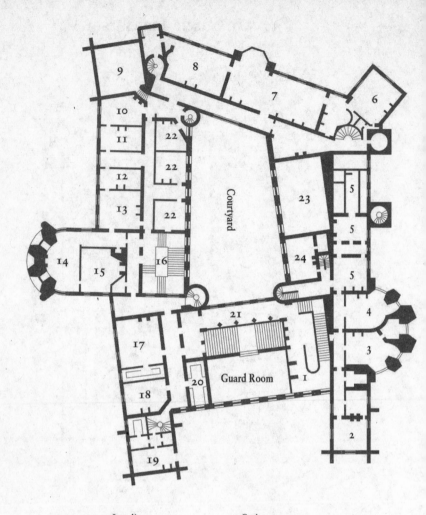

1   40-acre Landing
2   Night Nursery
3   Mr Gilkes's Bedroom
4   Schoolroom
5   Chapel
6   Tea Room
7   Drawing Room
8   Dining Room
9   Wine Cellar
10 Cellar Bedroom
11 Dressing Room
12 Dressing Room
13 Bedroom
14 Wellington Dressing Room
15 Wellington Bedroom
16 Ballroom Staircase
17 Tile Room
18 Still Room
19 Housekeeper's Bedroom
20 Linen Room
21 Carriage Landing
22 Marble Rooms
23 Kitchen
24 Bedroom

Fig 2. Belvoir Castle, First Floor

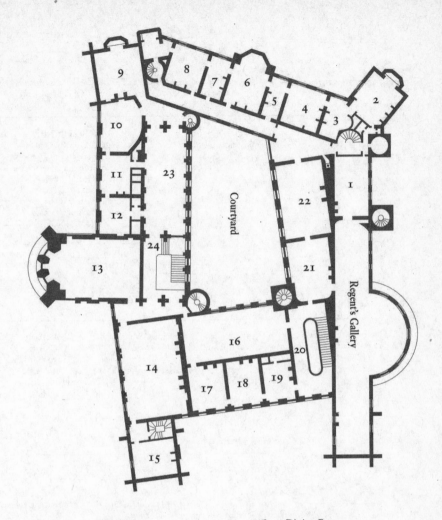

1 Chapel	14 State Dining Room
2 Bedroom	15 Fox Hunter's Dining Room
3 Anteroom	16 Picture Gallery
4 Bedroom	17 King's Sitting Room
5 Boudoir	18 King's Bedroom
6 Chintz Bedroom	19 King's Dressing Room
7, 8 Blue Rooms	20 Earl's Gallery
9 Tapestry Drawing Room	21, 22 Libraries
10, 11, 12 Chinese Rooms	23 Ballroom
13 Elizabeth Saloon	24 Ballroom Staircase

Fig 3. Belvoir Castle, Second Floor

Manners Family Tree

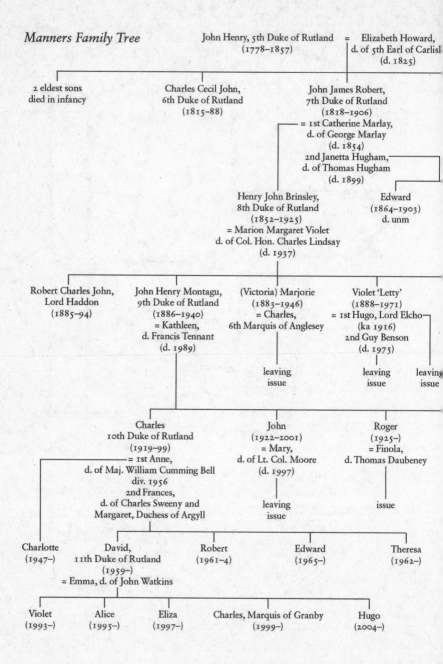

John Henry, 5th Duke of Rutland (1778–1857) = Elizabeth Howard, d. of 5th Earl of Carlisl (d. 1825)

2 eldest sons died in infancy

Charles Cecil John, 6th Duke of Rutland (1815–88)

John James Robert, 7th Duke of Rutland (1818–1906)
= 1st Catherine Marlay, d. of George Marlay (d. 1854)
2nd Janetta Hugham, d. of Thomas Hugham (d. 1899)

Henry John Brinsley, 8th Duke of Rutland (1852–1925)
= Marion Margaret Violet d. of Col. Hon. Charles Lindsay (d. 1937)

Edward (1864–1903) d. unm

Robert Charles John, Lord Haddon (1885–94)

John Henry Montagu, 9th Duke of Rutland (1886–1940)
= Kathleen, d. Francis Tennant (d. 1989)

(Victoria) Marjorie (1883–1946)
= Charles, 6th Marquis of Anglesey

leaving issue

Violet 'Letty' (1888–1971)
= 1st Hugo, Lord Elcho (ka 1916)
2nd Guy Benson (d. 1975)

leaving issue

leaving issue

Charles 10th Duke of Rutland (1919–99)
= 1st Anne, d. of Maj. William Cumming Bell div. 1956
2nd Frances, d. of Charles Sweeny and Margaret, Duchess of Argyll

John (1922–2001)
= Mary, d. of Lt. Col. Moore (d. 1997)

leaving issue

Roger (1925–)
= Finola, d. Thomas Daubeney

issue

Charlotte (1947–)

David, 11th Duke of Rutland (1959–)
= Emma, d. of John Watkins

Robert (1961–4)

Edward (1965–)

Theresa (1962–)

Violet (1993–)

Alice (1995–)

Eliza (1997–)

Charles, Marquis of Granby (1999–)

Hugo (2004–)

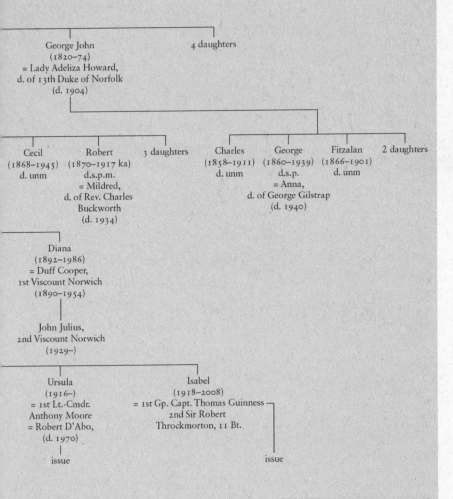

George John
(1820–74)
= Lady Adeliza Howard,
d. of 13th Duke of Norfolk
(d. 1904)

4 daughters

Cecil
(1868–1945)
d. unm

Robert
(1870–1917 ka)
d.s.p.m.
= Mildred,
d. of Rev. Charles
Buckworth
(d. 1934)

3 daughters

Charles
(1858–1911)
d. unm

George
(1860–1939)
d.s.p.
= Anna,
d. of George Gilstrap
(d. 1940)

Fitzalan
(1866–1901)
d. unm

2 daughters

Diana
(1892–1986)
= Duff Cooper,
1st Viscount Norwich
(1890–1954)

John Julius,
2nd Viscount Norwich
(1929–)

Ursula
(1916–)
= 1st Lt.-Cmdr.
Anthony Moore
= Robert D'Abo,
(d. 1970)

issue

Isabel
(1918–2008)
= 1st Gp. Capt. Thomas Guinness
2nd Sir Robert
Throckmorton, 11 Bt.

issue

d.s.p.	decessit sine prole (died without issue)
d.s.p.m.	decessit sine prole mascula (died without male issue)
d. unm	died unmarried
ka	killed in action

■ ■ ■ ■

PART I
18–27 APRIL 1940

■ ■ ■ ■

1

Two doctors were already at the castle; a third, Lord Dawson, Physician to King George VI, was expected. It was mid-morning on Thursday 18 April 1940 and they were gathered at the entrance to a suite of rooms. The door leading into them was made of polished steel; the colour of gunmetal, it was the type used to secure a walk-in safe.

The door was firmly closed.

The light from the dim bulbs along the windowless passage cast pools of inky shadows around the waiting figures. Piles of cardboard boxes were stacked against the bare stone walls. Marked 'Secret — Property of His Majesty's Government', they were secured with steel binding.

The doctors — Dr Jauch, a GP from Grantham, and Mr Macpherson, an eminent chest specialist — had been in and out of the rooms since dawn.

Shortly before eleven o'clock, the first footman, dressed in an azure tailcoat and navy-blue breeches, escorted Lord Dawson across the Guard Room. A coldly sumptuous hall, it was the first point of entry to the 356-room castle. Rows of muskets, taller than a man, and hundreds of swords, their blades sharp-edged and glinting, lined its walls. From the vaulted roof hung the tattered remnants of regimental colours, captured in battle. Directly in front of them, a magnificent staircase swept to the state rooms on the upper floors; and yet, as the footman led the King's doctor across the hall, he veered to the right, heading for its farthest corner. There, he ushered him through a discreet swing door. It marked the border between master and servant. They had stepped into the 'invisible world'.

Behind the Guard Room, the entire ground floor was devoted to the smooth running of the Duke's household. A gloomy hinterland of fifty rooms, some cavernous, some no larger than a priest's hole, it was where the servants lived and worked. From here, a network of passages coursed through the castle: hidden routes, which spiralled up the narrow turrets and towers to the splendid rooms above, enabling the servants to carry out their duties unobserved.

It was through this labyrinth of passages, deep in the servants' quarters, that the footman conducted Lord Dawson, arriving at the steel door where the other doctors stood waiting.

They were at Belvoir Castle in Leicestershire. Built in the Gothic style and situated on a ridge eight miles from Grantham, it belonged to John Henry Montagu Manners, the 9th Duke of Rutland. Aged fifty-three, he was one of the richest men in Britain. Three years earlier, he had carried the Sovereign's Sceptre at the coronation. His family had lived at Belvoir since the eleventh century. Looking south from the castle's Flag Tower, he owned the land as far as the eye could see.

Earlier that morning, the Duke's wife, Kakoo, had telephoned Lord Dawson. Her husband was desperately ill. He must come to the castle immediately.

2

Up in the Flag Tower, the clock struck eleven.
Ten minutes had passed since Lord Dawson's
arrival, but he had yet to be admitted to see
the Duke. The sounds of distant industry
drifted along the passageway: shouted orders;
the banging of tools; the clatter of footsteps
approaching on bare stone.

The sight of the King's doctor in the passage immediately caught the servants' attention.

'If there was something serious going on,
the housekeeper and the butler would try and
keep it quiet,' George Waudby, the third footman, recalled. 'They might talk together, but
they'd be tight-lipped in front of us lower
ranks. We were their inferiors. We were the
lowest of the low. We were never told anything. Everything we knew depended on what
we saw or overheard.'

'We all talked. We weren't meant to, but we
did,' said Dorothy Plowright, the daughter of
the boiler stoker. 'Every rank had its gossip:

the upstairs maids, the kitchen staff, the foot-men, they all had their grapevines.'

Until that morning, the servants' grapevine had had nothing to report. They had seen and heard very little. 'We knew the Duke was unwell. He had been ill for a week. But we didn't realize it was serious,' said George Waudby. 'We rarely saw the Duke. He spent all his time in his rooms. Every day, all day, he was in there. That had been the case for months. We knew this because they were in *our* quarters. Of course we had no idea what went on in there. Those rooms were absolutely secret. But we were told it was where the Duke worked. Nothing struck us as unusual. His routine hadn't changed. He had carried on working as normal.'

The servants had had no reason to believe the Duke's illness was life-threatening. Only two days previously, after spending the night at Belvoir, Lord Dawson had returned to London, satisfied that the Duke was on the mend. Before leaving the castle, he had is-sued a short statement to the press:

The Duke of Rutland is suffering from pneumonia at his home, Belvoir Castle, and is now stated to be making satisfactory progress. The Duke, who is 53 and suc-ceeded his father in 1925, was taken ill dur-ing last weekend.

That morning, however, the servants had reason to suspect that the Duke's condition had deteriorated. Shortly after breakfast, three mysterious-looking packages were delivered to the castle. From that moment, they were on tenterhooks.

The porter was on duty when the packages arrived at the lodge. Marked 'Urgent', they were addressed to Mr Speed, the Duke's valet. Two of the boxes were long and bulky; one was very heavy. The labels gave away their contents; they had come from Bartlett's of Jermyn Street, Suppliers of Oxygen Tents.

The castle's odd-job men were summoned to take the packages to the entrance of the Duke's room, where Mr Speed was in attendance. 'Besides the butler and the housekeeper, Mr Speed was the only servant the Duke allowed in his rooms,' George Waudby remembered. 'The rest of us were forbidden to go in there.'

Lord Dawson's hurried return confirmed what the servants suspected. The Duke was gravely ill. A thrill of suspense and excitement, usual in such circumstances, rippled through the household. *'Do you think he can last until morning?'* Along the passageways, in the vast kitchens, and in the still rooms, pantry rooms and preserving rooms beyond, this was the question whispered.

Even before the Duke fell ill, the castle had

been in a state of upheaval.

Six days after war was declared — on 9 September 1939 — a convoy of army lorries had turned off the Great North Road and trundled up the drive to the castle. For the last half-mile, the single-track road followed the contours of the ridge, coiling steeply through dense woods. The sound of the whining engines had shattered the peace, sending flocks of rooks wheeling gracefully skywards. Inside the cabins, fuggy after four hours on the Great North Road, the drivers had cursed the sharp gradient and the ruts and potholes. Double-declutching, they had inched their way along the unmetalled road.

The convoy, one of a number to leave London that week, was top secret. German bombing raids were expected at any moment: the nation's treasures were hurriedly being transported from the capital to various destinations for safekeeping. Works of art from the Tate Gallery had already left for Muncaster Castle on the remote Cumberland coast; the British Museum's collections had gone to Boughton, the Duke of Buccleuch's house, in Northamptonshire.

Belvoir Castle had been selected as a repository for the nation's most important historical documents — the records, spanning almost a thousand years, of the Royal Courts and the principal ministries of state.

At Chancery Lane in London, where the

records were kept, it had taken eight hours to load up the convoy. Seventy-five tons of documents, packed in bundles in specially made cardboard containers, had been stacked on to the lorries. Further convoys had been scheduled.

The oldest and most important records were evacuated first. Among them were parchment scrolls and rolls, stamped with the seals and signatures of every monarch since William the Conqueror. There were War Office papers dating from 1660 and Treasury, Chancery and Exchequer records going back to the eleventh century; contemporary Admiralty and Foreign Office records had also been included: these were the boxes marked 'Secret — Property of His Majesty's Government'.

Ten days earlier — on 30 August — the warrant to appoint the Duke of Rutland as Keeper of the Records had been rushed through Whitehall. The rules of the Public Record Office stipulated that, at all times, the records must be under the charge of a custodian appointed by the sovereign. The Master of the Rolls and the Lord Chancellor had sanctioned the Duke's appointment on behalf of King George VI.

At Belvoir, it had taken two days to unload the boxes. The Duke had supervised, directing his servants to the various locations that he had earmarked around the castle. Forty tons of documents had been stored in the ballroom; the remainder, along the passages in the servants' quarters. 'There were fifty-two steps up to the ballroom. It was a longer haul to the back passages on the ground floor,' George Waudby remembered. 'Every box had to be carried. Then they had to be unpacked, and the bundles of documents individually stacked. It was quite a chore, I tell you. I can see them now — all the boxes piled up in the ballroom and along the passages. All these documents. Boxes and boxes of them. They went back to Domesday, they said.'

A new shipment had been expected, when the Duke fell ill. With the prospect of a German invasion threatening, the remaining records at Chancery Lane were to be evacuated to Belvoir.

On the morning Lord Dawson was called to the castle, the servants had been busy making space in the Guard Room.

'We were expecting several tons of documents,' George Waudby recalled. 'The Guard Room was so big it made sense to put them there. The problem was, there were lots of boxes in there already. We had to sort them all out, and then shift them into rooms that had been allocated in the servants' quarters and upstairs. Some of the estate workers were brought in to help us. There were quite a few of us.'

The route to the storerooms in the servants' quarters took them past the Duke's rooms. 'The passage was only about four foot wide and there were hundreds of boxes stacked along it from previous convoys,' Jack Price, one of the estate workers, remembered: 'There wasn't much space to manoeuvre. Once the doctors arrived, we had to squeeze past them. We all felt uncomfortable about it. There we were, filthy in our working clothes, and we were brushing up against the King's doctor.'

Jack and the other servants had noted the precise time of Lord Dawson's arrival. It was ten minutes to eleven when the first footman had escorted him across the Guard Room. Fifteen minutes later, as they carried another load of boxes along the passage, they were amazed to discover that Lord Dawson and his colleagues were still there. 'We were all talking about it,' Jack recalled. 'We didn't know what to make of it. If the Duke was dying, what was the King's doctor doing in the passage? Why wasn't he attending him? It didn't make sense.'

A cold stone passage, filled with servants, was foreign territory to Lord Dawson, who was used to being ushered directly into the opulent state rooms where he normally attended his patients. Appointed Physician-extraordinary to King Edward VII, he had served the royal household for three decades. Famously, in 1928, when George V had almost died from a respiratory illness, Dawson had been credited with saving the King's life. It had made him a national celebrity — and the most sought after, most admired doctor of his generation. Invariably charming, he inspired his patients' trust. He had been by the King's bedside until the very end. It was he who had composed the memorable words on the notice posted on the railings outside Buckingham Palace: 'The King's life is drawing peacefully to a close.'

Lord Dawson had been in and out of the Duke's rooms throughout the preceding week. What, the servants wondered, could be so important that the Duke was keeping Britain's most trusted medical adviser waiting?

In a castle alive with gossip, a moment of absent-mindedness on the part of the fourth housemaid yielded a key piece of information.

3

It was a few minutes past eleven when the five housemaids trooped into the ballroom. Taking off their white starched aprons, they formed up in a line. The room was lofty, echoing the sound of their footsteps and voices, as in a church. Along one side of it, there were nine windows; between them, stone piers, with flowered capitals, arched upwards to the vaulted roof.

The oak floor — almost three thousand square feet of it — had to be polished by hand. It was an onerous task, one the house-maids least liked doing. Bending down, they placed their tins of wax on the floor. As they stooped on to their hands and knees, their long black dresses spread out around them.

Working in unison, they dabbed their cloths in the wax; then they rubbed the floor vigorously in quick, tight circles. Along the five-strong line, the action was synchronized, the movement rippling the full skirts of their dresses, fanned behind them. They chatted as they polished: about the war, the state of the Duke's health, and their families and children.

The housemaids had climbed the spiral staircase in the Flag Tower to get to the ballroom. On the ground floor, where they had come from, there were fifty rooms. On this, the second floor of the castle, which was of a similar square footage, there were just twenty-three rooms. It was where the Duke and his family lived and entertained.

Ahead, and a little off to the right, was the Elizabeth Saloon, a vast, fuchsia-pink drawing room of breathtaking opulence. Its painted ceiling depicted the myth of Jupiter and Io and the walls were fitted with panels of blue silk damask. Everything inside it was gilded: the ormolu console tables, the picture frames, the Louis Quatorze chairs and chaises longues, the fretwork on the walls and ceiling, even the curtain rails. Peacocks in their pride — the family's crest — were emblazoned on the specially woven carpet and on the fireback in the huge hearth.

The rooms beyond the Saloon were equally magnificent, and were filled with treasures the dukes had collected over centuries. There were the Chinese Rooms and the King's Rooms with their exquisite hand-painted wallpaper and great canopied beds; the Tapestry Room, where Poussin's *Sacraments* hung alongside the beautiful Mortlake tapestries of *The Naked Boys;* the two libraries, where the numbered bookcases — sixty in total — were lined with rare books. Then there were the two picture galleries which linked the rooms. Their walls were crammed with Old Masters: Holbein, Gainsborough, Stubbs, Reynolds and Rembrandt were but a few of the artists whose works were on display.

Perhaps the most stunning room of all was the 132-foot long Regent's Gallery, which the Duke used as his living room. Its walls were a pale pistachio green; the luxuriant velvet curtains and the fabric on the sofa and chairs crimson and muted pinks. Three Waterford chandeliers, sculpted from hundreds of tiny pieces of crystal, hung from the ceilings; marble busts, mounted on pillars, stood centurion-like along the gallery's length. Above the fireplaces there were gilded mirrors; beside them, the famous *Don Quixote* tapestries.

The ballroom, by contrast, was sparsely decorated. A hundred and twenty feet long and just twenty-four feet wide, it was rarely used for dancing; it was more of a corridor — a link to the state rooms beyond. That morning, it was looking more dismal than usual. Against the right-hand wall, piled six feet high, were hundreds of bundles of documents from the Public Record Office. All the furniture, with the exception of a glass cabinet, had been removed. The cabinet displayed a gruesome set of eighteenth-century surgical instruments. Neatly slotted in a faded leather case were the picks, scalpels, knives and hacksaws that surgeons had used to amputate the leg of Lord Robert Manners, an ancestor of the Duke's who was wounded at sea during the American War of Independence. The leg had turned septic and he had died shortly after the operation. Above the cabinet, there was a macabre painting of the death scene.

The housemaids hated working in the ballroom. The imposing staircase that took up one end of the room frightened them. 'That staircase was haunted,' a former maid remembered. We always did our polishing facing it. We wouldn't work with our backs turned to it. That way the stairs were straight ahead.'

The castle's Regency Gothic style was a pastiche of the classic 'house of horror' — the sinister ancestral home that formed the central convention of the Gothic novel. In the evenings, when the sun set behind it, the towers, turrets and crenellated battlements were forbiddingly silhouetted against the dusk sky. Ghosts had entered its mythology; in the servants' hall, many claimed to have seen them.

The ballroom staircase was the place the servants feared the most. Sweeping down to the Guard Room two floors below, it was the main thoroughfare in the castle. Family portraits of former dukes and duchesses, resplendent in ermine, adorned its walls. The steps, of bare stone — framed by a wrought-iron balustrade, topped by a mahogany rail — were wide and shallow.

'We were all scared of the ballroom stairs,' Sheila Osborne, a former maid, remembered: 'I was coming down them one evening. Halfway down, I felt somebody push me. They were behind me, trying to push me down the stairs. I turned round, and of course there was no one there.'

A number of the male servants, sceptical of ghosts as they were, had experienced a similar sensation. 'My father used to keep an eye on the castle when His Grace was away,' Dorothy Plowright recalled. 'He'd walk around in the dark with his dogs, no lights, no torches or anything. One night, he was coming across Forty-Acre — that's what they called the landing on the first floor — and he got to the top of the ballroom stairs and he felt this hot breath on the back of his neck. He turned round. There was nobody there. But the dogs wouldn't go any further; their hackles went right up. He said it was ages before he could get them to move.'

It was coming up to lunchtime and the housemaids had almost finished polishing the ballroom floor. They had drawn level with the macabre painting of Lord Robert Manners that hung above the glass cabinet containing the surgical instruments used in the operation that had killed him.

It was at this moment that Margaret, the fourth housemaid, ran out of polish. Mrs Ward, the housekeeper, often patrolled the castle to inspect her girls' work; to be caught with an empty tin of wax was a grave crime, punishable by a severe scolding or, worse, the loss of a day off. Margaret had forgotten to bring a spare tin with her; she would have to go and fetch one from the pantry on the ground floor. If she cut down the ballroom stairs and along the passage outside the Duke's rooms, she would be back within a couple of minutes.

Taking the dreaded stairs at a run, she darted across the Guard Room and was soon in the passage. Immediately, she was struck by its emptiness. There was no sign of the doctors. The steel door to the rooms was ajar, and she could hear the low murmur of voices coming from inside. The door opened outwards. Curiosity overcame her. Stealing up to it, she hid behind it.

Straightaway, she recognized the voice of Mr Speed, the Duke's valet.

'No, my Lord,' she heard him say. 'I'm sorry, but His Grace is not ready to see you.'

Margaret could not catch Lord Dawson's

reply, only its note of protest. But she heard Mr Speed clearly.

'I'm terribly sorry,' the valet said again. 'His Grace has something he must finish.'

Slipping out from behind the door, Margaret continued along the passage. What she had overheard gave her a pleasant feeling of her own importance; it was something to tell the other servants over lunch.

4

Lunch, in the servants' hall, was at twelve sharp. Three stone steps led from the Flag Tower up into the hall; the steps were rutted, worn down by the hundreds of feet that had passed through its doors. The hall, paved with flagstones, was dimly lit. The single window, set high in the rafters of the timbered roof, let in little light. In high summer the smell of rotting carcasses drifted through it from the fish and game larders in the courtyard outside.

The servants — maids of all descriptions, odd-job men, footmen, the flag man, the hall porter, the telephone boy, the boiler stoker and the stewards' room boy — were seated on the two benches that ran either side of a long table beneath a photograph of King George VI. The hall was solely for the use of the under-servants. The senior members of the Duke's household dined in the house-keeper's rooms, an appropriately gentrified suite in the west wing of the castle overlooking the splendid terraced gardens.

The under-butler, whose job it was to look after the Duke's gold and silver plate, sat at the head of the table. On his right sat the head housemaid, with her four assistants in order of precedence. On his left was the first footman; next to him, the second footman — and so on through the ranks.

The light from the fire in the huge grate flickered on the housemaids' starched aprons, touching them with orange; it shimmered in the gold buttons on the footmen's tailcoats. 'Their tailcoats were fitted at the waist with four gold buttons on either side and two at the join,' a housemaid recalled. 'There were eight gold buttons along the sleeves. They all had the peacock crest on them. That was the Duke's crest.'

Towards the lower end of the table, the other servants appeared drab by contrast. The kitchen maids, scullery maids and pantry maids were a blur of grey serge; the workmen and the coal carriers were in dark three-piece worsted suits. The dull colours of their uniforms reflected their position. They were lowest in the chain and rarely seen 'upstairs'.

Charlie Tweed, who was well into his eighties, kept a glassy eye on proceedings. 'He had a very long white beard did Charlie,' George Waudby remembered. 'He was in charge of the servants' hall. He was meant to keep us in order. It was his job to make sure the men behaved themselves and that they took their hats off.'

Born in the 1850s, Charlie Tweed had worked at the castle since he was six. When he was a boy, buglers, dressed in doublet and hose, had walked the corridors of the upper floors sounding their bugles to announce meals. 'Mr Tweed wasn't up to much,' George Waudby recalled. 'He was ancient. But the Duke kept him on. The castle was his life. One of his jobs was to bang the gong for dinner upstairs. I can see him struggling into his livery. He often forgot to do it. We used to have to cover for him, or else we'd have to remind him. "Come on, Charlie," we'd say. "It's time to bang the gong. It's seven o'clock." '

In the course of Charlie Tweed's long years of service, the faces around the table may have changed, but the names remained the same: Stannage, Draper, Coy, Thornton. They were old local families who had moved up and down the ranks of servants at Belvoir Castle for centuries.

They came from the picturesque cottages of brilliant yellow stone that stood in the lee of the castle, and from the hamlets and villages that nestled in the hollows and crowned the hilltops of the Duke's six by nine mile estate. It was rural country, barely touched by the twentieth century. The soil, a rich clay, was ideally suited to corns and grasses, and field after field stretched to the horizon, broken up here and there by ancient copses.

Many of the servants had been born in the Duke's villages; rarely had they travelled far beyond them. Sparsely populated, these villages, with no more than a few hundred inhabitants at most, were backward, inward-looking places. In the fields around them, big-barrelled Black Shires with white-stockinged legs, the descendants of the great working horse of medieval times, still ploughed the land. Horse Key, Pringle, Break Back Close, Low Warm, Top Abbot, Middle Abbot: every field had a name. All the names were known.

Outsiders rarely ventured on to the Duke's estate. It was a landscape that anyone crossing it was expected to know. The lanes were narrow, bordered by towering hedgerows, the slender spires of the village churches the only landmarks. On winter evenings, and at dawn on summer mornings, a thick mist rolled across the fields, obscuring all. At the junctions and crossroads, signposts were few and far between; now, with the coming of war, the Duke had ordered his servants and employees to scratch out the names of the villages, a precaution against a German invasion.

In the servants' hall, one end of the long trestle table was empty. War had reduced the size of the household: a number of the under-servants had been called up and were absent on active service. The diminished numbers, the excited notes of conversation, the light from the flickering flames, lent the scene an intimacy.

From the moment they had assumed their customary places on the benches, the conversation had turned on the bizarre events of the past twenty-four hours.

The Duke's secret rooms, by their very nature, held the servants in thrall. 'It was an area that we never entered, never saw, or ever knew what went on. It was a place of mystery,' George Waudby said. 'We knew there were five rooms — you could see the windows from the gun-carriage terrace. But what he did in there, we had no idea.'

The rooms were the subject of wild speculation, fuelled by the servants' fear of the Duke, and their knowledge of his eccentric interests.

To his servants, as George Waudby recalled, the Duke was a distant, Heathcliffian figure. 'He was fierce-looking, a very frightening man. About six foot tall and very thin. We never saw him that much — he spent all his time in those rooms. But when we did, he was not an easy person to work for. He was very sharp. Often very cross in nature. I don't think he was a happy man.'

'He was a peculiar man with strange interests,' said Footman Clarence Harper. 'He collected things. All over the castle they were. Birds' eggs, thousands of them; old brass fire-insurance plates; bits and pieces of pottery that he'd dug up. There was some as said collecting was what stopped him from going mad. On his right hand, he kept his nails an inch long. Curled they did, like talons. They said he kept them like that for scraping the mud off old tiles.'

It was the Duke's 'strange interests' that frightened his under-servants the most.

His morbid interest in tombs and ancient corpses was well known. On 11 February 1923, in the Valley of the Kings in Egypt as a friend of Lord Carnarvon's, he had been one of the first to see the interior of Tutankhamun's tomb. When he was a young man, the Duke had opened a number of tombs in the vicinity of Belvoir Castle — reportedly in search of King John's heart and the grave of Robert de Todeni, his eleventh-century ancestor. In the 1920s, there had been further exhumations. In the crypt at St Mary's Church in Bottesford, where his predecessors, the earls of Rutland, were buried, he had exhumed eight tombs. According to a theory in vogue at the time, the fifth Earl of Rutland was believed to have been William Shakespeare. The Duke had apparently wanted to find his tomb. But why it had been necessary to exhume all the earls of Rutland mystified his servants.

The Duke was also known to be fascinated

by the occult. Sir Oliver Lodge, the founder and president of the Society for Psychical Research, and La Mina, one of the most famous mediums of her day, were frequent guests at the castle.

His interest in supernatural phenomena played to his servants' fears. 'It wasn't just that the Duke dug up dead bodies. He thought the castle was haunted,' one said. He often had the mediums in. We never knew, of course, whether any ghosts or spirits were actually summoned. It all went on behind closed doors.'

In the Flag Tower, the clock struck one. The single chime of the bell signalled the end of lunch.

By the back door in the kitchen, the usual queue had formed. At this hour, every day, the poor from the nearby villages traipsed up the hill to the castle to collect the leftovers from the castle meals.

It was time to return to work but, in the exceptional circumstances, a number of the servants lingered. The Duke's sudden deterioration puzzled them. Two curses, one ancient, one modern — the details of which were discussed time and time again in the lower rooms of the castle — dominated their conversation.

'They said it was the curse of the pharaoh that was killing him,' Dorothy Plowright

43

recalled. 'The Duke was there when Tutankhamun's tomb was opened. They said that anyone who went inside it would die within so many years. It was in all the newspapers.'

The story of the pharaoh's curse was one the servants had followed closely. The Earl of Carnarvon had died five months after discovering the tomb. He — so the press had claimed — was Tutankhamun's first victim. Quickly, the legend of a curse had become firmly established as rival newspapers vied to announce the deaths of others who had entered the tomb.

In the servants' hall at Belvoir, each new report of a death was noted and debated. Over the years, Lord Carnarvon had often stayed at the castle. The servants had made his bed and served him his breakfast. His story was part of their story: it had lodged in their imaginations.

Upstairs, the Duke's diary for the year 1923 stood on display, carefully positioned on an occasional table in the library. One of the housemaids had peeked at it as she was dusting around it. It was open at the page for 11 February, the day the Duke had entered the tomb. 'The whole thing is stupendous,' he had written: 'I consider myself the luckiest man to have lived to see it. The sight of the inside of that tomb is a thing to have lived for alone.'

Among the Duke's under-servants, the

legend of the curse far outweighed any sort of truth. In April 1940, Howard Carter and countless others who had entered the tomb in the first weeks of February 1923 were alive and flourishing. 'They believed in the story of the pharaoh's curse,' Dorothy Plowright remembered: 'Oh yes. Anyone who entered that tomb was supposed to die within so many years.'

It was old Mr Tweed, the gong man, who spoke of another curse. 'Mr Tweed said His Grace was being taken by the witches' curse,' one of the Duke's tenants remembered. 'An ancestral curse, the family called it. We all knew about it. It had been going on for hundreds of years.'

The curse, so it was believed, had been cast in the early seventeenth century by a coven of witches living in the castle's grounds. In 1619, two of the women had been tried and executed at Lincoln for the murder by witchcraft of two of the 6th Earl of Rutland's infant sons. They had also, it was claimed, cast a curse over future generations: aimed at the Rutland heirs, it determined that the two eldest boys in the family would die before they reached the age of ten.

For more than three hundred years, it had seemed to the Rutlands and their servants that this was a curse from which the family could never escape. It had struck in all but three of the nine generations after the trial of the Belvoir witches. Four times, the family had lost their two eldest sons before they reached the age of ten; twice, the heir to the title had died in infancy.

The memory of the witches also haunted the villagers at Belvoir. When Mr Tweed was a boy, the belief in the power of witchcraft was still strong. Looking back to his childhood, he could remember the bottles buried beneath the hearths in the cottages below the castle. Filled with the urine and fingernails of their occupants, they were a type of counter-magic to ward off the maleficium of a witch. The bottles were a legacy from the trial at Lincoln. According to court records, the women tried for murdering the Earl's sons had wrought havoc across his estate. In two villages alone, five people were thought to have been murdered by the 'witches'.

'We didn't take any notice of Charlie Tweed,' George Waudby remembered. 'We thought he was a bit simple. His age, we supposed, had made him senile.'

In a voice cracked by his years, as Charlie went about his work, he often sang a ballad which the farm workers in the fields below the castle had sung when he was a boy. Written in 1619, it told the story of the Belvoir witches and their curse on the castle and its heirs:

These women thus being Devils grown,

Most cunning in their Arts
With charmes and with enchanting spells
They played most damned parts:
They did forespeak, and Cattle killed,
That neighbours could not thrive,
And oftentimes their Children young
Of life they would deprive.

Yet so their malice more increased
That mischief set in foot
To blast the branches of that house
And undermine the root.

On Saturday 20 April, the Duke slipped into
unconsciousness. That afternoon when Lord
Dawson was admitted to see him, he pronounced him beyond all hope. But in the
hours that remained before he died, his
under-servants would glean some information about the Duke's rooms which surprised
them.

At eight o'clock, two of the castle's footmen were called to wait at table in the Fox
Hunter's Dining Room.

5

The doctors — Lord Dawson and Dr Jauch — were dining alone, leaving the unconscious Duke in the care of his valet. Their mood was subdued, the setting sombre. The long table, carved from mahogany, took up most of the room, which was small and oppressive, in contrast to the state dining room. The walls were painted a baleful yew green and the heavy velvet curtains were black. All the paintings were of hunting scenes.

The two footmen stood at each end of the room and were privy to the doctors' conversation. From time to time, one would step up to the table to refill a glass, or to remove a plate.

What surprised the footmen was the doctors' description of the Duke's rooms. Gossip in the servants' hall had conjured vivid pictures of their interiors, of rooms filled with sumptuous fabrics and valuable treasures far surpassing those that adorned the state rooms. But, from what the footmen could gather from the conversation, this was not the case. 'They're not fit for a servant,' Lord Dawson had expostulated.

The fact that the Duke had refused to leave the rooms apparently puzzled the doctors. Throughout the week of his illness, they had tried to persuade him to move upstairs. The rooms, in their view, were inappropriate for a man who was gravely ill. They were dusty, damp and draughty. Only one of the five rooms had a fire. Lord Dawson described it as a stove: 'the sort that could be found in the maids' bedrooms up in the Flag Tower'. Worse still, there were no washing facilities. Water — hot or cold — had to be brought in from the servants' quarters.

It was in these rooms at sunrise the following morning that the Duke died. His death certificate states that he died of bronchial pneumonia. It is not known who found him, or who was with him during his final hours. The principal dramatis personae — his wife, his eldest son, his butler, his valet and the doctors — are no longer alive to tell us. The hours between ten o'clock in the evening, when the doctors retired from the Fox Hunter's Dining Room, and five minutes past six the next morning, when the Duke died, are blank.

Even in death, the Duke was reluctant to leave these rooms: his last wish was that his body should remain there until the day of his funeral. This singular request flouted a family tradition. Prior to burial, his predecessors had been laid to rest in the chapel in the south wing of the castle. Then their coffins had been moved to the Guard Room, where their servants, and the hundreds of workers and tenants on their estate, had been invited to come to pay their last respects. The Duke had specifically asked that all but his family and his closest friends should be barred from his last resting place.

At one o'clock on Wednesday 24 April, the day of his funeral, the great oak doors at the entrance to the castle were opened. The bier, a converted farm wagon, painted black and drawn by four chestnut horses, was brought inside the porch. In the enclosed space beneath the vaulted roof, the horses fidgeted, their hooves dancing on the polished stone.

Outside, rain poured from the leaden sky, which had looked threatening for some days. Pools of water collected in the potholes on the battlements where the crowd of mourners waited. 'The yeomen of the Vale of Belvoir put on their black broadcloth,' the local newspaper reported. 'And from all parts of the countryside made their way to the castle on the hill for the funeral of the Duke of Rutland, the ninth in an illustrious line. Because of the war, many of the notable county people were absent. Tenantry, servants and estate workers made up the greater part of the assembly that gathered on the turreted courtyard.'

Inside the castle, the pall bearers, servants nominated by the late Duke, reached the Guard Room, where they lowered the coffin on to the chequered marble floor and draped it with his flag. It was yellow and blue and bore his crest and his coat of arms.

The hall porter was at his post in the antechamber behind the Guard Room. It was his duty to keep up the visitors' book, a meticulous record of the date of arrival and departure of the Duke and his family and their overnight guests. 'His Grace the Duke of Rutland,' read the entry for 2 April 1940, the date the Duke had arrived at the castle. As the coffin was borne slowly through the Guard Room, the porter reached for his quill pen. In the departure column, he entered that day's date: '24 April'. Then, in brackets, with a flourish, in a befittingly neat Gothic script, he added the word 'Corpse'.

Punctually, at one o'clock, the wheels of the bier crunched over the gravel and the cortège moved off from the battlements and down the hill along the road to the mausoleum.

Less than a week after the Duke's death, the secret rooms were once again the focus of mystery. On the night of 27 April, three days

after he was buried, someone broke into
them.

6

It was shortly before three o'clock in the morning when a shadowy figure, dressed from head to foot in black, crossed the gun-carriage terrace. The night was cloudless, the moon almost full. A blackout was in force and the castle was shrouded in darkness. The light from the moon set tiny points of brilliance dancing in the blackened windows and on the barrels of the cannons that stood, pointing outwards, along the terrace. Up in the North Tower, the flag of mourning was at half mast. The barest crunch of footsteps moving stealthily across the gravel and the occasional cry of an animal from the woods below the castle were the only sounds that broke the stillness.

At ground-floor level, fourteen windows overlooked the terrace. Each offered a point of entry. Without hesitating, the figure approached the window that led into the room where the Duke had died. First a pane of glass was smashed; then a metal brace used to force the catch. The attempt at entry failed: the metal grille on the inside of the window was locked.

Had anyone been about at that hour, they would have described the intruder as male: he wore a long worsted jacket and his trousers were tucked into a pair of laced leather boots. Yet — as would become clear just moments later — 'he' was in fact a woman who had come disguised as a man.

Turning, and creeping back out on to the terrace, she stopped and looked up to take in the full expanse of the castle's façade.

A few paces to the right of the room where the Duke had died, two lead drainpipes, positioned a foot apart, ran up to the roof. Seen from the terrace, it looked an awkward climb. After pausing for a moment, she crept back up to the window; then, dropping the rose bit and the brace on the gravel, she grasped both pipes firmly and, using the brackets as footholds, climbed fifteen feet to the first floor. It was a precarious stretch to the window on the left, but it was possible to reach the stone ledge beneath it. The window was open and led into the nursery passage.

Moments later, the night watchman ran into her in the passage outside the Duke's rooms on the floor below.

Whoever she was, she was not caught. After being discovered, she fled along the passage and escaped from the castle.

54

The police arrived soon after dawn. When they interviewed the night watchman, he omitted to tell them that it was a woman, not a man, whom he had seen outside the Duke's rooms.

Missing this key piece of information, it was left to the police to try to make sense of the break-in.

Immediately, the police suspected espionage. It was clear that this was no casual burglary. The Duke's rooms had been specifically targeted. In the midst of war, all government establishments were on the alert for enemy agents. The police were aware that both a summary of the records stored at the castle, and a plan of the stacks, showing precisely where specific bundles of documents could be located, were kept in the rooms where the Duke had died.

Police reports of their investigation into the incident have not survived. But a report written by John Gilkes, the caretaker appointed to look after the records, is now held at the National Archives.

Midway through the morning, after inspecting the thousands of bundles of documents stacked along the passages and in rooms all over the castle, Gilkes communicated the facts — as he understood them — to the Keeper of the Records in London.

His report is confusing, the detail sketchy:

'I thought I ought to let you know of recent doings here,' he began. 'During last night an attempt was made to force the window of the Duke's room from the outside with a brace and a rose sinking bit. One pane of glass was broken, but the gates and bars outside were not forced. Also a man was spotted in the passage. He escaped having been seen by the watchmen. It is thought they got in through the window above the Duke's rooms. When told at breakfast of the occurrence, I walked all round our stacks but couldn't find even a slight alteration in the dust sheets, which I replaced in position on Friday last. Whatever they were after must have been in the room where His Grace died. The police were here early and I cannot say if any clues were found, except the brace and bit. So it is rather a mystery. So far nothing has been noted as missing.'

The break-in appeared motiveless: not a single document had been taken, nor a single item in the castle reported stolen.

At breakfast that morning, the servants had purposely kept Gilkes in the dark. Like the police, he was not aware that the 'man' was a woman. 'What went on up at the castle never went out the doors,' Gladys Brittain, the wife of the Duke's butler, remembered. 'The castle — by that I mean the family — was the castle. It was nothing to do with anyone else.' Gilkes, a cockney, and the police were outsiders as far as the servants were concerned; they belonged 'out the doors'.

So who had the night watchman seen? More than seventy years after the event, the trail is not quite cold. While the chief witness has long since died, among the descendants of those working at the castle on 27 April 1940, the memory of what happened that night lives on.

It was Philip Stubbley who saw the woman in the passage. He was one of three watchmen on duty on the night of the break-in. Security had been stepped up to protect the government records; the men were armed with revolvers and machines tracked their progress through the castle.

'The watchmen clocked into tachometer-type machines at various points on their round,' George Waudby remembered. 'They went everywhere. Up into the towers, out on to the roof, then they'd come down through all the different floors and levels. There were hundreds of rooms to go through, but they didn't miss a single one. It took them a full hour to go round. Then they'd start again. I don't know how many times they went round, but there were three of them circulating throughout the night.'

It was a few minutes past three o'clock when Philip Stubbley turned the corner into the passage outside the Duke's rooms. Bill

Hotchin, the boiler stoker, started work at dawn that morning. He told his daughter, Dorothy, what Stubbley saw: 'As he came round the corner into the passage a man ran past him. Or he thought it was a man. Philip shouted at him and *she* turned round. She was wearing men's clothes. All in black she was. I remember my father saying he ought to have got out his pistol and challenged her — the night watchmen were trained to fire below the knee, you know. But he didn't. He panicked and ran back to find the other watchmen. And of course, she got away. But she had been in the Duke's rooms.'

Stubbley — as Dorothy was later to discover from other servants at the castle — had every reason not to shoot. He had recognized the woman: 'He said it was "the woman from Eastwell". That's what they called her. She lived in the manor house in Eastwell village, just across the Vale. She was the Duke's mistress. Apparently, he used to see a lot of her. They said he'd left her a letter or some money, and that's what she'd come to collect.'

The moment's delay — when Stubbley went in search of the other watchmen — gave the woman the vital seconds she needed. Dashing across the Guard Room, past the stands of pikes and muskets, she escaped through the great oak doors at the entrance to the castle and vanished into the night.

■ ■ ■ ■

While the servants claimed to know who the woman was, *exactly* what she was doing in the Duke's rooms and what — if anything — she took away with her are among the many questions that hover over the strange events that occurred at Belvoir Castle in the week of his death.

With the passing of time, even her alleged identity becomes mere hearsay. But an important detail relating to the means by which she first attempted to enter the castle suggests there is some truth in the servants' second-hand recollection of events.

Of the many windows overlooking the gun-carriage terrace, the one leading into the room where the Duke died was the most secure. On the inside, a concertina-style iron grille operated in a similar manner to the doors of an old-fashioned lift: it could be pulled across and locked. So why then, when the woman arrived at the castle, did she make straight for this window? Why break the glass and force the catch when the internal grille surely rendered it impregnable? There is just one possible explanation: when she smashed the pane of glass and used the brace to force the catch on the window, she had anticipated that the grille would not be locked.

Someone, she presumed, had left it open for her.

The servants suspected the Duke.

According to George Waudby, the window was a route of entry that she had used many times before. In the servants' quarters, it was known that the Duke 'entertained the woman from Eastwell' in his rooms. They knew she entered the castle via the window; discretion was a priority: it was a way of avoiding the Porter's Lodge, where visitors were noted in a logbook.

So had the Duke instructed his valet or his butler to leave the grille open so that she could enter the rooms after he died? Had he told her to return in the dead of night after he was buried?

'His Grace has something he must finish.' Was the letter — or package — to his mistress the thing that preoccupied him in his final hours?

Nothing the Duke's under-servants saw or overheard explains what he was doing in those rooms before he died. Or why he chose to die in them. It is almost as if he died *for* them. Had he followed his doctors' advice and moved to the upper floors of the castle, possibly they might have been able to save his life. Nor were the servants able to explain why the Duke kept the rooms so secret.

'Never speak ill of the dead, they say, but some of us weren't sorry to see him go,' one of the housemaids said.

Yet there is another side to this man whose dark moods and morbid interests terrified the junior members of his household. Among the servants closest to him, he was loved and venerated. 'My father always used to say he was a very lonely man, but if you had him as a friend, you had him as a friend for life,' Tonya Pacey, the butler's daughter, remembered. 'I never heard my father talk about anyone in the way he talked about him. He loved him.'

Whatever it was that kept the Duke closeted in his secret rooms in the last hours of his life haunted his family too. Shortly after he died, his son, Charles, the 10th Duke of Rutland, closed them. In 1999, almost sixty years later, they were finally opened to outsiders. Today, only a handful of people have been inside them.

The closure of the rooms and the servants' stories are pieces in the puzzle. Now it is necessary to step back to the true beginning of this story — the moment when I first entered these rooms, before I even knew they concealed a mystery.

■ ■ ■ ■

PART II

■ ■ ■ ■

27 August 2008

It was one of those brilliant summer mornings that begins in a haze, promising the heat to come. A mist was rising from the fields as I dropped down the hill into the valley below the castle. I could see it ahead: a fairy-tale castle, all turrets and towers, standing majestically on the ridge.

I had arranged to meet Mr Granger, the Duke of Rutland's archivist, in the castle's Muniment Rooms. Then, I knew nothing of that sad day in April 1940; I did not know that John, the 9th Duke, had died in the rooms that I was about to see, or that they had been sealed after his death. Nor did I know that his servants had once called them the 'Secret Rooms'. I had come to Belvoir to research a different book entirely.

7

'There are five rooms,' Mr Granger said. 'I'll show you Room 2 first.'

We were standing in a small hallway at the entrance to the Muniment Rooms.* I peered along the narrow passage. Odd angles of light slanted across it; it seemed to recede into infinity, as if I was viewing it through the wrong end of a telescope.

A few minutes earlier, we had met outside the steel door. A tall man of military bearing, Mr Granger was in his mid-seventies. His manner was diffident. It was hard to catch his words.

'I think you'll find the rooms interesting,' he muttered. 'Follow me. I'll lead the way.'

He turned right into the passage. It was musty, the smell of damp rising from the bare floorboards. Rows of cabinets lined the walls on one side. Ahead of us, there was a small sign. Hand-painted in a plain font, it hung from the low ceiling. The sign was perfunc-

* See the plans of the castle on pages 11-13.

tory: 'Room 2,' it said. Beyond, there was a pool of bright white light.

The passage led directly into the room. Stepping in, it was as if we had entered an apothecary's shop. Tall white cabinets with glass doors jutted from the walls and formed bays at the centre of the room. There were sixteen of them, crammed into an area barely sixteen foot by ten. Tiny points of dust sparkled in front of us, caught in the light that flooded in from the single window. It was impossible to make out what was inside the cabinets: the glare from the sun struck the glass doors, obscuring their contents.

I moved closer, to alter the angle of light. Stacked along the shelves, I could see hundreds of box files. Every one of them was blue. Peacock blue: the colour of the Duke's crest.

'You'll find the family's private correspondence in there,' Mr Granger said, pointing at the cabinets. 'It's all in the blue files. The letters span almost five hundred years. They go back to the sixteenth century — to the time of Thomas de Ros, the first Earl of Rutland.'

He picked up a large, gold-embossed book from the desk beside him. 'In here,' he said, 'are examples of the handwriting of every member of the Manners family since the 1540s. John, the 9th Duke, compiled it. We use it as an aid to identify the correspondents in the blue files.'

Tall leather volumes crowded the shelves opposite us. 'Those are the household accounts,' he said, walking over to them. 'They go back to the eleventh century, when the Manners family first came to Belvoir.' Reaching up, he pulled down one of the ledgers and selected a page at random. The entries were in Early English, written on parchment. A spidery hand had listed the amounts spent on breakfast at the castle in the month of March 1541. The meal — 'collops, eggs, boiled mutton, braun and beef' — had cost three shillings.

'The household accounts and the family's letters form the backbone of the collection, but there are countless other treasures,' Mr Granger continued. 'It is probably one of the most important private collections of historical documents in the country.'

He handed me the catalogue to the collection. It was eighty pages long and contained a summary of the contents of each cabinet. There were ninety-four cases in the five rooms; together, they held over a thousand rows of shelving. The range of the material was breathtaking. Besides the family's correspondence and the Belvoir estate and household records, there were letters from King Charles I to Queen Henrietta, written days before his execution, and an unparalleled collection of printed broadsides published during the English Civil War. A large number of manuscripts dated from the Reign of Terror during the French Revolution; they included letters written by members of the *ancien régime* before they too faced public execution. Looking at the entries for the medieval period, two of the items, I noted, were extremely rare: the Chronicle of Adam of Usk — written in 1420 — and a map of Sherwood Forest, drawn in the fourteenth century, the time, purportedly, of Robin Hood.

'Everything in here, everything you see,' Mr Granger said, gesturing towards the rooms behind us, 'was put together by John, the 9th Duke. All the cataloguing and filing is his. It was his life's work. Most of his time was spent in these rooms.'

He paused, and looked down at the floor.

Then, looking at me quizzically, he said: 'The Duke died in here, you know.'

'He died in here?' I asked, surprised.

'Yes. In Room 1,' he replied. 'It was some-time during the last war. The place has barely been touched since then. The rooms are exactly as the Duke left them.'

He turned and headed back along the pas-sage. 'Come on, I'll show you the other rooms,' he said.

Rooms 3, 4 and 5 were situated at the foot of the Norman Tower, the central feature of the west front of the castle. They were indis-tinguishable; each was equally austere. The wooden floors were bare; aside from a number of desks and several pairs of heavy Tudor chairs, they contained no furniture. Boxes and files were stacked on every available surface; every inch of wall space was given over to cabinets and cases. Devoid of ornaments, or any attempt at beautification, they were rooms of hard lines and edges. There was nothing soft inside them.

Room 1 was the last Mr Granger showed me. Two wooden steps led down into it from the passage. It was square-shaped and smaller than the other rooms, and the ubiquitous white cabinets crowded three sides of it. Along the other wall there was a fireplace, fitted with a small, cast-iron stove. A large Chesterfield sofa stood beneath a barred window.

'That's where the 9th Duke died,' Mr Granger said, pointing at the sofa.

It was covered in faded green chintz. Its springs had broken and it looked badly in need of re-stuffing.

'What did he die of?' I asked, curious.

'Pneumonia,' he replied. 'He was relatively young. He was in his early fifties.'

He moved across to the sofa and propped himself against one of its arms. 'Most of these documents have never been seen,' he said, looking up at the cabinets around us. 'No one outside the immediate family has seen the twentieth-century papers. You are the first.'

To his right, there was a window, secured by a folding iron grille. A small desk had been built into the alcove beneath it.

'Why don't you work over there?' he suggested. 'Most of the papers spanning the First World War are in here, and in the cases in Room 2. I'll leave you to get on with it. If you need anything, you can find me at the end of the passage in Room 4.'

He disappeared.

I pulled up a chair to the desk. It felt strange to be working just a few feet from where the man who had assembled this remarkable collection had died.

I had come to Belvoir to research a book about this small corner of England in the years of the First World War.

In 1914, the Duke of Rutland's estate had embraced thirty villages. In the first weeks of the war, 1,700 men — a fifth of the estate's population — had left to fight on the battlefields abroad. They belonged to Britain's villages' lost generation: that mysterious army of ploughmen, horsemen and field workers who deserted the farms in the summer of 1914, many of them never to return.

The testimony of farm worker Leonard Thompson, who grew up in a village in Suffolk, had inspired the idea for the book.

In August 1914, at the age of nineteen, Leonard had volunteered for the Essex Regiment. 'We were all delighted when war broke out,' he remembered. 'A lot of boys from the village were with me and although we were all sleeping in ditches at Harwich, wrapped in our greatcoats, we were bursting with happiness. We were all damned glad to have got off the farms. We were all so patriotic then and had been taught to love England in a fierce kind of a way. The village wasn't England; England was something better than the village.'

Early in 1915, Leonard's battalion was drafted to Gallipoli. It is the confluence of what Philip Gibbs, the war correspondent, called 'This' and 'That' — the trenches, with life at home — which makes Leonard's account of his first experience of war so heartrending:

We arrived at the Dardanelles and saw the guns flashing and heard the rifle-fire. They heaved our ship, the *River Clyde,* right up to the shore. They had cut a hole and made a little pier, so we were able to walk straight off and on to the beach. We all sat there, waiting for it to get light. The first things we saw were big wrecked Turkish guns, the second, a big marquee. It didn't make me think of the military but of the village fetes. Other people must have thought like this because I remember how we all rushed up to it, like boys getting to a circus, and then found it all laced up. We unlaced it and rushed in. It was full of corpses. Dead Englishmen, lines and lines of them, and with their eyes wide open. We all stopped talking. I'd never seen a dead man before and here I was looking at two or three hundred of them. It was our first fear.

Of the men who left the Belvoir estate for the war, 249 did not come home.

At the edge of each of the Duke of Rutland's villages stands an oak or an ash. They mark the point where the volunteers had turned to wave to their families, who stood in the middle of the village streets watching them go.

Up at the castle, Henry John Brinsley Manners, the 8th Duke of Rutland, had played a large part in their going. Without his intervention, many of those who rushed to the colours in the summer of 1914 would not have done so. On the eve of the war, the Duke's hold over the men and women living on the estate had barely altered since his family had first settled at Belvoir. Then, and over the centuries that followed, the power conferred by their thousands of acres had enabled them to raise huge armies, for a succession of monarchs. While the feudal obligation of military service in return for land had long since been abolished, the Duke's power was undiminished: thousands lived in his cottages and were dependent on him for a living.

A few weeks after war was declared, a memorandum, signed by the Duke, appeared on the noticeboards at the gates to the churches in his villages. It was an appeal for volunteers: 'All who serve the Colours will have their situations kept open for them,' the headline read. The Duke had offered his tenants and employees further inducements: the families of men who volunteered would be entitled to live rent-free in their cottages; the men's wages — less their army pay — would continue to be paid to their dependants. The local newspaper had applauded the Duke's generosity: 'In common with all other great landowners of the country, the Duke of Rutland has come forward in a most patriotic manner. As an inducement to his employees who are able to serve with the Colours, he has made very generous guarantees, which no doubt will be accepted by a large proportion of the servants and workmen on the Belvoir Estate.'

For the majority of those who accepted the Duke's 'generous guarantees', it was the first time they had ventured more than a few miles beyond the villages where they were born. Aged between eighteen and forty, they belonged to a generation that knew little, if anything, of the realities of modern warfare.

There had been no war between the Great Powers since 1871. 'No man in the prime of life knew what war was like,' wrote A. J. P. Taylor: 'all imagined that it would be an affair of great marches and great battles, quickly decided.'

I wanted to follow the journeys of the Belvoir volunteers: to look at what became of them and how, when the war ended, their experiences rebounded on the way of life on the Duke of Rutland's estate. Yet it was not only the stories of these men that drew me to Belvoir Castle: it was the remarkable story of a ducal family.

In an age when the word 'nobility' conveyed a meaning that was entirely secure, a mystique and an aura attached to the dukes, unlike that which attached to any other members of the aristocracy. The title was the highest honour that the Crown could bestow. In the 577 years since its first creation, in all, fewer than 500 individuals had had the right to call themselves Duke (or *suo jure* Duchess).

In 1914, there were thirty dukes. Within living memory, they had enjoyed privileges that seem scarcely credible. Until the reforms of the nineteenth century, they were above the law: no one could arrest them; they could run up debts to infinity without punishment. In politics, they had control of Parliament, many of the seats in the House of Commons being within their gift. Such was their grandeur that, in the course of their public appearances, it was customary for trumpeters to announce their presence. 'Flattered, adulated and deferred to,' as Cecil Woodham-Smith wrote, 'they were the leading celebrities of their day.'

Of the ducal families, the Manners family was among the richest, most glamorous, most intriguing of all.

Through marriage and friendship, their tentacles stretched from the kings and queens of Europe to Prince Yusopov in Russia — the future assassin of Rasputin. In Britain, they were close to Prime Minister Herbert Asquith, and to other leading figures of their day. So opulent was their lifestyle at Belvoir that it prompted Julian Grenfell — himself the son of an Earl — to remark to a friend' 'Isn't it an absurd thing, really, that there should still be places like Belvoir? It's just like a pantomime scene.'

When war came, the family threw themselves behind it. At Belvoir, while the Duchess supervised the transformation of the castle into a hospital for Belgian refugees, the Duke was touring his estate, appealing for battalions of men. In London, Diana, their 22-year-old daughter, thought to be the most beautiful debutante of her generation, was working as a Voluntary Aid Detachment (VAD) nurse, and at Luton, John, their 28-

year-old son, who would later become the 9th Duke of Rutland, was training with his battalion, the 4th Leicestershires, as it prepared to embark for the Western Front.

Four years later, the scale of violence and destruction had altered reality, bringing an end to the life and values of Victorian England. 'It was not just that millions died,' Lady Mary Elcho, a relative of the Duke of Rutland's, remarked: 'it changed the world, *our world,* for ever, shaking all things to their foundations, wasting the treasures of the past, and casting its sinister influence far into the future.'

The breadth of the correspondence in the Muniment Rooms at Belvoir Castle offered a unique opportunity to chronicle their world as they stood on the cusp. Among historians and librarians, the reputation of the collection was unrivalled. The family, I was told, had guarded it jealously. Few, I understood, had been given permission to research in the Muniment Rooms. A mystique attached to the collection: 'It is the holy grail,' one historian had whispered to me.

8

I stood in front of Case 15 in Room 2, looking at the sea of blue box files. The case was nine feet tall; there were sixty files crammed along the five shelves. It held the family's correspondence for the first decades of the twentieth century; it was just one of nineteen cases I needed to go through.

I reached for the first file on the top shelf. It was labelled 'Personal Letters from Violet, Duchess of Rutland, 1914'.

Violet was to be an important character in the book. Aged fifty-seven in 1914, she was the granddaughter of the 24th Earl of Crawford. She was brought up at Sutton Courtenay, an impressive medieval hall near Oxford, and her father, Colonel Charles Lindsay, had been a favourite of Queen Victoria and an intimate friend of Louis Napoleon. Her life had been lived at the centre of events. Following her marriage in 1882, she had become one of the most influential and well-connected women of her generation. In the years leading up to the war, invitations to her parties were coveted. Besides politicians and other wealthy aristocrats, Rudyard Kipling, Feodor Chaliapin, Sergei Diaghilev and Sir Edward Elgar were among the guests she had invited to her townhouse a few hundred yards from the Ritz. A mother of four children, she was also the central figure in the Manners family.

I lifted the lid of the box. It was exciting to open it. Here was a time capsule. I was about to be transported into the Duchess's world in 1914. Inside, the letters were held in place by a metal clip. The spring on the clip was stiff; as I raised it, particles of rust scattered over the documents beneath. The letters had not been sorted: they appeared to have been bundled straight into the file from the case or drawer where Violet had kept them. The imprint of the clip, I noticed, was stencilled in rust on the top letter: clearly, no one had looked at them for many years.

Leafing through the pile, I pulled out the ones for August through to December. Mostly, they were letters that Violet had written to John, her son, who was with his regiment. Her handwriting was chaotic, her style breathless. The pages were punctuated with exclamation marks and words that had been heavily underscored. They captured the excitement and confusion of the first heady days of the war. 'John darling, No news of sea battles but news of 7 regiments of Germans having crossed Meuse, caught by Belgian Cavalry — practically annihilated,' she wrote from Stanton Woodhouse, the family's estate in Derbyshire, the week after war was declared: 'We stay here as long as you remain at Belper. I want to be buying comforts for you — what about <u>waterproof boots and coats,</u> for it rains here every day? Wire to me if you are going to be <u>under cover</u> — in <u>tents</u> or <u>barracks,</u> or factories and for pity's sake tell me if anything to <u>buy.</u> I may go to London 1 day soon — think of anything you want. Bless you my dear darling, Yr mother.'

John, Marquis of Granby, was Violet's only surviving son and the heir to the dukedom. On 4 August he had been fishing on the banks of the Wye when the river keeper came running to tell him that war had been declared. Immediately, he left for Leicester to join his regiment at its headquarters in Magazine Square.

Aged twenty-eight, John was a lieutenant in the 4th Leicesters, one of two of the regiment's territorial battalions. His family's association with the Tigers — as the Leicestershires were known — stretched back to the eighteenth century. John's namesake — John Manners, Marquis of Granby — celebrated for his courage in the Seven Years War, had commanded the Leicester Blues at the Highland Revolt; a long line of dukes, including John's father, the 8th Duke, had been honorary colonels of the regiment. The Leicestershires' depots were dotted across the Belvoir estate; historically, the regiment had recruited locally.

On 12 August, the 4th Leicesters marched the forty-four miles from their headquarters to a training camp at Belper. There, they were to await news of their next destination.

News, as Violet's letters revealed, was at a premium in those first weeks of the war. As soon as the British Expeditionary Force sailed for France, the War Office imposed a news blackout, with the result that the newspapers carried practically no news at all. Wild rumours circulated: 'There is still this "Russian Army through England" going on as a "fact". "I saw someone who saw them" was Mrs Abrahams story from Crewe!' Violet reported to her son on 1 September. The Russians, apparently, had landed in Scotland; they were on their way to rescue the beleaguered British Expeditionary Force and had commandeered trains to transport them rapidly south. That afternoon, Violet had instructed her chauffeur to drive her to the local railway station so that she could investigate the rumours herself: 'I went to see the Station Master at Ambergate, but no — tho' he had been warned of troops passing it was countermanded! Such a day! How happy we could have been here if it hadn't been for that tiresome old catspaw Austrian emperor!'

In the absence of any real news, Violet filled her letters with news from home. In the last weeks of August, there had been a flood of volunteers from among the servants at Belvoir Castle; they had all wanted to join John's battalion: 'All the footmen with us — Arthur, William, Charles — and Lamb, the groom, Chambers, the telegraph rider, and the motor cleaner, are going for soldiers. In the 4th Leicesters!! The two last have gone — to Grantham and on!' Attached to her letter was one from her brother, Charlie. 'Lil dear,' he wrote, 'I have a feeling that if John goes abroad, the more Belvoir people near him the better (if he is hit or if he is ill) to help him as they are all devoted to him.'

The two letters conjured an image from another age: of the young Marquis riding into battle flanked by loyal retainers. Yet in those first weeks of the war, people imagined that it would be won or lost by the cavalry. In France, the armies were still on the move: the horror of trench warfare was yet to come. War fever gripped the country. Violet, like everyone else, was caught up by the romance and glamour of it. On 4 September, in her capacity as patron of the Royal Leicester Hospital, she visited the first wounded soldiers to return from the Front. They were casualties from Mons, where the British

Army had been forced to retreat after finding itself outflanked:

Darling J

I was in Leicester Hospital yesterday. A wonderful experience!! Such gentlemen with speech like ours. Such longing to get back. I could not tear myself away. No excited exaggerations — all quite calm. Terribly pleased with their own feats and often saying, 'I don't think there were many left in my regiment.' I go back again today.

A great many small injuries, like 'a horse trod on my foot.' This was the only guardsman there and 'I'm quite all right now' (so beautiful), a 4th Hussar. A red-haired airman with a broken collarbone. Shrapnel in fingers and wrists and lots of cases of rheumatism and abscesses on feet. Some saying, 'England will never know what it was like!'

Lots of incidents told very graphically in groups of cribbage or card players — and then lots of men talking alone to me from their beds. One boy had his father killed and 2 brothers wounded. He doesn't want his mother told nor his sister. He's hoping they'll not know till the end of the war. He is a fresh, very young boy. Their chief misery seemed that when they thought they had just got the better of the enemy they were told to retreat (they almost hesitated at this!).

A few horrors were told in a whisper. One officer, German, forcing his men to advance into barb entanglements, cut their heads off with his sabre when they refused. The Plymouth boy's* death with 7 others was caused at night — he was guarding something and the Germans came dressed as French friends and killed them all.

I was lost in Violet's letters when Mr Granger appeared.

'I thought you might like to see this,' he said. 'It's the 9th Duke's war diary.'

He handed me the diary. It was bound in soft cream leather; the cover was grubby and worn. I read the first entry. It was dated 26 February 1915 — the day John left England for the Western Front:

Left Victoria by 5.55 train for Folkestone. The boat sailed soon after 8 pm. Good crossing and no sight of submarines, though the Captain was quite nervous. Hunlock, the King's Messenger, was on board. Reached Boulogne 9.20. Slept the night at Hôtel Meurice.

* Archer Windsor Clive, the third son of the Earl of Plymouth.

A newspaper cutting was pinned to the inside cover of the diary. John had been appointed Aide-de-Camp to the Commanding Officer of the 46th North Midland Division. The order to embark had been issued at short notice; in anticipation of a spring offensive, reinforcements were needed at the front.

A week earlier, on 19 February, King George V had reviewed the North Midlands at their training camp in Hertfordshire. They were the first territorial division to be sent out to France. 'The troops,' the newspaper reported, 'were honoured by the visit. But when the King addressed the twelve thousand men, the honour, he said, was his.'

John's father, Henry, Duke of Rutland, had accompanied the King. He had helped to raise the division's twelve battalions. They were drawn from the Midlands county regiments — the Sherwood Foresters, the Lincolns, the Leicestershires and the North and South Staffordshires. The Duke had a number of subsidiary estates in the Midlands; he had offered the same inducements to the young men in the villages he owned in Lincolnshire, Nottinghamshire and Derbyshire as he had offered at Belvoir.

The King and the Duke had wished the men good luck and God speed.

Attached to the news cutting was a photograph of John. He is dressed in uniform: the battle dress of a lieutenant in the Leicestershires. Written on the reverse of the picture was the date it had been taken — 11 February 1915, just two weeks before he left for the Front. He is smoking a cigarette and smiling. The shoulder strap of his revolver holster lies taut across his chest; the jacket of his uniform is immaculately fitted. His pose is relaxed, communicating an easy, unassailable authority. The silver tiger on his cap — the cap badge of the Leicestershires — is polished to a high sheen. The image is of a young man almost impossibly blessed. The bachelor heir to a dukedom, and one of the most substantial fortunes in Britain, he is strikingly good-looking.

I studied the photograph for some time. It was the first I had seen of John. Here was the man whom the servants at the castle were eager to serve alongside, the man who, a quarter of a century later, died feet from where I was sitting.

Leafing through the first few pages of his war diary, I could see that it had been meticulously kept. Hundreds of men from the villages on his father's estates had served with the North Midlands: the diary not only offered a record of his experiences, but theirs too.

It was an important discovery in the story that I had come to research.

However, that story was about to change

shape dramatically. Though I didn't realize it at the time, looking back I can pinpoint the moment exactly. Prosaic as it may seem, it came when I went to get a cup of coffee before settling down to read the diary.

Closing the heavy steel door behind me, I left the Muniment Rooms to find my way along the labyrinth of passages.

9

The castle was quiet and there was no one about. Mr Granger had given me directions to the kitchen: 'Follow the passage. Go past the servants' hall. You'll see a swing door. Go through there and you'll find it on your left.'

I stood in the corridor outside the Muniment Rooms. Doors and passages appeared to lead off in every direction. I was not sure which way to go. To the left, a long passage receded into the distance. It was gloomy, lit only by the strip lighting in the display cases that ran along one wall. Ahead, there was a solid oak door, carved in the Gothic style. Another passage led off to my right. I could see that it branched in two. One end led into a small hall. It was in darkness.

'No one goes in there,' a voice whispered behind me.

The woman gave me a fright; I had not heard her coming. I turned round. She was in her early seventies and dressed in the costume of an eighteenth-century parlour maid. A lace mobcap covered her head. Her black dress reached to the floor; her white linen apron was heavily starched.

She stepped forward. 'What are *you* doing in there?' she hissed, pressing her thin face close to mine. 'No one goes in there. Who's let *you* in?'

I realized she was asking about the Muniment Rooms. Startled by her appearance and her hostile tone, I explained briefly why I was there.

Reassured, she seemed keen to stop and chat. She was a tour guide, she told me. In August, from Sunday through to Thursday, the castle was open to the public. 'The visitors like us to dress in costume. It makes the tour more authentic,' she said. The guides, she added proudly, came from families who had served the Dukes of Rutland across generations.

After a few minutes, I said I must be going and asked for directions to the kitchen. She told me to take the passage to the left.

I went on. Some distance ahead, there was a kink in the passage. A man emerged from it, walking towards me. He was wearing knee breeches and a nineteenth-century coachman's jacket. As we drew level, he stopped.

'*Those* rooms are forbidden,' he said. 'What were *you* doing in them?'

On my way back to the Muniment Rooms, other members of the castle's staff approached me. Their questions were the same: 'Who are you? Who's let you in?' Invariably, after the questions, came a statement: 'No one goes in there. Those rooms are forbidden.' Then they would tell me it was where John, the 9th Duke, had died.

I didn't want to stop and talk; I was anxious to get back to work. I assumed that the guides were being proprietorial — that no one had told them that I would be working there. When they said the rooms were 'forbidden', I understood them to mean to visitors straying from the public route.

The clock in the Flag Tower struck twelve. I had been reading John's diary for almost an hour. I paused for a moment to listen to the bell; its tone was surprising: the high, musical notes seemed out of keeping with the castle's solemn Gothic style.

I was halfway through the diary. I had reached 18 June 1915. John and the 4th Leicesters had been out on the Western Front for sixteen weeks. I knew this was a key moment. I had read the battalion's war diary: a harrowing chapter in their story was about to begin.

On 19 June, after spending five days on leave in London, John returned to the North Midlands headquarters at St-Jans-Cappel, nine miles to the west of the front line at Messines:

June 19th 1915 Saturday
St-Jans-Cappel

Got up very late and did practically nothing. Caught 2pm train to go back to France. Punctured three tyres on the way from Boulogne to St Omer, getting there at 11.30pm. Got letter at Boulogne from Rothesay saying he and GOC* were on the water and that we are going to leave our happy home for Reninghelst, Poperinghe Road — damn.

It was against War Office rules to keep a diary. John's last sentence was obtuse, deliberately so. The letter waiting for him at Boulogne contained two pieces of momentous news. His division was about to be drafted to Sanctuary Wood in the Ypres Salient, the scene in recent months of the bitterest fighting on the Western Front. Within the fortnight the division would be 'going over the top'.

It was the first time the division was to be deployed in an attack. Since landing in France, the North Midlands had had a comparatively quiet time. Periodically, for the purposes of training and acclimatization, the three brigades had been rotated into the trenches on the western slope of the Messines ridge, but there was little fighting in

* General Officer Commanding.

their sector. Even so, in the sixteen weeks since the division had arrived in France, 325 officers and 1,600 other ranks had been killed or wounded.

These numbers paled in comparison to the casualties suffered by the divisions that had fought in the Ypres Salient. In the first nine months of the war, this small corner of the front, barely three miles by four, had claimed hundreds of thousands of lives. In April, the 1st Canadian Division had lost 7,000 men in forty-eight hours; the previous October, the 7th Division — named the 'Immortal Seventh' after its heroic stand — had incurred 8,373 casualties.

John's battalion, which was attached to 138th Brigade, was one of the first to be drafted into the Salient. On a warm summer's evening — Tuesday, 22 June — the four thousand men marched the six miles from their camp at Dranoutre to Ouderdom, a hamlet outside Ypres. By midnight, they were bivouacked in an open field. Here, the brigade was to wait until 19.00 hours on 29 June, when it was to proceed to Sanctuary Wood.

'It was a pleasant bivouac,' Captain Milne, an officer in the 4th Leicesters recalled. 'There was a farmhouse with its usual supplies of café au lait; there was a homely-looking windmill; there were one or two cows and a very young bull in a field; there was also "Les Trois Amis", an estaminet, where beer was supplied in a little back garden where one sat on a rickety chair by a tin-topped table and the daughter of the house (a rather plain girl) wearing a black dress and black cotton stockings came to and fro with glasses. It was warm weather and for a week it was not a bad war.'

But as Milne recorded, the thought of what awaited the battalion at Ypres cast a shadow over that week: 'Everybody knew what a visit there meant. Shelling by day and night, gas attacks, mines, bombing and all kinds of bloodiness.' As they waited to go up the line, their days and nights were spent watching the activity along the wagon track that ran to the south of the hamlet. The track led to the trenches in the Ypres Salient.

'What a track it was,' Milne remembered:

All sorts and conditions of soldiery passed along it; mounted staff officers with orderlies riding behind at a respectful distance; galloping Belgian interpreters hanging on by their spurs; limbered wagons with highly burnished hubs, obviously belonging to some Regular unit with a proper appreciation of spit and polish; Royal Engineers with mules bearing telephone equipment; an occasional Sepoy with thin legs and inscrutable countenance; an occasional section of field guns; an occasional platoon.

It was at night that the track became really

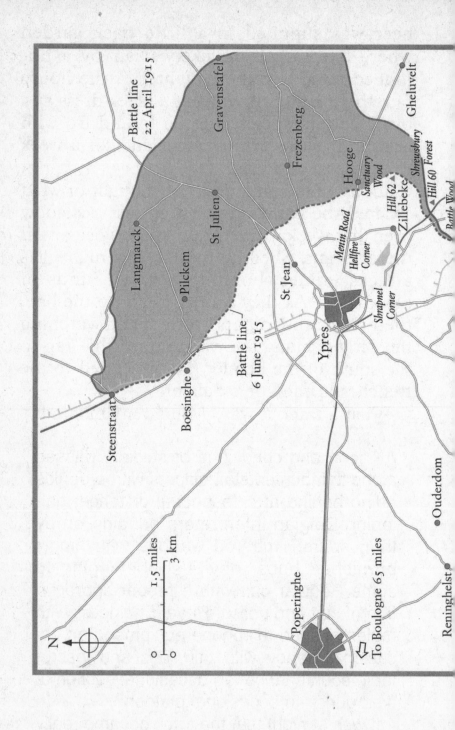

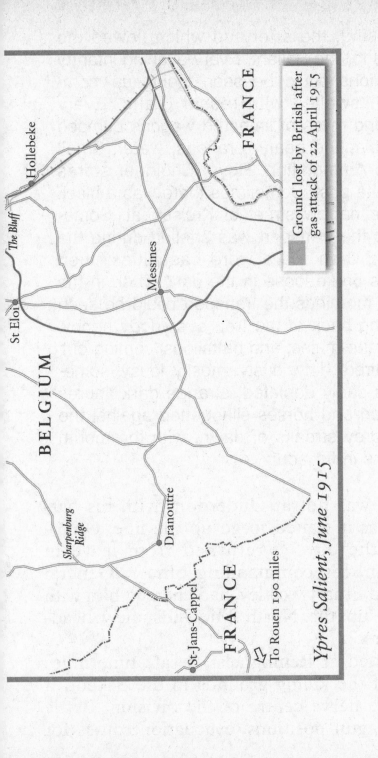

BELGIUM

Hollebeke

The Bluff

St Eloi

Messines

FRANCE

Sharpenburg Ridge

Dranoutre

St-Jans-Cappel

FRANCE

To Rouen 190 miles

Ypres Salient, June 1915

Ground lost by British after
gas attack of 22 April 1915

imposing, the artery up which flowed the blood for the Salient. Every evening infantry battalions could be seen 'going up' complete, swelled with recent drafts. Every evening miles of limbered wagons bumped and clanked bearing rations, water, Small Arms Ammunition, Royal Engineer stores and the post. Sometimes there was a block in the narrow street of Kruisstraat. Sometimes the transport was shelled during the block; then there were casualties, then mules broke loose in the dark. Then in the early mornings the transport could be seen coming back at the trot, everybody happy, even the mules; and battalions 'coming out' dog tired, dirty, dusty, mostly lousy, sometimes sadly depleted, strange dark figures of men and horses silhouetted against the first grey streaks of dawn, with the mouth organs in full song.

John was not at Ouderdom with his battalion as it waited to go up the line. On 19 June, the day he returned from leave in London, his commanding officer, General Edward Stuart Wortley, had charged him with setting up the North Midlands' new headquarters.

Situated at Reninghelst, a safe nine miles west of the killing grounds in the Salient, it was the nerve centre of the division. Battle orders, gun positions, evacuation routes for the wounded — details of the division's every move had passed across John's desk. I had read Milne's memoir and the battalions' war diaries for the weeks that followed: it was thrilling to think that his diary offered another contemporary record of the difficult days to come.

I turned the page expectantly. Frustratingly, the entries were brief. John had recorded only the barest of information:

June 20th: Spent most of the day looking at the farm and arranging how to place tents and huts etc . . .

June 21st: . . . Went over to our future head-quarters again — took Commander Royal Engineers round etc

June 22nd: ditto

'Ditto'? This was odd. The 22nd of June was the date his battalion had marched to Ouderdom: it was on its way to Sanctuary Wood, one of the most notorious sections of trenches on the Western Front. Yet he had not thought it worthy of mention.

I read on:

June 24th: Got up at 6 am, started seeing the headquarters packing up etc. I went on with the three motors full and Guthrie brought the wagons and horses on. I had a hard day pitching the camp and arranging everything — including all sanitary arrangements, building huts etc . . .

June 25th: Spent all day in camp as I am acting camp commandant.

June 26th: Spent all day in camp working hard. There is a lot to do to look after a Div. staff.

June 27th: In our camp all morning. Went over with General to see Corps Commander General Allenby. We are now in V Corps . . .

John's brevity was curious. Another week had passed, and he had said very little. Given the hectic preparations for the coming days, one explanation was that he had been too busy to keep up his diary. Except, I noticed, on 23 June, he had 'Spent most of the day doing nothing.'

The page that followed was even more puzzling. Four days — 28 June to 1 July — were entered on the one page.

On 30 June and 1 July, John had written just two words: 'Usual day.'

But then how could they possibly have been *usual days*? At 19.00 hours on the evening of the 29th, 138th Brigade had marched out of Ouderdom along the wagon track up to the front line. In their first forty-eight hours in the trenches they had come under heavy shellfire. John was at Reninghelst, the division's headquarters; he was ADC to its commanding officer: he would have seen the dispatches from the Front. On both 30 June and 1 July, he would have known that nine miles away, at Sanctuary Wood, all hell was breaking loose. So why hadn't he referred to the fighting?

I turned to the next page of the diary.

July 2nd 1915 Friday

Reninghelst, Poperinghe Road

Usual day. I went after lunch to Ypres Cathedral to get a few more fragments of the frieze of the screen — found a lot more.

Again, there was no mention of the war. John, it appears, had spent that afternoon souvenir hunting in the shelled ruins of the Cathedral.

He had already been there twice that week: 'Went to Ypres Cathedral,' he recorded on 28 June: 'The only thing left, curiously, is the marble and brass screen against the Chapel in the south side of the nave. A portion of the screen at one end has been destroyed. I picked up a bit of the fragments of the frieze.' The following afternoon, he was there again: 'Got a good few more pieces,' he noted: 'I

99

have put together the pieces I got yesterday and want to find more pieces to try and complete the frieze plaque which was broken to pieces.'

On 2 July — having spent the afternoon at the cathedral — John returned to headquarters. At 8 p.m., General Clifford, the Commanding Officer of 138th Brigade, sent a communiqué from the Salient. The brigade had suffered thirty-five casualties in twenty-four hours: its highest figure in a single day so far. A number of the casualties came from 'B' company in the 4th Leicestershires. It was John's own company; he had known the men personally. From 1909 — when the battalion was formed — they had spent their summers training together. It seemed incredible that he had failed to enter this distressing news in his diary.

As I read on, it was clear that pressure of work did not account for the omission. I was left with the impression that, while 138th Brigade was fighting in the Salient, neither John, nor his General, Edward Stuart Wortley, were overly occupied.

On the morning of 3 July, the brigade's fourth day in the line, they had left headquarters: 'Started at 8 alone with the General, and Tanner the chauffeur, to go to Rouen in the Rolls. Got there at one (two punctures), inspected the drafts. Then we went sightseeing.' They seemed to be in no hurry to get back to HQ; instead, they spent the night at the Hôtel de la Poste in Rouen. After dinner, John visited a nearby brothel: 'I rogered a woman in the Maison Stephane. Not good,' he records.

Something wasn't right. It was as if a different person was writing the diary. Throughout April, he had crammed the pages with vivid accounts of the progress of the war. Yet two months on, he appeared to have completely disengaged from the events going on around him.

I turned back to look at the earlier entries. On the night of 22 April, when the Germans had fired poison gas for the first time, he had been with the 46th North Midland at St-Jans-Cappel, twelve miles to the south-west of the Ypres Salient. On the morning of the 23rd, he and a group of officers had driven to Sharpenburg Hill to watch the battle from an official observation point. It had continued for the remainder of that week. Keyed up by the fighting, John had followed the course of the battle, often updating his diary twice in a day:

23 April: Up to Sharpenburg to see what there was to be seen of the battle just north of Ypres. Anxiously awaiting news all day. Canadians standing and attacking. Ypres completely wrecked by shells, half of it burnt. All inhabitants fled. The French are trying to retrieve the

3 miles they have lost. A perfect hell has been raging all last night and all day today and going on still (12 midnight). French sending up reinforcements as hard as they can — so are we. The gas felt by our own troops.

24 April: News this morning bad, what there is of it. The Germans have got a little further over the canal and I hear the Canadian left has had to fall further back. Both the French and us are badly outnumbered by guns. We have practically none. We have sent up the 4th Division and two Cavalry Divisions but without any guns. The French talk a lot saying they are sending up a whole corps and lots of guns, but the guns have not opened fire yet and their soldiers seem unable to hold the Germans . . . It all looks quite bad, unless we can push the Germans back a bit. I don't think the 27th and 28th Brigades will be able to hold out as they are being shelled from three sides. It looks as if we will have to give up the Ypres Salient and straighten our line behind Ypres.

11.30pm: News bad. Both English and French counterattacks failed owing to gas.

25 April: Battle has been going on all night with little result. The French are going to attack in force at 12 today. Again the French attack failed owing to gas. The French and English reserves

still coming up. The battle still going on without ceasing.

26 April: Battle went on all night again. The French and English now have over 200,000 men and a terrific battle has been going on all day. I watched it all the afternoon from Sharpenburg Hill. I never heard anything like the noise. The whole country is darkened by the smoke.

12 midnight: At last we have made a little headway. All day we have been held back by this damnable gas. My God, the Germans are the limit. The gas kills the soldiers by causing an acute attack of pneumonia and bronchitis which makes them die black from suffocation. I am off to Boulogne to try to buy 1700 yds of gauze for our men to tie over their mouths. The whole civilized world ought to rise up in arms and wipe out Germany for this. The Canadians have done perfectly wonderfully. They saved the situation for two days. My God, what a hell it must have been and is . . . We all pray for a change of wind then we should give them hell, but this gas is a knockout.

12.30am: News better just now — the French have made progress. The list of German prisoners will be small after this. I don't fancy much quarter will be given now — the buggers.

27th April: Started at 8.30am for Boulogne to buy gauze for the Division to put over their mouths to cope with this bloody gas. Bought a lot of gauze and we got back about 7pm. It takes three hours to get there. Not much news except the French can't make much headway, nor can we. The casualties must be terrific. The battle still goes on.

John paid for the gauze out of his own pocket. In that anxious week in April, he was viscerally engaged in the progress of the war and concerned for the welfare of his men. So why, two months later, when they were actually fighting in the Salient, had he become so detached? Did the terse entries, and the absence of any references to the fighting, or to the 4th Leicesters, conceal a bitter disappointment — even feelings of guilt on his part — at not being with them? His appointment as ADC to the division's commanding officer had been an order; on the night his battalion marched up the wagon track into the Salient, he had no choice but to remain behind at headquarters.

The 4th Leicesters left the trenches at Sanctuary Wood at 11.45 p.m. on 5 July. 'The Companies marched back independently to Ouderdom covering the eight miles by 5am the next day,' Captain Milne remembered: 'It was a wonderful summer morning: the sun shone, the air was fresh, there was not a cloud in the sky. It felt very good to be alive, and to be back again by the quiet, peaceful-looking old windmill, with the prospect of six days' rest, very good to be out of the wood, altogether too much stuff flying about up there.'

John had felt none of their euphoria. Nor did he refer to his battalion in his diary. 'Usual day — went to tea with Pulteney'* was all he wrote.

'Usual day.' It was a phrase that John had used repeatedly. Four of the days between 29 June and 5 July he had described as such. It did not make sense. Then I turned to the next page of his diary.

The date — 6 July — was written at the top. The rest of the page was blank. I looked at the one that followed, and the one after that. They were blank too. So was every other page, right through to the end of the diary.

It was frustrating. I knew that in the months to follow, there were dramatic events to come. After seventeen weeks in reserve, the North Midlands had spent most of that summer in the front line. In the autumn of 1915, at the Battle of Loos, it would experience its worst day of the entire war. On 13 October, in five ghastly hours, it lost a quarter of its strength: 3,763 men were killed or wounded — 180

* Lieutenant-General Sir William Pulteney, CO III Corps.

officers and 3,583 other ranks. John's diary had appeared to promise so much: a contemporaneous record, day by day. But he had abandoned it at exactly the moment the North Midlands had entered the thick of fighting.

I got up from my desk to fetch the catalogue to the Muniment Rooms. The blank pages in the diary were hugely disappointing. But at least the trail was not cold. On the shelves around me, there were John's letters home. There would be news of him in other family letters. I could follow his story through the correspondence in the blue files.

I made a note of the case and shelf numbers for every file relating to the year 1915. Two were of immediate interest: John's letters to his mother, Violet, Duchess of Rutland, and to his uncle, Charlie Lindsay.

John's letters to the Duchess were kept in Room 2. I looked at these first. Thumbing through the months to find the ones he had written in the summer and autumn of 1915, my heart sank. I had almost reached the bottom of the pile and it was only June. In July, the stream of letters stopped: John's last letter to his mother was dated the 6th.

The 6th of July.

The coincidence cast a shadow. It was the date John's diary had stopped.

Straightaway, I walked back along the passage to Room 1. John's letters to his uncle were kept there. The correspondence between them spanned twenty-five years; I pulled at the file for 1915. Even before I looked at it, I had an inkling of what I was about to find. Quickly, I flicked through the pages. John's last letter to Charlie was also dated 6 July.

Twenty-eight-year-old John, Marquis of Granby, had vanished. I felt a rising sense of panic. This was far from being the pristine archive I had imagined. I went across to my desk and looked at my list. I had identified a further twenty files that related to the year 1915. They contained the Duke and Duchess's correspondence, and that of their three daughters — John's immediate family. Surely their letters would yield clues to his whereabouts and the reason — or reasons — behind his apparent disappearance.

By the time I got to the fourth file, a clear pattern was emerging. It was not only John who had vanished. So, it appeared, had the entire Manners family. After 6 July, their letters *to* John — and theirs to each other — were also missing.

The tour guides' words kept floating into my mind. *No one goes in there.* But I was beginning to think someone *had* been in here. The apparent excision was meticulous. It extended with absolute precision from 7 July to 5 December 1915.

The discovery of such a significant void was a major setback. Without the letters, I had no means of chronicling the family's story — and the story of their great estate — at this important stage in the war.

But it wasn't just that. The fact that they were missing was so peculiar.

These were 152 critical days. They coincided with a period when John's regiment had incurred appalling casualties. On 13 October 1915 — the day the North Midlands had lost a quarter of their strength — the Leicestershires had suffered 820 casualties: the equivalent, almost, of an entire battalion. Twenty of John's fellow officers had been killed or wounded. These were men he had dined with in the officers' mess and alongside whom he had served day after day. A significant proportion of the regiment's casualties had come from villages on the Belvoir estate. They were the sons of the butcher, the blacksmith, the postmaster — and the sons of gamekeepers, farmers, estate workers and tenants. John's father, Henry, the 8th Duke of Rutland, had been Honorary Colonel of two of the regiment's battalions; he had personally recruited a large number of the soldiers. And yet there did not appear to be a single reference to this terrible day in the family's archives.

10

'What are *you* doing in there? Who's let *you* in?'

It was happening again. Another woman had approached me in the passage outside the Muniment Rooms.

'Those rooms are forbidden,' she said, pointing towards them. 'When I was a house-maid here, the housekeeper used to lock us in there while we were cleaning. She used to come and get us at coffee time. Then we'd be locked back in again.'

'You were *locked* in? Why?'

'It was to stop us taking anything out,' she said. 'No one went in there.'

'When did you work here?' I asked her.

'In the 1940s and '50s,' she replied. 'Those rooms were sealed. They were sealed after the Duke died.'

This woman seemed to be saying something other than the tour guides who had stopped me earlier. There really did seem to be a mystery attached to these rooms. I looked at her. She was in her early eighties and not in costume like the others.

'Which duke?' I asked.

'John, Duke,' she said.

'You mean the 9th Duke?'

The woman nodded.

'Why were the rooms sealed?' I asked.

'The family had secrets they wanted to hide,' she replied.

'What secrets?'

She gave me a thin smile and then turned and left.

Outside on the terrace, it was a beautiful summer's day. I walked over to the cannons to look at the view from the battlements. Beneath the parapet, the lawn fell gently away to the Rose Garden below. It was late August and the roses had faded; their petals scattered the walkways, vibrant pinks against the cool grey stone. A line of topiary stretched away to the right; the yew hedges were cone-shaped and clipped so smoothly you wanted to run your hand along them. Nearby stood the statues, sculpted by Caius Cibber in the seventeenth century, which the 5th Duke had acquired on a visit to Italy. Everything was so idyllic, so immutable, yet the beauty of it all jarred with what I had discovered: the sealing of the Muniment Rooms pointed to something dark beneath this perfect, ordered surface.

I stood there for some time. There were so many questions. Had I stumbled across something? Was there a link between the missing war letters and whatever it was the family had wanted to hide? The coincidence between the blank pages in John's war diary and the gap in the correspondence suggested that something had gone badly wrong for him on 6 July. But then if the void in the records concealed some sort of controversy, surely the present Duke of Rutland would not have given me permission to research this period in his family's history? Or was the former housemaid in possession of a secret of which he was unaware?

Thinking about it, there had to be a more prosaic explanation. Quite probably, I decided, the missing letters were stored in another part of the castle. I needed to find out where.

I found Mr Granger in Room 4. He was sitting at a large desk in the centre of the room, immersed in his work. The desk was cluttered; parchment rolls, reference books and hundreds of letters were piled on top of it.

He looked up, peering at me over the rims of his tortoiseshell spectacles.

'How are you getting on?' he asked.

'Not very well,' I replied.

I summarized the gap I had discovered in the family's correspondence. Mr Granger looked surprised.

'Did you know the letters were missing?' I asked.

'No,' he said. 'How odd.'

He paused, thinking for a moment. 'I haven't come across any gaps. But then I've only been here for a couple of years. There's so much material, I'm only just beginning to get to grips with it myself.'

'Perhaps — because they were written in wartime — the letters were thought to be of special interest and kept together as a separate collection,' I suggested. 'Could they be stored somewhere else in the castle?'

'I doubt it,' he said. 'As far as I've been given to understand, all of the family correspondence is stored here in the Muniment Rooms. It was as the 9th Duke wanted it.'

I asked Mr Granger if the rumour that these rooms had been sealed after his death was true. His response was cautious.

'The Muniment Rooms have been jealously guarded by the family. That I do know. In the last Duke's time — the 10th Duke, that is — I believe access was barred to researchers. The present Duke is very selective about who he allows in. But no, I wasn't aware the rooms had ever actually been sealed.'

'So even if they weren't sealed, you think it's unlikely that someone outside the family could have removed the letters?'

'Very unlikely,' he said. 'But why don't you

ask the Duchess? I would talk to her. She'll be here later on.'

It was shortly after three o'clock when the Duchess came into the Muniment Rooms. We had met before. A lively, elegant woman in her forties, she was writing her own book on the history of Belvoir Castle and had a detailed knowledge of the documents in these rooms.

Briefly, I explained what I had discovered: how, after 6 July 1915, until December of that year, there was a large gap in the family's correspondence, and that the start of this void coincided with the date John's war diary had stopped.

The Duchess looked at me, amazed. 'There can't be such a large gap,' she said. 'The letters must be here somewhere.'

'They couldn't be somewhere else in the castle?' I asked.

'No, everything is kept in here,' she said. 'The family's letters have been stored in here since John's time.'

'Could someone have removed them?'

She frowned. 'I can't see how,' she replied. 'My father-in-law closed these rooms after John died. No one outside the family has seen the early-twentieth-century material. The letters can't have been removed.'

'Why did the Duke close the rooms?' I asked.

'They were of no interest to him,' she said. 'Why, I don't know. But he didn't want to have anything to do with them. He just shut them up.' She paused for a moment. 'It was odd, given that his father had spent so much time in here.'

'Perhaps the letters have been lost?' I suggested.

'No,' she said firmly. 'John kept everything. Letters and historical documents were his great passion. Especially anything to do with the family. He spent his life cataloguing and filing their letters. They're all up there on the shelves,' she said, gesturing at the cases around us. 'Roger — John's youngest son — told me that his father always used to say you must never throw letters away. It is thanks to John that we have the Muniment Rooms. He created them. He was completely fascinated with history. Anything to do with history.'

'So when did he set the rooms up?' I asked her.

'It was soon after the First World War. The family's letters — some five hundred years of them — were scattered all over the castle. These rooms didn't exist then: or at least not as they are now. They were used as offices. John cleared them out, and he gathered together all this material. He also bought a lot of historical documents at auction. It was his life's work. He spent a lot of time in here.

In the last years of his life he rarely left these rooms.'

'He was supposed to have hidden five precious gems in here — rubies,' she added, laughing. 'A family myth, I expect, but his daughter, Ursula, told me. We've all had a good look for them, but they've never been found. Apparently, they were his insurance against bad times. Before he died, he was convinced the Communists were going to take over — this was where he died, you know — on the sofa in Room 1.'

'What did he die of?' I asked.

'Pneumonia,' she replied. 'He was only fifty-three. He had an oxygen tent moved in here. It was where he wanted to be, Roger said.'

The Duchess got up to leave. 'It's very peculiar. I can't believe the letters are missing. Are you sure you've had a really good look for them?'

I explained that I had only looked through the files relating to 1915.

'I'd go through the other boxes, if I were you. Maybe the missing letters have been misfiled.'

My face must have fallen. There were several thousand box files in the Muniment Rooms. It would take me days to go through them.

The Duchess laughed. 'Good luck,' she said.

She left the room. I could hear her footsteps receding along the passage. Then she stopped.

'Oh,' I heard her say. 'Wait a minute.'

She came back into the room.

'Have you tried the Tower Rooms? You might find the letters up there.'

'The Tower Rooms?'

'Yes, they're up in the East Tower. It was where John lived before he married. It was a sort of bachelor apartment. A lot of his things are still there.'

The East Tower, a fanciful structure with a canted end and Gothic buttresses and corner turrets, was in the far north-east corner of the castle. John's bachelor apartments were right at the top of the tower. Climbing the spiral staircase leading up to them, it struck me how remote these rooms would have been from those occupied by the rest of his family. At last — after ninety-four steps — I reached a landing. I kept straight on, heading towards the door at the end of the corridor.

It led into a bright, spacious hall. The view from the window that ran along one side of it was spectacular. Fields of crops stretched green and golden across the plain going towards Lincoln. It was exhilarating to be high up and in the open, away from the oppressive Gothic style of the floors below.

Three rooms led off the hall. Before beginning the search for the missing letters, I had

116

a quick look through them. It was evident that no one had lived up here since 1916 — the year John had married and moved out. The rooms were in a state of disarray: items of his furniture — worn leather armchairs, ancient lamp stands and boxes of old crockery — were stacked against the walls. In the room that he had used as a bedroom, the iron bedstead and the mattress that he had slept on were still there. It felt as if John had just left. Jumbled on the floor were the books and magazines that he had read. There were stuffed birds — the decoys he had used out shooting — and an old wooden globe. Even his hipbath was there. My spirits soared: the missing letters had to be in these rooms somewhere.

I began the search in the hall. It seemed the most promising place to start. Along one side of it, there were two Victorian writing desks; opposite them were three cabinets, each with sixteen numbered drawers. Beside them, piled up against the skirting boards, were rows and rows of boxes. These were places where the missing letters might be.

I started with the boxes. They were crammed with medieval corbels and gargoyles, each of the figures as grotesque as the next. I picked up one of the smaller ones; the severed stone head of a woman, clad in a wimple, sat easily in my hand. A label was attached to it. It had come from the site of Belvoir Priory, an eleventh-century abbey, which John had excavated in 1923. It was extraordinary to think that the carving, one of many that had lain, forgotten, in these boxes, was almost a thousand years old. I got up and walked over to the window. I could see the site where the priory had once stood: it was just below the castle, opposite the gates to the lodge.

Next, I tried one of the cabinets. The top drawer slid open easily. Inside were rows of glass boxes filled with birds' eggs. They were carefully labelled in John's hand. The kitsch way they were displayed was disconcerting; in each of the boxes, five eggs sat snugly in a tiny nest of delicately woven twigs and leaves. The twigs looked as if they had been specially gathered and cut to size. Had John made the nests himself, I wondered?

I opened the other drawers. These too were filled with eggs. There was something oddly compelling about the range of species and the meticulous way the collection had been ordered. The further I went down the cabinet, the bigger the eggs became: linnets, kingfishers, red-backed shrikes, snipes, dotterels, little grebes — until I got to the bottom drawer, which was full of puffin eggs.

I moved on to the two cabinets beside it, and began working my way through the thirty-two drawers. They contained yet more birds' eggs. In one drawer, I discovered some nightingale eggs that John had found on the Western Front in May 1915. Inside the box, there was a letter, which had been carefully folded. John had found the eggs at St-Jans-Cappel, a few miles behind the front-line trenches at Messines. The letter — to his uncle — was dated 23 May. It was a Sunday — a little over six weeks before John had vanished into thin air.

'Old Boy,' he had written:

Just a line to say good morning. I have no news whatsoever to give you. The French seem to be making gradual slow movements in the right direction. This afternoon Rothesay and I had nothing on earth to do so we went out into a jolly wood with books to read — very nice and quiet and peaceful, also lots of birds about.

I noticed a pair of nightingales and after a little trouble tracked them to their nest — which I took — a nice clutch of 5 — but also I forgot to bring my nesting appliances for blowing, etc. Would you look, old boy, in my bedroom, and on one of the bookshelves you will see a cigar box. Will you take out all the blow pipes and drills and send them to me in another box — and place the cigar box back on the shelf — I wanted a nightingale's clutch and also it will be interesting as taken in

France in 1915, won't it? I blew one egg this evening with a straw but it was an awful job.

Goodnight old cock — don't worry for the present.

It was the only letter I'd found. I looked through the two desks in the hall — and another chest of drawers. There was no sign of the missing correspondence.

Leaving the hall, I went into the room that John had used as a bedroom. Painted a pale shade of blue, it faced west, with a view across the terraced gardens. A tall glass-fronted cupboard stood against one wall. I turned the key to open it and peered inside. On the shelf directly in front of me was a large porcelain fruit bowl, prettily decorated with patterns of flowers. Looking closer, it appeared to contain fragments of bones. Gingerly, I read the label attached to it. The bones were the remains of the medieval monks that John had exhumed from Belvoir Priory. Next to the bowl, there were pieces of seventeenth-century slipware and saltglaze pottery. There was also a pile of clay cuneiform tablets dating from the Babylonian period. I knew that John had been passionately interested in archaeology: the things in this cupboard had come from the sites that he had excavated. But to have kept the fragments of human bone suggested a fascination that verged on the morbid.

I focused on the rest of the room. It was crammed with John's furniture. There were no other places where the missing letters might be. The large room at the end of the hall was virtually empty. There was just one room left to search.

As I entered, a wooden gantry, suspended from the ceiling, startled me. I had not spotted it earlier: it was in a corner to the left of the door. From a distance, the sinister-looking racks and pulleys lent it the appearance of some sort of instrument of torture. Littered across the floor in front of it were hundreds of small oblong wooden boxes; once stacked in piles, they had collapsed and fallen sideways.

Stepping around the boxes, I went over to have a look at the gantry.

At close hand, it was evident that it had been constructed as a housing for photographic equipment. A series of brass lamps, of different sizes, hung from the racks; the pulleys had been used to adjust the lighting. I bent down and picked up one of the wooden boxes. Inside it, there were some forty glass negatives, each wrapped in glassine paper. I held one up to the light. It was a photograph of John, aged four. The picture had a melancholy air about it. He stood, leaning against a pillar, holding the lead of a large dog which lay at his feet. He was wearing a velvet smock;

his delicate, elfin face had a forlorn expression. 'Myself. Belvoir Castle. 1890,' the caption read.

I turned to look at the hundreds of boxes scattered over the floor. Here was yet *another* collection. The gargoyles, the birds' eggs, the bones and the bits and pieces in the cupboard in the blue room were all things that John had collected. And now these. Thousand upon thousand of glass negatives — photographs that he had taken, and which he had catalogued himself. Then I thought of the rooms below, deep in the bowels of the castle, and the hundreds of files spanning nine hundred years of history: John, I knew, had also catalogued every one of those tens of thousands of documents.

This man's obsession with collecting struck me as pathological. The pursuit and ordering of objects appeared to lie at the core of his personality. It seemed to go far beyond mere interest — it was all-consuming, a compulsion. It looked as if these collections represented some sort of refuge, a form of escape into a private world. But what had he wanted to escape from? I had read Honoré de Balzac's *Le Cousin Pons,* the story of a man who was a dedicated collector. The novel was autobiographical. Balzac blamed his own obsessive interest in collecting on his mother's ill treatment of him. 'I never had a mother,' he said. Sigmund Freud had also suggested that a compulsive interest in collecting pointed to emotional deprivation, or abuse, in infancy.

I had been in the Tower Rooms for nearly two hours. I had searched every box, every drawer, every cupboard. I had found nothing to shed light on John's disappearance in the summer of 1915; the missing letters that I had hoped to find were not up here. All that I had discovered were the signs of an obsessive personality — a man who appeared to have been fascinated by order, and by things that were deathly and grotesque.

Retracing my route — down the spiral staircase and along the passages in the old servants' quarters — I made my way back to the Muniment Rooms. The only hope I had of finding the missing letters was if, as the Duchess had suggested, they had been misfiled.

11

I put the file back in its place on the bottom shelf of the case. It was the last one. It had taken me three days to go through the five rooms. Systematically, I had looked through 2,096 files. It was now clear that the missing correspondence was nowhere in the castle. The letters had not been misfiled. They were lost.

I shut down my computer and began to pack up my things. I was never going to find the letters. Without them, I would have to look for another setting for the book. It was bitterly disappointing. I had set my heart on writing about the Belvoir estate in the First World War. With the exception of the missing months in 1915, the material I needed to bring that world back to life was all here; the Muniment Rooms were a treasure trove. But the vital piece had turned out to be missing. It was only in the summer of 1915 that the horror of the war had begun to hit home. It was then, after months in training, that the volunteers from the Duke's estate — and John, the man who would one day inherit it — had been drafted into action on the battlefields abroad. I had no means of following their stories; extraordinarily, at this key moment, the record was blank.

But as I packed away my things, the puzzle kept turning in my mind. The four days at Belvoir Castle had left me with an uneasy feeling. It was not just that the letters were lost. A process of filleting had gone on. *7 July to 5 December 1915.* The *same* 152 days had been excised right across the different collections of correspondence. The fact that the letters had been extracted for the same period suggested that it was one person who had removed them. The precision with which the documents had been removed was unsettling. I'd found twenty-two files relating to the year 1915; a large number contained letters spanning the years on either side: whoever had extracted the missing months had assiduously rifled the files.

I found it impossible to shake off the niggling feeling that something peculiar lay behind the void in the records. I was not going to leave just yet. I wanted to know who had taken the letters and why.

It seemed a futile exercise, but I took out my notebook and began to jot down a list of possibilities. The Duchess, I noted, was sure that the letters had not been removed in the ten years since she and the Duke had been living at the castle. David, her husband, had become Duke in 1999; before that, his father, Charles — John's eldest son — had been Duke. The Duchess had dismissed the thought that anyone could have removed the correspondence in Charles's time; her father-in-law, apparently, had closed these rooms to outsiders. Yet it was impossible for her to be absolutely certain on this point. How could she be? She had not been there. Assuming the Muniment Rooms had remained out of bounds to outsiders, they would still have been open to members of the family.

John had had five children; they in turn had had children of their own. Between 1940 — when John died — and 1999 — when the present Duke had succeeded his father — upwards of twenty members of the Manners family had either lived at the castle or visited it regularly. The most likely scenario was that someone inside the family had removed the letters at some point in that period. Quite why they might have wanted to hide the entire correspondence for five months in 1915 was baffling, but as I didn't know the content of the letters, they could have had any number of motives. Whichever way I looked at it, the permutations appeared end-less, the trail to the missing correspondence completely cold.

Wearily, I set the notebook aside. In three

days, I had performed the same mechanical action 2,096 times: reaching for a file; lifting the blue lid; raising the butterfly clip; thumbing through the letters to check they matched the label on the box. The sheer tedium of it still resonated.

Then a thought suddenly struck me. *Surely the butterfly clips offered an important clue?* Every time I had opened a file containing material that spanned the early twentieth century, I had noticed that the clips, which had corroded, had left a single, pristine imprint on the top letter. The mark, stencilled in rust several millimetres thick, suggested that the letters had never been looked at. If someone had removed them after John died, the clips would have left a double imprint. In raising them, I had broken time's seal.

No one — aside from John — had had access to the files *before* he died. The most logical hypothesis was that the man who had created this historic archive had also created the void in the correspondence.

But was this right? It seemed so counter-intuitive as to be almost implausible. The empirical evidence, both in these rooms and in his rooms up in the East Tower, pointed to a man who had collected, ordered — even hoarded — historical papers and artefacts. He had devoted twenty years of his life to cataloguing and filing the tens of thousands of documents in the Muniment Rooms. In doing so, he had set out to build a seamless record of his family, going back to the mid-eleventh century. It was John who had compiled the volume 'Specimens of the handwriting of the Manners Family'; painstakingly, he had pored over the many thousands of their letters to select an example of each of their handwriting. Could he really have deliberately punctured the record — one that he had created, and which, up until the summer of 1915, appeared otherwise flawless?

It was his war diary that convinced me that he had. On exactly the date the diary stops — 6 July 1915 — so too did the stream of family correspondence. It was too much of a coincidence. I could only assume that John had destroyed these letters because they contained information about whatever had happened to him in the summer of 1915.

Possibly, by working back through the family's correspondence over the preceding months, I would find something to shed light on it. But before going any further, I wanted to check whether these were the only months that were missing. I was still troubled by the fact that the excisions contradicted what I knew of John's character. Was this the only gap in the correspondence? Or had he removed other chapters from his life?

I decided to look at the correspondence between John and his uncle, Charlie Lindsay.

There were twenty-two blue files. Beginning in the 1890s, when John was a small boy, their letters spanned more than thirty years and numbered several thousand in total. If there were other missing periods, these files would reveal them.

It was then that I discovered that John had created not one but three gaps in his biography.

The first began on 23 August 1894, a few weeks before his eighth birthday; the second on 6 June 1909, when he was twenty-two. Including the void in 1915, he had obliterated 356 days from the archive. It was clear that the gaps were no accident. They recurred in each of the collections of letters.

What I discovered next served only to heighten the mystery. In the months leading up to 6 June 1909 — the start of the second gap in the records — John, who by then was Honorary Attaché at the British Embassy in Rome, had sent a flurry of telegrams and letters to Charlie. For the most part, they were written in cipher.

12

British Embassy, Rome
23 February 1909

Old Boy,
Just a line to let you know what I think of the 24906 35427 11411 53702 66892 27490 4732 21131 54224 it 89231 79619 23604 83705 72630 79967 83294 69631 50011 is 54123. 92141 77117 38519 72432 14041 60903 to the 14066/ 50215/ 12001/ 20039 77129/ 21115/ 61232/ 72603/ 19731 83220 69699 65906 and, 50999 70901 83110 21166 82915 70444 61291 23615 — and so 50000 53741 47314 54330 83309 86154 and 53131 78042 40319 62731.

I forgot if I told you to put the following numbers down for 'ing': 956 957 958 960 — as one uses 'ing' so often and it is so noticeable.

Goodnight old cock, J

This was one of thirty-four letters that John

had encrypted to his uncle. Looking at the rows of meaningless numbers, I began to feel overwhelmed by the strangeness of what I was finding. John was evidently using a complex cipher. So how had he become such an accomplished cryptologist?

My first thought was that he had been involved in intelligence work at the embassy.

But then why would he have encrypted his letters to his uncle? A quick check through the records in the Muniment Rooms revealed that Charlie Lindsay was a well-known antiquarian and bibliophile. Cryptology was one of his hobbies. Most probably, he had taught John to write in code. So was it simply a game between them? Or did the cipher conceal important information?

The fact that John had used it in the weeks leading up to the moment when, for the second time in his life, he vanishes from the record was surely significant. Yet without the key to the cipher, there was no means of knowing what it concealed.

I turned to the other letters. Interspersed between the pages of numbers, there were paragraphs of text. These were the things he was willing to communicate. What was to be gleaned from his authorized version of events?

Rome was John's first diplomatic posting. He joined the embassy as Honorary Attaché on 27 January 1909. In the months that followed, he made several trips to Sicily, where, on 28 December 1908, a massive earthquake had devastated the region, killing upwards of 180,000 people.

John was charged with coordinating the relief efforts organized by the British government. Messina, situated on the northern coast of Sicily, was the first city he visited. It had been destroyed by the 40-foot-high tsunami that followed the earthquake and more than seventy thousand of its inhabitants had died. Throughout January and February, the aftershocks continued to claim more lives. On 1 March, the day John arrived, thousands of bodies were still buried under the rubble.

'Old Boy — I got down here last Monday,' he wrote to Charlie on 6 March:

On our way out we went from Naples to Messina in a little boat and had a terrible crossing, but you will be pleased to hear that I was the only one out of the four who was not sick.

We got to Messina in the early morning with splendid sun. The sight was quite extraordinary. We went straight to the American Consul who lives at the end of the town, where we had some food. Then he took us all over Messina — I never saw such a sight — practically every house is down. It is quite impossible for me to explain what a state the whole place is in.

There are little bands of people everywhere looking for their dead relatives. One can always tell where the bodies are owing to the smell. All the inhabitants that remain live in huts made out of anything they can get hold of. The stench of the bodies with the present filth of the people living among the ruins is very bad.

Everywhere one sees the whole of a house down except for perhaps one or two rooms which are open to view like a section of a doll's house and in one place I saw a man who had been dead since the earthquake caught up on a beam 3 storeys up — but he could not be got down.

From Messina, John crossed the Straits to Catona, a small town on the Calabrian coast. Like Messina, it had been badly devastated. Over two thousand people — two thirds of its population — had been killed in the earthquake. Some weeks earlier, Herbert Asquith, the British Prime Minister, had dispatched a Royal Navy ship to Catona to set up a relief camp. With aftershocks posing a constant danger, its crew had pitched the camp along the sandy dunes at the edge of the beach, away from the hazard of falling masonry.

'We are living in tents on the seashore about 150 yards from the sea,' John wrote to Charlie, a few days after he arrived:

133

Etna is in full view of us and when it is fine the view across the Straits is quite splendid. The weather at one moment is lovely and at another thundery and lightning, like nothing I have ever seen before. There are little earthquakes going on all day. Last night we had quite a nice one that lasted about 15–20 seconds. There are two sorts that we get here. We call them 'Bumpers' and 'Rockers'. The Bumpers are up and down movements. The Rockers are from side to side. The one last night was a Rocker. When it is quiet in our camp it is quite uncanny the noises that go on. The sea is about 150 to 200 yards off. Even when it is calm, the little ripples coming in sound like large Atlantic rollers owing to the earth being so thin and hollow that it transmits the sound like a telephone. There are always rumbles going on underneath — which sound like thunder underground — and water bubbling and boiling.

The swallows here just arrived and they don't know what to do as all their homes have been destroyed.

Must go to bed as it is very late and must be up by 5.30.

A hospital tent had been set up at the camp to treat the victims of the earthquake. John was shocked by the sights he witnessed:

'The hopeless state the people are in is too appalling,' he told Charlie: 'In our hospital tent the cries and groans are terrible. People were brought in absolutely covered in wounds all over, great chunks out of their bodies. One man I saw had a large chunk taken out of his arms, showing the bone about six inches long, the same thing on one of his legs, the whole calf being taken away — the other leg broken. This is nothing to some of the people — and the worst part is that owing to many of the people being underground amongst the debris their wounds have become rotten and the smell is too terrible. Many in the hospital have died from lockjaw. A curious thing in the hospital tents was that when Vesper time came in the evening all the patients stopped groaning and screaming from their wounds and sung some prayers for 1/2 an hour, even people who were on the point of death did the same and one woman actually died after she had finished her chants.'

Though John was based at the camp, most of his time was spent in the countryside around Catona. 'Our work,' he explained to Charlie, 'is to go to the little villages and towns both along the coast and inland and find out the state of the people, what their losses are, how many of each family are left. Then we come home and the next day take up the blankets and boots etc on mules.

Tomorrow we go to the mountains for two days.'

There was nothing controversial — or any hint of a secret — in the paragraphs of normal text in John's letters. The impression I was left with was of a privileged young man who appeared genuinely moved by the suffering and devastation he had witnessed. And yet woven through the graphic descriptions were pages and pages of cipher. The central question remained unanswered. What had John regarded as so important, so confidential, that it could only be communicated in a secret code?

I was becoming more and more caught up in the mystery behind this man, and starting to follow a different story — his story. In creating the gaps in his biography, he had erased so much of himself — and so thoroughly. What I had discovered in these rooms — and in his rooms up in the East Tower — was disquieting; in my imagination, he had become the dark force preventing me from writing the book that I had set out to write. Yet in the few glimpses I had had of him — the fragments that I had read, written in his own words — he struck me as a likeable, straightforward character.

So why were there these mysterious encrypted letters? And why had he filleted three chapters out of his life?

Whatever his story, it seemed that it was one that he had been determined no one should ever know. The fact that he had pruned the records for three different periods — 1894, 1909 and 1915 — could suggest that there was a single act or event and that the subsequent gaps covered times when there were repercussions from that original event. Equally, the gaps could relate to three separate acts or events. But could he really have had *three* secrets?

I returned to the encrypted letters.

John had first used the cipher on 11 February 1909. He had been at the British Embassy for a week. 'I hate the sight of Rome and everything in it,' he complained to Charlie: 'I don't think there is the slightest chance of being able to get away even for one day. So it would be no use you coming out this way to pick me up. 368 369 53 82 415 359 44 14 68 92 46 219 156 270 223 369 98 100 96 11 337 35 105 285 203 175 20 387 240 379. I am going to make a 279 94 105 4 200 some time and will send it you for your approval. Goodbye old boy, J.'

Did the numbers represent words or letters? And why, at times, had he used two numbers, rather than three? A letter, written a few days later, offered a steer. 'If I send you a telegram in cipher,' he told Charlie on 8 February, 'this is the way to read it':

Suppose the sentence which is in cipher is:

'I hope you are quite well' and that the numbers are: 52 109 110 11 16 400. Well — you have got to make each block of numbers up to 5 figures. So in the telegram you will have to cut off either 3 figures or 2. And let us say that we can put any numbers we like to make up the block — thus it would become 52063 10942 11072 11072 16704 40000.

It was helpful, but only up to a point. I could now see that the numbers represented words, not letters; I could grasp the principle of adding random numbers to make up a block of five. Yet how John had arrived at '52' for 'I' and '109' for hope, and so on, was flummoxing. Without the key to the cipher, it was impossible to know.

The next letter provided a vital clue:

Old Boy, I enclose a new key. Let us use it in future. The way to use it is like this.
    In old cipher key
    Every word is of three figures. So in future 305 any 44.15.11. figures 415. 238x. after each word so to make each word 386. 368.181.389. figures therefore it will be like this.
    In old cipher
    204. 156. 415. 413. 489

In new cipher

51342. 35910. 94631. 93249. 10000

There is a note at the top-right-hand corner of the second page of the key which you should read carefully. Every time you write or wire in cipher, when you look up a word and do not find it, you should make a note of it and say in your next letter what you have given it.

The enclosure was missing. The 'new key' that John had sent to Charlie was lost. Nor was there anything to be drawn from the numbers. They were nonsensical. It was the information in the last paragraph that caught my attention. The clue to the cipher lay in the reference that John had made to the 'note at the top-right-hand corner of the second page of the key'; he had instructed Charlie to 'look up words' and make a note of the ones that he could not 'find'. Implicit in the letter was the suggestion that some sort of key to the cipher already existed. I kicked myself for being so slow. Countless times, working my way through the pages of the Muniment Rooms catalogue, I had passed the entry for the volume entitled 'Key to Cyphers'.

The volume was listed in the section relating to the seventeenth-century material. The rooms held a large number of documents dating from the English Civil War, including a collection of coded letters which Charles I had sent from Carisbrooke Castle in the last months of his life. The 'Key to Cyphers' contained the King's secret code. Carisbrooke, on the Isle of Wight, was where he had been imprisoned before he was executed on the scaffold in January 1649. It seemed barely credible, but I was sure that John was using the cipher that the King had used in the letters that he had sent from the castle.

The cipher was one that Charlie Lindsay had known intimately. Through painstaking work, conducted over many years, he had managed to decipher a large number of the King's letters. It was a remarkable achievement. For almost three centuries, historians had puzzled over the cryptic messages, the means by which they had been smuggled from the castle adding to their notoriety. The King had concealed them in his gloves before giving them to the gentleman usher, whose job it was to hold the gloves while he was at the dining table. He had hidden other messages in the water closet in his bedchamber. The maid who emptied his chamber pot had collected these.

I got up from my desk to fetch the catalogue. John's code had looked impossible to decipher, but with the key to the King's cipher, it ought to be possible to crack it.

John had filed the 'Key to Cyphers' below the rows of files containing his correspondence with Charlie. The two volumes beside it were also important: 'Transcripts made by Captain Lindsay of a volume of original letters from Charles I in the feigned hand whilst prisoner at Carisbrooke in 1648' and 'Letters in Cypher'. Both were bound in crimson leather; the titles, and the edging on the volumes, were embossed in gold.

I pulled down the 'Letters in Cypher' and turned to the first page. There were two inscriptions on the inside cover. The first was written in Charlie Lindsay's hand:

This volume contains transcripts of letters (Reign of Charles I & Interregnum) which are written either wholly or partly in cipher, none of which to my knowledge (after enquiry and research) has ever yet been deciphered.

Some of them I have been able to decipher without difficulty, either by applying the various 'Keys' of the period which I have collected, or by comparing them with other letters in the same cipher which possess the contemporary decipherment.

With regard to others I have been fortunate enough to work out the 'Key' myself.

A considerable number still remain undeciphered, in spite of some labour already spent over them.

On the page opposite, John had added his

own inscription:

Left to me by Captain Charles Lindsay 1925 now at Belvoir Castle and I hope and wish that as long as the Castle remains the property of a Manners, this book will be kept and carefully preserved as part of the Belvoir archives.

I took the three volumes over to the sofa and spread them out, together with the bundles of his letters from Rome.

13

Outside, the sky had darkened. The afternoon was warm and close; I could hear the sound of the wind in the trees along the battlements and the low, nagging rumble of distant thunder.

Several hours had gone by and I was still struggling with the cipher. John, I had quickly discovered, had not used the King's cipher. The numbers did not match. The volume 'Key to Cyphers' lay open in front of me. Besides the King's cipher, it contained the keys to some seventy others. It was an extraordinary historical document. Here were the secret codes of the leading figures of the English Civil War and the Interregnum: Oliver Cromwell, Archbishop Laud, the Earl of Strafford, Charles II, and the Earls of Northumberland and Leicester.

The keys ran to 195 pages. I was sure that John had used one of them. But which? In the hope of identifying his cipher, I had tried comparing the blocks of numbers in his letters with those in the different keys — so far, without success. I had reached page 27, Cipher no. 10. It was the cipher that Charles I's adviser, Sir Edward Nicholas, had used in his letters to Lord Jermyn.

In the spring of 1646, Lord Jermyn had been with Queen Henrietta Maria in exile in France. He was her closest confidant; later, in the winter of 1649, it would fall to him to break the terrible news of her husband's execution.

The key to Sir Edward's cipher ran to eight columns:

No.		No.		No.		No.	
1	Null	66	F	131	day	196	have
2	Null	67	G	132	did	197	had
3	Null	68	H	133	doubt	198	hear
4	Null	69	I	134	doubles	199	he
5	S	70	K	135	draw	200	him
6	T	71	L	136	sing	201	hold
7	U	72	M	137	die	202	hope
8	W	73	N	138	delay	203	houses
9	X	74	O	139	deliver	204	his
10	Y	75	P	140	desire	205	here
11	Z	76	Q	141	down	206	how
12	Null	77	R	142	da	207	hundred
13	Null	78	S	143	do	208	high
14	Null	79	T	144	di	209	heart
15	Null	80	U	145	ece	210	hap
16	A	81	W	146	end	211	halfe
17	B	82	X	147	ever	212	I
18	C	83	Y	148	earl	213	is
19	D	84	Z	149	ed	214	en
20	E	85	all	150	ef	215	if
21	F	86	about	151	eg	216	im
22	G	87	after	152	eh	217	it
23	H	88	am	153	ene	218	ill
24	I	89	an	154	en	219	idle
25	K	90	are	155	e/o	220	ing
26	L	91	at	156	eques	221	inch
27	M	92	aw	157	ex	222	ick
28	N	93	and	158	ee	223	ist
29	O	94	act	159	eh	224	know
30	P	95	ad	160	ev	225	knew
31	Q	96	ax	161	ey	226	knave
32	R	97	ay	162	for	227	knot
33	A	98	although	163	from	228	knight
34	B	99	always	164	fra	229	lay
35	C	100	altogether	165	free	230	live
36	D	101	be	166	faith	231	love
37	E	102	by	167	form	232	lovely
38	F	103	both	168	fix	233	like
39	G	104	but	169	fast	234	last
40	H	105	because	170	first	235	late
41	I	106	business	171	fall	236	luck
42	K	107	ble	172	fill	237	little
43	L	108	bly	173	follow	238	least

I stared helplessly at the page, scanning the numbers against the ones in John's encrypted letters. Yet again, they did not appear to match. It would take hours to go through the rest of the book. I decided to photograph the pages and show them to a cryptologist.

It was three o'clock in the afternoon; with the sky heavy outside, the room was almost dark. I got up from the sofa to put the light on. The switch was at the top of the stairs, by the entrance to Room 2. Turning to come back down them, I paused, struck by the fall of light across the room. Illuminated by the naked bulb, the sofa on which I had been sitting, and on which John had died, now seemed to dominate the room. It bore the marks of its long service; the springs protruded from the faded chintz cover; one end of it sagged heavily. It was at this end, presumably, that John had sat so many times.

I had been so absorbed by the missing episodes in his life that I had barely given any thought to his death — or rather, to his manner of dying. He had died on this sofa of bronchial pneumonia. *It was not as if he had died suddenly.* He must have lain on it, seriously ill, for some days.

I looked around me, trying to visualize the scene. An oxygen tent had been brought in here. I could almost hear the sounds of despair: the shallow, rapid breathing of the dying man, the judder of the oxygen pumps.

I imagined him lying under the canopy, isolated in the centre of the empty room, dwarfed by the tall glass cabinets that surrounded him.

A draught coming along the passage rolled a ball of dust across the bare floorboards. I watched it as it drifted past. It was such a perverse thing for John to have done, to have willingly immured himself in these rooms in the last days of his life. It was where he had wanted to be, Roger, his son, had said. But it simply didn't make sense. There was a rudimentary form of under-floor heating — hot air blasted up through vents from the floor below — but otherwise the coal-burning stove in front of me was the only source of heat in the Muniment Rooms. John had died in April when the rooms would have been damp and the nights still cold. Not one of the five rooms had washing facilities or running water: the nearest bathroom was a good distance away beyond the old servants' hall. On the upper floors of the castle, there were suites of bedrooms. Lavishly furnished, they had huge four-poster beds with soft linen sheets and great stone hearths for blazing fires. During his final hours, any one of these rooms would have been more comfortable, a more fitting place for a Duke to die. Instead, he had died in a cramped, sparsely furnished room deep in the servants' quarters. *Why?*

It was a question I puzzled over for weeks. In some way, it felt as if the peculiarity of the circumstances of his death held the key to him. I spoke to numerous members of the Manners family, and their relations — men and women born in the early 1920s who remembered John. But they were unable to tell me why he had chosen to spend the last days of his life in the Muniment Rooms. With the passing of time, his final hours remained shrouded in mystery. It was not even clear whether there had been anyone with him when he died.

It was then that I began the search for a contemporary witness: someone who had been working at the castle and had been inside the Muniment Rooms before he had died.

The pool of potential witnesses, notwithstanding the decades that had intervened, was far smaller than I had imagined. The former servants I spoke to painted a vivid picture of the events at Belvoir in the last days of John's life, but their memories were confined to the corridors and back passages of the castle. John, it emerged, had barred them from entering the Muniment Rooms. Just three members of his household were permitted inside them: his butler, Mr Brittain; his valet, Mr Speed; and Mrs Hayward, the housekeeper. They were all dead: Mr Speed was killed in 1941 as he cycled along the main road into Grantham; Mrs Hayward died in the 1960s; and Mr Brittain in 2005.

There was no one left alive to explain why John had closeted himself away in the Muniment Rooms in the final hours of his life. Nonetheless, what I learned from the servants who had been on duty at the castle was startling. Evidently — based on what they had seen and overheard — they had been as mystified as to why he had chosen to die in a cramped suite of rooms in their quarters as I was seventy years after the event. The speed with which his illness had claimed him had also surprised them. It was then, in confusion, that those in the servants' hall fell back on the two curses: the first cast by the three witches in the seventeenth century; the other, by the pharaoh prince, Tutankhamun.

Yet these accounts, however extraordinary, brought me no closer to the answer I sought. Much of what the servants had to say belonged in the realm of gossip and conjecture. Without a first-hand witness, the circumstances of John's death remained as bizarre — and as mysterious — as the blanks that he had created in the blue files. The notion that two curses — one ancient, one modern — could have a bearing on his story struck me as utterly fanciful. I could only assume that the rumours and theories that had circulated through the servants' hall were gossips' handiwork — the sinister embellishments, a consequence of the mystery and secrecy that surrounded the 'Secret Rooms'.

I focused instead on the few fragments of fact. It was the servants' observations of the doctors' movements that were particularly intriguing.

In the last hours of his life, John, apparently, had kept his physicians at bay. Before he became unconscious, one of the castle's housemaids had overheard his valet instructing the King's doctor to wait in the corridor outside the Muniment Rooms. The Duke, Lord Dawson was told, had something he had to 'finish'. This revelation could only mean that he had been working on something right up until the end. According to the servants, the doctors had urged him to rest. They had even tried to persuade him to move from the rooms to one of the bedrooms upstairs. John had ignored their protests. It reinforced my conviction that whatever it was that had occupied him in the days before he died mattered to him to the exclusion of all else — even at the risk of shortening his life.

So what had kept him from seeking the medical attention he had so urgently needed? *What had he wanted to finish?*

The one theory circulating among his

servants was that it was a letter, or a package, for his mistress — the woman who broke into the Muniment Rooms a week after he died. None of the servants I spoke to could remember her name, but a former housemaid told me that she had lived at Eastwell Hall. It was an important lead. Situated three miles from the castle, the Hall belonged to the Belvoir estate. Whoever she was, she would have been a tenant of the Duke's. It was more than probable that the rent books in the Muniment Rooms would reveal her identity.

The rent books were kept in Room 2. Going back to the 1820s, they recorded the names of the Rutlands' tenants — and the amounts of rent they owed. The books took up three cases. Each was identical: bound in burgundy leather, with the words 'Belvoir Estate Rental' — followed by the year — embossed in gold on the ridged spine. Above and below the title was a delicate, hand-stitched row of tiny fleurs-de-lys, also embossed in gold.

I took down the volume for 1940. The Duke's properties were listed by parish. Turning the pages, I could see that his tenants had paid rent twice yearly: on Lady Day — 25 March, the annunciation of the Blessed Virgin Mary — and at Michaelmas — 29 September, St Michael's Day. There were some four hundred properties in total, yielding a rental income of nearly £20,000* per annum.

I found 'the Woman from Eastwell' in a matter of seconds. The Hall was one of six entries listed for the parish and her name — Hilda Lezard — was entered beside it.

A quick search on the internet provided further details. Born in Suffolk in 1891, Hilda was the daughter of Sir Daniel Cooper, 2nd Baronet, and his wife Harriet. On her mother's side, her grandfather was Sir James Grant Suttie, the 6th Baronet of Balgone. She had been married four times; first, at the age of nineteen, to Viscount Northland, the heir to the Earl of Ranfurly; then, two years later — after Northland was killed in action on the Western Front — to Geoffrey Mills, a younger son of Lord Hillingdon, who had also died soon after their marriage; third, in 1918, to Captain John Wardell, an officer in the 10th Hussars; and, lastly, after their marriage was dissolved in 1929, to Julian Lezard.

Intriguingly — so the links from his name revealed — in the Second World War, Lezard had worked for British Intelligence. His code-name was Église. According to records held at the National Archives, he took part in Operation Cathedral, a secret SOE mission in the French Alps.

Among the documents in Lezard's file was

* £852,000 at today's values.

a personnel form. 'Next of Kin: Hilda Lezard'; 'Marital Status: Married'. This was in 1944. Before joining SOE, Lezard had served in Egypt with the Parachute Regiment. As the form showed, from 1939 he had been absent abroad, allowing Hilda to carry on her adulterous affair.

The details of Operation Cathedral were fascinating. Lezard was evidently a brave man. In August 1944, he had been parachuted into France with four other agents; enclosed in the file were the orders they had been given at the start of their mission:

OPERATION ORDER
    Operation: CATHÉDRALE

1. INFORMATION
    Operation CATHÉDRALE is being sent out to form an Allied Mission with ST SAUVEUR, VOILIER, RICHESOIR, CATHÉDRALE and INOCERE.
2. METHOD
    A. you will be parachuted into the Basses Alpes on or after the 3rd August 1944.
    B. you will be received by ARCHDUC on ground ASSURANCE; lat. 44 deg 19'29" 4 1/2 km N.W.AVRET, longitude 6 deg 16'49". 9 1/2 km. E.S.E.BAYONS
    C. should you by any chance miss the committee you will go to the follow-

ing safe house:-
Mme TURRE
SEYNE-LES-ALPES
Mot de passe: *'je viens voir le vélo'*
D. you will wear uniform in the field and maintain your proper status as an Allied Officer save in exceptional circumstances.
E. you will take with you two letters, one from the Allies, the second from the French which will accredit you with the local resistance authorities.

3. FINANCE

You will take with you the sum of 100,000 francs.

The next document in the file was the report Lezard wrote on his return to England. From the start, the mission had gone wrong for him.

REPORT OF CAPTAIN J. J. LEZARD
(Église)

I was dropped in the Basses Alpes area near SEYNE on 5th August 1944.

Unfortunately I badly injured my spinal column as I landed on some rocks and rolled down a fairly considerable slope. I consider that we were dropped a good deal too high (at least 2,500 ft) and I landed about 2 kms away from the lights on the

154

landing ground. There appeared to be no reason for this as it was a clear night, but from this height I experienced a good deal of wind.

I was a complete liability as I was unable to move at all for the first seven weeks. In the first days conditions were difficult as I was in great pain and I had to be moved each night to new hiding places for reasons of security. Colonel ROGER had been captured about this time so people were naturally uneasy. The French looked after me extremely well and never left me alone at all in spite of the fact that I was a great nuisance to them and they all had plenty of other work to do.

After eight days when things had settled down I was taken to Doctor JOUVE's nursing home where I was x-rayed and it was considered that I should be fit to jump again in about 6 weeks' time. Whilst lying in this nursing home I was visited continually by numbers of resistance people and got to know them very well. The intelligent French are very worried about the future of France and count tremendously on their friendship with the English. Colonel ROGER was loved by everybody and was undoubtedly one of the most outstanding figures in the South East.

It is impossible for me to enumerate all the French who helped us since I was in bed most of the time, but from my personal experience two families were outstanding. Doctor JOUVE and his wife (a doctor) both well known in the South of France, whose work was invaluable and who never failed to give any assistance that was in their power, and Monsieur and Madame TURREL, small shopkeepers in SEYNE. These two represented the finest types one could hope to meet in any country.

I am now proceeding to LONDON with Major Karl NURE. And am a volunteer for work in the Far East, but if at any time there is further work to be done in France I should be pleased to do it.

This was Julian Lezard. But aside from the brief biographical details that I'd found on the genealogy sites, there was no other information about Hilda.

I returned to the rent books. The tenancy at Eastwell Hall was in her name. Working back through the years, I was able to establish that Hilda had moved into the Hall in 1938. The rent was £350 p.a.*; on arrival, she had paid an additional £10 for 'the installation of electric light'.

Interestingly, at the time of John's death, the rent was in arrears; she owed the estate £370 — the equivalent of a year's rental. The

* Approximately £14,300 at today's values.

implication was that she could not afford to live there or at least had been allowed to fall behind with the payments.

I asked the archivist if the Muniment Rooms held a description of the Hall. He steered me in the direction of the 1919 sales catalogue. That year, John's father — the 8th Duke — had sold a large portion of his estate. The Hall — Lot 457 — had been included in the sale before it was withdrawn at the last minute.

The particulars of the property were listed in the catalogue; clearly, it was a substantial residence:

A very desirable old-fashioned seventeenth-century Manor house situated in the centre of the village of Eastwell and known as Eastwell Hall, together with Stabling, Gardens, Lawns and Spinneys, the whole comprising an area of approx. 4 acres.

The residence is Stone-built and Slated and contains Entrance Hall, Inner Hall, from which the staircase ascends, Dining Room, Dråwing Room, Smoke Room; Lavatory, Panelled Billiard Room, Kitchen, Scullery, Pantry and Cellar; five principal Bedrooms and Dressing Rooms, Bath Room and W.C., five Servants' Rooms, and Attics.

The Muniment Rooms yielded several further pieces of information. According to the visitors' book, Hilda had first stayed at the castle in October 1936; her husband had not been with her. Four months later, she was there again. On both occasions the other guests were Hubert Duggan and Phyllis de Janzé. They, I discovered, belonged to the Kenyan 'Happy Valley' set. Had they introduced Hilda to John? Possibly, it was around this time that their affair had begun.

I also found a list of the floral tributes that had been sent to John's funeral. Hilda's was the last name on it. Some forty people had sent flowers; they were referred to by their full name or title. The suggestion was that those who didn't know who 'Hilda' was didn't need to know.

These were fragments; not one explained why, three days after John was buried, Hilda had returned to the castle in the dead of night and broken into the Muniment Rooms.

She was almost fifty in 1940. In the pitch dark, she had climbed fifteen feet up a drainpipe and then negotiated a precarious manoeuvre to an adjacent window ledge. She was obviously determined to get into the castle at any cost.

Importantly, however, before climbing the drainpipe she had first tried the window leading into the room where John died. According to his servants, this clandestine route of entry was one that she had used countless times before. It offered a means of seeing her lover without being seen. Their affair had been going on for some years; long enough for her to take a considerable personal risk in scaling the castle wall. She had evidently been breaking in for a reason. But was it because she wanted a keepsake — something to remember him by? Or because they'd arranged that she should retrieve something?

John hadn't known he was going to die; five days before his death, he appeared to be on the road to recovery. Had he spoken to her on the telephone and told her that he was leaving something for her? Or had he somehow managed to relay a message to her? The fact that it had been necessary for her to break into the Muniment Rooms suggested they had not seen each other during his final hours.

So if she was there to retrieve something, the question of course was *what*? Was it something incriminating — love letters they'd exchanged? Or had he left her something of value?

It was pure speculation of course, but there were the five rubies the present Duchess had mentioned. In the 1930s, John had apparently hidden them somewhere inside the Muniment Rooms. Discretion prevented him from leaving Hilda anything in his will. But the rent books suggested that she might have been hard up. If he had loved her, he might have wanted to provide for her future. His family knew the rubies were hidden in the Muniment Rooms — though where exactly they hadn't known. Had he told Hilda to retrieve the jewels? If he had, it was understandable that he had not wanted his family to know.

This was simply a theory — and one that was completely unsupported by facts. Hilda had died in 1961; it looked as if she had taken her secret to her grave. My only hope was that someone in her family might be able to resolve the mystery. In one last attempt to get to the bottom of the break-in, I wrote to her grandson. Until I heard back from him, there was nothing more I could do.

I returned to the question of what John had wanted to 'finish'.

The servants at Belvoir had offered one further piece of information. In September 1939, the Public Records had been evacuated to Belvoir Castle for safe-keeping. Under the Act of Parliament that governed the stewardship of the records, it had been necessary for King George VI to make John their official custodian.

So was it urgent war work that had kept him in the Muniment Rooms? Had a patriotic sense of duty compelled him to keep the King's doctor waiting?

14

I tapped in my reader number and selected 'Search the Catalogue'. It was a bleak afternoon in late November and I was at the National Archives in Kew.

According to the servants, sixty tons of records had been delivered to the castle in the winter of 1940. Further deliveries had been imminent when John died. I wanted to look at the official correspondence relating to this material.

When I entered 'Evacuated Records' in the search box, three references came up. One looked promising: 'Public Record Office: Repositories for Evacuated Records, War of 1939–1945'. Following the link, all seven of the wartime repositories were listed. I selected 'Belvoir Castle' and ordered up the documents.

It was entirely plausible that John was working on the records when he died. April 1940 had been an anxious month in the progress of the war; France was on the verge of surrendering to Germany. With the threat of a Nazi invasion escalating, the pressure had been on to evacuate the last of the records from London; it could have been work relating to the transfer of this material that he had wanted to finish.

The documents arrived in a large cardboard box. It was the letters between John and the Keeper of Records — the Head of the Public Record Office — that I was interested in. Sifting through the box, I found twelve. As I began to go through them, it quickly became evident that, while John had been a conscientious custodian, his appointment as Assistant Keeper of the Records had been titular. The arrangements for evacuating the records had been handled by London; once they had reached the castle, John had had nothing to do with them. There was no reason why he would have been working on them when he died.

But the other documents in the box were intriguing. The decision to use the castle as a wartime repository, I discovered, had been controversial.

On 24 April 1939, Cyril Flower, the Keeper of Records, received a phone call, which he reported in a memo to a senior official at the Office of Works: 'I've just had a call from the Duke of Rutland, who suggested that Belvoir

Castle might be a good place for the Public Records in an Emergency. I explained to him that at the outbreak of War we should be fully occupied in evacuating to the two buildings already allotted to us.'

At the time Flower was writing, the plan was to evacuate the records to Shepton Mallet Prison in Somerset, and to St Luke's Hospital in Market Harborough. While the Keeper's memo does not reveal why John believed the castle 'might be a good place', it is clear his offer was politely refused. 'I did not feel I could accept His Grace's offer,' Flower informed the official at the Office of Works. 'I told him that your office kept a register of buildings available for similar purposes during an Emergency. His Grace agreed that I should write to you and that you would let him know whether you could accept his offer to have the castle put on the list.'

The previous year, realizing that armed conflict with Hitler's Germany was inevitable, the Committee of Imperial Defence had instructed the Office of Works to compile a register of buildings that could be utilized when war came. Britain's historic houses played a key part in the plans for mobilization. They offered large-scale accommodation that could be adapted to a variety of purposes — hospitals and convalescent homes, intelligence and military headquarters, billets and training premises for the armed forces, even prisoner-of-war camps.

The register, detailing which buildings would be requisitioned and for what purpose, was top secret. That it remained secret was imperative. Not only was the committee anxious to prevent disclosure of its plans to the enemy, it was also keen to avoid the volume of protest that would erupt were the register to come to light. If there was a war, Britain's historic homes were to be compulsorily requisitioned: their owners would have no say over the purpose for which they were being taken over, or any right to reject the government's decision.

When John telephoned the Keeper of Records, neither he nor Flower knew that the Ministry of War had already staked a claim to the castle. Its size and its commanding position meant that it was ideally suited as a military headquarters. On the government's secret register, it had been earmarked as a billet for troops.

And yet at the eleventh hour, just seven weeks before war was declared, the decision to use the castle as a military headquarters was reversed.

Out of the blue, on 12 July, Flower received a short communication from Edward Normann, the Assistant Secretary of Defence at the Office of Works: 'Arrangements have now been made for Belvoir Castle not to be used for billeting purposes, so you can proceed to make arrangements for evacuating there.'

No explanation was given for the last-minute switch. But, clearly, the decision infuriated senior officials at the Public Record Office. Far from believing the castle to be a 'good place in an Emergency', as John had suggested, they regarded it as hopelessly ill suited to their needs. In every respect, it failed the criteria they had so carefully laid down.

The search for an emergency repository for the records had involved months of investigation. The Keeper of Records, in a memo written after the war, explained the factors that had governed the search: 'There were two main dangers to which records might obviously be exposed in time of war: aerial bombardment and invasion. There was obviously very little we could do as a direct precaution against the dangers arising from invasion. Aerial bombardment was, from the first, the danger which those responsible for the custody of the records were bound to take mainly into account.' With this in mind, the Keeper had explored the possibility of storing the records on the Piccadilly Line beneath Aldwych station. But as his investigation concluded, 'It was found that the tube as a whole was too damp for the storage of documents for any length of time.' He had also considered using a special train, which, should it become exposed to attack — either from the air, or by invading enemy troops — could be moved at short notice from its siding. Finally — early in 1939 — he had selected the two emergency repositories: the prison at Shepton Mallet and the hospital in Market Harborough. Located as they were in sleepy market towns, both were thought to be discreet, secure locations.

Unlike Belvoir.

'I wish I could consider it a safe place,' Michael Dawes, the Deputy Keeper of Records, lamented to his colleagues after seeing the castle for the first time: 'It is a landmark for miles around and I can quite imagine the Germans bombing it for the sake of effect, or attempting to seize it for a time and overawe the neighbourhood.'

To the senior officials at the Public Record Office, the government's abrupt decision to evacuate the nation's most important historical documents to a building that was dangerously vulnerable to enemy attack appeared cavalier. No clearer indictment of the mistrust with which the Keeper of Records regarded the castle can be found than his decision — on the day war was declared — to send the most valuable document in his collection elsewhere.

On the evening of 3 September, a small, unmarked van left Chancery Lane. Travelling under armed guard, it headed west out of

London. Its precious cargo, wrapped unobtrusively in brown paper, lay beside the driver on the front passenger seat. The parcel contained the Domesday Book. It was on its way to Shepton Mallet Prison, where it was to be hidden in a secret hiding place in the women's wing for the duration of the war.

So why, given that Belvoir Castle was infinitely better suited to military requirements, had the government suddenly changed its mind?

From the outset, it was John who had pressed Whitehall to use the castle as a repository for the records. In doing so, he had joined a queue of anxious dukes. In the weeks leading up to the war, rather than see their historic homes wrecked by troops, the Dukes of Marlborough, Bedford, Portland, Devonshire, Beaufort — and others — had been quick to offer their houses to the government for non-military use. For the most part, the offers had been accepted: Blenheim, Woburn and Welbeck had been taken over by the security services; Chatsworth had become a girls' boarding school; and Badminton a country retreat for the elderly Queen Mary — the widow of George V.

John knew the Prime Minister personally; he also knew the members of his Cabinet. It looked as if he had pulled strings to stop the Ministry of War from taking over his castle.

But was it because he had simply wanted to prevent it being used as a billet for troops?

Or had he had a specific interest in the records?

What I found curious was that, from the moment the first convoy arrived at Belvoir, John had insisted that two classified documents — a summary of the records stored at the castle, and a plan of the stacks, showing exactly where they were located — should be kept in the Muniment Rooms.

I found this detail in a report, filed by Mr Gilkes, the caretaker appointed by London to look after the records. He had travelled up to Belvoir with the first convoy. 'Everything is in order here,' he informed the Keeper a few days later: 'Every bundle is sorted and stacked. The slips are sorted in a leather box and I have a plan of the stacks, so bundles can be found at a moment's notice. These are kept with a Summary of the Records in the Duke's rooms.'

By Act of Parliament, the records had to be accessible to government departments and court officials at all times. It was Gilkes's job to locate and retrieve them. Tens of thousands of bundles were stacked along the passages, and in the ballroom at the castle: without the summary and a plan of the stacks it would have been impossible to find any particular bundle.

But why had John insisted that these two

important documents be kept in his rooms? Though he had been appointed temporary custodian of the records, they were not his business. Was it because he had wanted to be able to locate specific records himself?

Gilkes's report hinted that John might have had some ulterior motive in pressing the government to use the castle as an emergency repository. But there was no further correspondence to suggest what his motive might have been.

I drove away disheartened. Once again, I had drawn a blank. It had been raining all day; gloomily, inching my way through the traffic, I mulled over the precarious state of my research. A depressing pattern was emerging. Every avenue of enquiry seemed to lead to a dead end. Either that, or it compounded the mystery behind this man. The search for the missing letters had revealed that John had created not one but three gaps in his biography; his encrypted letters had proved impossible to decipher — unless a cryptologist could make something of them. I had spent weeks chasing the mystery behind the circumstances of his death inside the Muniment Rooms, yet all that I'd managed to establish was that there had been something he had wanted to finish before he died. I had talked to the family; I had talked to the servants: I had run out of leads to follow.

And yet I couldn't escape the feeling that I had overlooked a crucial element, one that was important in a way that I didn't yet understand.

One detail, which the servants had supplied, was particularly baffling. A few days before he died, John had made an unusual request. Flouting a centuries-old tradition, he asked that his body should remain in the Muniment Rooms until the day of his funeral. At Belvoir, the burial of a duke had always been a very public event. His predecessors had been laid out in the Guard Room, where hundreds of the family's tenants and employees had filed past their coffins.

Even in death it seemed John was wedded to these rooms. His singular last wish was yet another mystery, as seemingly insoluble as whatever it was that he had regarded important enough to risk his life in order to finish. Why had he needed to be in the Muniment Rooms to finish whatever it was that he was doing?

Why these rooms and not elsewhere?

It was then that it dawned on me that I was faced with a puzzle that no one else had tried to solve. The Muniment Rooms had been sealed immediately after John died. They had been frozen in time. They were *exactly* as he had left them. I thought of the large, black Bakelite telephone on his desk and the vintage Anglepoise lamps with their round-pin plugs and braided gold flexes. In one of the drawers of the desk I had found packets of the brand of cigarettes that John had liked to smoke; in another, I had even come across a half-filled ashtray. Were the traces of whatever it was that he had wanted to finish still there?

15

I was anxious to make an early start. The next morning, I left London at seven. It was soon after nine when I drew up at the gates below the castle. The morning was cold and overcast. There had been a hard frost overnight and a thin mist hovered over the fields in the valley. As I drove up the narrow track through the woods, the mist thickened. At the top of it, coming over the brow, I could barely make out the castle. Its lower floors were obscured: only the Gothic turrets were visible, ghostly shapes, rising out of the fog.

I parked my car on the terrace by the battlements. The oak door to the portico loomed ahead. It was thirty feet high, and the Duke's crest, emblazoned in gold and peacock blue, glinted above it, a tiny splash of colour in the murk. I tried the small priest's door inset in the corner of it. It was locked. The other entrance was on the opposite side of the castle. In the thick fog, it was impossible to see more than a few yards. Hugging the pale stone walls, I walked the two hundred yards or so around the battlements.

A small door led into the estate office. Stopping briefly, I collected the key to the Muniment Rooms. Then I cut across the ground floor of the castle through the passages in the old servants' quarters — past the entrance to the spiral staircase that ran up to the Central Tower, then left, into the long passage by the servants' hall. I saw no one.

It felt odd to be turning the key to the rooms. I had searched them many times before, but this visit was different. Previously, I had been looking for letters; this time, I did not know what I was looking for.

I began in the room where John had died. First, I went through the cases looking for things that I might have missed on a previous search. Then I pulled out the sofa and looked behind it and underneath it. Next, I examined the floor for loose-fitting boards — places where something might have been concealed. I did not find anything. Then I checked Room 2 and the six cases along the passage. Again, I could see nothing of note. I repeated the process in Rooms 3 and 4.

It was when I got to Room 5 that I realized there was one place I had not searched.

Trunks and boxes, stacked one on top of the other, crowded the centre of the small room. Situated at the foot of the Round Tower, it was little more than a cupboard off

Room 4. I had already had a quick look inside the trunks on the top of the pile. They had been empty. But I had not looked through the others. I had assumed they were empty too.

There were twelve boxes in total: gun cases, metal hatboxes, old leather suitcases and sturdy-looking wooden boxes that had once stored breakable items. The ones at the bottom of the pile were awkward to get at; four of the larger trunks had been stacked on top of them.

I levered the first trunk from the pile. It was black and made of metal and had thick brass studs. John's initials were stamped on the side of it. Dating from the end of the nineteenth century, it was a travelling trunk — the type that would once have been strapped to the roof of a horse-drawn carriage. The other three trunks were smaller and easier to shift. But when I tried to move the box underneath them, it was too heavy. I lifted the lid. To my astonishment, it was crammed with letters. There appeared to be several thousand in total. They were still in their envelopes, neatly tied in bundles with slivers of pink ribbon.

My first thought was that this was the missing correspondence that I had been searching for all along. But, flicking quickly through the bundles, I saw that the letters were not confined to the missing months in 1894,

1909 and 1915, as I had hoped. They spanned fifty years, starting in the 1870s. Mostly, they appeared to be addressed to John's mother, Violet, Duchess of Rutland. The family crests and stately addresses of the correspondents were embossed on the backs of the envelopes — men and women who had belonged to the Upper Ten Thousand (the term used in the late nineteenth century to denote Britain's ruling elite). This was a huge cache of letters: they looked important. So why had John left them to gather dust in these trunks?

It was when I began to go through them that I realized their significance.

At first sight, it seemed these were letters that John had not managed to look at before he died. They were unlike any others I had seen in these rooms. John's comments filled the margins of the letters that he had catalogued in the blue files; he had added dates to those that were undated; he had inserted the full name or title of the correspondent when it was unclear. The pages of these letters were unmarked. There was nothing to suggest that he had begun the process of sifting through them. They appeared to be original source material — the raw material from which he had intended to construct what would have been a long series of blue files.

But it soon became clear that he had in fact

been through them. John had rifled these bundles. The months in 1894, 1909 and 1915 were missing. The gaps in the correspondence coincided precisely with the gaps in the blue files.

On close analysis, it seems that John had been working on these letters when he died. They explain why, after he fell ill in April 1940, he had refused to leave the Muniment Rooms. They also explain why, in the two years leading up to his death, his days and nights had been spent in them.

The letters belonged to Violet, Duchess of Rutland. In creating the gaps in the family record, John had had plenty of time to work on the rest of his family's correspondence. But he had had to wait for his mother's papers. It was only after her death in December 1937, when her letters finally came into his possession, that he could complete the task of constructing his version — the authorized version — of this period in his family's history.

It was a formidable undertaking. Violet, Duchess of Rutland, was born in 1856. Over the course of her lifetime, she had been an inveterate letter writer: frequently, she wrote to those she was closest to several times a day. When John inherited her correspondence, the collection encompassed many thousands of letters.

In a note written shortly before her death, Violet had expressed the wish that her son should be the arbiter of what was left for history to judge of her life: 'He [John] may look and destroy, or keep everything,' she had instructed. The task had consumed him. From the moment she died, he had rarely emerged from the Muniment Rooms.

Yet still, in April 1940 when he fell ill, he had not completed the work he had begun in December 1937. Some three thousand of his mother's letters remained to be sorted.

These were the ones that I had found in the trunks.

John had failed to mark these letters because he hadn't had time. As he was dying, it was the pruning of these letters to which he had had to give priority. In doing so, for the first and only time, he had deviated from his own exacting standards.

His previous excisions had been meticulous. His passion for history meant that he saw himself as both curator and censor: this was why the dates that signalled the beginning and end of the gaps that he had created had been so precise. But he had approached the last of his mother's letters in a panic. Instead of reading through them, he had reached straight for the envelopes. He had known exactly what he was looking for: postmarks dating from the three periods which it had taken him twenty years to obliterate from the rest of his family's correspondence. Had he thought that he would have time to return to them, had he intended to read through them, it was a method he would never have chosen. The postmarks on the envelopes were not always clear; often, the ink was blurred, or the hand stamp only half rolled. Without reading the letters, he could not be certain whether there were any he had missed. Scrupulousness had been John's hallmark, yet in his haste to remove the evidence that he believed to be incriminating, this fallible method had been the one option open to him.

I had not doubted that John had something important he wanted to hide, but this pointed to something of vital importance.

There was an intense pathos in this immensely rich man spurning the trappings of wealth to die in discomfort for the sake of these letters. For John to have walled himself up in these dank rooms must have required a remarkable act of will. He was gravely ill: his body must have craved rest and comfort. Instead, ignoring its demands, and against the advice of his doctors, his overriding concern had been to finish the process of sifting his mother's letters. Something had hounded him up until his last breath. Whatever it was, he had made its concealment his final act.

The trunks stood open on the floor around me, the bundles of letters piled high inside them. I had barely looked at them. In my haste to fill in the gaps in his biography, I had done exactly as John had done: I had looked at the postmarks on the envelopes.

I took the bundles of letters out of the trunks and spread them over the long map desk. Until now, it was as if I had been locked in a chase with him; whenever I had searched for something important, he had got there first. It seemed brutal, but, at last, I had the upper hand. I was looking at the work of a dying man. As he had hurried through the bundles, it was likely that he had overlooked something. He had had no time to read these letters. There were bound to be ones that he had missed.

There were about eighty bundles, spanning the years 1870 to 1920; some contained only a handful of letters; others, forty or fifty.

First, I had to identify those that might contain sensitive material. I focused on the three missing periods. There was the gap in the summer of 1915 when John had been on the Western Front, and which had begun with the blank pages in his war diary. Then there was the one in the summer of 1909 — the year he was at the embassy in Rome. The third gap — in 1894 — was the most mysterious of all. The thought that John had felt compelled to cover up an event in his childhood was disquieting.

Scrutinizing the postmarks, I combed through the envelopes keeping a careful eye out for any postmarks that were illegible. These, possibly, were letters that John had missed. I was also looking for any dated either side of the gaps: these too might shed light on the periods he had been trying to protect.

After several hours, I had three piles of letters: one for each of the years 1909 and 1915 — and a collection of around sixty letters that I had been unable to date. There were no letters at all, I noted, for the year 1894.

The pile for 1909 was the smallest. It seemed logical to begin with these. This was the year John had used the cipher to encrypt his letters from Italy. The events of that period were still fresh in my mind.

As I began to go through the pile, the content of the letters struck me as utterly bizarre. A few weeks before John had arrived at the British Embassy in Rome, Violet had approached Lady Rodd, the wife of the ambassador. Here was a mother asking another woman to spy on her son.

■ ■ ■ ■

PART III

■ ■ ■ ■

16

John arrived in Rome on the evening of 27 January 1909. The embassy, an impressive neo-Palladian villa, was situated inside the walls of the city, next to Michelangelo's Porta Pia. Once the home of the Duke of Bracciano, its splendid reception rooms on the *piano nobile* were the setting for the party the ambassador and his wife hosted to welcome him.

A little before midnight, Lady Rodd showed John to his room. After bidding him goodnight, she retired to write to his mother:

My dear Violet — your John has arrived looking well, and is charming to talk to. He has plenty of aplomb and conveys an atmosphere of dignity and calmness by his manner. We do not find him in the least shy — much less gauche which is remarkable considering age and circumstance. I am sure he will find the rest of the staff very friendly and good company.

They are all delightful people and they have promised to look after the boy and teach him everything and put him au courant of the diplomat's duties! You may be quite at rest and whenever I have time I will send you a line.

A month later, the ambassador's wife wrote again. Her letter contained a series of remarks that went far beyond the ordinary. Violet had evidently given her carte blanche to say what she liked about John. This in itself was unusual. More peculiar, however, was the fact that Violet had felt it necessary to seek the opinion of a woman who had only known her son for a matter of weeks:

Dearest Violet,
John went off again last night to Messina where he is really happy — doing useful work and coming into daily contact with working people who he likes so much better than folks he meets in drawing rooms.
We all like John immensely — he is fuller of good qualities than bad. He has the most charming manners I have ever seen and is full of consideration and kindly thought for everyone. Of course, he is not socially inclined but he always does his duty and talks to anyone he sits next to. I wish he would take up Italian — he would find it useful and the knowl-

edge of it would make travelling about so much more enjoyable. I have suggested it several times and he always seems eager to begin — but somehow he puts it off till a more convenient moment. The same with golf — he wants to begin, but seems shy of making the first effort. The fact is, he is very proud, and unless he does a thing well he hates doing it at all. I hope when he knows us better he will lose that sort of shyness — it is nothing else but a sort of self-consciousness which is not uncommon in boys of John's age. He is developing very much and I expect when you see him you will be immensely struck with his increased personality. If only he would smoke less — but how we are to compass this baffles me. The best way would be for him to fall violently in love with some fair lady, but that is a dangerous solution to try, and as far as I know John very unlikely to happen for some time to come.

I wish you could manage to come out and see him some time this spring. I should like to know if he is really happy. He seems so but one never knows.

Goodbye and rest assured we will look after him all the time.

Violet forwarded Lady Rodd's letter on to her brother. His reply was odder still. Charlie was writing from London; he had no plans to visit his nephew in Rome, yet he appeared to be acting in *loco parentis.*

'Lil dear,' he wrote:

Thank you for sending me Lady R's letter, which I now return.

I will, as you suggest, have a go at Jack about smoking, golf, and Italian. As to smoking, you know I am entirely converted and believe it is the root of most evils, if not, perhaps, quite all. Of the use of knowing Italian there can be no question. With regard to golf, it won't be so easy to urge it wholeheartedly. To me it seems the rottenest of all exercise games which young people should play.

I am not much impressed with Lady R's letter, with the exception of the smoking, about which she is right. The rest is unconvincing. Self-consciousness is <u>not</u> one of John's failings. I sometimes think his character must be a difficult one to read — it is so seldom one hears it rightly described.

Violet, above anyone else, ought to have understood her son's character. Nonetheless, Charlie proceeded to describe it to her:

John's tastes are formed and no persuading or fault-finding will ever alter them. It

186

is not self-consciousness which makes him prefer to pore over old manuscripts, to grub about amongst ruins, to go and see old sights, than to play golf and enjoy society — they are his formed tastes, part of his character. Rare and wonderful tastes to have — for his friends to understand and congratulate him upon. Not one in a hundred is so fortunate as to possess them. It is a pity, as he is young, that he does not better combine and enjoy all the good things — the society and the games and company — but it's no use not understanding or trying not to see the real motive in his actions. You cannot, and never will get him to take active pleasure in things which don't interest him. It is, quite possibly, a matter for argument, whether the time may not soon arrive when it would be wisest to urge him towards things he has a turn for and will do well, rather than push him towards things which you preconceive to be better and which certainly are better for other people.

I believe I can in a way visualize the life he is leading now. He finds himself in a 'profession' which, for the small fry, means little else but society, parties and things of that nature, for none of which he cares a two-penny damn. A good deal of the day is occupied in it, and he probably does the work conscientiously. When he is free he occupies the rest of the day with his books and old things. He hates and detests the life at the Embassy. These Messina expeditions are his only enjoyment and makes it all the worse when he returns from them.

The picture Charlie painted was of a withdrawn, antisocial young man who appeared to prefer 'books and old things' to people. John's character, Charlie admitted, was a 'difficult one to read'. But why had Violet found him difficult to read? The impression I was left with was of a mother who barely knew or understood her son. More than that, she appeared to have lost her way in trying to understand him. Why else would she have felt the need to benchmark her perception of his character by eliciting the opinion of others? Violet had asked Charlie to persuade John to give up smoking, and to take up golf and Italian. These were straightforward things that any mother could have broached with her son. The fact that they were so prosaic served to suggest some sort of rift between them.

I went back to John's blue files for the period. He had barely written to his mother from Italy. In the handful of letters that there were, his tone was cold and aloof. Frequently, when writing to Charlie, he had added the postscript 'Don't show this to mother,' or 'Keep this private.' Their content offered no explanation as to why he had stipulated this. There was nothing secret or controversial about them: it seemed that he added the postscript purely because he had wanted to keep his mother at a distance. Had they quarrelled before he left for Italy? Or did these letters — and the ones from Lady Rodd and Charlie — point to a more serious estrangement?

Looking at Violet's correspondence with Charlie in the years before John left for Rome, it quickly became evident that this was no ordinary family row.

'Darling Charlie, I have not and cannot say much to John naturally. I can never speak to him,' she told her brother in the autumn of 1907: 'It does hurt me so, I can't tell you how much. Don't let him dream I have spoken to you, will you, dear. And you, please don't lose your temper with me on the subject of John.'

Violet had written endlessly to Charlie on the 'subject of John'. She had poured out her heart to him; 'You see,' she told him, 'I have no one else I can confide in.'

The complexity of her relationship with her son, and the friction it caused, leapt from the pages. Jealousy — sparked by the hold Charlie had over John — consumed Violet. She was convinced that her brother had turned her son against her. The letters pointed to a profound, often histrionic insecurity. At times, she pleaded with Charlie; at others, she was manipulative and mistrustful. Fear — that John would discover her letters, or that Charlie would betray their contents — also gripped Violet: 'Burn'; 'Destroy'; '<u>Please</u> don't tell him we've spoken,' she had written in large capitals whenever she confided in her brother. Whether it was because she was afraid of alienating John further, or whether she was actually frightened of him, it was impossible to tell.

But it was the depth of Violet's anguish that was so startling. It was as if the rift with her son had driven this woman to the point of distraction. 'Darling C, I think you always think I speak to you about John in a fault-finding humour,' she told Charlie after John failed to apologize to his sister, Marjorie, following a trivial row at Belvoir:

If I say John ought to say he's sorry it is not for <u>my own</u> satisfaction because I may think he is wrong and I right! It is <u>not</u> that. It is that in his future (people don't get <u>gentler</u> as they get older but rather, <u>harder</u>) to be able to say 'sorry' to a woman — <u>a sister</u>, or a <u>mother</u>, is a most helpful thing, whether sorry or <u>not</u>. Still, for the sake of peace and gentleness at home just 'Sorry', which doesn't bind you to anything — but it turns away wrath! And soreness! And is like sunshine and hurts no one.

I left Belvoir next day for 1 night and wrote John a darling letter saying just say 'sorry' to Marjorie for she is so hurt. Get it over before I get back, darling, do.

If you had perhaps added 1 word to my prayer, John would have thought it a nice thing to do, not a stupid thing — and would have done it, and Marjorie also would have been taught to see how 'sorry' helps all round — and would have said 'sorry' too!! and all would have been smooth. As it was my long deeply felt and affectionate letter to him was taken absolutely no notice of because he thought it grand not to unbend.

The one and only time you spoke for me to John he rushed back and said so sweetly, 'I am sorry' and it warmed me and surely did him a world of good as never before or since!

You see, if you are silent as if to keep peace it makes his young mind think Charlie is right. You know dear, it is just you siding with him that makes him like that!!

On the face of it, Violet's letter was about a trivial row between John and his sister. But it wasn't an apology she was wanting: it was his affection she craved.

It was clear the rift had gone on for some time. But, working back through hundreds of letters, it was impossible to establish what had caused them to fall out in the first place. It wasn't as if John was incapable of forming loving relationships: he had obviously been exceptionally close to his uncle. So why had he denied Violet his love?

A vituperative letter, written in the summer of 1907, provided an important clue. The note scribbled on the back of the envelope suggested that Violet had had second thoughts about sending it: 'Read in the train and tear up,' she instructed her brother: 'And forgive if I have said anything I have not time to go over and alter.'

Extraordinarily, the letter, which was entirely about John, was thirty-one pages long.

Aged twenty at the time, John, who was studying for his final exams at Cambridge, was living with his uncle at his house in Chelsea. Relentlessly, in what amounted to little more than a stream of consciousness, Violet accused her brother of failing in his 'parental duties':

'What do I fuss about his <u>cavern</u> of a chest for?' she snapped at Charlie:

Half for health — those who expand their

lungs, it is now well proved, are the people who send good blood through their veins! Half for looks! Look at all the men you know who look 'poor creatures', naturally well made but for want of care in their 17 to 22 years — having no wish to be <u>proud</u> of their <u>upstandingness</u> and honest look — become stiffened in a stoop. You may not see it, but I fret very very much about John not holding himself up <u>because he can't</u> — unless <u>exercising</u> helps him to biggen the muscles of chest to counterbalance the very much too big muscles across his shoulders. Therefore, even at the risk of worrying him, you might say every morning, 'I say, let's both make a run of 5 minutes — exercise is good for both of us.'

<u>Exams!!</u> You both wrote promises that the French should be taken up earnestly and thoroughly and pursued right through the holidays. Whenever these kind of promises are given to me — and broken — you distinctly ought to make a point of saying, 'I say, John, if you can't manage to keep your promise, well, I'm not going to help you waste your time.' By this I mean that a little displeasure on your part, and not always being ready to amuse him at your house, might make him see that play is better when some 'bit' of work has been accomplished.

The letter bore the hallmarks of others I had seen of Violet's on the subject of John. Her frustration was out of proportion to the things she was complaining about — as if it stemmed from a hidden cause. But, on this occasion, anger provoked her into levelling an accusation against Charlie, which previously she'd left unsaid. For thirty pages, her frustration had gathered momentum, until, on page 31, in one final outburst, she at last revealed the root cause of her resentment:

You see dear, from the age of 9 he became your boy. Therefore you who took him, with your spoiling kindness away from his home, have a stern duty in it I think, and your saying now to me 'Well, please do place him in his father's hands' comes when it is too late.

'From the age of 9 he became your boy . . .'
The rift between John and Violet had originated in his childhood.

The revelation was startling in itself. But there was something else. The break with his mother appeared to coincide with the first gap in the family records.

17

The Duchess frowned. 'That's not right,' she said. 'It wasn't Charlie who took John away from Violet. Violet sent him away.'

I had run into the Duchess by chance in the passage outside the Muniment Rooms; briefly, I had explained what I had discovered.

'*Sent* him away?' I said. 'Why?'

'She couldn't bear the sight of him,' she replied.

We were standing by the fire in the Guard Room; the light from the flames flickered on the blades of the sabres displayed on the walls.

'Violet sent John to live with Charlie after Haddon, her eldest son, died,' she continued. 'Haddon was the apple of her eye. He was her favourite. He was only a year older than John. The story in the family is that John was sent away because Violet found the sight of him too painful. He reminded her of Haddon.' She paused for a moment, looking down at the fire. 'It must have been awful for

John. But then in Victorian times I suppose that sort of response was quite common. Families didn't necessarily talk about things. It was the great tragedy of Violet's life. She never got over it.'

'When did Haddon die?' I asked her.

'In the autumn of 1894. He was only nine. There's a scrapbook full of newspaper cuttings in the Muniment Rooms. You might want to have a look at it.'

'But that's extraordinary,' I said. 'His death coincides with the first gap in the records. Why would John have wanted to remove all mention of his brother, even if his death had caused the rift with his mother?'

The Duchess looked puzzled. It was some weeks since I had seen her. The last time we had spoken was when I had been looking for the missing letters. I was about to explain how I had failed to find them and how I had pieced together that it was John who had removed them, but she was in a hurry.

'I'm late for a meeting. Let's talk about it later,' she said. 'It sounds very intriguing.'

'Have you seen Haddon's tomb?' she asked as she was leaving. 'You must see it. It's in the chapel. Violet sculpted it. She was an extremely talented artist. Her pencil drawings are wonderful but the tomb is her best work by far. It really is terribly moving. One of the tour guides will show you the way.'

■ ■ ■ ■

Before going to see Haddon's tomb in the chapel, I decided to look at the newspaper cuttings. Potentially, these were key documents.

In peeling back one layer in the mystery, another had revealed itself. John had concealed not one but *two* important events — the break with his mother *and* the death of his brother. Violet's abandonment of him explained their later estrangement. No wonder, when he was older, he had wanted to keep his mother at a distance: he was unable to forgive her for the hurt she had inflicted on him when he was a small boy. It also explained Violet's anguished letters to her brother; her distress over their broken relationship was laced with guilt. But it did not explain why John had wanted to remove all mention of his brother's death from the Muniment Rooms. Haddon had died in September 1894. The family correspondence for the one month prior to his death — and for the two months after — was missing. Aside from the newspaper reports, he had made certain that not a single document remained to shed light on this tragic episode. Why?

I left the Guard Room and made my way back to the Muniment Rooms.

I found the newspaper reports in a large, leather-covered scrapbook. It had belonged to John's grandfather, the 7th Duke of Rutland, who was living at Belvoir Castle the year Haddon died.

The Duke had cut the articles out of local newspapers. Densely printed, they ran to many column inches; the sudden death of this small boy, the heir presumptive to the dukedom, had evidently rocked the neighbourhood.

The report in the *Grantham Journal* began portentously:

To all of us — high or low, rich or poor, renowned or obscure — death must come sooner or later. It is the unalterable law of the universe. But how different when a young life is cut off! The ancients had a beautiful saying — 'Those whom the gods love die young.' When the dreadful King of Terrors takes a youthful victim it often happens that his fatal dart strikes the fairest, the best beloved, the most promising. The ducal house of Belvoir has this week to mourn the loss of such a one.

The news that the eldest son of the Marquis of Granby has succumbed to an attack of illness, of very short duration, was received with feelings of deep sympathy and regret throughout the whole district.

A fortnight ago, Robert Charles John Manners, better known by his courtesy title of Lord Haddon, was leading a happy country life at Hatley Cockayne, Bedfordshire, the residence of his parents. Today, he lies interred in the family Mausoleum at Belvoir.

In the evening of 22 September, Lord Haddon was suddenly seized with an illness, and the condition of the sufferer became so critical that on the Wednesday following it was deemed advisable that he should undergo a serious operation. This was carried out, but we are grieved to record that the little fellow gradually sank, and he died on Friday, September 28th.

The child, so loving and beloved, rests in the Mausoleum, under the ancient yews, on a mound near the castle at Belvoir.

The newspaper had printed a number of tributes to Haddon. One, written by a friend of the family, was particularly touching:

He was a boy of singular promise. His chief characteristic was his generosity. All he had given to him he at once wished to share, and he would almost insist on giving up any little pleasure to another. His parents arranged their plans so that their boy, who was remarkably active, should lead a really country life; and though he was only nine years old when the swift and sudden blow fell on them, he knew more about flowers, birds and animals, than many far older. He loved his dumb friends: his life, in fact, was full of happiness. His gentle, natural, simple ways, his remarkable power of observation, and his activity made him a charming companion. He was in perfect health, and revelling in the many joys he had at Hatley, the very day he was stricken. During the days and nights of extreme suffering that followed, he showed the same sweetness and sense that always characterized him, thanking all who ministered to him in his usual, gentle, winning way. I grieve for his parents; but I also grieve for a wider circle: not only his kin, but his country, seem to me the poorer for his loss — for the boy is but the forerunner of the man, and a career such as all might envy seemed to be before him.

The remainder of the article was devoted to an account of Haddon's funeral. I imagined that this bleak event would have taken place in private; that his devastated parents would have buried him quietly. But the 9-year-old boy was accorded the equivalent of a state funeral: thousands of the family's tenants and employees attended it.

Few who gathered on the battlements at Belvoir Castle that morning in October 1894 can have forgotten it. They were meant to remember it. Full of pomp and ceremony, it was a deliberate display of status and authority by a family who had ruled over the neighbourhood for eight hundred years.

The newspapers listed the family members who were staying at the castle. John was among them. But it was the detail that followed which was truly horrifying: John had left the castle with his uncle a few hours after the funeral. I checked the visitors' book. It was three years before John returned to Belvoir. It looked as if Violet had sent him to live with Charlie immediately after Haddon's funeral.

Less than a year had separated the two brothers — John had lost his friend and playmate; as the younger son, he had lived in his brother's shadow, then, suddenly, it was he who was destined to become Duke. These were traumatic things in themselves. But then to be abandoned by his mother on this day of all days can only have been one of the most painful moments in his life.

It is in picturing what he had seen before he left the castle that her cruelty becomes incomprehensible.

18

The spectacle of mass grief began the day before the funeral, when Haddon's body, enclosed in a coffin of unpolished oak, with plain silver mountings, was brought to Belvoir by train.

Haddon had died at his parents' house at Hatley Cockayne, a tiny village near Sandy in Bedfordshire. It was forty miles from there to the castle. Early that morning, Henry and Violet left the house in a shuttered carriage, taking John with them. They were travelling ahead of the coffin, leaving the Duke of Rutland's assistant to oversee the arrangements for the transportation of their son's body.

The coffin left Sandy — a tiny station on a branch line of the Great Northern Railway — on the 12.55 train to Peterborough. There, it was transferred to the London–York Express. Special dispensation had been obtained for the express to make an unscheduled stop at Grantham, where another train waited to convey the coffin the last eight miles or so to Belvoir.

In the village below the castle, a crowd of thousands had gathered outside the station. They had come from all points on the Belvoir estate, crossing the recently harvested fields in large walking parties that had set out from the Duke's villages soon after dawn.

The train bearing Haddon's body pulled into the station shortly after two o'clock. Outside, on the forecourt, the coffin was loaded on to a dray, drawn by three grey shire horses, and covered with a pall of green velvet edged with a gold band. As the dray turned into the village high street, the lone figure of Mr Marvel, the Duke's butler, walked ahead of it. The road to Belvoir — which was straight and two miles long — ran across flat, open country. The villagers followed behind the coffin as it progressed slowly towards the castle. On reaching the gates to the lodge, they dispersed. The long drive up to the castle was private; the 'sad carriage', as one paper described it, progressed the last mile alone.

Up on the terrace, John was the only small boy among the group of family mourners. They were assembled beneath the portico. The drive, which dropped steeply from the battlements, lay directly in their line of sight; on one side, it was flanked by tall yew hedges; on the other by an avenue of maple trees. As the three shire horses, led by Mr Marvel, appeared over the brow below, and the coffin made its slow, final approach up to the castle, the bell in the tower began to toll.

John walked behind the dray as the Duke's stud groom led the horses through the great oak doors to the portico: in the confined space, he watched as the small coffin was lifted off the carriage and the green velvet pall that concealed it was removed. It was replaced with a white pall, 'a symbol,' so the *Grantham Journal* reported, 'of innocence and youth'. Then he followed behind his parents and grandparents as the coffin was carried through the Guard Room, and along the passages, to the family's private chapel, where it was placed in front of the altar.

The Duke's indoor servants — 110 of them — joined the procession to the chapel. Seated in the family pew beside his brother's coffin, John listened as his grandmother, Janetta, the Duchess, addressed the household: 'It will, I am sure, be of the greatest consolation to the bereaved parents, my beloved husband, and to my children, to think that on this occasion, when our darling child has been released from pain and suffering to go, as we firmly believe, to a better world, we should greet him on his arrival here with sounds of prayer and praise. I thank you most gratefully for all your great kindness.'

The next morning, well before noon — the appointed time for the funeral — thousands of spectators made their way up the castle's steep drive to the gun-carriage terrace.

Amid the throng of people, it took the cortège several hours to form up. Strict rules of protocol determined the order in which the mourners progressed. First to follow were the immediate members of the family, led by the Duke, and his son, Henry, Marquis of Granby. Precedence dictated that, because the Marquis was the father of the deceased, it was his personal servants, rather than the Duke's, who followed next. Then came the household servants, dressed in mourning suits that had been specially bought for the occasion. They were led by the heads of the departments: the house steward, the house-keeper, the head forester, the head gardener, the stud groom, the head keeper, the coach-man, the Duke's factor and Monsieur The-venot, the *chef de cuisine;* behind them, in long, flowing black robes, came the clergy-men from the forty-three churches on the Belvoir estate, followed by the Duke's out-door servants, and the huntsmen and whips of the Belvoir hounds, wearing scarlet hunt-ing coats. Bringing up the rear came the huge numbers of the Duke's tenants and em-ployees.

The one person who was not in the cortège was John. He was inside the castle. Had a servant kept him away from the window as the cortège prepared to move off to the mausoleum? Or had he watched the distressing scene on the terrace below? The newspaper reports of the funeral did not include this detail, but, at twelve sharp, his brother's coffin, hoisted on the shoulders of six of the Duke's wagoners, was carried from the Guard Room and lowered on to the funeral carriage. Some moments earlier, his mother had left for the mausoleum ahead of the cortège. Policemen, mounted on black horses with mourning ribbons plaited through their manes and tails, had held back the crowds to allow her carriage through. The curtains in the windows were tightly drawn.

The family mausoleum stood on a hill opposite the castle. It was a Romanesque folly, built in the 1820s by the 5th Duke to commemorate his wife. A contingent of local militia, in full dress uniform and wearing brass helmets, formed a guard of honour along the route. It was half a mile from the castle to the mausoleum; such was the crush that the tail end of the procession was still on the battlements when the burial service began. Violet had chosen 'There is a Green Hill Far Away', a favourite of Haddon's, as the first hymn. Twelve choirboys from the Duke's churches — all of the same age as the dead boy — had been specially invited to sing.

As the clear, haunting notes of the hymn broke the stillness and carried along the line of mourners, up at the castle, John would have heard the thousands of voices that had joined in the singing.

A little after half past three, when the crowds had gone, the carriage taking John and his uncle to the railway station clattered down the deserted avenue below the battlements.

The image of the solitary carriage on the empty road — and the small boy huddled inside it — was heartrending. Along that very same route, only a few hours earlier, John had seen the thousands that had gathered to honour the memory of his brother. Yet he was being cast out. Had he been given a reason? Had his mother gently explained to him why he was leaving?

Violet had not sent her three daughters — Marjorie, Letty and Diana — away. They were aged ten, six and two. Her cruelty in banishing her only son was inexplicable.

So what drove Violet to send him away? This was a question that, unsurprisingly, the newspapers did not answer.

I put the scrapbook back in its place on the shelf and left the Muniment Rooms to look for a tour guide to show me the way to the chapel. I wanted to see the tomb that Violet had carved in memory of Haddon.

19

We turned a corner and entered a long passage, crossed a large hall and stopped in front of a sturdy oak door. The guide unlocked it and led me into a small, windowless hallway. We were in the depths of the old servants' quarters. It was a part of the castle I had not been to before. A warren of pantries and sculleries ran off the passage to our left; to our right, a staircase descended into darkness.

I stopped and peered down it. The bare brick steps were broken and uneven. 'Where does that lead to?' I asked the guide.

'Down to the Doom,' she replied. 'It's where they kept the coal for heating the castle. They used to bring it here by barge from the Dukes' collieries in Derbyshire.'

'Why is it called the Doom?'

'I don't know,' she answered. 'It's always been called that. There are forty or fifty rooms down there. It runs the whole length of the castle.'

I followed her into a long corridor. Our

footsteps echoed on the stone flags as we passed a series of doors. They were firmly closed. These were the rooms where the servants had lived and worked in Haddon's day. The family had employed 110 servants then. On the day of his funeral, it was along this corridor that, dressed in mourning livery, they formed up in order of rank before joining the crowds of mourners outside.

Ahead, the guide turned right into a narrow, crescent-shaped passageway; a few yards along it was a door that led into a turret. As we climbed the spiral staircase, she told me the story behind Haddon's tomb. Violet had modelled the effigy of her son from a death mask. Sir Alfred Gilbert had cast the mask the morning after the boy died. Gilbert — who was famous for his statue of Eros in Piccadilly — was a friend of the Duchess's; under his tuition, she began work on the effigy a few days later. It had taken her forty-two years to finish it. Throughout that time, she had continued to work on it, keeping the unfinished tomb in the basement of the family's house in St James's.

At the top of the stairs, we arrived in a circular hallway. 'I'll leave you here. The chapel is through there,' the guide said, pointing at the door ahead.

Stepping into the chapel, I was taken aback by the scale of it. The vaulted ceiling rose to the full height of the castle; along one side of it, the windows were set high in the rafters, the light entering tempered by the lattice of circular muntins that separated the panes of glass. Huge tapestries, depicting biblical scenes, hung beneath the windows. The plain white walls, and the black marble floor, accentuated their rich colours.

I went through the arch that led into the inner chapel and walked up the aisle, past the rows of empty chairs. The light cast from the high windows was subdued and mysterious, falling equally on everything. A heavy stillness pervaded.

I found Haddon's tomb at the far end of the chapel. It stood in a corner to the left of the altar. Beside it, mounted in a wooden display case, there was a printed notice:

Here lies an effigy of the eldest son of the 8th Duke of Rutland, Lord Haddon, who died at the age of nine of tuberculosis. His mother, Violet, was consumed with grief at the death of her eldest son and was responsible for the moulding and sculpting of this effigy as a final token of her love.

The effigy, which was life-size and cast of plaster, was breathtaking in its simplicity and beauty. The little boy lay on top of the tomb, his head inclined to one side, sleeping. He was wearing a loose nightshirt and had a blanket wrapped around his shoulders. The intensity of emotion in the detail was remarkable: the curls of hair falling across his face, the tiny dimple in his chin, the contours of his neck where his shirt lay open. The thought that Violet had moulded these things with her own hands — and that she had spent more than forty years working on them — filled me with a sharp sadness.

I bent down to read the inscription that she had carved at the foot of the plinth:

HOPE OF MY EYES
SOMETHING IS BROKEN THAT WE
CANNOT MEND

WITH GRIEF, REMEMBRANCE,
PRIDE AND LOVE, I DECORATE
HIS MEMORY

DEAR DEAR LITTLE BOY
YOU GAVE US ALL PERPETUAL
BENEDICTION

ENTIRELY DESIGNED AND MODELLED
BY HIS MOTHER

It was the dissonance between the outpouring of grief over the loss of one son and the apparent cruelty with which she had treated the other which was so extraordinary. Yet Violet undoubtedly loved John: her letters to Charlie revealed her distress at their later estrangement. So why hadn't she wanted to cherish him after losing her elder son?

There was something else I found puzzling. Violet had accused Charlie of treating John with *spoiling kindness* after Haddon died. It was such a strange phrase for her to have used. Following his brother's death, and her abandonment of him, John had been in need of every bit of kindness. If Violet, paralysed as she was by grief, had been unable to give him the love and attention that he had needed, why had she begrudged Charlie his kindness?

I turned to walk back along the aisle; I spotted the line of stone coffins that stood, some yards further down, against the wall of the chapel. The effigies of nameless medieval monks lay on top of them, their hands clasped in prayer. Reading the inscriptions, I could see that John had excavated the coffins from the site of Croxton Abbey, a thirteenth-century monastery a few miles from the castle. He had exhumed other tombs from sites on the Belvoir estate: according to his servants, he had disinterred eight of his ancestors in the crypt at Bottesford Church.

The contrast between this man's morbid fascination with death and the peaceful, sleeping boy I had just seen was disturbing. I thought of the things I had discovered in John's rooms in the East Tower: the bowls of human bones, the boxes of gargoyles, the bits and pieces of old pottery and the tens of thousands of glass negatives, all meticulously catalogued and labelled. Then I remembered the theory that a compulsive interest in collecting often pointed to a traumatic event in childhood.

Without the letters that John had removed, it was impossible to determine the exact course of events in the autumn of 1894. But what had happened to him in the years after his brother had died? The catalogue in the Muniment Rooms had listed a small collection of letters that John had written between 1895 and 1901. These, possibly, would offer an insight into what had been going on in the mind of this small boy.

20

The file contained a photograph as well as letters; intriguingly, some of the material dated from the years before Haddon died.

I looked at the photograph first. It was of the two brothers — John and Haddon — aged three and four. The composition of the picture, which had been taken in an empty panelled hall, was haunting; Haddon stood, leaning against a long footstool, in the centre of the large room; to his right, at a distance of some yards, John was seated, curled up, in an elaborately carved chair. In the background, the door to the room stood at an odd angle, as if it had come away from its hinges. This, and the emptiness of the scene, seemed to foreshadow the tragedy to come; and yet, of course, the two boys had been oblivious to it.

The photograph was rendered the more poignant by the letters that followed. They were from Haddon and John. Full of love, and an innocent delight in small things, they testified to the happy times the family had shared before Haddon's death.

There were two letters from Haddon; one was a letter that he had written to his mother on her birthday, when he was six:

Belvoir Castle

Dearest mother — very many happy returns on your birthday.

I wish you had been here yesterday then I would have given you loving kisses!

This morning when I got up I found it had been snowing in the night. Have you got snow in London. Do you know dear mother I am writing this letter all by myself, no one is holding my hand. I am copying it from another paper. I hope you will like it.

Your own dear little son Haddon.

The other letter — also written when he was six — was to Father Christmas:

Dear Father Christmas
I will try to be a better boy and not so naughty at my lessons and not give so much trouble to those who take pains to teach me. I am afraid I have been too naughty to ask for anything.

But dear Father Christmas I should be so pleased if you would be kind enough to give me a box of pencils.

Please help the poor and give clothing to all the poor little children. Haddon.

The two letters from John dated from the summer of 1894. He and his brother — and their elder sister, Marjorie — had been staying at Belvoir with their grandparents:

Dear Papa
Every day we fish in the pond and have caught lots of fishes; carps, tench, perch.

On the heap of sticks in the paddock we have made a lovely hut. We get up to it by ladders and have the goats, Quiz and Rosey, with us.

I have found a beautiful robin's nest in the hay-stack near Marjorie's hut. I took an egg out of it.

Please give my love to all.
Your affectionate boy
Little John

Some days later, John had written to his father again:

Dear Papa
I have found a spotted flycatcher nest with four eggs. We have lots of butterflies, some are very pretty. Mamma arrived yesterday and took us all to the station to give us a drive.

I hope you are enjoying yourself with Uncle Bobby. We are going to London on Monday and I hope you will soon be there. Please give him my best love.

With lots of kisses to you
Your affectionate boy
Little John

Just six months later, Haddon's death had evidently altered his relationship with his father. In his letters to him, he was no longer 'Little John'; instead, he signed himself Roos — which stood for Lord Roos, his courtesy title.

John had been writing to his father from Evelyn's, a small boarding school of around a hundred pupils in Uxbridge, where he was sent in the spring of 1895. He appeared to be frightened of his father: his letters — which also suggest that he was depressed — were full of apologies for his poor performance at the school: 'Dear Father, I hope you won't be angry with me if my report is not very good because I am in a new class and I find the work very difficult indeed, but I am working very hard': then again, a few days later: 'Dear Father, You must remember I am in a new class and the work is awfully difficult. I am trying very hard. You don't know how dull it is here, so that I have to think for about five minutes and then find nothing to say. Goodbye. Roos.'

As John had anticipated, his report was terrible:

Dearest Father — I am horribly sorry to hear about my report — it is dreadful of me but I don't know why it was so bad but I will with all my might try and have a good one next time, do please forgive me, I will try very hard. Roos.

John rarely saw his parents. He spent most of his school holidays with his uncle, whom he clearly adored. In early February 1900, around the time of the Siege of Ladysmith, John was anxious that Charlie, a bachelor in his forties and a former Guards officer, would be recalled to the Boer War: I do hope you won't have to go to South Africa,' he told him, 'and if you do I shall have to come with you.'

The letters that John wrote to Charlie from school paint a picture of a desperately lonely boy. I had seen others written by boys of his generation — and of a similar age and class — but John's were different. The usual references were absent; he didn't refer to the sports he played, or to the boys he made friends with; apart from the insects he kept, he didn't mention other pets; there were no tales of pranks, or practical jokes. Though his uncle was being kind to him, it clearly wasn't enough for this unhappy little boy. One constant refrain ran through them:

I wish you could come down . . .

Do try and come and see me I would love it
so . . .

<u>Do</u> try and come down some time soon . . .

Oh, do come down and if you do, mind you
bring chocs and pear drops. Do try and bring
them, rather than send them. But don't come
down if you think it would bore you . . .

Oh please come Wednesday because I shan't
be able to live without you . . .

If you can't come, please write. I do love your
letters so much they make me jump all round
the room when I see one from you . . .

Sometimes, the plea for a visit was all that
John had written:

I won't write to you any more if you don't
come down some time soon. Yours affectionately, SITM.

The nickname that John had chosen for
himself was sadder still: the initials SITM
stood for 'Stick in the Mind'.

It was awful to discover that, despite John's
pleas, and despite the fact that Charlie lived
just fifteen miles from the school, he never
visited him once in his five years at Evelyn's.

There were times, too, when John appears
to have been completely abandoned. The dual
parental authority had caused confusion; at
half term, he was often left behind at the

school after his parents had failed to write to Matron. 'I am so sorry that I could not come for my Exeat this week,' he told Charlie one weekend in the summer of 1899, when he was twelve: 'None of my family wrote to Miss Evans and told her I was to go, so I was not allowed to go without my people's word. I hope you will be able to read this because I am writing with an etching nib. Dear Old Boy, one of my Emerican Buggs have come out innormous green — one with taills 2 inches long. I hope you will be in London on Saturday because I will come next Saturday.'

In May 1900, at the age of thirteen, John left Evelyn's to go to Eton. His arrival there coincided with an invitation his parents received to stay with Queen Victoria at Windsor Castle.

Both Henry and Violet had close links to the Queen; Henry's uncle, the 6th Duke, had served as Lord of the Bedchamber to Prince Albert in the 1840s; some years later, Violet's father, Colonel Charles Lindsay, the second son of the 24th Earl of Crawford, and a great favourite of the Queen's, had held the post of Groom-in-Waiting.

Henry and Violet spent four days at the castle. While they were there, they arranged for John to be presented to the Queen.

Afterwards, his father formally noted the occasion:

Lord Roos Presentation to the Queen

On Wednesday, May 16th 1900, my son, Roos, was by command of the Queen presented to Her Majesty.

He, being then aged 13 years and three quarters, was told to be at Windsor Castle at 11.30 am. He, together with my wife and myself, was shown into Princess Beatrice's sitting room, where Her Majesty was.

The Queen asked several questions of him — as to whether he liked Eton (he had only been there a fortnight this being his first half there); how old he was; what his amusements were. He with considerable composure having answered Her Majesty's questions, was finally permitted to kiss the Queen's hand and the 'audience' was then concluded.

I do not know how many boys have during their Eton career been presented to the Queen, but that Roos should have been thus honoured by Her Majesty just before her 81st birthday, is a most gratifying fact to me and my wife.

John supplied his own version of the presentation to Charlie: 'I had to go up to the Castle at 10.30 and so I got off all the morning work,' he wrote: 'I stayed at the Castle till 1 and then Mother and Father went and before they went, we went all over the Castle and I saw the caliph's Black flag and his bible and a Car and all the Queen's Jubilee presents. Please excuse writing but in awful hurry. Goodbye.'

'P.T.O.,' he had added at the bottom of his letter: 'As none of my family are coming on 4th June you must.'

Henry and Violet had found the time to stay with the Queen at Windsor Castle, but they hadn't found time to return to Eton a few weeks later.

The fourth of June was the biggest day of the year in the Eton calendar. A glittering social occasion, it involved games, races on the river and elaborate picnics. It was an important ritual for boys and their families to share; it was also the chance for Old Etonians to revisit the scenes of their youth and to catch up with their contemporaries. Henry had been at Eton in the 1860s; it was John's first term at the school, his first 4 June. Yet both he and Violet decided not to go. They were unlikely to have had a more pressing engagement; 4 June was part of the summer season — the day London society decamped to Eton.

Though his brother had been dead for six years, it seemed they still preferred to have little or nothing to do with John.

There can have been few boys whose parents were not at Eton that day. For John as a new boy, the stigma attached to the absence of his own can only have added to the challenges that he was facing. A few days before the event, he hinted in a letter to Charlie that he was being subjected to some form of abuse. Whether he had made a neat copy of it and in doing so had missed words out, or whether the missing words pointed to his distress, it is impossible to tell. But his letter made no sense whatsoever:

Dear Charlie — I am writing to bother one more for those photos which we look out but you did not cut them all they are all in a envelope I have which I am sory to do and that is that chap Bourke is the very worst chap in the School in for the thing which we talked about before I came here and so I have by letter let him know that I am going to have absolutely nothing to do with him. I would as you know let no one except you know about it.

I am still looking forward to seeing you on the 4th.

Goodbye
Your affectionately
Jack

Given their neglect of him, it was hardly surprising that 'Jack' had chosen to confide in Charlie, rather than his parents.

■ ■ ■ ■

Two short notes from Henry and Violet had found their way into the file; they revealed the extent to which the loss of their elder son had overwhelmed them.

One was a bleak note that Henry sent Violet on her thirty-ninth birthday, a few months after Haddon died.

Darling
So it's your birthday. Well I wish I could make you happier on it, but as I feel myself to a large extent what you feel, empty phrases about 'happy returns' and so forth, are but of little use. Anyway, no one in the world wishes you more personal happiness than I do, or more earnestly prays that you may in the future be spared any such suffering as you have gone through.

The other was a note that Violet left for Henry in the winter of 1899. 'To open if I die,' she had written on the envelope. In expressing her last wishes, her overriding concern, to the exclusion of all else, was Haddon's unfinished tomb:

My Dearest,
If I die, have a little bust of Haddon cast at once by Gilbert and put the big thing

of Haddon in the middle of the chapel,* looking towards the East with the back of his head lit by the West window. Gilbert to make the base and me and you to be buried in the ground on either side with nothing but stone slabs deeply engraved. His little body to be brought there. Your wife V.

Violet had not even included a final message of love to her husband.

Reading these letters, it was awful to see the evidence of the wreckage the death of this 9-year-old boy had caused. Here were three individuals — Violet, Henry and John — locked — cut off from each other — in their own worlds of misery.

One letter remained in the file.

It was from John to his father: he was almost fourteen and had failed his exams at the end of his first year at Eton:

Darling Father — I have failed. I am a fool, but it is not my fault. My Tutor is going to try and keep me on but I don't want to, because I don't think it does me any good.

You had better send me abroad with a man.

* Violet was referring to the chapel at Haddon Hall, the family's house in Derbyshire.

I have never been quite so depressed as I am now though I have been very near it before.

For goodness sake don't keep me here. I shall never do anything in life so please don't suspect it.

Goodbye
Roos

Presumably, John had meant to say 'don't expect it'.

I closed the file. The damage to this boy was undeniable. He had come from one of the most privileged backgrounds in England: to be confronted with the evidence of the neglect that he had suffered as a child was shocking.

Yet these letters failed to resolve the central mystery.

Precisely eighty-seven days were missing from the family's correspondence. Haddon had died on 28 September. The gap in the Muniment Rooms began on 23 August — *thirty-six days before Haddon's death* — and extended to 19 November.

I could understand why John had wanted to erase the traumatic events that occurred *after* his brother had died. It had been an intensely painful moment in his life. It had also been a shameful one. He had been thrown out of the family home that he would one day inherit, as if he were unworthy of it.

But the void covered the period when Haddon had been ill.

What had happened then?

From what I knew of John, the length of the excision was no accident. In putting together this historic collection, his primary objective had been to preserve the record. In removing material he had been meticulous. So why, if he had simply wanted to conceal the fact that he had been sent away after his brother died, had he removed the correspondence for the weeks *before* Haddon died?

In those days, there was no cure for tuberculosis; the family's world would have turned on Haddon's illness: the weeks leading up to his death would have been agonizing for them. But this alone did not seem reason enough to explain why, half a century later, as John himself lay dying, he had felt compelled to remove the letters dating from this period.

What I discovered next changed the course of my research entirely.

It was the note that Violet enclosed inside the box containing Haddon's death mask which cracked the mystery open.

But this is to jump ahead.

First, I had a long conversation with the Duchess.

21

It was a two-mile drive to Knipton, a pretty village of yellow stone houses in the valley below the castle. The Duchess had asked me to meet her for lunch at the Manners Arms. The hotel, which had once been the 6th Duke's hunting lodge, belonged to her husband, David, the 11th Duke.

We met in the stone-flagged hallway. 'This was one of our first projects after David succeeded,' she explained. 'We wanted to turn it into a really nice country-house hotel. I designed all the bedrooms myself. They're all named after the family's ancestors — the Flying Duke, the Hunting Duke, the Gentleman Duke, and so on. There are things of theirs in the rooms — and photographs and portraits of them.'

I followed her into the dining room. The tables were decorated with white linen cloths and horn-shaped glass vases, filled with peonies and lilies. One wall was dominated by a set of large windows which overlooked the garden outside; the others displayed pictures of horses and hunting scenes.

'I'm longing to hear what you've discovered,' she said as we sat down. 'I've only had a quick look through the twentieth-century papers. You must have found some wonderful material for your book.'

I began by telling her that the book had changed course, and that my focus was now on John and the missing periods in the correspondence in the Muniment Rooms. I also told her it was now clear that he was responsible for the gaps in the letters. I went through them in detail: the gap in 1894 when John was eight, and which concealed his brother's death; the one in 1909, when he was Honorary Attaché at the British Embassy in Rome, and which the coded letters presaged; and the gap in 1915, when he was twenty-eight, and serving with the 4th Leicesters on the Western Front. As we discussed them, the Duchess could not think of a single reason why John would have wanted to remove the correspondence. His motives were as mysterious to her as they were to me.

'You know Charles — John's eldest son — closed the Muniment Rooms after his father died,' she said. 'It's never been clear why. He appeared to have some sort of a block about them. It was almost as if he attached some sort of feeling of fear to them. Perhaps it was because John kept him at a distance. He never confided in him.'

'Didn't Charles get on with his father?' I asked.

'No, their relationship was complicated. John adored his second son, who was also called John. He was his favourite. No one thought Charles would live to succeed — he was a sickly child. It was why John lavished all his attention on his younger brother.

'I know it sounds strange,' she continued, 'but it goes back to the witches' curse. They lived in the castle's grounds — up on Blackberry Hill, where the mausoleum is now. Two were hung at Lincoln for murdering the Earl of Rutland's sons. It was some time in the early 1600s, I think. The women were said to have placed a curse on future generations. It has haunted the family ever since. Time after time, their eldest sons — or one of their sons — have died in infancy. It skipped that generation — John's children. But Charles lost his second son. He was my husband's brother. After we moved into the castle, I asked a priest to exorcize it. I was frightened the curse would strike our sons too.'

Our conversation returned to the closing of the Muniment Rooms. I mentioned the trunk of correspondence that I'd found which suggested that John was working on his mother's letters when he died.

'Charles was at the castle when his father fell ill. There was a stove in the Muniment

Rooms. Perhaps he saw John burning the letters. We don't know. But if he knew there was
something he wanted to hide, he must have
realized that the race to destroy whatever it
was had not been completed when he died.'

'I don't understand,' I said. 'Why close the
rooms? Wouldn't he have wanted to find out
what the letters contained.'

'No, not necessarily,' she replied. 'Family
papers and historical documents were of no
interest to Charles. He hated those rooms.
His father had created them. It was a place
John had warned people off from entering. I
think Charles felt intimidated by them — a
sense that his father was the great expert,
and he didn't know what was inside them.
Perhaps it went back to his childhood — the
memory of being kept out of this dark, secret
place when he was a small boy. He knew
there was something bad in there, but he
couldn't bring himself to confront it. The
simplest solution was to close the rooms. That
way, there was no danger of anyone discovering what his father had wanted to hide.'

22

I returned from lunch to find a note on my desk. Beside it, there was a bundle of letters, and a thick, well-thumbed journal.

The note was from the archivist:

Have you seen this? I found it at the back of the drawer in John's desk. I can't find the death cast — or the box. Both appear to be missing.

I've left you the letters of condolence that Violet and Henry received after Haddon died.

The journal is Violet's.

The 'this' to which he had referred was the small pale-cream envelope that he had pinned to the note. Six ominous words were written on it: 'A Death Cast of Lord Haddon'. The words — written in Violet's hand — had been heavily underlined.

Cautiously, I opened the envelope; it obviously had something to do with the death mask Sir Alfred Gilbert had cast the morning after the boy died. Inside it was the note that Violet had enclosed in the box that had contained the missing cast:

April 9 1907

A cast of my best beloved boy of nine years old who died on 28th September 1894 after six days agonies and starvation from an accident twisting something inside. And then my heart was broken. He was my Joy and Pride.

But I hid it away. For it was not like my beautiful big fair child of beauty. And yet I cannot destroy it and shut it up now in this box to be sent to Belvoir Castle to rest there.

His mother
Violet Rutland

I leant back in the chair, stunned. This was a major discovery. Here, at last, was the secret that John had been determined to hide. His brother hadn't been ill; he had died as a result of an accident 'after twisting something inside'. The notice on the plaque beside Haddon's tomb stated that he had died of tuberculosis. Contemporaneously, the newspapers had been told that the boy had died from 'an illness'. Clearly, it wasn't only John who had wanted to cover up the accident: his family had clearly been at pains to conceal it at the time.

Why?

Violet's note pointed to some sort of internal obstruction: a blow to a vital organ. But what had caused the accident?

I made three further discoveries that afternoon.

By law — according to the Coroner's Act of 1887 — any violent, sudden or unnatural death was subject to a judicial investigation. A call to the Bedfordshire Record Office revealed that there had been no inquest following Haddon's death. Nor had there been a police investigation. The appropriate authorities had not been told that he had died as the result of an accident. The information on Haddon's death certificate corroborated Violet's note: 'Cause of death — Intestinal Obstruction'. But the *underlying* as opposed to the *actual* cause of death had been omitted. In failing to report the accident, Violet and Henry — then Marquis and Marchioness of Granby — had broken the law — a crime, which, had it been discovered, would have resulted in a criminal prosecution.

Henry, it seems, had also concealed the truth from Queen Victoria. The day after Haddon died, he sent a telegram to Balmoral. I found the Queen's reply among the letters of condolence:

I am most deeply grieved at the news you give me and much surprised as we knew nothing of the dear boy's illness. Was it sudden? Say everything most kind and sympathizing to dear Violet.

The third thing I discovered was that Haddon's accident had occurred on John's birthday. This grim detail was buried in the pages of the journal which the archivist had left on my desk. Violet had kept the journal in the mid-1930s. At the time, she had been thinking about writing her autobiography. In mapping out the chapters she proposed to write, she had noted the things that had happened to her over the course of her life. The entries were chaotic; no more than fragments. But still, the few lines that she had written about Haddon's death struck a jarring note. They were hidden among a jumble of memories of the places she had visited and the people she had met in the weeks before he died:

Aug 14 Go to White Lodge. Draw Royal baby, future King Edward VIII. Difficult won't go to sleep. Start at 9, finish at 4.30. German governess will clap her hands to wake him and make him open his eyes! I sit for Shannon. On 16th I go again to White Lodge.

I go down to Hatley — Haddon lovely at Station. To Longshawe. Babies with me. [Earl of]

Wharncliffe, Charlie L [Lindsay], Sir Henry James, Miss James. Darling children arrive towards evening (Spt 7) cut Haddon's hair. Lockinge — Manoeuvres — Blues and Horse Guards etc. in Camp. Big children arrive from Longshawe next day. Happy day for Haddon. He dines down. He sits next me. No hurrying to bed. Dance and play after. Haddon plays harmonium. Tea party for John's birthday. Play after. Haddon ill that night — Sept 22. Operation 26th successful. Worse on 27th, despair. On 28th a spark of hope! Died at 10 pm.

Violet had not mentioned the accident. It was as if it had never happened. All that she had said was 'Haddon ill that night.' The loss of her eldest son had been the central tragedy of her life — 'my great sorrow', as she repeatedly referred to it. But half a century after his death, as she planned her autobiography, she had drawn a veil over it. She had opted to keep to the official version of events.

Clearly, the death of this 9-year-old boy had been no ordinary accident. It had happened at the family's home at Cockayne Hall in the tiny village of Hatley Cockayne. If it had been straightforward — if Haddon had fallen from a tree, or a pony — his parents would not have gone to such lengths to cover it up. Someone must have been to blame for it: someone they had wanted to protect.

Awful though this was to contemplate, the finger of suspicion pointed at John. It would explain why he had been sent away within hours of the funeral. His parents had wanted him out of the way.

And there were the excisions that John had made in the family's correspondence. The accident resolved the mystery behind the length of the gap he had created in the records. The correspondence in the weeks leading up to it would have revealed that Haddon had not been suffering from tuberculosis. Over the course of the six days it had taken the boy to die, the letters and telegrams that had flown between Belvoir Castle and Cockayne Hall would have contained details of his condition, exposing the myth of illness. In reporting the accident to the Duke and Duchess, in all probability, Henry and Violet had described *how* it had happened.

But what had actually happened?

If John *was* to blame for Haddon's death, had it simply been a tragic accident, or had there been more to it than that?

The lengths to which both John and his parents had gone to cover it up presented the chilling possibility that he might have actually killed his brother. Of course, the likelihood that he had killed him by design was infinitesimal. But he might have wanted to hurt him.

My best beloved boy. My joy and pride. These

were the words Violet had written in the note she enclosed in the box containing Haddon's death cast. As the second son, John had lived in his brother's shadow. He had had every reason to be jealous of him. The accident had occurred at his birthday party. Had the two boys been fighting? Or had a game they had been playing gone wrong? Had something provoked him to harm his brother in a fit of jealousy?

I found myself completely torn. In sending him away so soon after the funeral, it was possible that Violet and Henry had wanted to punish him. It would also explain why Violet had resented Charlie for the 'spoiling kindness' he had shown towards John at the time. But if it had genuinely been an accident, then his parents' behaviour towards him was unforgivable. Ordinarily, the loss of a sibling would have been damaging, but John had been made to feel murderously responsible for the death of his brother. In casting him out, they had prevented his mourning from progressing in the usual way; they had failed to give his feelings a proper hearing. Cumulatively, his parents' behaviour would have fuelled a belief that he was dangerous — dangerous to the people that he loved.

So was he innocent or guilty? Worryingly, when he was older, John had shown an unhealthy fascination with things deathly and peculiar. As a young man, he had exhumed numerous tombs. He had also collected human bones. Was this a manifestation of the psychological damage his parents had inflicted on him? In clinging to the deathly had he been clinging to his dead brother? Or did his morbid obsession with death point to something more sinister?

The challenge, more than a century after the event, was to construct a narrative of the accident. I needed to find out how Haddon had 'twisted something inside'. John had removed his family's correspondence, but the letters of condolence that friends and relations had sent to his parents were still in the Muniment Rooms. It was just possible that among them I would find someone who had been privy to the details of the accident. I was not expecting them to be spelt out; John would not have left the letters there otherwise. But the correspondence might at least offer pointers as to what exactly had occurred.

23

The letters were mostly to Violet. In the bleak days following the loss of her eldest son, her friends had rallied round. Mary, Countess of Minto, had written on 6 October, two days after his funeral:

My darling — it <u>was</u> dear of you to write to me and every word just cut my heart like a knife. I know exactly, exactly how you are feeling — the rebellious indignation at the sorrow coming to you, and taking your best most beautiful cherished one. Oh I understand it all.

I quite know <u>how</u> difficult <u>faith</u> must be when things go wrong. I don't think you can <u>really</u> feel that death is death. I am so sure there is a future, and about his being frightened and alone remember that he is now the strong one, and you the weak. And fancy what the certainty of happiness must be to a child, without one sin staining their record — it must be absolute happiness. I shouldn't grieve for <u>him</u>, but for you, for Henry, for the children, for all who loved him. This sorrow has come home to me almost as if it was one of my own children, the sickening feeling 'can this awful tragedy be true'.

Am I writing a sort of sermon? I don't mean to. Oh how well I know how watching those agonies must have taken all belief in God away — why can't I say anything to do you good! I think of his lovely angel face illuminated with intense joy and peace, and somehow that brings me comfort, for I know he is unspeakably happy. Then I think of you without him — the anguish and misery and how <u>can</u> I pity him? My heart longs to comfort you. I know till you can think of him as he is — 'around the throne of God in heaven' — you will never find one ray of hope.

Bless you darling

Mary, Countess of Wemyss, whom Violet had known since she was a child, had also written. Mary had lost her own son when he was three years old:

Darling Violet
I was so touched at your writing to me telling me all about yr darling beautiful boy. It is difficult for me to say all I feel about it, because my heart answered every

word in yr letter — every pang, every sigh, every bitterness, that terrible terrible longing and feeling of regret — that something might have been done differently — the cruel burning thought of the tender one's pain and suffering and one's own helplessness, the longing to live the time over with one's experience and the horror of the pain endured — oh! dear Violet, I feel for you so much and alas!

I know that one is tormented, maddened for months and months. The only comfort is that as far as <u>they</u> are concerned the pain once over is as if it had never been but it lives in one's own memory. Then you have the consolation of feeling that yr love and care eased his suffering — what a brave splendid little fellow he was! One cannot think his pure little life was in vain, as you know he was happy and well every minute of it and died like a hero. But it's so true, what you say, of when people write and tell one that Death is best. It's small consolation and does not remove one's sense of pity and wrong at the bright happy useful life so full of promise being snapt off — seemingly in such a wanton meaningless way.

When the Spring comes and the flowers or games or anything bright and beautiful that they would have <u>loved</u>, when one sees the others <u>rejoicing</u> in life and when <u>all</u>

<u>other</u> people have forgotten then one's heart bursts within itself with grief, that they are not there too and nothing ever replaces the silent aching gap in one's own heart. To a mother it is the sorrow of all sorrows that leaves one not the same, the place can never be refilled.

I hope my letter may not pain you in any way you poor dearest. I hope the other children are well and I hope they are some comfort and distraction to you. I hope Henry is well. I wonder where you are? I've heard nothing of you since you wrote. I have left Gosford and go to Panshanger tomorrow and Loseley on Sat.

yr loving
Mary

Lucy Tennant, a cousin of Violet's, had written from Glen House, the family's castle in the Scottish borders:

Oh darling Violet — poor poor Darling. My heart is all bleeding for you — how cruel how dreadful to have your best your lovely lovely child taken away. It is too terrible a stroke almost for a human being to bear. So sudden and relentless and fearful.

Your wonderful letter goes to our hearts — Darling — what fearful agonies you have been thro'. That lovely darling child.

It is too fearful to think of — a most cruel fate — and it all seems dark and blind and a mad wicked waste of goodness and beauty and strength, in which no glimmer of intentions or wisdom pierces. Try to be glad he had such a perfect child-life, the happiest that could be — with an ideal Father (the most delightful I have ever seen) and a Mother who was perfect and heavenly to him, and then he had not even had the small childish sorrow of leaving for school. His little lovely flower-life was cruelly broken, but so complete and flawless and exquisite while it was with us. His whole self and beauty was most like you — the others are much less like you — I do mourn him very truly and deeply and am glad I saw him twice at Hatley.

Daisy [Countess of Warwick] and Etty [Ettie Grenfell, later Lady Desborough] were here but left today. I showed them your heart-wringing letter thinking you wd forgive my doing so, and you said Daisy might see it.

This in haste
Yr loving and sorrowful
Lucy

The love and sympathy that Violet's friends expressed was terribly moving. Their heartfelt words brought the tragedy of Haddon's death — and the sudden shock of it — to life. But none of the letters revealed the cause — or the circumstances — of his accident.

Interestingly, however, Violet had written to some of her friends immediately after Haddon died. A number were writing *in reply* to her. Had she told them what happened? If her letters were preserved in other family collections, I might find the answer there.

There was something else. Several of the correspondents had had the temerity to ask for further details of Haddon's illness. 'What was the matter that an operation was necessary?' Cecil Drummond, Henry's second cousin, had asked. 'What illness was the poor boy suffering from?' another had enquired. His sudden death had clearly prompted questions to be asked at the time.

So what was the gossip? More than likely, it had also circulated in the servants' halls. In those days, lady's maids and valets accompanied their masters and mistresses on the constant round of country-house visits. Had the Granbys' servants told other servants what they had seen or heard at Cockayne Hall? Had they, in turn, reported the gossip — as was customary — back to their employers?

I jotted down the names of those who had written to the family. Then I made a list of the friends and relations who had attended Haddon's funeral. The long roll call of aristocratic families pointed to the archive collections that I needed to search.

For months, the search proved fruitless.

The pool of collections turned out to be far smaller than I expected. A significant number of the families who were close to the Rutlands in the 1890s had died out. Their possessions had been dispersed to distant heirs, and their papers lost.

Besides scouring national and county records offices, I contacted archivists at the historic houses where Violet and Henry had stayed in the 1890s, and where the letters of those they were visiting were still held. Even here my hopes were dashed. Winnie, Duchess of Portland, and Mary, Countess of Minto, had been great friends of Violet's, yet while large numbers of their letters had been preserved, there wasn't a single one from Violet, or any that referred to Haddon's death.

At times, I came tantalizingly close to finding what I was looking for. At Cadlands in Hampshire, the home of the Drummond family — the Rutlands' cousins — I found a wonderful cache of letters dating from the 1870s and 1880s. They were full of family gossip and vivid descriptions of visits to Belvoir Castle, but in the 1890s the letters came to an end. There wasn't anything sinister behind it; it was simply that the next generation of cousins was not as close.

Working my way through collections of correspondence belonging to other families on my list, I came across occasional references to Haddon's death, but there was no mention of how his 'accident' had occurred.

I found the answer to the question that had eluded me for so many months at Stanway House, the home of the Earl of Wemyss, near Toddington in Gloucestershire. There, in the family's archives, was Violet's reply to the letter of condolence Mary, Countess of Wemyss, had sent her — the only surviving reply to the mountain of letters Violet had received.

She was writing three weeks after Haddon's death. Mary's third son, Colin, had died of an illness at the age of three. Knowing her friend would understand what she was feeling, Violet had poured out her heart to her.

Violet's letter, which was twelve pages long, brought the traumatic events of the last days of Haddon's life into sharp focus. Yet it is only on the fifth page — *en passant,* and in one short sentence — that she mentions the accident. In her own words, she explains *how* it happened. But in light of the fact that she sent John away almost immediately afterwards, the glaring omission was that she failed to tell her friend *why* it happened. Particularly when, as she describes it, the accident itself was so tragically — and innocently — prosaic:

Mary dearest

It was dear of you to write. You know poor dear what it all means — and how bad it is!

I couldn't have imagined it could be so awful — and it all gets worse and worse. The memory of him ill and dying and the week's agonies is torturing enough — and the cruel little bits of hope that gave one breathing time while watching and nursing and the dashing of hopes, and the tortures he suffered are maddening to live over again — and yet the thought of him alive, and strong and brimming over with eager happy life — the beautiful, beautiful face, and lithe, agile, peaceful body, and the darling, tender, artistic, dexterous hands and all that <u>never</u> again for my poor eyes to feast on — that is too heartbreaking to bear.

Poor Henry misses his <u>eldest</u> son! Sees no joy or reason for the future in life and suffers dreadfully to have lost his companion. They were such <u>friends</u> and the boy was devoted to him, and Henry so proud of him.

<u>I</u> haven't got to the future yet. That's got to come. I am only still raging that <u>why</u> should that beloved have suffered such tortures. Why should he have been given his beautiful life — and then have it taken away before having a chance of us-

ing it! Of making it! I fret at it being so unfair, so unjust to <u>him</u>. I am not thinking of what matters to me, or the missing him yet, but him, him, him.

If he had been killed dead, it would have been easier to be patient now. Or if he had had an illness!

But he was always so strong. So well. Never ill. And it was just only a tiny acrobatic trick that twisted something inside — and gave him intolerable tortures for 6 days.

The operation was a successful one because they found the twisted thing and untwisted it. But just a day too long had he suffered — just <u>too</u> long had the thing been twisted. It could not regain power. The Drs marvelled at his wonderful strength and vitality — no weakness or collapse from the operation. And he just died of starvation — just the most awful death imaginable.

The Drs loved him, and wondered at his strong character and will, and his clear brain (a strong constitution that would fight to live) and his patience. I heard one Dr say to him 'Do you know what a hero is? You are one!'

The Drs nursed him in the most devoted way. But I cherish a tiny thing he said — 'Oh, you Drs, you are all so clumsy! Mother must do it — she is the only one who knows how to do it.' And then: 'Mother dear, if you hadn't thought of doing that, I think I should have died really.' I was stroking his forehead with a wet handkerchief and he kept saying 'Lovely, oh lovely, Mother dear.'

There is no comfort <u>anywhere</u> yet! No daylight. Nothing but gaping wounds.

Nothing can be the same again. Nothing, also, can hurt again like this.

If all the others were swept away, it would mean nothing more of pain to me.

Mary dear, he was the best, the kindest, the tallest, the most beautiful amongst them all. The one who loved to draw, and to play, and who had the darlingest hand touch — the simplest, the most generous.

If only he had not been so beautiful! My eyes govern me! And they seem now blinded to all else. All grieve who knew him, not for us, I mean, but just that they find he was a thing to miss.

People write and say I ought to be pleased that he is out of this world, away from the troubles and the bufferings that must come to those who live, and that Death is better than Life.

I say Death is good for those who are tired and sad and hopeless, and for those who are crushed and maimed and disappointed. It is good for those who have gone through fire and flames and tragedies. But it is <u>not</u> best for those who only know life's sunshine and brilliant lookings forward!

Dearest M, will you tell that dear Ld Wemyss about me and Haddon. I have not courage to write more to him than dear thanks for his sympathy. I have let my pen run away with me to you and I know you won't mind. You know and understand.

Yr most loving VG

(What is so dreadful to me is, that if any of the others had the same thing happen, we could save them easily with our experience. I rage to think we had no experience ready for <u>him</u>, the best treasure of all.

I do not blame anyone. It is a risky thing to have an operation if nature was likely to put itself right by itself. But another time I would not wait at all.

They mentioned hoping till the end, because he was not <u>ill</u>. Only starving. What a selfish letter. Why do I harrow you? But you will forgive.)

The letter, as Violet acknowledged, was desperately harrowing — not least in its exposition of a grief so overwhelming, so excluding, that it had stifled her love for her other children.

'*He was the best, the kindest, the tallest, the*

most beautiful amongst them all . . . If all the others were swept away it would mean nothing more of pain to me.'

Yet in one short sentence, Violet had glossed over the event that was the source of all her pain. *'It was just only a tiny acrobatic trick that twisted something inside.'* She had even said, 'I do not blame anyone.'

But all the circumstantial evidence points to the fact that Violet *had* blamed John, and that he himself had felt to blame for the accident — or, at the very least, had wanted to conceal the fact that his mother had held him to blame. She had sent him away after Haddon had died: he had spent a good part of his life removing all trace of what had happened from the Muniment Rooms at Belvoir. And if the cause of Haddon's death was 'only a tiny acrobatic trick', why had the family gone to such lengths to cover it up at the time?

So much of what Violet had to tell Mary was in flat contradiction to the official version of events.

'He was not ill' . . . 'So well' . . . 'Never ill.'

Yet the newspapers were told that he was ill. Then there was the notice beside his tomb which stated that he had died of tuberculosis. By Violet's own admission, this was entirely untrue.

■ ■ ■ ■

My first thought after seeing her letter was that it was in fact John who had injured his brother. Violet was claiming that Haddon's injury was self-inflicted. But could he really have 'twisted something inside' simply by performing some sort of 'acrobatic trick', or was his internal injury caused by an external blow? Had John hit his brother in the stomach or caused him to fall awkwardly against some kind of obstacle?

I showed Violet's letter to a gastroenterologist. He immediately dismissed the theory. Based on the medical procedures she described, Haddon had died from a twisted gut. More than likely, it was a condition that he had been born with. At any stage in his life, even 'walking down a garden path', his gut could have twisted of its own accord. He had not hit, or been hit by something or someone. It *was* the 'acrobatic trick' that had killed him.

A handstand, a cartwheel, a somersault off something — it was awful to think that something so innocent had had such tragic consequences. Haddon's death haunted both John and Violet for the rest of their lives, and yet with the benefit of modern medical knowledge, it is clear that it was an accident waiting to happen.

But I still hadn't discovered why the blame fell on John. In one final effort to shed further light on the episode, I spoke to David, the present Duke. I told him about the discrepancy between the information contained in Violet's letter to Lady Wemyss and the notice in the chapel beside Haddon's tomb.

John was David's grandfather. Yet it was the first time he'd heard that Haddon had died as a result of an accident.

'It must have been a cover-up,' was his immediate reaction.

But a cover-up of what, or why, it is impossible to know. I could only think that in some way, whatever the trick Haddon was performing, John had egged his brother on. After all, almost by definition, an acrobatic trick is something performed for someone. Less than a year separated the two boys; they played together constantly. The most likely person *was* John.

This was as far as it was possible to go in reconstructing the story behind the first gap in the records at Belvoir; midway through researching it, I received a lead to the events that lay behind the second.

■ ■ ■ ■

PART IV

■ ■ ■ ■

24

I was at Cadlands on the Solent looking at the Drummond family archive, when I got a call from George Davies, a computer analyst with an interest in cryptology. He had managed to decipher John's letters from Rome.

Potentially, it was an important breakthrough. Just nine letters remained at Belvoir for the period between 6 June and 28 October 1909. John had used the cipher in the months leading up to the gap.

There were thirty-four coded letters and telegrams in total. The first, a letter to Charlie, sent from the British Embassy in Rome, was dated 11 February 1909; the last, a telegram that John had wired from Rome Terme, the main railway station in the centre of the city, was dated 5 June. The void in the correspondence at Belvoir began the *day after*. The gap in 1894 had concealed a series of truly awful events; the natural suggestion was that something startling had also occurred in the summer of 1909.

The question, of course, was what.

Until now, I had drawn a blank. Looking at the letters that John was working on when he died, I had found nothing to shed light on what he had wanted to conceal — or why. But something had clearly been going on in the run-up to the gap: something of such importance that John had felt compelled to communicate it in a secret code.

George was sending the decrypted material through by email. In 1909, post boys had delivered the original coded messages from door to door, but a century later, I needed a wi-fi signal to read them, and Cadlands, which was in the New Forest, was an internet blackspot.

I left the house and drove off in search of a signal. As I turned out of the long drive that led up to it, the light in the forest was magical. High above, the leaves of the oaks formed a canopy. It was early evening and the sun was at a low angle, casting checkerboards of light through the shadow. I thought about my conversation with George. John had apparently created a replica of the King Charles I's cipher. Evidently, it had been more than just a game to him: mimicking the patterns of numbers the King had used, he had gone to considerable lengths to devise a numerical vocabulary. It was a substitution cipher: the numbers represented words, syllables and letters: using it would have been both laborious and complicated.

By a strange quirk of coincidence, Carisbrooke Castle, where Charles I had been imprisoned before his execution, was nearby. It was at Newport on the Isle of Wight. Weeks before the King faced the scaffold, hundreds of encrypted letters were smuggled in and out of his bedchamber. The long sequences of numbers concealed details of the last, desperate plots to spring him from the castle and restore him to the throne. Two hundred and fifty years later, John had created a similar cipher to encrypt his secrets from Rome.

It was such a bizarre thing for John to have done. Why replicate Charles I's cipher? Given his knowledge of cryptology, he could have invented one of his own. Had the 22-year-old felt some sort of affinity with the Stuart King? Had something about the King's life or character drawn John to him?

At this stage in his life, I realized I understood very little about John. His letters sketch only the faintest picture of him. His personality remained hidden, as if he were guarding it. From Messina in Italy, he wrote graphically of the devastation caused by the earthquake, and the scenes that he had witnessed at the British relief camp. But this was reportage. After the pain his parents had inflicted on him as a child, it was hard to determine what sort of young man he had become. I certainly had no inkling of what he was hiding in the pages of encryption.

I knew where he had been in the months before he went out to Italy. Having left Cambridge in the summer of 1908, he was living at 97 Cadogan Gardens — Charlie's house in Chelsea. Their life together appears to have revolved around their shared interests: antiques, books, rare manuscripts and John's bulldogs — Ariel and Togo. Though Charlie was thirty years older, they seemed inseparable. Most weekends, they went shooting or fishing together. Then there were expeditions to excavate archaeological sites on the family's numerous estates. In September 1908, they spent three weeks at Croxton Abbey, the medieval priory close to Belvoir Castle, where John found the monks' tombs.

When he wasn't with Charlie, John saw his friends. In London, he belonged to a fashionable, bohemian set; besides other wealthy aristocrats, it included the leading lights of the day — painters, writers, actresses and musicians. Their evenings were spent at the theatre, or at dinner parties hosted at houses in Mayfair and Belgravia. After dinner, they raced their cars along the Mall, or joined in the midnight treasure hunts that were all the rage.

This was the surface of John's life — but I wanted a sense of the person beneath it.

There was a telling photograph of him in the family album the Duchess had shown me. It is late in the summer of 1909 and John is standing with a group of friends. He is leaning against a wall, looking down, his arms folded. There is a cigarette in his mouth, which is unlit. He has dark, glossy hair; his handsome face is caught in profile. There is an aura of rebelliousness about him; his striking looks single him out: he appears more worldly, more sophisticated than the conventional, awkward-looking young men he stands beside.

There are other pictures of him taken that summer: posing with his sisters on the battlements at Belvoir; at Croxton Abbey, with his sleeves rolled up, digging an excavation trench; on the banks of the River Wye in Derbyshire, fishing for trout; The impression they leave is of an active, engaging young man. But there is also a hint of distance. John, I noticed, never looks at the camera. His gaze is always averted.

Thirty years later, as he was dying in the Muniment Rooms, he returned to the events of that summer. Something had happened that he was determined no one should remember.

I parked by the thin strip of beach. I'd finally found a wi-fi signal in a small village overlooking the Solent. Directly opposite, about two miles distant, I could see Cowes. It was a still summer's evening and the sea shimmered. There were yachts and motor cruisers out, their wakes dazzling white against the blue. Three hundred and fifty years ago, in the depths of winter, Charles I's devoted servants had risked their lives crossing this very stretch of water to deliver the encrypted letters from his exiled courtiers. It was incredible to think that I was about to see the text that John had hidden in his replica of the King's code.

The signal was weak; it took a while for the document to download. Watching the blue indicator flickering slowly forwards, I wondered why John had left the encrypted letters in the Muniment Rooms. Why hadn't he destroyed them? Was it because he thought his version of Charles I's cipher was unbreakable?

25

There were 148 pages to go through. John and Charlie had used the cipher throughout their letters; frequently, they had encrypted a single word within a sentence. For this reason, their entire correspondence was included in the document.

The letters were in date order. I scrolled down to 11 February, when John had first used the cipher. It was his second week at the embassy and a letter had come from Charlie in that evening's post. Before joining the ambassador and his wife for dinner, he had replied immediately:

'My dear Old Boy,' he began:

During the course of this letter I am going to put one or two things in cipher but do not trouble to make it out in a hurry as it will be of no importance . . .

It looked as if this was a practice run. I stopped reading and scrolled back up to Charlie's letter to see if he had mentioned anything that would have prompted John to use the cipher. I couldn't see anything of consequence. Having spent the weekend at Belvoir, Charlie was missing his nephew; the letter was mostly devoted to news of John's dogs, Ariel and Togo:

Belvoir Castle

Jacko — I am here till Sunday, with little Ariel who is extremely well.

I am now writing at your centre table and the little boy is lying spatchcock by the fire, thinking of you. It is almost painful to see the way he dashes into this room and then his deep disappointment not to find you here, and he is by no means the only one who misses you really badly here. Togo is also well, as long as he doesn't swallow bones. He was very sick the other night and produced a chicken's pelvis.

Charlie relayed other news from the castle. 'We had a ball for the servants last night. I danced the opening dance with Mrs Walker* and a valse (!!) with Miss Tritton,'† he reported. Then, after telling John about the proposed reorganization of the library at Bel-

* The housekeeper at Belvoir.
† The Duchess's lady's maid.

264

voir, he asked whether he could use the diplomatic bag to send out the parcels of cigarettes he wanted.

I returned to John's reply:

I find out now that the Foreign Office will not send out anything at all in the bag, except in the form of a letter, so that is no good for cigarettes. So if you could send out some more as soon as you can, I should be very glad.

I wonder if you know of any references to cipher letters and keys in the Vatican Library? If so, I might go and do some work there some time. I think I shall go there on the chance and have a look about.

He continued by asking Charlie to do one or two chores for him:

When you have a chance I should be awfully grateful to you if you would telephone to Mr Rye* and get as much information as you can out of him about the roof and ask him when he is going to send me the plan and the vellum and powder. I am also writing soon to Cousins† to ask

* The caretaker at Haddon Hall, the family's medieval castle in Derbyshire.
† A breeder of British bulldogs.

him again to look out for a wife for Ariel
and will tell him if he finds a good dog to
get your approval first. You don't mind
this, do you?

Then came the cipher:

51349 44695 35963 59823
83358 27472 79901 12211
54370 54151 94731 77336
695 514 543 831
390 921 946 236
837 dogs it isn't the being 390 910 489
that 501 650 but it is the 200 771 231
441 358 385 140 695 444 122 not only to
body but to mind never 433
130 120 543 one has got a moment to one's
self — even while I am
93245 54372 84006 44601 24200
24329 91034 53592 61271
59445 69226 54364 behind
83305 81273 50139 53121
80647 69685 13092 is coming in.

Decrypted, the numbers read as follows:

how i Do Long
to Be si T.
ing in Your ro
om have. ing teA. with you And
the dogs it isn't the being A. wa Y
that i mind but it is the D. re ad

full Di S. C. om for T. not only to body but
to mind never fe E. L. ing
one has got a moment to one's self — even
while I am
write ing this i Am
All wa Y
Lo ok ing behind
to see i F
some on E. is coming in

John had told Charlie this was of 'no
importance'. But it was important to me. I
was seeing a side of him that I had not seen
before. The vulnerability which the cipher
concealed was absent from his other letters.
It was also at odds with the assured,
handsome-looking man I had seen in the
photographs.

I read the translation again:

How I do long to be sitting in your room having tea with you and the dogs. It isn't the
being away that I mind, it is the dreadful
discomfort not only to body but to mind,
never feeling one has got a moment to
one's self — even while I am writing this, I
am always looking behind to see if someone
is coming in.

His paranoia was disconcerting; he seemed
at pains to conceal his unhappiness from
those around him. The 'looking behind' as he

was writing, and the fact that he had chosen to express his unhappiness as a series of mathematical equations that only Charlie could understand, suggested that he was afraid of anyone knowing what he really felt.

John had written 'important' by the blocks of cipher in the letters that followed. I was expecting the translations to reveal the details of a particular event, or a sequence of events: something that had happened to him, or that was about to happen to him. But he hadn't used the cipher to communicate information. Time after time, he had used it to encrypt raw emotion — feelings of deep loathing for his father:

238 385 503 592
As S. ho le.
312 541 401 122
C u N. T
50000 53741
47314 54330 83309 86154
and 53131 78042 40319 62731
he is
go ing to Try
and F right En Me

Quickly, I scanned the rest of the pages. There were gaps in the translations; places where the cipher hadn't been broken. John was obviously locked in a bitter row with his father, but it wasn't clear what they were fighting about.

I wondered whether the hatred concealed in the strings of numbers stemmed from the way the Duke had treated John after his brother died — and whether the row was in some way a byproduct of that. But, on closer reading, it looked as though it had something to do with money. Family heirlooms, and the terms of John's allowance, appeared to come into it. Yet it was impossible to pinpoint how — or why — the Duke had wanted to frighten him. Or why John had loathed him so intensely.

Until now, the Duke had played only a small part in the story I was following. He was a remote, mysterious figure; I knew very little of substance about him. At Belvoir, I had come across just one letter of his: the short note that he had sent to Violet on her birthday, a few months after Haddon died. He had barely featured in the other letters that I had seen: his family rarely mentioned him.

In the few glimpses I'd had of him, he struck me as a kind, socially responsible man. On becoming Duke, his concern for the welfare of the poor in his villages had led him to donate generously to local charities. In 1914, in the first weeks of the war, he had offered to support the families of men anxious to fight abroad. But it was the strength of emotion that he had shown at Haddon's funeral that jarred against the crude insults that John was levelling at him. Unable to maintain the stiff reserve of Victorian times, the Duke had wept throughout his son's funeral: his own father had had to support him as Haddon's coffin was lowered into the ground.

Fifteen years later, this same, apparently sensitive, man had wanted to 'frighten' his only surviving son.

Whatever John's feelings towards his father, Charlie clearly shared them. Looking at the decrypted material, it seemed the two of them were tapping into a conversation that had been going on for some time. 'Blitherer'; 'rotten'; 'cheat'; 'liar': these were all words Charlie used to refer to the Duke.

The suggestion was that there was a hidden side to Henry Rutland. The material at Belvoir was thin, but what had his contemporaries made of him? Printed sources — the newspapers, and published letters and biographies of the period — seemed the obvious place to start.

Henry's life passed his contemporaries by. They had little to say about him. Famous only for his handsome looks and his putative charm, he was, so the press baron Lord Beaverbrook believed, 'a man of considerable stupidity'.

Born in 1852, the year the new Houses of Parliament were completed in Gothic Revival style, he was the only child of John Manners, the 7th Duke of Rutland, and his first wife, Catherine, the granddaughter of the 2nd Earl of Lanesborough.

The newspaper reports published around the time of his birth pointed to the family's reach and power. At that time, his grandfather, John Henry Manners, had been Duke. Within his domain, he inspired awe. As a matter of course, whenever he entered the villages on his estate, peals of bells sounded and his flag would be hoisted on top of the parish church.

Further afield, in the Midlands cities where

the Duke had political and commercial
interests, the adulation was on a grander
scale. At Leicester, a few weeks after Henry
was born, a crowd of fifty thousand turned
out to see the unveiling of a statue of his
grandfather. The Duke himself was the guest
of honour. He had arrived in a gold carriage,
emblazoned with his coat of arms, and accompanied by retinues of servants and his
own personal band; trumpeters had walked
ahead of the carriage to announce his presence. Later that evening, a magnificent
firework display was staged, the details of
which the local newspaper rapturously reported in advance:

A beautiful set piece, formed by thousands
of diamond lights, will represent the Duke of
Rutland's coronet, supported by a motto of
'God Save the Queen' in beautiful-coloured
fires, surrounded by double rainbow-wheels,
and mounted with a great variety of beautiful colours. Another beautiful set piece will
represent his Grace the Duke of Rutland's
crest, formed by thousands of beautiful-
coloured lights, supported by the motto
'Three Cheers for the Duke' in beautiful
diamond lights, the whole surrounded by
Chinese flyers, with coloured centres fronted
with emerald fires. Several splendid bal-
loons will ascend during the evening, and
the illumination of the ground will be superb

in the extreme. Special trains will run from Derby, Nottingham and Peterborough, taking up passengers at most of the intermediate stations. A medal will be struck for the occasion, the children of the schools will be regaled with tea etc, and the day will be a general holiday.

Such veneration was Henry's birthright. From the very beginning, wealth and prestige on a scale that seems scarcely credible awaited him.

Fifty-four years later, when he succeeded his father to become the 8th Duke, he was a man of few achievements. Briefly, in the 1880s, he had been private secretary to Lord Salisbury, the Tory Prime Minister — a job secured by family connection. Derided by his contemporaries for his old-fashioned courtly ways and his lack of intelligence, he was known as 'Salisbury's Manners'.

In 1895, after serving as MP for North Leicestershire, a seat his family had held since the beginning of the century, Henry retired from public life.

The 8th Duke was six feet two inches tall, with a firm set to his jaw and a powerful physique; pheasants, dry-fly fishing and actresses were his principal interests. Famously, he and King Edward VII fought to seduce Maxine Elliot, America's most celebrated actress, who had made her debut on the London stage in 1905. Henry's charms proved the more alluring and he and Maxine began a long affair. Simultaneously, he was seeing Violet Vanbrugh, another actress, by whom he had a child.

Elegant, affable, a legendary philanderer: this was the public face of Henry Rutland. But, at home, as the memoirs of Lady Diana Cooper, his daughter, reveal, his family saw a very different character.

The picture she paints of him is of a brutish, unsophisticated man with a 'ferocious temper' who hated 'abroad' and 'soap in his bath', and who terrorized his children with the prospect of nemesis. 'Ruin stared us in the face — everything sold, beggars in the street,' she recalls.

Day and night, Henry's financial worries gnawed at him, sparking the flashes of 'ferocious temper' so feared by his staff and family. His moodiness seeped into the atmosphere at Belvoir Castle. On a low day, he was approached with trepidation; whenever Diana and her siblings wanted to talk to him, they would first ask his butler if it was a propitious moment to disturb 'His Grace'.

The enormity of his financial difficulties had apparently induced a sort of paralysis. Though he 'worried and fretted' and forced himself to do a 'good two hours of tiresome work every morning', he was ineffectual and prone to distraction. When in London, as Diana describes, he worked in the library of the family's fifty-room townhouse behind the Ritz in Piccadilly. 'Seated at a large writing table, surrounded by bound copies of the *Burlington Magazine,* the current works of Conan Doyle and Kipling, *Burke's Peerage* and Turf Guides, he wrote letters to Drummond's Bank, the Leicestershire Agricultural Club, the Sun Insurance Co, occasional articles on dry-fly fishing for the *Badminton Magazine* and a blue-moon letter to *The Times*' On the stroke of twelve, this 'tiresome routine' would end, to be followed by one more agreeable: he laced on his boots at midday and walked down Bond Street, taking off his top hat to bow to acquaintances at every other step.'

Diana went on to become one of the most celebrated society figures of the twentieth century. Her memoirs run to 753 pages; yet her father's death, in the spring of 1925, merits one short paragraph. 'Sadness fell from the air one bright day in May,' she recalls:

The Gower Street telephone rang to tell me, and my mother with me, that my father, slightly ailing and in bed, had been seized with a heart attack. We got home as quick as could be, but it was too late. The good old man (he was over seventy) was dead. He had been a loving and wise father. What hot tempers he had started with had long since abated into serenity.

As I read these few words, and the cold, sparse entries that preceded them, it seemed there was much that Diana had left out.

The castle was wreathed in late-summer sunshine, the rays slanting through the iron bars that secured the windows. I was back in the Muniment Rooms.

I levered the book down from the shelf. Bound in burgundy leather, the year '1899' was embossed on the spine. It weighed twelve or thirteen pounds. Stacked along the shelves beside it, there were seventy others like it.

These were the castle's ledger books. Henry's preoccupation with money had dominated Diana's characterization of him; money, so John's decrypted letters had indicated, was the most likely cause of the row with his father. I was interested to see whether the family's financial records for the period would shed light on it.

The year 1899 was an important one. When Henry's accountants had presented him with the ledger, it had marked a rite of passage. His father was in failing health; this was the year he had taken over the running of the family's financial affairs. The pages of this weighty volume had shown him how he had fared in managing his father's estate for the first time.

The ledger was in pristine condition. The leather binding, and the expensive cream paper, a millimetre thick, exuded the smell of newness — just as they must have when Henry had first looked at it. The pages listed the annual income and expenditure in each of the castle's various departments: 'Farms in Hand'; 'Game and Fisheries'; 'The Household'; 'Forestry'; 'Minerals'. Each receipt, and every item of expenditure, had been entered. The figures were fascinating, conjuring up the way life had been lived in this remote rural community in the last year of the nineteenth century. On the home farm that winter, £1 was spent on turnip seed; £8 18sh 1d was paid to Nottingham City Corporation for night soil — human waste — to spread on the fields; W Sopps had charged £4 2sh for mole-catching at Woolsthorpe; and William Wright, one of the Duke's farm labourers, received £3 3sh for castrating the lambs and other newborn livestock. The figures, written in a neat, confident hand, ran to 420 pages.

At the centre of the ledger, where the stiff pages opened flush with the spine, there was a profit and loss summary. Presumably, it was to these pages that Henry had turned first.

Income was summarized in the left-hand column: expenditure, on the right. The results for his first year in charge showed a deficit in the region of £41,559.*

The ledgers for the decade that followed told a similar story. Year after year, Henry's losses had mounted. So had the interest on the huge sums he was borrowing. No wonder he had terrorized his children with the threat of bankruptcy.

Looking at the ledger books prior to 1899, it was painfully evident that the family's financial difficulties went back several decades.

Henry had taken over from his father at a time when the farming industry was caught in the grip of the longest depression that anyone could remember. From the mid-1870s, cheap food imports from abroad, made possible by the new refrigerated ships, had caused food prices to collapse and land values and agricultural rents to fall. At Belvoir, the consequences were catastrophic. Steadily, as the depression bit deeper, the large profits the family had grown accustomed to expect from their 65,000 acres evaporated until, by the early 1880s, the estate was operating at a loss. In 1897, the position was made the more precarious by

* £3.6 million at today's values.

the need to write off another £31,000 in rental arrears from farm tenants hit by the depression.*

Henry's father's solution had been to borrow huge sums of money. By 1899, his estates were heavily mortgaged: £234,000 was owed to various creditors, the interest payments alone coming to £10,474 a year.† Ten years later, Henry had only succeeded in adding to the debts — in 1909, they stood at £289,000.‡

Henry's problems were intractable; but the ledgers for this period do more than illuminate the cause of his anxiety. They offer a telling insight into his character. Leafing through them, it is clear that he was the sort of man whose private troubles made his public face all the more important to him. Faced with the collapse in land and rent values, many of his contemporaries, including the Dukes of Bedford, Devonshire and Westminster, were cutting their losses and starting to sell off their subsidiary estates. Pride prevented Henry from taking such a prudent step; instead, he kept on spending. Regardless of the reality of his financial position, he was determined to keep up appearances. Despite the staggering levels of debt

* £2.7 million at today's values.
† £20.5 million and £920,000 at today's values.
‡ £22 million.

attached to his father's estates, in the early 1900s, he made little attempt to balance the books, or rein in his expenditure. Evidently, all that mattered to Henry was that his father should be seen to be maintaining the lavish *tenue* expected of a Duke.

To sustain this pretence, between 1899 and 1907 he sanctioned an outlay of £12,887 per annum.* The ledgers disclose that he found the money by juggling the overdraft limits on his father's various bank accounts; a glance at the payments summaries for any one of these years tells us exactly what he spent it on:

HOUSEHOLD ACCOUNTS FOR THE YEAR ENDING 1899
(The figures in parentheses represent modern values)

Castle Expenses [repairs, furniture and refurbishments]	£2,223 (£195,000)
Consumption and Caterers [meals consumed by the family, guests and servants]	£3,318 (£291,000)

---

* £2 million at today's values.

Servants' Wages	£2,005 (£902,000)*
Stables	£595 (£52,000)
Straw	£59 (£5,200)
Granary [bread and Belvoir buns made at the castle]	£215 (£18,900)
Grooms' Wages	£552 (£248,000)†
Servants' Liveries	£389 (£34,200)
Game and Fisheries	£1,489 (£131,000)
Gardens	£960 (£84,300)
Pleasure Grounds	£348 (£30,600)
Bounties and subscriptions [servants' pensions and donations to charities]	£107 (£9,400)
Coals	£602 (£52,900)

* Calculated using average earnings as opposed to RPI.
† Calculated using average earnings as opposed to RPI.

| The Duke's chaplain's salary | £25 (£11,200)* |
| Total | £12,887 (£2,065,700) |

These were the figures; Diana's recollections of her father's regimen at Belvoir offer a glimpse into the lifestyle they purchased.

There was never an hour when a servant of one sort or another was not labouring away in some far corner of the castle. Heated only by coal, in 1899, it had no electric light. Above the ground floor there was no water, hot or cold, and no baths or lavatories.

As she looked back nearly sixty years later, the armies of servants who traipsed its corridors and on whom the family depended for their basic amenities loomed in Diana's memory: 'The watermen are difficult to believe in today,' she wrote: 'They seemed to me to belong to another clay. They were the biggest people I had ever seen, much bigger than any of the men of the family, who were remarkable for their height. They had stubbly beards and a general Bill Sikes appearance. They wore brown clothes, no collars and thick green baize aprons from chin to knee. On their shoulders they carried a wooden yoke from which hung two gigantic cans of

* Calculated using average earnings as opposed to RPI.

water. They moved on a perpetual round. Their job was to keep all jugs, cans and kettles full in the bedrooms, and morning or evening to bring the hot water for the hip-baths.'

Joining the watermen on their round were the castle's lamp men. Paraffin lamps, candles, and the glow from the many coal fires were the sole sources of light after dark. 'There was no other form of lighting. Gas was despised, I forget why — vulgar, I think,' Diana recalls. As dusk fell, it was the lamp men's job to light each of the castle's 356 rooms. Working their way through them, they placed the lamps they had cleaned, and fine candelabra, on tables and sills, and lit the wall sconces along the corridors. Later, when the Duke and his guests had retired from the state rooms, they busied themselves turning wicks down, snuffing candles and de-waxing extinguishers.

Throughout the night, watchmen patrolled the passages, terraces and battlements. 'They were ghostly figures one never quite saw,' Diana remembers: 'They frightened many a newcomer to death. There was a little of the watermen about them, but they were dreadfully silent and they padded. Always if one woke in the night, as the fire flickered to its death, one would hear a padded foot on the gravel outside and a voice, not loud enough to waken but strong enough to reassure, saying "Past twelve o'clock. All's well." '

Then there was Betsy, the still-room help, who was well into her nineties when Diana first met her: 'She was born in the castle, no one quite knew how, and for seventy-five years she washed and dried the plates for the lesser meals. She was felt to be one of the castle's treasures, together with the Benvenuto Cellini ewer and basin. The visitors were always shown her. She had never learned to read or write — no disgrace, I think, to the family, as what child of her class did learn to read before Waterloo? But maybe she was the happier for her ignorance, for she was always laughing, lived to over a hundred and had a grand funeral.'

Diana's favourite was the Duke's tailor, who worked in the upholsterer's room at the foot of the East Tower: 'He was exactly like a Hans Andersen tailor. Cross-legged he sat in a tremendous confusion of curtains and covers, fringes, buttons, rags and carpets, bolsters, scraps, huge curved needles like scimitars, bodkins, hunks of beeswax to strengthen thread and hundreds of flags. The flags on the tower-top, I suppose, got punished by the winds and were constantly in need of repair. I never saw him actually at work on anything else. There were slim flags for wind, little ones for rain, huge ones for sunshine, hunting flags, and many others.'

■ ■ ■ ■

And there were countless others on Henry's £900,000 wage roll.

In 1899, the castle had a groom of chambers, a house steward, an usher of the hall, a chef, a pastry chef, a confectioner, a plate butler, a clockman, a steward's room boy — and housemaids, kitchen maids, scullery maids, footmen, odd-job men, and porters galore. These were just the indoor servants. In the castle's grounds, there were hundreds more: grooms, stable lads, dairy maids, studmen, brewers, rat catchers, mole catchers, millers, mechanics, gardeners, groundsmen, gamekeepers, river keepers, huntsmen, kennelmen, slaughtermen, stockmen, horsemen, farm hands and woodsmen.

This vast establishment, paid for largely with borrowed money, revolved around just one person: Henry's father, the elderly John Manners, 7th Duke of Rutland.

As the century turned, the Duke entered his eighty-third year. His bent frame and his shock of shining white hair marked him out as he went about his castle. 'I can see him very clearly walking down the endless corridors of Belvoir, wrapped warmly in a thick black cape buttoned down the front, for these passages in winter were arctic — no stoves, no hot pipes, no heating at all,' Diana remembered: 'He would unbutton his cape at the drawing-room door and hang it on a long brass bar with many others. He joined his large family at lunch, but I do not remember his talking very often.'

After serving in three Tory cabinets as Postmaster General and Chancellor to the Duchy of Lancaster, the Duke had retreated to Belvoir. His life there was sybaritic and self-regarding; from Diana's description of his daily routine, the *tenue* Henry was keeping for his father served no other purpose beyond being — *and being seen to be* — a Duke.

Every day, after lunch, the old Duke liked to tour his estate. 'Tingaly the bingaly, Farver,' one of his daughters would say at the end of the meal — the 'bingaly' being the small gold bell that stood on the table beside him. 'The groom of chambers, thus summoned,' Diana recalled, 'would ask what orders for the stables. Some days, the answer was "Perfection round at a quarter before three, if you please." '

Perfection — 'snow-white and very fat and quiet' — was the Duke's horse. Watched by Diana and his other grandchildren — a footman in attendance to hold the horse's bridle — the Duke would clamber on to the horse from the mounting stone at the entrance to the castle. As he set off, he was always accompanied: 'Either one of his sons or Mr

Knox, his private chaplain, would ride beside him, while a smart old groom, liveried in blue and buttoned in silver, top-hatted and cockaded, jogged behind.'

On the days he chose not to ride, the Duke would tour his estate by carriage. 'A lengthy discussion,' Diana recalled, 'would be carried on between him, some aunts and the groom of the chambers as to whether it was to be the landau, the Victoria or the barouche that should be used for the drive. I never understood what the issue was — the size of the vehicle, the state of the roads or the condition of the horses. Anyhow, the decision was made and the children were dressed for the drive. I remember genuinely hating it, I don't know why. Perhaps it was because I, for one, always felt sick and dreaded the smell of the blue leather padding and the hot horses, and sitting backward, sometimes on the vast landau seat, sometimes on the minute stool of the Victoria. We would drive for an hour and a half through country roads of very little interest. There was no town within eight miles and scarcely any neighbours to leave cards upon. So round and round the muddy lanes of the estate we splashed, with an immense apoplectic coachman on the box and an alert footman in a fawn boxcloth liveried coat, check-lined and almost to the ground, who sprang up and down to open the too many gates.'

Often, as the Duke's carriage wound its way back up the single-track road that ran through the woods to the castle, large crowds of tourists were gathered on either side. 'My grandfather would uncover his head and bow very slightly with a look of pleasure and welcome on his delicate old face. He loved his tourists. They represented to him England and liberty and the feudal system, and were a link between the nobility and the people.'

On Sundays, the Duke's post-lunch routine altered. Instead of Perfection — or the landau or the barouche — a pony chaise was ordered for the purposes of touring the castle's grounds. In all weathers, the Duke expected his family, his guests, his gentlemen secretaries and his chaplain to follow on foot. As Diana recalls, this ritual was as tedious as the carriage drive, involving as it did a 'trudge of a good three miles'.

The stables, located at the bottom of the long drive up to the castle, were the first port of call: 'Mr Durrance, the head groom, would be standing there in blue and silver, carrots in hand, to receive us. The gigantic Princes, Belvoirs and Wellingtons that drew the carriages, lined up hind-end foremost, were given a pat on the withers by my grandfather's withered hand, and a carrot was proffered to each twitching muzzle.' A quick inspection of the harness room followed, where armies of grooms had polished the deep mahogany leather saddles, and the solid-silver peacock crests on bit-rings and blinkers, until they gleamed.

After the stables came the kitchen garden, a walk of several hundred yards along the Park road. Its high walls, encompassing fifty acres, were topped at intervals by yet more peacocks — these ones carved in stone. At the wrought-iron gates leading into the garden, Mr Divers, the head gardener, a sombre figure clad in a black cutaway coat and a Homburg hat, waited to show the party around. 'He would cut us off a fine bunch of white grapes from the thousand hanging clusters in the vinery, pick us a camellia apiece and offer us apples to munch on the walk. My grandfather would congratulate him on his last-won horticultural medal and pretend to understand the Latin names of his flowers.'

The inspection continued at the poultry yard, followed by a tramp across the fields to the dairy to see the prize-winning Stilton cheeses and the creamy yellow butter pats, churned by Miss Saddlebridge, the Duke's dairy maid. These too were stamped with peacocks.

Last came the kennels, which housed the famous Belvoir foxhounds and 'smelt of dead horse'. Only then, after 'a good two to three hours', would the Duke allow his followers to process back up the hill, through the beech woods, to the castle.

Somewhere among them was John. The Sunday inspection was obligatory; on his visits home, he would have been there too.

Vividly, Diana describes its route and its rituals. But what were the dynamics within the family group?

*'Asshole. C***.'*

The ferocity of the language John used to describe his father suggested a murkier reality beneath the glittering surface. Over the course of the 'good two to three hours', who had walked with whom? Where were John and his father in the straggling line of followers? Had they positioned themselves as far away from each other as possible?

Diana's memoirs delineated the *tenue* her father insisted on maintaining; they hinted at a cantankerous side to his character. But they did not account for the hatred John had concealed within the pages of encryption.

Money — or the lack of it — appeared to lie behind the row between them. But what had sparked it? And why had Henry wanted to frighten his son?

Somewhat desperately, I asked the archivist at Belvoir whether there was any other material for the period. He steered me towards two boxes of correspondence.

The documents inside offered a dark answer

to the mystery.

The key to it was an auctioneer's report, submitted by Messrs Cox of St James and addressed to His Grace the Duke of Rutland in the autumn of 1907. Henry had regarded the contents of the report as absolutely secret; for almost two years he kept it in a locked drawer in his writing desk.

But on 5 January 1909 matters came to a head when, over breakfast at the castle, Henry told Violet that he needed to find £76,000 (the equivalent of £6 million at today's values) — *immediately*.

28

Later that day, Henry caught the train to London. At some point during the course of the eighty-minute journey, he composed a note to Violet, which he handed to a delivery boy on his arrival at King's Cross. Mindful of his bad temper at breakfast, and the humiliation of the situation, his tone was apologetic:

On Train

Darling, I know it must have annoyed you awfully, but I cannot avoid selling to clear as far as possible all liabilities from off the properties. Should this new deal come off it will practically effect this.

Always yr beloved

PS 'Lumby' [lumbago] made me dull and unappreciative this morning.

The threat of bankruptcy, rather than backache, was the true cause of Henry's ill temper. His financial position had now reached a crisis. It was almost three years since his father had died and the £40,000 he owed the government in death duties was still outstanding; so were the 'children's portions' — the £36,000 he owed his brothers and sisters under the terms of his father's will.

Other liabilities loomed. At White's, his club in St James's Street, and at the House of Lords, rumours of punitive tax increases in the forthcoming budget were circulating. David Lloyd George, the Chancellor of the Exchequer, was in the process of preparing his 'People's Budget'. Its aim, he announced, was 'to wage implacable warfare against poverty and squalidness'. To raise the money for the sweeping welfare reforms he proposed, the chancellor was also waging war against the rich. He planned to increase income tax *and* inheritance tax: further, in the most significant redistribution of wealth hitherto seen, he intended to introduce a 'super tax' on incomes over £5,000.

All of these measures threatened to reduce Henry's income and increase his costs. 'The estate cannot bear any further burdens,' he wrote to John: 'Something <u>must</u> be done.'

His remark was specious. What he was actually doing was concealing the truth from his son. As Henry had confided to Violet that morning, he knew exactly what was to *be done.* To settle the amounts outstanding, he was proposing to sell £76,000 worth of family heirlooms.

While land remained sacred to Henry, paintings and 'joux-joux' — his pet name for the jewels and precious *objets* he presented to his mistresses — were dispensable. Unsurprisingly for a man whose interests were confined to the maps that marked out the boundaries of his estates and anything he could hunt, shoot or fish within them, he had no interest in the treasures his predecessors had amassed over the centuries. The contents of his many properties — the precious collections of Old Masters, furniture, rare books and manuscripts — bored him. They were simply 'old things'.

At Belvoir, when possible, he would get his daughters to show his guests around the castle. 'My father was frankly philistine,' Diana recalled: 'The unfortunate guests, after the Sunday walk and a tremendous tea, were handed over to Letty* and me to be instructed about our family history and heirlooms and any legend we had picked up. If we were not to be found and he was forced to show them himself he would, with a gesture, wave a whole wall away — a wall studded with the finest Nicholas Hilliard miniatures — with a "Don't worry about those: they're all fakes."'

It was imperative that Henry kept his plan

* Diana's sister.

to sell the family heirlooms secret. They were not *his* to sell. They belonged equally to John. Under the terms of a complex legal agreement, drawn up by the 6th Duke in the mid-1850s, they had been formally annexed to the family's estates. The word 'heirlooms', as defined in the agreement, had a far wider significance than in popular usage: from the gilt tableware in the butler's pantry to the elaborate Gobelin tapestries that adorned the walls of the Regent's Gallery, the term included any item of value. The agreement made Henry's position quite clear: the heirlooms were 'settled', meaning they were held in trust for the next heir. He could not sell them without John's permission.

Regardless, Henry had not allowed this detail to stand in his way. As Cox's report tells us, his plan to sell a number of valuable heirlooms had been in place for some time.

Secretly, in the autumn of 1907, Henry had selected the items himself. Realizing that, in a worst-case scenario, the castle's treasures offered a means to raise the £76,000 he needed without having to sell land, one afternoon, he had taken a stroll through the state rooms and upstairs corridors at Belvoir. With only a cursory glance at the paintings he passed, and after rummaging through the fine porcelain and decorative silver displayed on the many occasional tables, he had picked out some fifty 'old things' for the saleroom.

His selections were made without thought or care. He simply chose the paintings and 'joux-joux' he liked the least.

Then, choosing a day when John was in London, Henry invited Messrs Cox up to Belvoir to value them. As he showed them around the castle, pointing out the things that he had earmarked, he instructed them to put together a list of items which, if sold, would yield somewhere in the region of £76,000. Their report, submitted a few days later, reveals twenty-five of the treasures that he had selected at random:

VALUATION OF SELECTED HEIRLOOMS
Pictures

£1,000 T. Gainsborough, R.A.	Portrait of Charles, 4th Duke of Rutland 49in × 39in.
£4,000 Murillo.	The Virgin and Child with St Rosalie 74in. × 57in. The Adoration of the Magi. 74in. × 56in.
£3,000 Rembrandt.	Portrait of a Young Man, in black cap 31in. × 26in.
£500 A. Dürer.	Portrait of a Man, in fur cape on panel 32 1/2in. × 26 1/2in.

£1,000 T. Gainsborough.	The Woodcutter's Home
	57 1/2in. × 47 1/2in.
	A Woody landscape, with a Youth, Girl and Cattle
£3,000 Rubens.	The Crowning of St Guthrie
	40in. × 83in.
£300 Rubens.	The Holy Family — on panel
	21in. × 19in.
£200 Rubens.	Hercules and Antaeus — on panel
	25in. × 19 1/2in.
£100 Robert Walker.	Portrait of the Artist
	29in × 24in.
£500 D. Teniers.	The Quick Doctor — on panel
	9in. × 7in.
£300 D. Teniers.	The Ox Stall
	18in. × 23in.
£400 P. Wouvermans.	Horseman outside a Farrier's forge
	14in. × 16in.
£150 D. Teniers.	A group of Storks among rushes
	14 1/2in. × 21in.
£2,000 A. Cuyp.	A River Scene, with figures and cattle
	14 1/2in. × 19in.
£1,000 D. Teniers.	Dutch Proverbs

	51in. × 81in.
£100 Rubens.	A Shepherd embracing a woman.
	57in. × 50 1/2in.
£500 Wynants.	A Landscape, with a hare hunt.
	39 1/2in. × 33in.
£40,000	A suite of 8 panels of old Gobelins Tapestry, with subjects from Don Quixote; in flower festoon borders, on pink ground.
£10,000	An Elizabethan Rosewater Ewer and Dish, of chased Silver-Gilt and Agate.
	Ewer 15 1/4in high.
	Dish 18 3/4in diam.

£77,050

I VALUE the foregoing Pictures, Tapestry and Silver-gilt plate, for the purposes of Sale, at the several prices fixed against each, making a total sum of Seventy seven thousand and fifty pounds.

Tom Cox

A few weeks before John left for Rome, when Henry could no longer put off paying the £76,000 he owed, he was confronted with the problem of how to realize these valuable assets. Quietly, on the side, and without telling John, he had already sold a few 'heirlooms'. But even Henry, 'philistine' as he was, realized that the sale of works of art of such calibre would leave glaring gaps on the walls of the state rooms at Belvoir. He had to get John to agree to his plan.

On 5 January, after confiding in Violet, he had caught the train to London to see his lawyers. In the course of their meeting, he instructed them to alter the 6th Duke's settlement agreement. Its original purpose was to ensure that the castle, its contents and the land that surrounded it stayed within the main line of succession. Under the terms of the agreement, they could not be sold, bequeathed by will or otherwise alienated: by operation of the law of entail they *had* to pass from one Duke to the next. Henry was asking his lawyers to break the entail. If the heirlooms were to be separated from the family's 'settled' estates, they would no longer belong equally to John.

There were thousands more besides the twenty-five items on Cox's list. Over the years — by the very fact that the heirlooms were formally annexed to the settled estates — lawyers had meticulously listed them. The lists — one for each of the family's properties — ran to pages and pages and encompassed any item worth more than £100: down to the last Fabergé egg, the lawyers had been careful to see that nothing was missed out. The potential cash reserve offered by future sales, as Henry recognized, was huge. Rather than haggle with John over the sale of specific heirlooms, it was far simpler to have them made over to him.

Still, however, he was confronted with a problem. The 6th Duke's settlement agreement was a legal document; it had been specifically designed to protect the interests of the next in line. It could not be altered at whim. To *resettle* the heirlooms — i.e. to *'unsettle'* them — he needed John's agreement.

What is extraordinary is that Henry didn't even talk to him about it. Effectively — and very obviously — he was disinheriting John; he was proposing to take away a portion of his inheritance worth millions. Yet he did not explain why he was doing it; far less did he make any effort to persuade John to go along with it. Instead, he simply instructed his lawyers to courier the resettlement agreement to him for signature.

John received it two weeks before he left for Rome. There are no letters in the Muniment Rooms at Belvoir to tell us how he felt, or what his reaction was, on first reading the agreement. But a remarkable letter from Violet survives.

On 19 February — more than three weeks after John had arrived in Rome — Violet handed the letter to a footman at Belvoir. It was marked 'Urgent: Delivery by Hand'.

In the grey light of a cold winter's morning, a pony trap took the azure-coated footman to the railway station at Grantham. From there, he caught a train to London. Arriving at King's Cross, he hailed a hansom cab to 97 Cadogan Gardens in Chelsea.

Violet's letter was to her brother Charlie. The previous day, Henry had told her that John had appointed his own lawyers to contest the resettlement agreement.

Violet was reporting the conversation that had followed.

29

Belvoir Castle
19 February 1909

Charlie dear,
Henry let out his heart to me yesterday
and I was touched — and <u>fussed</u> — re
John and him.

He says it is unheard of that in annals
of father and son etc that there should
now be 2 lawyers. Therefore he thinks to
<u>start</u> with that it was most unfriendly to
make the 'business' like this — 'never has
happened in his family before'. He
thought he had always been an indulgent
and kind father — John certainly <u>never</u>
having done <u>anything</u> to please him —
(<u>quite</u> true).

John must not be allowed, Charlie dear,
to make any more breach. It is <u>most</u>
impolitic, I can see.

Henry at this moment says quite gently
and calmly and sadly that he can <u>never</u>

forget or forgive John's dreadful attitude to him.

I can't disguise from you, C. dear, that it hurts me also to the quick that John should have slowly, and behind my back, brought such pain and hurt to his Father — it is a big slap in his face — from an unexpected quarter.

If only I had been told at the beginning. Why can John never have confided in me — he might have known I should have seen to his interests. He might have known that H. would also (considering him to be his _only son_). I can't bear it — I think John is being ungrateful. Oh, it's a cruel mess. It may mean a real break.

To me it's all an earthquake — to a _sweet_ home — when we are all such a happy family! I think we have _all_ been wrong to let John think we despise Henry for his tempers etc. Anyhow, Henry is tender-hearted enough never never never to have behaved to _his_ father like that. I think John has been _terribly_ badly advised and I think the sooner he undoes the 'fighting feel' of it the wisest.

Loving VR

Of course, I shall write to John. My _gentle_ views.

I must admit Henry was quite gentle and _not_ in a temper or violent but _just_ I thought in all he said.

There can be few 'happy' families in which a child encrypted his letters to his uncle to describe one of his parents as a 'c★★★'. Violet was being disingenuous. She was writing to the man who had looked after her son since he was a boy; until a few weeks before, when John had left for Rome, Charlie was still looking after him. During his childhood, she and Henry had barely seen him: they had sent him away. Yet here she was supporting her husband's belief that 'he had always been an indulgent and kind father'. Behind the dissembling, what her letter actually amounted to was a naked appeal to Charlie to bring John into line.

Looking at other letters from the period, the attempt to browbeat John was part of a greater pattern. It wasn't the absence of a loving relationship with him that mattered to Violet and Henry: their overriding concern was to bludgeon him into becoming the son they wanted him to become. They had not moved on from the death of their beloved Haddon. John could never replace him: he had failed to come up to their expectations.

On 25 January, two days before John left for Rome — and before he contested the agreement — Henry wrote to him:

'Dear Boy,' it began:

I don't want to preach, but this is just the

beginning of whatever you choose to make of your life. You'll be well advised if you throw yourself thoroughly into the job, and pick up and absorb all the information of all sorts of which you can get hold. Make yourself quietly popular if you can!

Go about and see and talk to people and things — all comes in useful later in life: and remember always that you've got to fit yourself for a troublesome heritage here when I slip my cable.

Don't shut yourself up with books entirely: that is an unhealthy process for anyone, and leads to no practical end. In fact, in Kipling's words, 'buy an "am an" and see life'.

If you keep your head screwed on right in so doing, then your experience thus gained is most valuable in enabling you to gauge human beings and their ways.

Seeing this letter, and others like it, it was obvious that Violet and Henry thought John odd. His scholarly interests were alien to them; his rejection of the values and lifestyle of their world infuriated them. Socially, as one of the most eligible bachelors in England, he was in constant demand; yet he refused to attend the customary round of balls and Saturday to Monday house parties hosted by their friends. Why he should prefer to shut

306

himself away in museums and libraries, or to spend weeks on an archaeological dig in some obscure part of the country, was a mystery to them. Among their friends and acquaintances, they put it down to shyness. Privately, they thought him peculiar.

Time after time, Charlie had tried to persuade them that there was nothing wrong with their son. This explained his letter to Violet of 1 April 1909, which I had discovered among the bundles of letters John was working on when he died. 'Society and parties are things for which he does not care a twopenny damn,' he wrote: 'It is not self-consciousness which makes him prefer to pore over old manuscripts, to grub about amongst ruins, to go and see old sights, rather than enjoy society — they are his formed tastes, part of his character. Rare and wonderful tastes to have — for his friends to understand and congratulate him upon. It's no use not <u>understanding</u> or trying not to see, the real motive in his actions. You cannot, and never will get him to take active pleasure in things which don't interest him. It is, quite possibly, a matter for argument, whether the time may not soon arrive when it would be wisest to urge him towards things he has a turn for and will do well, rather than push him towards things which you preconceive to be better.'

Charlie's pleas fell on stony ground. Violet

and Henry persisted in their efforts to stifle John's academic interests. After leaving Cambridge in 1908, John told them he wanted to become a dealer in rare manuscripts and medieval ceramics. Henry refused even to contemplate this ambition. 'If you are entirely without a profession it becomes a condition of things most eminently condemnable,' he told him: 'In these days, to be a loafer is more to be despised than even formerly (when he was more or less acknowledged). Now such a position is impossible.'

The label 'loafer' could better apply to Henry than to John. By the age of twenty-two, John had become a leading expert in medieval ceramics; others in the field consulted him. He had worked hard at it, teaching himself both the history and the languages of the period. He could read Early French and Middle English; he was also proficient in Greek, Latin and Coptic. Yet these achievements meant nothing to Henry; instead, in a series of threatening letters, he pressed John to look for an alternative career. 'In your case it must be obvious that I could never even consider handing over to you during my life any portion of my property unless you had qualified for such a proceeding by putting in 8 or 10 years' steady work at some profession where you are under discipline and compelled to work so many months in the year. Unless some part of the Estate is so given to you, when you succeed the death duties will smash you utterly. So, for every reason, as soon as you settle, or signify on what profession you wish to embark, I shall be delighted to assist you in any way I can.'

The word 'settle' was key. So hopelessly broken were the lines of communication between John and his parents that they were unable to articulate the true reason for their anger. The many rows over John's choice of career were a smokescreen: they concealed the one issue that obsessed both Violet and Henry. *Whom was he going to marry?* His long-term happiness did not enter into it: it was all about blood lines and *money.*

Their preoccupation with the subject, as their letters reveal, was entirely self-regarding. Theirs was the highest title the Crown could bestow: they stood at the pinnacle of society, above all other subjects in the realm. If John failed to produce an heir, the dukedom held in direct line since 1703 would pass out of their branch of the family. For their progeny it would mean a drastic demotion in rank. Both Violet and Henry could trace their aristocratic lineage back to the Middle Ages: in the absence of an heir to the dukedom, their direct line, blue for almost eight hundred years, threatened to turn an ordinary shade of red.

The future social prestige of the family was not all that was at stake. They were counting on John to resolve their financial problems by marrying a wealthy heiress.

That he *should* marry — and marry *well* — went without saying. Unthinkable, but lurking in both their minds, was the suspicion that he might not marry at all. 'Peculiarity' — the word Violet used to refer to any behaviour that deviated from her conventional view of the world — ran in the family. Both she and Henry had numerous relations who had failed to marry. Lady Kitty, Henry's half-sister, had brought disgrace on the family by becoming a Catholic and a nurse. Then, one Sunday afternoon in 1903, decked in all the jewellery she possessed, and leaving her parasol behind her, she had jumped from a bridge below the castle and drowned herself in the lake. Lord Cecil, Henry's half-brother, was homosexual. On Violet's side of the family, Charlie was thought to have male lovers too. Their anxiety regarding John's reclusive personality was driven by the fear that he had inherited his aunt's and uncles' 'peculiarities' and that, like them, he would prove disinclined to marry. Even if this was not the case, if he shunned society and immersed himself in books and 'old things', how would he ever capture the heart of a wealthy heiress?

Regardless of John's feelings on the subject, the search for a daughter-in-law consumed Violet.

In her hunt for an eligible candidate, she spurned the traditional ducal marriage market. For centuries, the dual obsessions of marriage and rank had united all ducal families. To avoid a dilution in rank, more often than not the sons of dukes married the daughters of other dukes. The result of this vast incestuous dance was that, in 1900, all thirty-three dukes were related. But, as Violet recognized, she was unlikely to find a suitable bride for John among the family's cousins.

The thirty-year depression in the farming industry threatened to bring an end to the intermarrying. Until its effects began to be felt, wealth had never previously been an issue in the marriage alliances between ducal houses. No Duke owned fewer than 75,000 acres: his daughters were guaranteed to bring in a handsome dowry. But as land and rental values had collapsed, so too had the value of dowries, knocking the daughters of land-rich but cash-poor dukes out of the market. Only those whose families were protected from the crisis by coal, or other commercial interests, could offer the traditional combination of rank and fortune which every Duchess sought for her son. Consequently, the competition for the handful of eligible candidates was intense.

Violet did not rate John's chances. She had known his rivals since they were children.

There was the dashing George Stafford, the Duke of Sutherland's boy. Also in the running was Hastings Tavistock, the heir to the Duke of Bedford. An intrepid explorer, he had recently returned from China, where he had been gathering zoological specimens for the British Museum. Then there was Sonny Titchfield, the eldest son of her great friend Winnie, Duchess of Portland. He stood to inherit the family's coal fortune. Against such stiff opposition, how could her reclusive son hope to compete? But, Violet calculated, if wealth were to take precedence over rank, there was an alternative and, potentially, extremely lucrative marriage market.

In the early 1890s, American girls had begun to descend on London in droves. The daughters of America's new billionaires — steel magnates, railroad owners, real-estate and stock speculators — they had come in search of the one thing their money couldn't buy at home: a title.

'Until then,' New York heiress Jennie Churchill, the mother of Winston, remarked, 'the American woman was looked upon as a strange abnormal creature with habits and manners something between a Red Indian and a Gaiety Girl.' Among Britain's cash-strapped aristocrats, dollars — millions of them — changed this perception.

In 1895, the Duke of Marlborough set the precedent by marrying Consuelo, the daughter of American railroad billionaire Willie Vanderbilt. Her dowry was a staggering $2.5 million dollars.* That year alone, nine American heiresses married members of the English aristocracy; by the end of the century, a quarter of the House of Lords had a transatlantic connection.

In this brisk, burgeoning marriage market, Violet had the advantage — a title was the only necessary credential.

In 1903, after seeing off the Duke of Manchester, Henry, the 8th Duke of Roxburghe, won the heart of May Goelet, the daughter of Mr Ogden Goelet, a New York real-estate broker. Her personal wealth was estimated to be in the region of $5 million.† Violet could see the equation was simple: the grander the title, the greater the chance to capture fortunes so huge they were almost unimaginable.

One other factor persuaded her to jettison the all-important criterion of an ancient lineage, and this was the collapse of the Duke of Marlborough's marriage to Consuelo.

Their recent separation was the talk of London. Consuelo, it was reported, had not wanted to marry the Duke; Alva, her socially ambitious mother — famous for her remark to her daughter, 'I do the thinking, you do as

* $67 million at today's values.
† $128 million at today's values.

you are told' — had apparently forced her into the marriage. As she stood at the altar, Consuelo, it was whispered, had wept behind her veil. The Duke had never loved her: almost from the start he had been hopelessly in love with raven-haired Gladys Deacon, the daughter of a murderer. Secretly, he had continued to see her throughout his marriage. Now Gladys was a regular visitor to Blenheim. Her carriage, paid for by the Vanderbilt millions, was a familiar sight on the long drive up to the palace.

It was the Duke's enviable temerity, rather than the loveless marriage, that had caused a sharp intake of breath in the gilded drawing rooms which Violet frequented. Consuelo's dowry was non-refundable: cynically, the Duke had used his illustrious title to pocket $2.5 million worth of Vanderbilt railway stock while carrying on his amorous activities as usual.

His behaviour was an object lesson to Violet. No matter if John was 'peculiar' and his marriage failed to last: come what may, if she could only find an American heiress and persuade him to marry her, the mere exchange of vows would secure the future of the Belvoir estate.

In the spring of 1908, as John entered his final term at Trinity College, Cambridge, Violet's search began in earnest.

After carefully scrutinizing the lists of American debutantes in London, and after making enquiries via her *new* friend, Mrs Whitelaw Reid, the wife of the US ambassador, she selected her target: Miss Margaretta Drexel, the daughter of Anthony J. Drexel II.

Margaretta Drexel was the wealthiest of all the American heiresses in London for the season. Her grandfather, worth a reputed $40 million, was the Philadelphia-born merchant banker, Anthony J. Drexel I. Beautiful, with a curvaceous figure and tresses of auburn-coloured hair, Margaretta was also the most celebrated: 'Those who supply the matrimonial gossip of Europe,' one newspaper reported, 'have already married her off to the son of the German Emperor, the son of the King of Greece, several Dukes, and a few French Counts.' Writing to her from America, her best friend remarked, 'I've stopped reading fiction, I just read about you.'

The Drexels had arrived in style, renting 22 Grosvenor Square in Mayfair, complete with Holbeins, Romneys and Chippendale furniture. They were to spend August grouse shooting at Dalgross Castle in Inverness-shire; they had also taken a house at Windsor for the Ascot Races, and at Cowes for the Regatta. There, moored in the harbour, Mr Drexel's 300-foot yacht waited, having sailed across the Atlantic manned by a 68-strong crew. The yacht was named after Margaretta.

No sooner had Violet selected her future daughter-in-law than a rumour circulated that Margaretta had received a proposal of marriage: 'Miss Dresel [sic] is going to be engaged to Reginald Fellowes! I go on hoping it is not true,' she wrote to a friend from Belvoir: 'I wish we had had a really good look at her — like having her here for a week to see if she is really the darling I think her. Jack Gilliat who has adored her — afar — says she is just a perfect darling, but not happy. Rather hating being dragged about to balls and parties to please her mother — and very lonely and sad. She is never allowed to leave her mother's side — that is the way the correct Americans treat their daughters when they first come out. I can't see a better daughter-in-law! I hunt about and it's the only one so far that has beauty and gentle sweetness and music.'

And, of course, *money*.

Some days later, Violet learned that 'Miss Dresel', whom she had yet to meet, wasn't in fact engaged to be married. Springing into action, she invited Mrs Whitelaw Reid to tea and asked her to engineer an invitation for John, and her daughters Letty and Diana, to stay with the Drexels for Ascot Week.

The invitation duly secured, John, however, turned it down. Refusing to be thwarted, Violet approached the long-suffering Charlie.

Disguising the fact that it was she who had wheedled the invitation in the first place, and pretending that her motive had nothing to do with the 'idea' that John should marry 'Miss Dresel', she begged her brother to persuade him to go:

Darling C — Your help! Listen — the 2 girls go to a house for Ascot the Dresels [sic] have taken for the week. John was asked to take them. I should <u>love</u> him to go!! Simply love him to — not because of the 'idea' I have talked to you lightly and laughingly about — because that <u>is</u> so far in the <u>future</u> to be thought of improbably — but because, as he will never be an idler and will never get <u>too</u> fond of society, I believe a <u>little</u> is just the very thing for him now.

If 'Foreign Embassies' are to be worked for he must be seeing a little more of people and society or else it will be too difficult and distasteful to him. Whatever in his character he gets from <u>me</u> would make him, if he had everything in his own hands, shun everyone and be a recluse! and <u>that</u> must be guarded against.

In this case I would like him to go — as a kind of protection to his sisters! I could give him this reason — a chaperone to them.

It is the week of 17th June — 18th —

and he can get away on the Friday <u>or not,</u> it would depend on how he felt. He might <u>like</u> it by then and want to go to a <u>cricket match,</u> or to Windsor, or something. If there is a ball at Windsor it is a nice thing for him to do. Oh, I <u>do</u> want it so. I want to do it the cleverest way I can and if <u>clothes</u> are wanted I will provide money with greatest ease.

He was asked by <u>word of mouth</u> by Mrs Dresel [sic] but he said NO on plea 'of not able to leave Cambridge', I believe. But she is <u>wanting</u> men so it's quite easy for me to arrange it, and the Dresel [sic] boy will be there and so all is made easy for John.

I wish his dress coat could be made better.

I go to Belvoir this afternoon late, girls go earlier. I return earlyish Monday. Do help me about John — but don't let him think it is anything to do with <u>the girl.</u> I mean that my real true object now is to get him not to shun people and to go to look. Everything about 'Races' is made so easy by motors and so the hours spent there are short and he could always leave a day sooner.

Loving VR

Charlie persuaded John to go, but whether Margaretta appealed to him — or he to her

— the letters at Belvoir do not relate. In any event, the following summer, she married Guy Finch-Hatton, the heir to the 13th Earl of Winchilsea.

The material dating from the period before John left for Rome was revealing. But I couldn't understand why John had put up with his parents' interference and their constant sniping. On every point of contention — even small things — he appears to have caved in. After first refusing the Drexels' invitation to Ascot, he had agreed to go; at his father's instigation, he had abandoned his ambition to become a dealer in ceramics, and settled instead for a career as a diplomat. John hadn't wanted to go to Rome: it was Henry, via his friendship with the ambassador, Sir Rennell Rodd, who had found him the job and forced him to accept it.

So why hadn't John stood up to his father? The rigid social mores of the time may have demanded a measure of acquiescence, but not complete subjugation. Particularly when, judging from the note he wrote to Charlie soon after arriving at the embassy, he hated himself for having given in.

30

The British Embassy
Rome
27 January 1909

Old Boy,
Here I am. Arrived at 7.30. My first
impression is just about as bad as can be,
but I hope it will improve. The whole of
Rome is covered in snow and bloody cold.

I had a very comfortable journey, empty
carriage the whole way.

The life here as far as I can judge at
present is the very worst for me (bloody
fool as I am) but I shall be able to form a
better opinion later.

Will write again when I am in a position to know if I am standing or sitting.

Jack

Things did not improve. Two days later, he
was seething with resentment. His 'job' was
superfluous; there was very little for him to
do. He was embarrassed that his father had

pulled strings to foist him on the staff at the embassy; equally, it was humiliating to feel that he was there under sufferance.

'My God, this place is a caution,' he told Charlie. 'At present this is my day':

I have to get up at 7. Breakfast at 8.30 alone with the Rodds who don't want me at breakfast, but have not the pluck to say so.

Then I am not supposed to go to the room of work till 10, so from 9 to 10 I sit in my bedroom. Then at 10 I go to the work room, where I say good morning to the three secretaries, then silence. They never talk or give me more than 1/2 hour's work all the morning. So I sit there for 2 1/2 hours doing nothing (dreadful). They leave the room at 1.15. Then comes lunch at 1.30 with the Rodds. I never know if they want me or not. Then, after lunch, I wait about outside the work room to see if the other men come in again. But they have never come in after lunch yet. When I think it is safe to leave, I go out to see something such as the Forum which I already simply hate the sight of.

Then home about 4 to 5, where I wait in my bedroom to see if the Rodds want me in to tea. If they don't I go without it. I wait up in my room till about 7.30, and if the Rodds dine in, I dine too. If they dine out, I go to the Grand Hotel where I dine alone.

I am trying to look at this in a funny light but at present my imagination will not go as far.

Goodbye, old boy

Yours truly, Jack

Not a word of this, old boy, to anyone.

By 'anyone', he meant his parents.

'It makes my heart ache, old boy, to think of you alone at the Grand Hotel,' Charlie replied. 'I can picture the whole scene, even to the seat and the liqueur table. I have read your letter many times. I think your present worries will, to a great extent, pass off quickly. I see them as no more than the extraordinary miserable experience of first joining the Army. I arrived at my Battalion in the south of Ireland, for all purposes as far as you are, into a nest full of people I did not know and cared for still less, all intent on their own affairs, leaving me absolutely stranded, high and dry, with nothing but discomfort, nervousness and home sickness to look forward to each morning. I think most fellows go through something of this kind, but it doesn't last, thank the Lord, and as a fact, recovery is extremely quick. You will be at your ease very soon, and able to arrange for yourself the best sort of life that the circumstances will permit. I rather wonder

Lady R hasn't tumbled to the unease of the meals. If she doesn't I should rather be inclined to ask her in confidence what she prefers. I can see the tiresomeness of it.'

'I quite understand what you say about recovering oneself after a time,' John replied, 'but I don't suppose your life consisted of paying and receiving calls, tea parties, luncheon parties and dinner parties from morning till late at night, which is what the job comes to.'

'Bloody fool as I am.' His anger at being there appeared to be eating away at him. The impression I had was of a petulant, unhappy and rather helpless man. He was twenty-two years old; his life was his own, and yet he seemed incapable of taking charge of it. Was he just pathetic? Or was something holding him back?

Three weeks into the job, he was still miserable: 'No new news. But most disagreeable at present,' he wrote to Charlie: 'I had to go to a ball on Saturday night, which was too dreadful for words — hundreds of people, none of which I knew. All yesterday I had to try and make myself pleasant to about a dozen dreadful old Italian women. All like the very worst kind of Billingsgate fishwives. I don't think I ever saw such nasty old hags as this Roman-English society is composed of. I think by the end of this week I shall be able to form a very good idea of what this existence will be like — I must confess that at present I put it down as just as bad as it could be. Love to Togs.'

John was writing to Charlie on 15 February. It was at the end of that week that the row over the resettlement agreement erupted.

Only on 18 February, a month after the document was couriered to John for signature, did Henry discover that he was contesting it.

In doing so, John was defying his father for the first time. 'I'm damned if I'm going to give in, so help me God,' he told Charlie before he caught the train to Rome.

'I will warn you of every move that occurs,' Charlie promised him.

The first 'move' came on 19 February when the Duke's footman appeared on the doorstep of Charlie's house in Chelsea. The footman had come all the way from Belvoir to deliver the letter that Violet had written that morning.

Clearly rattled, the minute he read it, Charlie fired off a letter to John.

31

97 Cadogan Gardens
Friday, Feb 19 1909

Jacko,
I have just received the most astonishing letter from your mother. I do not write this in cipher, as I have not time before the post goes, and I don't want to miss it. Besides, as you will see, it is no use keeping this letter so please destroy at once.

  Your mother says that your father 'opened his heart out' to her yesterday upon the subject of you — he apparently has taken it very much to heart that you should have done anything in the matter. He said it was an unheard of thing in the annals of Father and Son that there would ever be 2 lawyers and that it was therefore unfriendly of you to start with, considering that he had always been an indulgent and kind father to you, and so on and so on (evidently making your mother extremely sad).

Then comes a good deal about the pity of you not having confided in her, then that she intends to write to you 'when she has seen Dowling' [Henry's lawyer].

That is all, but it is a letter of the greatest excitement and full of injustice, etc. I really believe the matter in this way — that Dowling has invariably put the case to your father in the worst way — that your father, with some justice, imagined you were doing the whole thing underhand, and that your mother has been convinced by your father.

I believe that you would do well to put that matter right at once, and it seems to me there will not be much difficulty, as you have many strong points to bring forward, i.e. the gibberish of the document originally sent to you; the rudeness of Dowling in answering your questions; your waiting always for your father to speak to you at Belvoir. A good letter could easily be made out for you to write to him. I think this is imperative as he may really have been put up to all sorts of suspicion of you by Dowling.

You must not show that you have heard from me at all about it. I imagine your mother intends to write you a letter which will give you all the needful excuse for writing to your father, so don't do anything until you hear from her.

What a bombshell — your father believes I know nothing at all.

Yrs, Charlie
DESTROY

Clearly worried, at midnight, Charlie writes a second letter. Again he urges John to placate his father by writing him a 'friendly' letter: 'Remind him that you came and told him in his bedroom in London what you were doing and asked his permission to send particulars to the man, and he did not seem to object . . . I should like to know by wire, whether you mean to send the letter . . . Wire in cipher, of course.'

Three days later, John answers. He appears relaxed; contrary to his uncle's instructions, he had not bothered to encrypt his telegram:

Just received your letter. Yes, it is a bombshell but not really I think so bad as it looks. I have wired my man [Wilson, his lawyer] to be careful not to give information to anyone — in case she [Violet] might go there herself.

But then suddenly his position alters. Overnight, his lack of concern switches to alarm. Someone has evidently alerted him to the Duke's motive in seeking to alter the agreement. John knows that his father wants to sell the heirlooms to settle his debts. The records at Belvoir do not reveal the source of his information, but, straightaway, he encrypts a letter to Charlie. It is at this point that he tells him that the Duke is about 'to try and frighten him':

23 Feb 1909
British Embassy Rome

Old Boy — just a line to let you know what I think of the 24906 35427 11411 53702 66892 27490 47232 21131 54324 to 89231 79619 23604 83705 72630 79967 83244 69631 50011 is 54123 92141 77117 38519 72432 14041 60903 to the 14066/ 50215/ 12001/ 20039 77129/ 21115/ 61232/ 72603/ 19731. 83220 69699 65906 82915 70444 61291 23615 and so 50000 53741 47314 54330 83309 86154 and 53131 78042 40319 62731 [Old Boy — just a line to let you know what I think of the affair. The ★★★★ Duke of Rutland is now beginning to understand the position he is in with respect to the children's★ portions and so he is going to try and frighten me.]

Decrypted, the note remains as cryptic as

★ The £36,000 Henry owed his brothers and sisters under the terms of his father's will.

the code it is written in. Yet Charlie clearly understood his meaning. Panicking, he arranges to see Violet. 'I hope you understand and approve of my taking her into confidence,' he tells John:

I do it for reasons which I think are sound:-

1. That it is the only means I have of learning what goes on behind the scenes (I remaining, as always, absolutely incognito).
2. That she has an influence on your father which might just possibly be the means of solution.

On 25 February — a day when the Duke is at Belvoir — Violet and Charlie meet at the family's townhouse in Piccadilly. Aware of John's encrypted note, Charlie presses his sister for an insight into her husband's state of mind. As soon as the meeting is over, he reports back to John.

His letter does not tell us how the Duke is proposing to 'frighten' him, but he is anxious to impress upon his nephew exactly what his father thinks of him.

'It appears that this talk your father had with your mother was even more serious than I first reported,' he begins:

He has apparently got it into his head that you have treated him very badly. He was, it seems, very much cut up, in a state bordering on collapse and broken-hearted about it, talked about his son being the last person he wanted to defraud, saying he could never forget the way you had behaved and ending by saying he was absolutely determined not to give in any more etc. Of course the thing's all rot . . .

My advice is (or I am very strongly of the opinion) that you ought to correct this present mood by a friendly letter to your father, explaining that you never had any intention of behaving in an unfriendly or behind the back manner towards him. But I should leave the actual matter of the Agreement alone until later, or until some development occurs. I reason that you cannot possibly do any harm, or in any way give your case away by writing in this manner, whereas it might be the actual means of getting something out of him — you know the blitherer — he'll probably be delighted with your letter.

'No one of course knows that I am writing to you,' he continued:

To my mind the only thing to save the situation is for your mother to tell him he is all wrong. Your mother was fearfully against you when we began our talk, but I so put the matter that she altered her views and when I asked her point blank whether she would take the responsibility of advising you to sign the deal as it stood, she said certainly not.

She means to write to you today — so do nothing till you get it.

Therefore till my next

Yours Charlie
BURN

Violet had broken Henry's confidence by reporting their conversation to Charlie; he, in turn, had betrayed her trust by relaying it to John. Henry was claiming to be 'broken-hearted' when, purposely, he had set out to cheat his son. The deception and the double-dealing exposed the poisonous relationships within the family but, a hundred years later, they rendered it impossible to work out what was actually going on.

It was Charlie's advice to John that I found completely mystifying. The Duke was trying to divest John of a substantial part of his inheritance, yet three times in the course of a week he had urged him to write a 'friendly letter' to his father. And this despite the fact that John had told him that the Duke was going 'to try and frighten him'.

Why was Charlie being so conciliatory? In his coded letters to John, he had called his father 'a liar' and 'a cheat'.

And why the subterfuge?

Charlie was tiptoeing around the Duke: 'Burn'; 'Destroy'; 'No one knows I am writing.' The secrecy and the whispered conversations with Violet implied that John was guilty. But he wasn't. Before he left for Rome, he had *told* his father that he would be appointing his own lawyer to look at the resettlement agreement: the charge that he had 'gone behind his back' was completely trumped up. It was Henry who had gone behind *his* back; he hadn't discussed the agreement with him — the first John knew of it was when it was presented to him for signature. As for the agreement itself, the law was on John's side: to alter the legal status of the heirlooms, Henry needed his permission.

It was almost a month since John had left for Rome and he had not heard from either of his parents since 2 February; yet, there he was, a thousand miles away, reading the dreadful things they were saying about him. Charlie had long since replaced them in his affections; still, they were his parents.

At this stage in the proceedings, we can only imagine his feelings. Charlie is denying him a voice. His instructions are explicit: 'Do nothing until you hear from your mother.'

'Tiring, isn't it all?' he remarks acerbically in a note to Charlie. But what was he *really* thinking?

It is only on 28 February, when, at last, Violet's letter arrives at the embassy, that John's voice kicks in.

The letter came a few hours before he was due to catch the night train to Calabria. He was on his way to Reggio to coordinate British aid efforts following the devastating earthquake.

Before leaving for the station, he wrote to Charlie:

Old Boy,
I'm off in an hour — no time for cipher.

I have written the best letter to father that I could in the time, I am afraid it is not as good as I should have liked, but I am dreadfully pressed for time in getting things ready. On the other hand I think my letter will put things right for the time being.

Mother's letter was a lot of rotten 'hurt feelings' etc. My God, what rot the whole thing is — I still believe it is all got up to try and make me give in — but we shall see. I expect to be round about Calabria for a week and will write to you when I get back as I don't suppose I shall get a chance till then.

What a bombshell — and especially at this moment most unlucky.

I wish I was with you. Mother says I don't understand everything.

Goodnight, old boy

But a postscript, hastily scribbled on the back of the envelope, reveals that John did not send the letter he had written to his father. At the last minute, he had substituted one that Charlie had drafted for him:

PS. Your draft is much better than mine. So have sent yours. My dear old boy, I can't tell you how awfully grateful I am to you for helping me.

The letter was among the Duke's papers at Belvoir. Judging by John's handwriting, which lacked its usual neatness, he had evidently copied it out in a rush:

British Embassy
Rome
28 February 1909

My dear Father
I have just received a letter from Mother which has surprised me very much. I am very sorry indeed that you think that I have tried to be unfriendly and distrustful with you because I had no intention of doing anything underhand and I certainly did not think that what I was doing was

making you feel miserable all the time, or I think I should have come and talked to you about it at once.

Mother says you told her it was an unheard of thing going to another lawyer. As a matter of fact some man <u>had</u> been appointed by Dowling to represent me, for he sent me his name and address, just as if it was the usual thing, without my ever asking him to, and it was only because Dowling had been so rude and offhand when I wanted the epitome paper explained (not a word of which I could understand) that I thought of getting someone else who wasn't a Dowlingite. Perhaps you have forgotten that I came and told you at once, in your bedroom in London, what I was doing and asked your permission to send particulars to the man, and you did not seem to object at all.

I can see now that it would have been much better if I had come straight to you about it but it was very difficult to decide what to do. I had several messages from you through the lawyers, and I thought it was very likely you would rather not talk to me privately at all, especially as when we were at Belvoir together you were as friendly as possible. All that time I felt very uncomfortable not knowing what I had better do and expecting every moment that you would say something yourself. I did not tell Mother anything about it and the only time I asked Charlie he said I had better go straight to you, which I wish I had done.

I don't know whether I have explained myself properly but anyhow I hope you will see that I never meant to be un-friendly.

I wish I was in England and could have a talk with you alone — without anything to do with the lawyers. If you would like it, I will write and explain everything that I can remember about it.

Yours affectionately, John

Given that his father was trying to take away a significant proportion of his inheritance, the emollient tone was astonishing.

I imagined that John had torn up the letter that he had had second thoughts about sending. But he hadn't. It was in the file of papers that he had kept from his time in Rome. This one was written from the heart; still, the anger I expected to find was absent:

British Embassy, Rome

My dear Father
I have just received a letter from Mother which distresses me very much and the worst of it all is that it has arrived at a most inconvenient moment as I start for

the Reggio Relief Camp in an hour, and so am dreadfully pressed for time in getting things ready and so can't put on paper well what I want to.

I can't tell you my dear Father what rot this all is, and can't make out what you have got into your head, about trouble between Father and Son etc. This must be put right at once. I don't believe for one moment that you really feel hurt, as Mother says you are.

I originally went to the lawyer (which by the way I told you I was going to do) because of two reasons.

The first was because Dowling was so infernally rude to me and would not help me to understand that enormous amount of writing which was just the same as Hebrew to me — that I should never have believed or trusted him — and as you have always instilled into me the one principle of never putting one's name to anything one does not absolutely understand, I did not sign it.

As to the not mentioning it to you, that was a just a matter of not bringing a subject of this kind into the family home. And, as a matter of fact, as you did not mention it to me, I thought that you thought the same thing — that it was unnecessary.

I am afraid this letter is making no sense

but I hope it will just put the one item right, which is that it is absolute rot for you to feel hurt and distressed. This is not a question of feeling that one's son thinks that his father is going to have him.

I beg of you to put all this out of your mind at once.

I hope you will be able to read this and that it will convey my feelings to you of how sorry I am that you should have felt as no doubt you have over this matter. If you had only mentioned it before I left you would have had none of this hurt feeling — but I am sure this rotten letter will wipe it all out.

Your loving son

It was what he wasn't saying that was revealing. While his anxiety to placate his father was undoubtedly real, the sentiments he was expressing were completely at odds with his true feelings. He hated his father. In the letters and telegrams he had encrypted to Charlie he had called him a cunt. He had gone out of his way to sooth his 'hurt feelings'; but he hadn't believed in them. As he told Charlie, he thought they were 'got up' to make him give in. Charlie had agreed with him; yet, though equally contemptuous of the Duke, he had been as obsequious.

Given the true state of their feelings, the suspicion arising from both their letters was that they were conceding ground for a reason. It seemed they had an ulterior motive for wanting to keep relations on an even keel.

I could only think it was because the Duke had some sort of a hold over John, one that he and Charlie had not needed to spell out in their letters to each other, not even in cipher, because it was so obvious to them.

32

The missing piece in the puzzle was not a huge debt, or an embarrassing relationship, but an abandoned medieval manor house. Ghostly, falling slowly to ruin, it stood on a limestone escarpment in the Derbyshire Peaks.

The discovery gave me an uneasy feeling. The house was Haddon Hall. I knew that in 1909 it had mattered more than anywhere else to John.

The clue lay in an angry outburst from Violet: 'That Haddon Hall is at this moment nothing to do with John,' she told Charlie: 'Henry can sell it! Henry can let it go to ruin — he need not spend a penny on it!'

The Hall, built of grey Derbyshire stone and dating back to the twelfth century, had come into the Rutlands' possession in the 1560s, when Dorothy Vernon, a wealthy heiress, married John Manners, the second son of Thomas, 1st Earl of Rutland. At the time Violet was writing, the family had not lived in it for two hundred years. In 1703, after Sir John Manners, 9th Earl of Rutland, was created Duke of Rutland by Queen Anne, he had abandoned the Hall in favour of the larger Belvoir Castle, a more fitting residence for a Duke. Surplus to the Duke's requirements and ill suited to Belvoir, much of the heavy oak medieval furniture housed in it had been left behind. Ever since, the Hall, a fortified manor house of turrets and battlements, had stood suspended in time.

The romance of Haddon had captivated John. In the summer months, while staying at the nearby Stanton Woodhouse, he and Charlie had picnicked among the ruins. Steeped in the history of the Middle Ages and the Reformation, the Hall appealed to John's fascination with the past. He was drawn too by its fine architectural features, and as a boy his ambition had been to make its restoration his life's work. In 1907, when he came of age, he began work on the project, spending the bulk of his £1,500* allowance on building materials.

The knowledge that Henry could at any moment take Haddon away from him was what had kept John in his thrall. It was the hold his father had over him. It explains why John accepted the job at the embassy and why, in the period before he left, he was

* £612,000 at today's values.

beholden to his parents. It also explains why, in the row over the resettlement agreement, both he and Charlie had been so contrite.

In 1909, the Hall, and the 20,000 acre estate that surrounded it, belonged solely to Henry. Under the terms of the complex legal arrangements that governed the passing of the family's property from one generation to another, the Haddon estate was classed as 'unsettled', meaning it was not entailed and therefore did not automatically pass to John. As Violet had angrily — and correctly — pointed out, Henry could do with it as he liked.

Henry had used the threat to sell the Hall to bully John into signing the resettlement agreement. While there is no evidence to prove the point, it is more than probable that this was John's meaning when he told Charlie that his father 'was going to try and frighten him'.

So central was Haddon to the argument, and such was the depth of feeling vested in it, that the protagonists had not needed to mention it; it is only in the resolution of the row that its importance becomes apparent.

On 12 June, five months after the row began, John told his father that he would sign the agreement. He did so only because he had extracted a promise that Haddon would be made over to him. Such was the mistrust between them, he asked his father to confirm his promise in writing. Three days later, the Duke wrote back to him: 'The question of Haddon has been safeguarded in the settlement.' Only then did John sign the agreement.

They had fought each other to a standstill. While John was forced to concede his legal interest in the family heirlooms, so anxious was the Duke to raise the capital he needed to pay off his debts, he had had to surrender the one thing he had never wanted his son to have. It had nothing to do with the Hall's material value. It was simply because it bore the name of his dead son.

A letter — from John to his mother — written seventeen years later, offers a chilling coda. In August 1926, when the restoration works at Haddon were finally completed, John moved into the Hall. As he wrote to Violet, it was the fulfilment of a lifetime's ambition; yet she defaced his letter.

The cruelty of her gesture becomes apparent only after reading it:

Haddon Hall
Bakewell
Derbyshire
28 August 1926

Mother darling
I hasten to write to you on notepaper with an address on it, which I have been hop-

ing to use for now just on 20 years. Although the house is not ready yet for occupation, I feel justified in making you the recipient of the first letter written from Haddon by a member of the family since they left for good in 1703. I am writing from my sitting room which is the uppermost room in the Nether Tower — the whole tower being finished and ready for occupation. My dreams, as far as my sitting room is concerned, are fulfilled. It is a perfect room with the sun pouring in.

There is only one cloud over this moment and that is that old Charlie* is not here with me — then indeed my spirits would be overwhelming. But perhaps he may know that I am writing at his own writing table.

Goodbye for the moment.

Yours, John

It was the address that Violet had defaced:

---

* Charlie Lindsay had died of cancer, aged sixty-three, the previous spring.

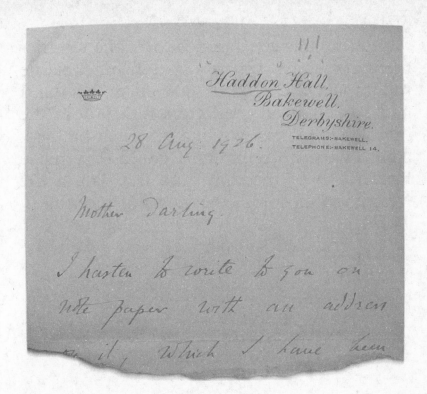

The stabs of her pen spoke volumes: John was unworthy of the house that bore his brother's name. The implication of her gesture was that she wished it was Haddon who was living there, not him.

John's encrypted letters had exposed the tensions inside this troubled family. Evidently, the scar left by Haddon's death had not healed: the loss of the 9-year-old boy had continued to haunt their relationships.

The central mystery, however, remained.

What had happened to John in the summer

of 1909?

I had no answer. The row over the resettlement agreement was resolved in June, before the gap in the records at Belvoir begins. I had looked at all the letters for 1909 in the bundles John was working on when he died. There were no pointers. I could only move forward — to the third and last gap in the Muniment Rooms: the missing months in 1915.

PART V

33

7 July–5 December 1915. The correspondence from 152 days was missing from the Muniment Rooms. From what I knew of John, he had hidden things that were painful to him: I could only think that the excision related to some traumatic event that had occurred on the Western Front.

It was where he had been in the summer of 1915. Aged twenty-eight at the time, he was aide-de-camp to General Edward Stuart Wortley, the commanding officer of the 46th North Midland Division. The division had arrived at the Front on 26 February 1915. John had been there for just over four months.

I went back to the notes that I had made when I first discovered the missing letters.

The last sighting I had of him was on 5 July. That afternoon, at around 4 p.m., he drove his general to Goldfish Château, the headquarters of III Army Corps at Vlamertinge. British troops had named the château, situated a few miles to the west of the canal sector at Ypres, after the fishponds in its gardens. There, according to the entry in John's war diary, they had tea with Major-General Sir William Pulteney, the corps commander.

It is at this point that John vanishes from the record. From 6 July, the pages of his diary are blank.

The date coincides precisely with the start of the gap in the letters at Belvoir. Not a single document remains in the blue files that crowd the shelves of the Muniment Rooms to explain what occurred between then and 5 December 1915. John had made certain of this. My only hope was that something — or some clue — lay in the pile of letters that I had extracted from the trunk of correspondence he had been working on when he died.

1. Belvoir Castle, looking east towards Woolsthorpe, *c*.1935.

2. The Guard Room at the castle. The door leading to the former servants' quarters is to the left of the fireplace.

3. John, 9th Duke of Rutland, with his wife, Kathleen, and Roger, his youngest son, at King George VI's coronation in May 1937.

4. Room 1, where John died in April 1940. The sofa on which he died is at the centre of the picture.

5. The Elizabeth Saloon, one of the many state rooms at the castle.

6. The Guard Room, March 1940. Boxes containing documents from the Public Record Office are stacked to the left of the arch.

7. The Muniment Rooms (at the base of the Round Tower), as seen from the gun-carriage terrace. The two drainpipes that Hilda Lezard scaled to break into the castle are to the left of the tower.

8. Violet Lindsay and Henry, Marquis of
Granby (later 8th Duke and Duchess of
Rutland), on their engagement in 1882.

9. Violet and Haddon.

10. Haddon, aged three, at Cockayne Hall,
the family's home in Hatley Cockayne,
Bedfordshire, in 1889.

11. John, aged four, at Belvoir.

12. Haddon.

13. John.

14. Haddon, aged nine.
The photograph was
taken shortly before
his death.

15. Haddon's tomb.
Violet's inscription reads:

Hope of my eyes
Something is broken that
we cannot mend

With Grief, Remembrance,
Pride and Love, I decorate
his memory

Dear, dear little boy,
You gave us all Perpetual
Benediction

Entirely designed and modelled
by his Mother

16. Violet on the terrace at Belvoir in 1895, the year after Haddon died.

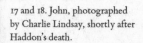

17 and 18. John, photographed by Charlie Lindsay, shortly after Haddon's death.

19. John, aged thirteen, at Stanton Woodhouse, the family's home in Derbyshire.

20. A portrait of John by Sir James Shannon, painted in 1908, a few months before he was appointed Honorary Attaché at the British Embassy in Rome.

21. The seafront at Messina after the earthquake on 28 December 1908.

22. Violet, Duchess of Rutland, by Sir James Shannon, *c*.1890.

23. Henry, Duke of Rutland, and Charlie Lindsay, *c.*1920.

24. Violet, Duchess of Rutland, *c.*1915.

25. John (*first on the left*) in the summer of 1909.

26. The War Office in the autumn of 1914 – the scene of Violet's meeting with General Sir Edward Bethune. The police have cleared a passage through the crowds of men waiting to volunteer to make way for the car at the entrance to the building.

27. General Sir Edward Bethune.

28. Lord Kitchener of Khartoum.

29. John in the courtyard at Arlington Street before leaving for the Front in February 1915.

30. George Gordon Moore.

31. Lady Diana Manners, c.1915.

32. Field Marshal Sir John French (*right*) picnics with his ADC, Lt.-Col. Fitzgerald Watt, on the Western Front in June 1915.

33. *Left*: Field Marshal Sir John French in his dress uniform.

34. *Below*: Walking wounded at Vermelles, during the later stages of the Battle of Loos.

35. OFFICERS OF THE 4TH LEICESTERSHIRE REGIMENT AT LUTON, OCTOBER 1914

Back row: 2/Lt. G.E.F. Russell*, 2/Lt. J.F. Johnson*,
2/Lt. W.N. Dunn, Lt. G.A. Brogden,
2/Lt. F.M. Waite.
Next row: 2/Lt. M.B. Douglas, 2/Lt. H.F. Papprill,
Lt. J.G. Abell, Lt. F.N.Tarr*, Lt. W.B. Jarvis,
Lt. G.J. Harvey, Lt. A. Silver, 2/Lt. H.C. Brice*,
Lt. F.S. Parr, Lt. A.E. Ball.
Next row: Capt. R.A. Faire*, Capt. B.F. Newill,
Capt. A.C. Cooper*, Maj. L.V. Wykes,
Lt.-Col. W.A. Harrison, Capt. R.S. Dyer-Bennet,
Capt. T.P. Fielding-Johnson, Capt. J.C. Baines,
Capt. H. Haylock*.
Front row: Lt. T. Whittingham*,
2/Lt. A.C. Clarke*, 2/Lt. R.C. Harvey*,
2/Lt. L. Forsell*.

* Killed in action, 1915. Of the other officers,
all were wounded on 13 October 1915,
the day the North Midland Division
incurred 3,700 casualties.

36. Goldfish Château, where John had tea with General Pulteney on 5 July 1915,
the day his war diary stopped.

37. Gassed soldiers at Casualty Clearing Station No. 8, Bailleul, which John visited on 2 May 1915.

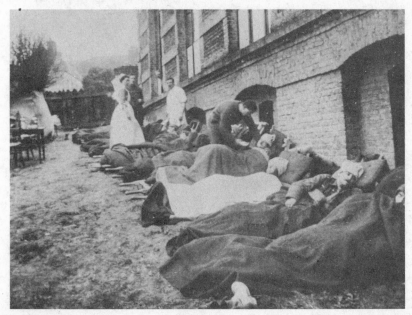

38. General Edward Stuart Wortley.

39. Rothesay Stuart Wortley.

40. Marjorie, Marchioness of Anglesey, and her daughter Caroline, Belvoir Castle, 1915.

41. John and Kakoo's wedding at St Margaret's Church, Westminster, on 27 January 1916.

A family celebration at Belvoir Castle, June 1918.

42. Henry, Duke of Rutland, is toasted by his family after receiving the Order of the Garter from King George V. He was awarded the Order for his work in raising recruits for the war. Diana is seated on the left. Opposite her, on Henry's left, is Marjorie, Marchioness of Anglesey, and, next to her, Kakoo, Marchioness of Granby.

43. John and Kakoo.

44. Henry and his daughter Diana.

45. Kakoo and Charlie Lindsay, 1918.

46. John at the christening of John, his second – and favourite – son, Haddon Hall, 1922.

48. Haddon Hall by Rex Whistler. John commissioned the painting in the early 1930s. He and Charles, his eldest son, are the two figures in the foreground. The withered tree suggests that Whistler sensed – or was aware of – the tragedy in the family's recent past.

47. Haddon Hall.

49. John's sons at King George VI's coronation, May 1937. *Left to right*: Charles, Lord Granby, Page to the Duke of Gloucester; Lord John Manners, Page to Lord Ancaster; Lord Roger Manners, Page to his father.

50. John poses with the local cricket team and his bulldog Belvoir, a descendant of Toto, 1937.

51. The funeral of Violet, Duchess of Rutland, Belvoir Castle, January 1938. John leads the procession, followed by his three sons.

52. The cortège arrives at the mausoleum in the grounds of the castle.

53. David, the present and 11th Duke of Rutland.

54. Emma, Duchess of Rutland.

34

First, I counted the envelopes; there were sixty-three. Then, working from the postmarks, I made a quick note of the dates the letters had been sent. Fifty-seven were dated before 6 July, and two after 5 December. Four were impossible to date: the 'killers' — the rippled lines that prevented the stamp from being re-used — were sharp. So was the year. The rest of the information — the date, the time, and the month they had been delivered — was blurred.

I began with these. Potentially, as John hurried to cull the last of his mother's papers, these were letters that he missed.

The first, written from Belvoir, was from Violet to her daughter, Marjorie, Marchioness of Anglesey. At the top of the dove-grey notepaper, a miniature of the castle, the size of a large coin, was embossed in white against a black background. Beneath it, there was a date — 15 June 1915.

The date was interesting. It was around the

351

time that I had noticed a change in John —
from engaged and engaging to terse and
secretive. In his war diary, in April and May,
he had written long, vivid accounts of the
fighting at Ypres. He had expressed his
thoughts and feelings on the progress of the
war. But in these last weeks in June, just days
before he mysteriously vanishes, he records
very little: the short, flat entries amount to
no more than one or two sentences.

Only once had he expressed any emotion.
This was on 19 June. That morning, he left
London to return to the Front after five days'
leave. When his ship docked at Boulogne, he
learned that his division was about to be
drafted to Sanctuary Wood in the Ypres
Salient. There, for the first time — and in
one of the most dangerous sectors on the
front line — it was to take part in an attack.
'Damn,' he wrote later that evening.

After this brief eruption, his diary offers no
further insight into his state of mind. Day
after day, he had written just two words to
mark the passage of war: 'usual day'.

His brevity was troubling. As I had established, these were far from 'usual days'. For
the first time, the North Midlands were in
the front-line trenches; they were coming
under attack. Although John was nine miles
away at division headquarters, he was aide-
de-camp to the commanding officer: the
dispatches from the Front had passed across

his desk. Soldiers from his own battalion — men who came from the villages on his father's estate, many of whom he had known since he was a child — were being killed and wounded. Yet, in his diary, he fails to make a single reference to the fighting, or to the casualties incurred by his regiment.

So what had changed between May and June? Something must have happened to account for his detachment. The terse entries suggest that he was preoccupied by something else — something he was not prepared to confide to his diary.

Was there a link between the change in his mood and his mysterious disappearance after 6 July? Violet's letter to her daughter, written at such a crucial time, might point to what had occurred.

'Darling — such a day as we've had — a great success — telegrams all day,' her letter began:

Buckets of rose leaves, the nursery all roses. Caroline like a little drunk Bacchus with a wreath of red roses over one ear and as naughty as you please. All the rose effect done by me this morning. Also chairs and cushions and rugs in your top garden. Caroline got a new ball and a new perambulator. Great gossiping amongst the grown-ups and playing with the children, and so on, until tea — with a wonderful chocolate and sugar birthday cake with rose red candles.

It was not what I was hoping for. Violet, who was obviously an indulgent grandmother, was writing of a tea party that she and the Duke had hosted to celebrate their 2-year-old granddaughter's birthday.

I read on, hoping to find a reference to John. 'Lovely it was,' Violet continued, 'and Caroline getting naughtier and naughtier. Then George Paynter produced a walking stick that shoots cartridges like a gun and Father shot off at a swallow with it and it nearly knocked his front tooth <u>out</u>! This is terrible! I'm <u>so</u> sorry about it. Now the children are in bed, but Caroline won't sleep a wink, I expect. The whole day was a great success and very pretty to look at. Father's shooting out his own tooth the only sad moment. I feel <u>worn</u> out. My love, darling. VR.'

The absence of any mention of the war appeared to be a family trait. A few hundred miles away, on the other side of the English Channel, the British Army was sustaining heavy losses in its attempt to hold the trenches east of Festubert. Yet here was the Duke firing a makeshift gun at a swallow for fun. This, and the rose-festooned party for the 2-year-old baby, seemed to belong to another age.

I turned over the page. Violet had at least

mentioned John. On the back of her letter, she had added a postscript:

John home on leave, I hear. I _am_ glad. I wish he'd come here for a day. Will you tell him from me I shall leave here Friday, so if he doesn't come to see me before that he must make a point of seeing me in London.

The imperiousness of her tone was bemusing. John had left for the Front in February; this was his first visit home. Violet appeared anxious to see him, yet evidently they were not in communication. She was asking her daughter to act as messenger. Her letter hadn't pointed to anything that might have caused John to turn in on himself. But then judging from her request to Marjorie, she was not in a position to know. The suggestion was that her relationship with her son remained as problematic as ever.

I moved on to the second of the four letters. As I unfolded it, the paper, brittle after almost a century, emitted a sharp crack.

Immediately, the date caught my attention. _Tuesday 19 October._ The gap in the records extended from 6 July to 5 December: this was the first letter I had come across inside the missing period.

The date had a further significance. Six days earlier, on 13 October, the North

355

Midlands had suffered severe losses at the Battle of Loos. In the space of just a few hours, 3,700 men had been killed or wounded as they fought to recapture the Hohenzollern Redoubt — a small piece of high ground made up of coal-mining waste. John's battalion, the 4th Leicesters, had gone into the battle a thousand-strong; the morning after, just 188 men had answered the roll call.

The letter, written from Belvoir Castle, was from the Duke to Violet:

Dear,
My blasted tooth has gone wrong these last two days, and if it goes on I must come to London Tuesday for 1 night to have it looked at. So don't be surprised at my movements.

The 4th and 5th Leicesters have had a bad knocking — very heavy casualty lists, I am told. 110 men and 10 (!) officers go from the 3/4th Leicesters to the 4th Battalion from Belton at once.

Your affectionate husband

Evidently news of the battalions' severe losses at the Hohenzollern Redoubt had only just reached the Duke. Yet his letter seemed remarkably casual. In breaking the news to his wife, the absence of any heartfelt reference to the fact that their son had survived unscathed was surprising.

356

That same day, the Duke had written to John. This was the third of the four letters. On 19 October, John, it appeared, was back from the Front — or due back at any moment. It was the first indication I'd had of his whereabouts since he had vanished from Goldfish Château on 5 July:

19 October 1915

Dear Boy,
Re: Longshaw on Saturday next. I can't come as I have arranged for some time past to be in London that night. Returning here the following day.

But as you know, of course, shoot there if you can arrange it. Mr Kerr will do this for you.

You had better arrange for the hire of a car to bring you back here after shooting, as the cars here will be pretty busy on Saturday, and could not get over to Longshaw.

I've just had your General's divisional order thanking the Division for their gallant conduct in a recent engagement couched in very highly appreciative language. I hear the Leicester losses are very heavy.

Your affectionate father
Rutland

I found the letter as puzzling as the one to Violet. Longshaw, high on the moors in the Peaks, was the Duke's shooting lodge in Derbyshire. If John was hoping to shoot there on 23 October, he must have obtained leave from the Front almost immediately after the battle. But then why, if he had been in communication with his father earlier that week, had he failed to tell him what had happened at the Redoubt? The Duke had referred to the division's 'gallant conduct in a recent engagement'; evidently he had no other information. The North Midlands had suffered close to 3,700 casualties. Surely, at the very least, John would have told his father of their appalling losses? But he hadn't: he hadn't even mentioned the battle. The first the Duke had heard of it was via the North Midlands' commanding officer, General Edward Stuart Wortley.

The last of the four letters explained the omission. It was from the general himself. He was writing to John on 16 October, a few hours after he had ordered the last of the North Midlands' shattered battalions to withdraw from the trenches beneath the Redoubt.

It took a while for the implications of the letter to sink in:

My Dear John
Very many thanks for all the partridges

358

which you are sending to us — they are most acceptable.

We had a great fight on the 13th, but the task given to us was much too big.

The Division advanced to the attack in successive lines with the greatest gallantry but were mown down by machine guns from many directions. We had a tremendous artillery bombardment but experience has taught us that it has little effect upon deep and narrow trenches. The enemy know that an attack is coming and remain in dugouts in their trenches until the bombardment is over. They then jump up, get their machine guns in position and rake the advancing infantry. Our losses were very severe. 160 officers and about 3,500 men, but many slightly wounded.

We gained and held the Hohenzollern Redoubt, which was an important advance but at great cost.

However, the Division is very cheery and well. We are now resting for a few days.

Yours ever,
Edward Stuart Wortley

John had not been with them. No wonder he had had nothing to tell his father. As his fellow soldiers were being raked by the enemy's machine guns, it looked as if he had been shooting partridges in England.

Attached to the general's letter was a list of the officer casualties in John's battalion. He had been one of thirty to embark for the Front the previous February. On the afternoon of 13 October, twenty of them had been killed or wounded:

4th Leicesters

Killed:

Capt. R. D. Faire
Capt. F. S. Parr
Lt. T. Whittingham
Lt. R. S. Green
Lt. A. R. Forsall
Lt. R. C. Harvey
2 Lt. G. E. Russell
2 Lt. W. P. Scholes
2 Lt. B. E. Mogridge
2 Lt. F. T. O'Callaghan
2 Lt. F. W. Walker

Wounded:

Lt.-Col. R. E. Martin
Capt. R. S. Dyer-Bennet
Capt. B. F. Newall
Lt. J. F. Johnson
2 Lt. W. A. Riley
2 Lt. F. C. Blunt
2 Lt. O. H. Cox

Missing (reported wounded):

Capt. Corah
2 Lt. J. E. Barken

Somehow, John had managed to escape the battle. Loos had been the centrepiece of a major autumn offensive. The battle — the largest attack by the British Army since the start of the war — had opened on 25 September. In the weeks prior to it, all leave had been cancelled for the 75,000 soldiers assigned to take part.

So why wasn't John there? When had he left the Front, and what — beyond shooting patridges — was he doing in England?

It was on re-reading the Duke's letter of 19 October that I realized that the prosaic details regarding John's hire-car arrangements for the shooting trip to Longshaw were significant: 'You had better arrange for the hire of a car to bring you back here after shooting, as the cars here will be pretty busy on Saturday,' he had told John. The Duke was writing from Belvoir; the implication was that John was planning to stay there on the night of the 23rd. Quite possibly, he had stayed there on other occasions when he had been shooting at Longshaw.

Unusually, the castle's visitors' book listed the names of family members in residence as well as their guests. Potentially, it offered a means to track John's movements. If I could pinpoint his visits to the castle that autumn, it ought to be possible to determine roughly when he returned to England from the Front.

The visitors' books were kept on the top shelf of Case 12 in the Muniment Rooms. They dated back to the 1820s, when the 5th Duke of Rutland had moved into the newly built castle.

The one I was looking for spanned the years 1905–33; it was bound in black leather, with the words 'Visitors' Book Belvoir Castle' inlaid in gold on the cover.

It was the hall porter's job to compile the visitors' book. Seated at his desk in the lodge off the Guard Room, he had a clear view of the comings and goings at the castle: he could see the carriages and motors drawing up on the terrace outside. Meticulously, as the Duke's footmen hurried to and fro with the visitors' luggage, he had noted the arrivals and departures.

I turned to the first page; the names were entered in black ink in a neat, italic hand:

DATE OF ARRIVAL	NAME	DATE OF DEPARTURE
January 3rd	Miss Lindsay	January 7th
" "	Miss Horner	" 9th
" "	Miss Drummond	" 7th
" 4th	Mrs Cust	" 7th
" 4th	Courtauld Thompson Esq.	" 7th
" 4th	C. J. H. Pollen Esq.	" 7th
" 4th	Raymond Asquith Esq.	" 7th
" 7th	Capt. Charles Lindsay	" 16th
" 9th	Mrs Page	February 3rd
" 10th	Marquis of Granby	January 15th
" "	Lord Robert Manners	" 12th
" "	The Rev. F. W. Knox	" 25th
" "	Mrs Knox	" 20th
" "	Miss Knox	" 20th

Leafing through the pages, it was fascinating to see whom Violet and Henry had invited to the many house parties they hosted before the war. Among the hundreds of names were men or women whose wealth or fame had granted them a passport into what was otherwise an exclusively aristocratic circle. Interspersed between the titles were some of the most celebrated figures of the early twentieth century. In December 1911, at the height of the success of his Peter Pan novels, J. M. Barrie had stayed at the castle. Robert Baden-Powell, the founder of the Boy Scouts, the conductor Sir Thomas Beecham, and Madame Nellie Melba — the acknowledged prima donna at Covent Garden — had stayed that year too.

John's name cropped up frequently among the eclectic mix of guests. The visitors' book delineated his world, as much as his parents'. Senior politicians and leading figures from the international stage had also been invited. As the tension in Europe increased, it was surprising to see that Counts Benckendorff, Metternich and Mensdorff, the Russian, German and Austrian ambassadors, were frequent guests — often simultaneously. I counted four prime ministers: Lord Rosebery, Arthur Balfour, Herbert Asquith and Andrew Bonar Law. There were other famous figures too: notably Alice Keppel, Edward VII's mistress, and Prince Yusopov, the future assassin of Grigori Rasputin.

Looking at the pages for the summer of 1914, the entries dwindled and the great house parties came to an end, a grim reminder of the passing of an epoch. After August, the Duke and his family were mostly alone at the castle. Only occasionally did they invite one or two guests.

I skipped through the months that followed to October 1915. I found John's name halfway down the page: 'Marquis of Granby 23rd to 28th October'. He *had* stayed at the castle the night he was shooting at Longshaw.

I looked at the previous page. There he was again: Marquis of Granby, 9th–14th October.

This was where he had been as his battalion was fighting to capture the Redoubt.

I turned back another page. And another. I could not believe what I was seeing. John had been at the castle for most of the summer. He not only missed the Battle of Loos: his visit in July coincided with the fighting at Hooge, when the Germans attacked the North Midlands trenches with liquid fire.

So when did he return to the Front? Quickly, I skimmed through the entries after 28 October. 'The Marquis of Granby November 20th to November 22nd'; 'The Marquis of Granby, December 11th to December 14th'; 'The Marquis of Granby December 16th to December 22nd': his name appeared on every page until the following spring. From the frequency of his visits to the castle, it looked as if he was in England from July 1915 until April 1916.

Nine months. It seemed impossible. It had never occurred to me that John was not where he ought to have been. He had embarked for the Western Front with the 4th Leicesters on 26 February 1915. When he volunteered for the war, he had signed the Imperial Service Obligation. It committed him to 'active service in any place outside the United Kingdom' for its duration. Bar injury or illness, the pledge, signed by every territorial soldier, was unbreakable. He should have been with his regiment.

1915 Date of Arrival.	NAME.	Date of Departure.
Oct" 9th	Lady Elcho	Oct" 11th
	Lady Mary Charteris	" 11th
	Master David Charteris (baby)	" 11th
" 13th	His Grace The Duke of Rutland	" 14th
" 14th	Marchioness of Anglesey	Nov" 8th
" 16th	His Grace The Duke of Rutland	Oct" 23rd
	Her Grace The Duchess of Rutland	" 18th
	Lady Robert Manners	" 27th
" 18th	Mrs Ralph Peto	" 23rd
" 23rd	Her Grace The Duchess of Rutland	" 25th
	Miss Cunard	" 25th
	Marquis of Granby	" 28th
	Captain Charles Lindsay	" 28th
	Captain Harry Lindsay	" 25th
	John Gilliat Esqr.	" 24th
" 24th	His Grace The Duke of Rutland	Nov" 8th
" 30th	Her Grace The Duchess of Rutland	" 1st
	Lady Diana Manners	" 1st
	A. Duff Cooper Esqr.	" 1st
Nov" 13th	Her Grace The Duchess of Rutland	" 15th
	Lady Diana Manners	" 15th
	A. Duff Cooper Esqr.	" 15th
	Marchioness of Anglesey	" 22nd
" 16th	His Grace The Duke of Rutland	Dec" 6th

■ ■ ■ ■

I returned to his war diary.

John had arrived at Belvoir on 14 July. He must have left the Front at some point between 6 and 13 July. His departure accounted for the blank pages, but, now that I was armed with this new information, would the last entries explain why he left?

The week leading up to 6 July filled just one page. The entries were disappointing. John hadn't even hinted at the fact that he was about to return to England. But then had he known he was leaving? And if he had, was this why he seemed so detached?

Re-examining the curt entries, it was impossible to judge:

July 1st 1915 Thursday
Reninghelst Camp
Poperinghe Road

Usual day.

July 2nd 1915 Friday
Reninghelst Camp
Poperinghe Road

Usual day. I went after lunch to Ypres Cathedral to get a few more fragments of the frieze of the screen — found a lot more.

July 3rd 1915 Saturday
Hôtel de la Poste Rouen

Started at 8 alone with the General, and Tanner the chauffeur, to go to Rouen in the Rolls. Got there at one (two punctures) inspected the drafts. Then we went sight seeing. I rogered a woman after dinner in the Maison Stephane — not good.

July 4th 1915 Sunday
Reninghelst Camp
Poperinghe Road

Started at 7am back, arrived 12.20, two punctures. Spent the rest of the day here.

July 5th 1915 Monday
Reninghelst Camp
Poperinghe Road

Usual day — went to tea with Pulteney with GOC.

This was John's last entry.

In the course of the next eight days something happened to him which haunted him for the rest of his life. At his instigation — until 14 July, when he arrives at Belvoir — the record is completely blank.

Working from the visitors' book, and the

game books that were kept in the Muniment Rooms, I was able to build a picture, albeit a faint one, of John's routine once he got to Belvoir.

His days, so it seemed, were spent fishing, shooting and entertaining beautiful debutantes. Nancy Cunard, the bohemian and striking-looking daughter of Emerald Cunard, the legendary Edwardian hostess, stayed at the castle three times while John was there. The Comtesse Jacqueline de Portalès, the granddaughter of the Comte de Portalès — a favourite of the Bourbon King, Louis XVIII — was invited on numerous occasions; so was Miss Felicity Tree, the daughter of the theatre impresario Sir Beerbohm Tree; and Miss Violet Keppel, the daughter of King Edward VII's mistress.

The game books for the months of July and August conjured images of an idyllic summer; of picnics by the lake below the castle and grouse-shooting parties up on the Duke's heather-covered moors in the Peaks. The constant round of sporting activities continued through the winter months. Evidently, John was fit to fight. So why wasn't he with his battalion in France? In the spring of 1916, his visits to Belvoir became less frequent; after 20 April he was absent from the castle for six months. Was this when he finally returned to the Front?

It was then that I checked the contemporary

Army Lists. Updated quarterly throughout the war, they listed the names and regiments of all serving officers and, importantly, the theatre of war to which they were assigned.

What I discovered was startling. In flat contradiction to the evidence in the visitors' book, the Lists clearly showed John as being on active service with the 4th Leicesters until April 1916. Further, they revealed that, when he left Belvoir that month, it was not to rejoin his battalion on the Western Front. On 4 April he had been appointed ADC to Field Marshal Sir John French.

The previous December, Herbert Asquith had sacked Sir John for his incompetent handling of the Battle of Loos. The much-vaunted offensive had ended in failure; far from forcing a German retreat, not a single yard of ground had been gained. British losses amounted to 50,000, and yet to save the field marshal's face — and the morale of the hundreds of thousands of soldiers formerly under his command — the prime minister made him a viscount and appointed him Commander-in-Chief, Home Forces.

From April 1916, John was based at French's headquarters in Horse Guards. There, in luxurious surroundings, he served out the remainder of the war.

The information contained in the Army Lists was bafflingly at odds with the scant evidence held at Belvoir. More troubling though, was the revelation that John's departure from the Western Front in the summer of 1915 marked his retirement from active service for good. I had seen his name on the war memorial in the chapel at Belvoir. So why, if he hadn't been with the 4th Leicesters after July 1915, were the words 'Capt. 4th Leicesters' inscribed beneath his name?

The plaque stood on the wall, facing the altar. An oblong-shaped tablet of pale-grey stone, it commemorated the members of the household who had served in the war.

Violet had commissioned the memorial in 1919; she was responsible for its design, and for the tribute inscribed beneath the names:

George Allcroft	Frank Palmer
Cadet RAF	Pte 8th Lincs
Died in hospital 1918	Killed in France July 1916

———

Charles Coy	The Marquis of Granby	Frank Patience
Pte 3/4th Leicesters	Capt. 4th Leicesters	Cpl M.G.C.

Edward Doubleday	James Lamb	John Price
Pte R.A.S.C. M.T.	Cpl 5th Leics	Chauffeur B.A.C.
		Croix de Guerre

David Gibson M.C.	Edward Nixon	Charles Tweed
Lieut R.I.F.	Lieut R.A.F.	Cpl R.E.

THIS MONUMENT TO THEIR COURAGE IS SET UP BY
THOSE WHO LOVE THEM AND ARE PROUD OF THEM.

There at the centre of the plaque was John, his name flanked by those of the family's servants. Frank Palmer, killed at the Somme at the age of twenty-two, had been the 4th footman at the castle; George Allcroft, the 19-year-old son of the Duke's Master of Hounds, had worked in the kennels. Nixon, Doubleday and Tweed were gardeners; and Lamb, Coy and Patience were grooms. John Price, who had received the Croix de Guerre, was the Duchess's chauffeur; David Gibson, awarded the Military Cross, one of the highest awards for gallantry, was the Duke's valet.

Among these courageous men, John's name did not appear to merit inclusion. He had served as a soldier for just four months of the war. During that time, his battalion was held in reserve. At the very moment it was drafted into the front line, he left for England. The castle's servants had fought for the duration of the war. Two had won medals for their bravery. John had not fought at all.

Capt. 4th Leicesters; the reference to his battalion was extraordinary. The impression left to posterity was that John had been with them. The 4th Leicesters had spent close to four years on the Western Front. They had fought at Ypres and Loos in 1915; at the Battle of the Somme in July 1916; at Hill 70, Thiepval and the attack on Lievin in 1917; and at the battles of Cambrai, Selle and Sambre during the Final Advance in Picardy in 1918.

I found the injustice of the inscription — and the apparent deception — disquieting. Opposite the war memorial, at the far end of the chapel, stood Haddon's tomb; there beside it was the notice that stated he had died of tuberculosis. This hallowed room appeared to have become a repository for myths the family was anxious to perpetuate.

But then how had Violet been able to get away with including John's name on the plaque? In 1919, everyone — from the castle's servants to the villagers on the Duke's estate — would have known that he had not been with the 4th Leicesters; they would also have known that he had not fought in the war.

It pointed to just one conclusion: John's reason for leaving his battalion must have been entirely honourable. The letter General Stuart Wortley sent him after the catastrophic action at the Hohenzollern Redoubt reinforced this theory. There was no suggestion that John had evaded active service, or that he had left the general's staff under a cloud.

So why, if John's reason for leaving his battalion was honourable, had he gone to such lengths to conceal it? His departure from the Front coincided *precisely* with the start of the excisions he had made in the family records. Not a single document remained to explain why he had left, or what he was doing in England.

Given his determination to kick over the traces of this chapter in his life, I had assumed that in seeking to bury his secret in perpetuity, he must have believed that excising this period from the family records would do the job — that there were no other records elsewhere which would reveal his secret.

But his military career was a matter of public record.

Over the course of the First World War, the War Office kept a file on every soldier in the British Army; they contained the details of promotions and postings, and the periods of service in various theatres of war. The files were now held in the National Archives at Kew. If I could find John's file, it ought to explain why he left the 4th Leicesters in the summer of 1915.

Then I remembered that at the outbreak of the Second World War a significant proportion of the nation's records had been evacuated to Belvoir. Some three hundred tons of documents had been sent up to the castle in the months before John died.

Had the service records of soldiers who had served in the First World War been among them?

The government's decision to use the castle as an emergency repository had been taken at the last minute, largely thanks to John's persistence. He had not been responsible for the records; yet he had insisted that the catalogue to the many thousands of documents be held for 'safe-keeping' in the Muniment Rooms.

Had John pressed the government into using the castle as a wartime repository because he had wanted to find — *and remove* — his own War Office file?

The priority now was to return to the National Archives at Kew.

35

'WO 374. Piece Number 28523. The Marquis of Granby, Capt. J. H. M. Covering Dates 1914–1919'.

The file was buff-coloured; the pages inside loose leaf and frayed at the edges. It was impossible to determine whether John had looked for it and failed to find it; it wasn't clear whether it had actually been among the records transferred to Belvoir in 1940. The main thing was that it was here.

I began to go carefully through it. It held around thirty documents; printed reports that had been dated and rubber-stamped; numbered army forms that had been signed and counter-signed. Scrawled in ink across the pages were the hieroglyphics of anonymous civil servants. Four million British men had served in the First World War: the acronyms and strings of numbers were a bureaucracy's means of imposing order on the horror and chaos.

It was the third document in the file that

caught my attention. *Form A. G. 4A.* The date — 9 July 1915 — leapt off the page: this was just three days after John's war diary stopped. The print was faded; the tiny creases in the tissue-thin paper, a wartime economy, obscured some of the details. I smoothed out the form and studied it closely. It was a notice of embarkation:

Rank and name	Lieut. The Marquis of Granby
Corps	A.D.C. to G.O.C 46th Division
Date of Leaving Unit	July 9th 1915
Date of Embarkation	July 9th 1915
Port of Embarkation	Boulogne
Port of Disembarkation (England)	Folkestone
Date of Arrival in England	July 9th 1915
Cause of Return	Sick

Cause of return, sick.

A form, filled in by an orderly in the Transport Corps on the quayside at Boulogne, had given away John's secret. But then why would he have wanted to keep this information secret? He had been invalided home from the Front: it was a legitimate reason for leaving his battalion: he could hardly be blamed for the fact that he had fallen ill.

Shell shock — or a nervous collapse of some kind perhaps; it must have been an illness of which he had been ashamed, one to which some kind of stigma was attached.

I turned to the next form in the file. It was marked 'Confidential: Proceedings of a Medical Board'.

John had attended the board at Caxton Hall, opposite Westminster Abbey, on 23 July. Quickly, I scanned the form to find out what had been the matter with him. At the bottom of the page, in the space that had been left blank for handwritten notes, the examining surgeon had filled in the details:

The above-named officer [Lt. J. H. M. Marquis of Granby] was sent back from France on 9 July suffering from diarrhoea, the effect of old malarial poison contracted some time ago in Rome; of a very obstinate character, with abdominal pain and symptoms of dyspepsia. It is surmised that the abdominal discomfort may indicate a condition of chronic appendicitis. He is, at present, quite unfit for duty. Recommended for two months' leave. To apply for a Board before its expiration should he feel fit to return to France.

The account of his illness contradicted the

evidence in the game books and the visitors' book at Belvoir. Chronic appendicitis was a life-threatening condition; usually, it was necessary to remove the appendix before it burst. John, as far as I could tell, had not had his removed. On 25 July — two days after the medical board — he had returned to Belvoir. More puzzling still was the fact that the examining surgeon, a lieutenant-colonel in the Royal Army Medical Corps, had declared him 'quite unfit for duty'. John had spent the entirety of his two months' leave shooting, fishing and entertaining his friends at Belvoir. There was nothing to suggest there was anything wrong with him. So why, if he *was* fit, hadn't he applied to return to the Front before the expiration of his leave, as the army surgeon had recommended?

I read the next report — the proceedings of a second medical board, which John attended on 22 September. This was three weeks before the battle at the Hohenzollern Redoubt.

It wasn't surprising to see that the 'chronic appendicitis' that the doctors initially suspected had failed to develop. What was surprising though, was that John was given a further two months' leave. According to Lieutenant-Colonel Brown, the examining surgeon, the intemperate conditions in the trenches would 'aggravate' his illness: 'He is distinctly better,' he reported, 'but his general condition is unsatisfactory and is susceptible to the slightest climate change as regarding his gastro-intestinal system.'

The diagnosis explained how John had managed to escape the fighting at the Hohenzollern Redoubt on 13 October, but it did not explain how, if he was 'susceptible to the slightest climate change', he had managed to spend a number of days that month shooting partridges on his father's moor in Derbyshire.

The meteorological records were held at the National Archives. A quick check revealed that October 1915 had been memorable for its appalling weather. In the Peak District, where the Duke of Rutland's Longshaw estate was situated, the mean temperature — accompanied by strong winds and torrential rain — remained well below average. Surely, if John had been fit enough to stand for hours on a wet, windswept moor, he had been fit enough to stand in a trench?

On 4 November, three weeks before his leave expired, John presented himself at Caxton Hall for a third board. This time, the examining surgeon judged him fit for active service. So why hadn't he returned to the Western Front? He had passed the medical board; he was under orders to rejoin his regiment immediately; yet, according to the visitors' book, he remained at Belvoir.

I skimmed through the rest of the documents in the file. They were all medical reports. Within weeks of his third medical board, John had suffered a relapse. He had not recovered from his gastro-intestinal problems. Between 4 December 1915 and 16 October 1918, he appeared before a further fourteen medical boards. He failed every one of them.

The insignia of His Majesty's Government was stamped across these documents; on seventeen separate occasions a panel of eminent army doctors had ruled John unfit for active service. On the face of it, despite the discrepancy between their findings, and what I had found in the scant records available at Belvoir, there was no reason to doubt the veracity of these reports. But if this official version of events was true, why did John want to conceal the fact that illness had kept him out of the war? He was suffering from a stomach condition. He had no apparent reason to be ashamed of his illness, yet he had removed all mention of it from the letters in the Muniment Rooms.

I had come full circle. The reports in this file resolved two mysteries: I knew why John had left the Western Front in the summer of 1915; I knew why he hadn't returned to fight. But I was no closer to understanding why he had wanted to obscure the months after he was invalided home. Something of vital importance to him had occurred between 7

July and 5 December 1915 — so important that he had spent a good part of his life — and his final hours — expunging it from the record.

The excisions were tantalizingly precise. The gap in the correspondence at Belvoir began with his illness. But why did the letters resume on 5 December? What was the significance of this date?

Then it suddenly struck me. The defining moment in John's military career was the board of 4 December: at all subsequent boards he had been deemed unfit for active service.

I went back through the file and took out the report of the board's findings: 'Proceedings of a Medical Board assembled at the War Office on 4 December 1915. By Order of the Army Council'.

Straightaway, I noticed that the details were different. John's previous boards had taken place at Caxton Hall by order of the GOC, London District. This one, convened by the Army Council, had taken place at the War Office. The Army Council was the highest military authority in Britain; chaired by Lord Kitchener, the Secretary of State for War, its sixteen members included the Chief of the Imperial General Staff, the Adjutant-General, the Quartermaster General, the Master General of the Ordnance and a number of permanent secretaries. Of what possible interest could John's health have been to them?

One further detail suggested that the board had been far from routine. The fourth of December was a Saturday; medical boards were usually held on weekdays.

I ran my eye down the page to find the examining surgeon's explanatory note. It was short and unilluminating:

The Board, having assembled pursuant to order, proceed to examine Capt. J. H. M. Marquis of Granby and find that he has not yet recovered from the gastro-intestinal symptoms for which he was invalided home in July. *Vide* attached certificate.

John's GP, Dr Donald Hood, had supplied the medical certificate. It was addressed to the Director General, Army Medical Services:

43 Green Street,
Park Lane
2 December 1915

Sir,
I have this day seen and examined the Marquis of Granby, who has been well known to me since his birth.

He is naturally of a delicate susceptible constitution and some seven years ago suffered from a rather severe attack of dysentery contracted in Rome, since which he has constantly been affected with gastro-intestinal disturbances.

Lord Granby was invalided home from the Front by Colonel Beevor on July 8th 1915 as suffering from gastro-irritation. Since that date he has had several similar attacks, so much so that I have questioned whether he may not have chronic appendicitis trouble. His heart action is far from satisfactory and he is in my opinion unfit for active military service.

Donald W. Hood CVO, MD, FRCP
Examining Physician, Foreign Office
Consultant Physician, West London Hospital
Physician, Roland Gardens Hospital for Officers

The second paragraph contained what seemed to be a barefaced lie.

Emphatically, Dr Hood had stated that John's symptoms stemmed from 'a rather severe attack of dysentery contracted in Rome'. John had been to Rome just once before the war. This was in 1909, when he was Honorary Attaché at the embassy. I had seen every one of his letters home; they were in the blue files in the Muniment Rooms at Belvoir. Not one of them had contained any mention of illness, least of all 'a severe attack

384

of dysentery'.

'Since which,' Hood had continued, 'he has constantly been affected with gastro-intestinal disturbances.'

But how could he possibly have been 'constantly affected' when he hadn't had dysentery in the first instance?

It looked as if I had found the answer to the mystery behind the gap in the records in the summer of 1909. John had returned from Rome on 10 June. On his return, he had been ill with a stomach complaint. The gap in the correspondence began on 6 June but I'd found a stray letter from the Duke to John. Until now, I hadn't thought it of any consequence. 'Dear boy,' he wrote on 14 June. 'Glad to hear you've recovered swiftly.' This was the only evidence of illness I'd discovered in the period: it didn't point to a 'severe attack of dysentery'. So was John's 'illness' an echo of Haddon's 'illness'? Had he destroyed the family's correspondence for the weeks following his return from Rome to conceal the fact that he hadn't after all been seriously ill?

I re-read Hood's medical certificate. Evidently, he was trying to keep John out of the war indefinitely. He wanted to convince the panel of RAMC surgeons that John was suffering from a condition that was ongoing and likely to recur. Hood knew the army doctors would not question his diagnosis. Why would they? He was examining physician to the Foreign Office and one of the most respected doctors of his day.

His name cropped up frequently in the letters at Belvoir. Aged sixty-eight in the summer of 1915, he was a close friend to Violet and Henry and had been their GP for more than thirty years. He had delivered all five of their children, and was regularly invited to shoot and fish at Belvoir.

That he was capable of falsifying John's medical certificate did not surprise me.

In the autumn of 1894, it was Hood to whom Violet and Henry had turned after Haddon's accident. At their request, he arrived at Hatley the morning after it had happened; he spent the next six days there, battling to save the boy's life.

The note that Hood had sent to Violet on 30 September 1894, two days after Haddon had died, was at Belvoir:

43, Green Street
Park Lane. W.

My dear Lady Granby
After being with you so much it seems strange and trying not to know how you are today. I cannot tell you how my heart bleeds for you in this awful trial. It has been a bad time for me, but for you and Lord Granby, too terrible for words.

You have shown such true courage that I trust you will keep well and able to bear up against the overwhelming truth.

If you feel at any time that a little talk would do you good, or give you any comfort, send me a note.

My Best From
Donald W. Hood

There had been no inquest after Haddon died; the authorities had not been informed of the accident. Legally, the obligation to report a 'sudden, violent or unnatural' death fell equally on the attending physician and the deceased's relatives. In failing to report Haddon's accident, Hood had been as much to blame as Henry and Violet.

In the years after Haddon's death, Hood went on to become one of the leading doctors in the country. His obituary, published in the *British Medical Journal* in the spring of 1924, paid tribute to his distinguished career:

We announce with much regret the death on March 15th of Dr Donald W. C. Hood. He was born in June 1847 at Market Lavington, Wilts, the eldest son of the late Sir Charles Hood, a Lord Chancellor's visitor in lunacy.* From Harrow he went to Caius College, Cambridge, and afterwards to Guy's

* Senior physicians appointed by the Lord Chancel-

Hospital, and graduated M.B. in 1871, proceeding M.D. in 1879, and was elected F.R.C.P. in 1892. After a few years in general practice in the country, he was appointed consulting physician to the West London Hospital and until a few weeks before his death he remained in close touch with that institution. Dr Donald Hood's other appointments included those of examining physician to the Foreign Office, a manager of the Royal Institution of Great Britain, governor and member of the committee of management of Bethlem and Bridewell Royal Hospitals and examiner in medicine to the University of Cambridge. He received the C.V.O. in 1901 for services rendered in connection with the fund for the relief of wounded and sick officers during the Boer war.

Twice, despite his impeccable curriculum vitae, it appeared that Dr Hood had perverted the course of official proceedings; he failed to notify the authorities that Haddon had died as a result of an accident; he fabricated the illness that had led a succession of army medical boards to deem John unfit for active service.

These were serious charges.

---

lor to examine wealthy Chancery patients in asyhms throughout England and Wales.

Having failed to save one son, had he wanted to save the other? Or was he simply carrying out the family's instructions?

His papers have not survived to answer these questions.

The medical certificate, written in the doctor's cramped, barely legible hand, was a damning piece of evidence. Until now, I had thought John an innocent victim in the traumatic events that he had erased from the records at Belvoir; it had seemed that he had wanted to obliterate things and relationships that were painful to him. But it was impossible to escape the conclusion that, in removing this chapter, he had sought to remove evidence that would incriminate him. He had used an invented medical condition to escape the front line. Effectively, he was guilty of desertion, a capital crime, for which the penalty was execution by firing squad.

It was not just his reputation that it had been necessary to protect. His father had raised thousands of men for the war. Day after day, the Duke had toured his estates, addressing school halls crammed with villagers who had turned out to hear him speak. In appealing for volunteers, the Duke had championed the chivalric ideals of honour, valour and sacrifice.

'If we had attempted to keep out of this war, we should have violated every honourable principle,' he told his audience at Red-mile, a few weeks after war was declared:

> We should have been guilty of one of the most cowardly actions that a country and a Government has ever been guilty of. We should have forever stained the name of Great Britain with an infamy which could not be borne.
>
> This war is not going to end in 48 hours or 48 days. It is a big thing. Half a million men are needed. It is to be a big knock-out, and the opponents that must be knocked out are the Germans. Yes, it's going to be a knock-out of a genuine kind. None of that slipping down to avoid punishment. We have to knock them out and cripple them. They have to get a dressing-down from which they will not recover for the next fifty years. There are to be no half-measures. It must go on until we have them on their knees. And go on and on until we have their noses on the ground.
>
> We want every available man to come forward to enlist and sacrifice themselves for the good of the Empire and of their country. I hear from Leicester that two more battalions of the Leicestershire Regiment — the 6th and 7th battalions — are to be formed. That is an additional two thousand men required. The more of you who go, the quicker the war will be over. Come Forward.

This is what I want. And what England wants. And I am confident that what England wants, you will not forget to give her.

Invariably, in those early weeks of the war, the Duke quoted John as an exemplar of the courage and patriotism he was demanding of his tenants and employees:

The North Midland Division are now all around London and my son is on the Staff there. I've heard that they will shortly be going to the Front. If so, they will be one of the first Territorial Divisions to go to France. As for me, the Government will not take me. I am 62. But at any rate, my boy is on the path and he will do whatever he can when he gets there. I am proud of him.

In the summer of 1915 he must have known that John's 'illness' was a sham. Yet for the next six months — until conscription was introduced, in January 1916 — while concealing his son's desertion, he continued to urge the men from his estates to step forward and sacrifice themselves for 'the good of the Empire'.

Much of the mystery surrounding this episode in John's life had vanished; his War Office file had explained a great deal. I now understood why his name was inscribed on the memorial in the chapel at Belvoir. It was there to reinforce a lie. Violet included it because the family's employees had been led to believe that, while illness had kept him from fighting, John had served dutifully for the duration of the war.

I could also see why there was a discrepancy between John's actual whereabouts and his whereabouts as recorded in the contemporary Army Lists. Though published quarterly, the lists did not indicate periods of leave resulting from illness or injury: until an officer was killed in action, or transferred to another unit, he was listed as serving with his regiment. It explains why, between July 1915 and March 1916, when John was in England, he was listed as being on active service with the Leicestershires.

But a number of things still puzzled me.

I had found nothing to account for the marked change of tone in his war diary. This had occurred in mid-June, three weeks before he left the Western Front. Suddenly, for no apparent reason, he appears to have withdrawn from the events going on around him. *Why?* Was it because he was already planning his escape?

And how had he managed to get himself invalided home from the Front in the first place? In supplying him with a fraudulent medical certificate, Dr Hood had given him a passport out of the war. But this was *after*

John had returned to London. So who was behind his escape from France? Or had he somehow convinced his superiors he was ill?

And there was one very obvious question that nagged at me. Five months after John arrived back in England, the Army Council convened his fourth medical board at the War Office.

This was on 4 December, the day before the records resume at Belvoir.

I had checked the proceedings of other medical boards held that month. I couldn't find one that had taken place on a Saturday, or one that had been convened by the Army Council at the War Office. They had all taken place at Caxton Hall by order of the GOC, London District.

So why had the Army Council, the highest military authority in Britain, intervened to call what appeared to be some sort of an emergency board?

What was so special about John?

His War Office file had revealed this mystery; it did not resolve it. The irregular circumstances of the board — and its co-incidence with the resumption of the records at Belvoir — convinced me that, in making his meticulous excisions in the correspondence in the Muniment Rooms, there was something else that John wanted to hide.

I now had a clearer idea of what I was looking for. There were sixty-three letters at Belvoir; I had looked at four of them. Fifty-nine remained in the pile that I had extracted from the trunk of correspondence that he was working on when he died.

36

As soon as I saw the letters, I knew there was something special about them. Carefully, I spread them out on the long map desk in Room 4. It was hard to tell in the dim light but, if I peered closely, they had a peculiar sheen to them; they appeared to be coated in a thin film of translucent powder. I ran my finger along the surface of a page; the powder felt silky, rather than gritty.

Going over to the window, I tilted the page to and fro against the light; the paper sparkled as if it had been dipped in fine filaments of gold. It looked like compact powder, or some type of pigment used in mixing paint.

It was the first time I had come across it. I had found the letters, stuffed inside one large envelope. Violet had evidently kept them separately. The mysterious substance suggested she had put them inside something — as if she had wanted to hide them. Had they once lain in the box or drawer where she had kept her painting materials? Or had she secreted them in one of the compartments of her dressing table?

I settled down to read them. When I saw their contents — and the names of the correspondents — it was obvious that Violet *had* been at pains to conceal them.

Woven through these letters — seventeen of them, spanning the first thirteen months of the war — was a web of intrigue that stretched from the Duchess to the highest military authorities in the country. Evidently, her position at the very top of society had allowed her to call in favours, no matter how dishonourable, whenever and from whomsoever she pleased.

It was a telegram from John that changed everything. Dated 23 September 1915 — the day after he attended his second medical board — it was to his sister, Marjorie:

Six weeks more leave STOP Damnation STOP Bitterly disappointed STOP.

The letter pinned to it explained the source of his disappointment. It was not cowardice that had prevented him from fighting in the Battle of Loos. It was Violet.

The week before, she had written to a senior official at the War Office to ask him to fix the outcome of the board.

'Darling — I must fight! Don't be cross with me!' she told Charlie afterwards: 'Other mothers do <u>nothing</u>. What do they get for their bravery? <u>The worst.</u>'

The two documents cast John in an entirely different light. Here was proof of a conspiracy to which he was unwitting. Far from wanting to escape the fighting, he had wanted to be in the thick of it.

But how had Violet succeeded in keeping him in the dark?

I had stumbled across a treasure trove. The names and details contained in this small cache of letters offered a route map to sources outside the Muniment Rooms that finally enabled me to piece together what had happened.

Together with the letters in John's blue files and the others that I found in the trunk of correspondence he was working on when he died, they from the basis of the narrative that follows.

The story begins on a summer's day in August 1914, when Violet received news from General Stuart Wortley, John's commanding officer. What he had to tell her came as a bolt from the blue.

PART VI

37

It was first light on the morning of 27 August 1914 — the twenty-fourth day of the war — and Violet lay, half awake, in the master bedroom at Stanton Woodhouse, the family's home in Derbyshire. A low, rambling Tudor mansion, with gables and lattice windows, it stood, nestled in a cluster of trees, at the end of a mile-long drive. Outside, wood pigeons cooed in the boughs of the tall elms that framed the house; beneath her window came the soothing sound of running water from the stream that ran through the steep hillside garden. Earlier, while she was sleeping, her maid had crept into her room to draw the curtains. The view stretched before her: over the sculpted yews and the gravelled pathways in the garden below, to the moors beyond, pale mauve in the hazy morning light.

By any standards Violet's appearance at this hour was eccentric. Her silk-frilled nightdress was worn under a cream flannel kimono-shaped garment and her head was bound, seemingly in a knitted vest, the long sleeves of which wound around her chin. This elaborate structure, designed to keep her hair in place, accentuated the coarseness of her features. Forty years before, when she was eighteen, Mrs Patrick Campbell, the actress and muse to George Bernard Shaw, had described her as the 'most beautiful thing I ever saw'. While her former beauty was still evident in her bone structure, age had added a fleshiness to her face. There was a ruthlessness about it too. Unkindly, Margot Asquith, the prime minister's wife, likened her to a 'Burne Jones Medusa'. Her daughter-in-law, Cynthia, had been crueller, noting 'the faintly sinister strangeness of her eyes so deeply set in shadowy caverns'.

Propping herself up in the Elizabethan four-poster bed, Violet opened her mouth wide and screamed. Invariably, this was her first action on waking. The 'stylized scream', as Diana, her daughter, described it, was the signal to Tritton, her maid, to bring in her breakfast tray.

It would be lunchtime before Violet left her bedroom. The first half of her day followed a set routine. 'My mother spent the mornings in bed,' Diana remembered: 'I see her sitting cross-legged writing endless letters with a flowing quill pen. On her knee was balanced a green morocco folding letter-case, with blotting paper and a pot of ink which, curiously enough, never got splashed on the Irish linen sheets.'

Downstairs, Henry was up and dressed for breakfast. Seated at a long black oak table in the panelled hall, he was going through the morning's post.

Among the letters was one from John's general:

Headquarters, North Midland Division
Stockwood Park
Luton

My Dear Henry,
One line to tell you that your boy is doing excellent work. He is really first rate, and I am very glad to have him on my staff. I hope we shall all be over the water in about 6 weeks' time, prodding the Germans in the back part of their front!

Yours ever
Eddy Stuart Wortley

Reaching for the fountain pen he kept in the breast pocket of his suit, Henry wrote a note to his wife:

I think you ought to see this.

R [Rutland]

Then he summoned a footman to take the note, and the general's letter, up to Violet's bedroom.

'John <u>going</u>!!! At any moment!!!' Violet wrote to Diana: 'I am cracked with fear.'

The letter from General Stuart Wortley lay beside her on the bed. His news was the last thing she had anticipated. The North Midland was a territorial division. On 4 August, the day war had been declared, the government had announced that all territorial divisions would remain in England. The war was expected to be over by Christmas. Violet had not, for an instant, imagined that John would actually be drafted to the Front.

Only the previous week, her great friend Winnie, Duchess of Portland, had written to congratulate her on her luck: 'How heavenly for you that J is only to be in England. Gen. E. Wortley, I hear, is to stay <u>here</u> and defend us!!' On numerous occasions, the general himself had written to reassure her. His last letter — sent to Belvoir by dispatch rider the night the North Midlands arrived at Luton — had been particularly avuncular:

North Midland Headquarters
Stockwood Park
Luton
15 August 1914

My dear Duchess,
Your boy drove me in the Rolls Royce to
this place today — he drove very well —
and we came from Derby in 3 hours!
    I have told him to join my Staff tomor-
row as Galloper (I hope he will not
tumble off his gee!) and he will remain
with me — so do not be worried.
                            Yours ever,
                    Eddy Stuart Wortley

Now, out of the blue, she had every reason
to worry. In a panic, and determined to find
some means of stopping John from going to
the Front, Violet turned to her brother:

Charlie darling,
Eddy Wortley writes 'I expect we shall all
be over the water in 6 weeks' time'!!
    Now what can you and I do secretly —
think and tell me? Surely J could go on
the staff of someone remaining here to
teach new army? Think hard — I am up
to anything secret.

Sir George Arthur* — is he any use to us? Or shall I come to London soon and see Kitchener of Khartoum, or what or what!? Shall I write a little secret letter to Eddy Wortley begging him to tell to me when he knows his own news, and telling him of my intense wish to keep J under a General left in England?

I wish you were here. Find out all you can.

There was no time to write any more. 'Post going,' she scrawled.

The calling in of favours was Violet's métier. Until her late middle age, she had traded on her beauty to obtain what she wanted. Her many admirers had been only too happy to oblige, even to the extent of lending her husband huge sums of money. In the 1890s, she had persuaded the Duke of Portland to lend Henry £20,000 to purchase their London house, Number 16 Arlington Street. A large Queen Anne mansion, it was situated behind the Ritz in Piccadilly. The terms of the loan, which Violet had negotiated, were absurdly favourable: only the capital sum was repayable — and this only when Henry could afford to pay it. Before then, Lord Brownlow,

* Sir George Arthur, Private Secretary to Lord Kitchener of Khartoum, Secretary of State for War.

one of the wealthiest men in Britain, and the uncle of her then lover Harry Cust,* had provided their first family home. This was Cockayne Hatley Hall in Bedfordshire, the house where Haddon had died.

Now approaching her late fifties, Violet had only her charm — and her position — to fall back on. The former, when she chose to deploy it, was considerable: 'I had a letter from Violet Rutland on Saturday that really would have melted one, if one were not so convinced of her evil character and falseness,' Lady Desborough reported to a friend.

Violet spent the rest of that morning going through her address book. By the end of it, she had drawn up a list with six names on it:

General Sir Ian Hamilton [Aide-de-Camp to King George V]

Field Marshal Lord Grenfell [former Commander-in-Chief of the British Army in Ireland]

Sir John Cowans [Quartermaster General to the Armed Forces]

* Henry Cust, politician and editor, 1861–1917. His affair with Violet began soon after her marriage and continued into the early 1900s. He was the father of Diana, Violet's youngest daughter.

Major-General Frederick Hammersley [Commanding Officer of the 11th Division]

Lord Curzon of Kedleston [former Viceroy of India]

Sir George Arthur [Private Secretary to Lord Kitchener of Khartoum, Secretary of State for War]

These were the men Violet believed could help in her bid to keep John back from the war. She knew each of them personally; they had been guests of hers at Belvoir. The difficulty was, if she was to avoid both her husband and her son getting wind of her plan, she would have to approach them surreptitiously; then she would have to persuade them to collaborate with her in secret.

At Luton, as Violet plotted a means to stop John from going to the Front, the machinery of war was gearing up to send him.

38

Three weeks later, on an overcast morning, John stood with General Stuart Wortley at the centre of a windswept parade ground. They were dwarfed by the scene around them. Ahead, some four hundred yards distant, was the magnificent neo-classical façade of Luton Hoo, the home of diamond-mine heiress Lady Wernher. Behind them, drawn up in razor-straight lines, were five thousand soldiers.

They were waiting for King George V, who was on his way to review the North Midlands. John, ADC to General Wortley, had taken the call from Buckingham Palace to say that the King would be with them at half past ten. It had been a long day already. To allow plenty of time for the troops to form up on the parade ground, after reveille at five, they had marched the two miles from the North Midlands headquarters at Stockwood Park. The infantry were lined up along the boundary, with the Field Ambulance on the extreme right, and the artillery on the slope of the ground to the left. A significant number of the men were still dressed in civilian clothing; with just a few weeks to go before their departure for the Front, their uniforms had yet to be supplied.

Opposite the troops, in the far corner of the ground, half a dozen cars were drawn up. Beside them, huddled against the wind, stood the mayor and the town clerk of Luton and the handful of guests General Stuart Wortley had invited to watch the parade — among them, John's father, who was Honorary Colonel of two of the division's battalions. To the left of this group — gathered at a respectful distance — were a small number of estate workers. There were no other spectators. The parkland that framed the ground was deserted. The King had insisted that his visit be kept as private as possible. This was business, not public ceremony.

Morale among the troops was high. As they formed up into position, a local newspaper reporter spoke to some of them. 'We are the first Division in the Territorial Forces to be selected for service in the field,' one soldier boasted: 'other Divisions have been accepted for Colonial and Garrison services abroad whereas we, the North Midland Division, are bound for France early next month. Hurrah!'

Until the King arrived, the order was to 'Stand easy'. With five thousand pairs of eyes directed at him, John watched the small ripples of movement that ran up and down the lines of men as they shifted about on their feet and clapped their hands to keep warm. While he did not share their enthusiasm for the war, he was stoic in his approach to it. 'It is a mouldy business. God knows how long it will last,' he confided in a letter to Charlie: 'As far as I can see there is no reason why it shouldn't last for over a year, or even two years. Anyhow, there it is. It will have to be seen through.'

At Stockwood Park, it was the long evenings in the officers' mess, rather than the interminable route marches and the monotonous hours spent drilling on the parade ground, that John found challenging. The week after war was declared, he had turned down the opportunity to switch from the Leicestershires to one of the smart Guards' regiments. His duty, he believed, lay with his county regiment: he felt obliged to serve alongside men who came from the estates that he would one day inherit. His decision set him apart from his fellow officers: the North Midland Division was composed entirely of other county regiments, with the consequence that he was the only titled officer on the staff. The others — the sons of brewers, woollen hose manufacturers, and colliery, brick factory and tannery owners — had grown up in the industrial towns that gave the Black Country its name. Feeling friendless, and anxious to ingratiate himself, John had sought Charlie's help: 'He made a <u>great</u> point of getting his father to send some grouse as soon as possible for his Staff mess,' Charlie told Violet after seeing John briefly in London: 'They are 10 people. So 5 or 6 brace would be the least to send, and if it can be done, it should be done <u>at once</u>. The idea is that it would be thought a very nice attention from Henry, and also it would be a great thing for John, who is, of course, very shy among people none of whom he knows, and wants to be as nice and attractive as he can be. Vegetables from Belvoir he also wants. The General is fond of good young salads. He says it would be best to address these things to the General himself at Stockwood Park.'

Facing the prospect of months — if not years — in close proximity to his fellow officers, John was hoping to persuade General Stuart Wortley to find places for his friends in the division. Having failed to obtain a commission in other regiments, a number of his contemporaries from Eton had written to ask if they could join the Leicestershires. One of them was Henry Bunbury, the son of Sir Charles Bunbury, 10th Baronet:

The Manor House
Mildenhall
Suffolk

My dear Beaver
In desperation I am sending you a line to
ask if you could get, by any chance, myself
and Reggie[*] commissions in your Regiment? We have been trying every known
bloody thing, but the answer is 'we will
let you know later' or 'you are not
wanted.' So here we are doing bum all
and thoroughly well fed up.

Reg has tried Needham[†] — he, I believe,
is in the front of the show somewhere. Julian Martin Smith,[‡] I hear from Reg, has
got out with the Intelligence crowd. By
the way, all the soldiering we have had
was in the dog porters at Eton. I did
about 18 months I think as a tommy, and
Reg was in the band, if I remember right,
but does that matter much?

I don't suppose you will have a minute
to write a long letter, Beaver, but if you
could, just drop either of us a line to say

[*] His elder brother, Charles Bunbury, later 11th
Baronet.
[†] Francis Charles Needham, 4th Earl of Kilmorey,
Captain, Life Guards.
[‡] Great-grandson of the Marquis of Bute, killed in
action, 1914.

413

what you think we had better do. If we could get into your show so much the better.

So long, Beaver, and the best of luck.

Guy Charteris, the second son of the Earl of Wemyss, had also written:

My Dear John,
I have been unable to join Ego's* regiment and am making frantic efforts elsewhere. I suppose you could not get me a commission in yours?

I got the news of the fall of Namur yesterday and food for much thought it gave me. Things look bloody bad. Our troops are bound to lose heavily whilst retiring, especially cavalry. People will cease to laugh at German shock tactics soon. I hope you are enjoying yourself and that your men are giving short shrift to all deaf mutes who fail promptly to answer a challenge. Please give me a sketch of your life.

I am just off to London to importune the War Office in general and 'Uncle Jack',[†] the Under Sec. in particular.

* His elder brother, Hugo, Lord Elcho, killed in action at Gallipoli, 1915.
† Harold Tennant, Under-Secretary of War 1912–16.

8 battleships and 2 cruisers spend considerable amounts of their time off Littlesham protecting the Dab Beds and Kentish Plovers, presumably for the Prussian foe.

Yours, Guy C

It was a quarter to eleven when the King's car, a 'fine six-cylinder Daimler', drew up on the parade ground. As General Stuart Wortley and John greeted the King, the order was given for the General Salute. 'Just as His Majesty took the salute,' the local paper reported, 'the sun was making a pretty successful effort to shine boldly through a rift in the clouds. With no brightly-coloured uniforms or brave trappings to catch the eye, it would have been a dull scene but for this touch of sunlight, which was reflected in myriads of flashes as swords and rifles, with bayonets fixed, were brought to the "present".'

Following the salute, the King went over to inspect the troops. As he did so, one of the battalion's bands struck up the national anthem, the notes of which were barely heard above the wind.

Only a portion of the twelve thousand-strong division could be accommodated on the makeshift parade ground, which until August had been the polo ground. Yet still, it took the King half an hour to inspect the five thousand troops. 'The faces of those he spoke to wore one common expression,' the newspaper reported: 'of enthusiasm at the prospect of leaving shortly for France, and of devotion for His Majesty, who stood in front of them, dressed in khaki, like them. "We're counting the days to the off, Sire"; "We'll be in Berlin before you know it," they replied to his solicitous enquiries.'

As he progressed through the ranks of infantry and artillery, the King, a slight figure, barely five foot six inches tall, had to look up to every one of the soldiers he passed. In September 1914, a man had to stand five feet eight to get into the army. A month later, so great was the need for recruits, the minimum height requirement was lowered to five foot five; in November, after the losses sustained in the First Battle of Ypres, it was lowered again, to five foot three.

After completing his inspection, the King returned to a spot near his car to watch the troops march past. The Duke of Rutland joined him. Through their grandparents' friendship, they had known each other since they were children. For a full thirty-five minutes the troops streamed past, before splitting into columns to march through the park. The infantry led the way, then came the artillery, with the Field Ambulance bringing up the rear; the beat of a drum and the sound of a bugle set the pace.

Standing only a few yards from the soldiers, Henry looked on with pride. Many of the faces were as familiar to him as they were to John. He knew a large number of the men in the two Leicestershire battalions — of which he was Honorary Colonel — and there were others he recognized. The soldiers in the Sherwood Forester battalions came from Alfreton, Ilkeston and Bakewell — towns that lay within his Derbyshire estates.

From the outset, Henry had embraced the war wholeheartedly. He subscribed to the view — widespread in the popular press — that war would be good for the country: the unity, dedication and sacrifice that it demanded would shake England out of the sloth induced by years of peace and prosperity. It was a view promoted by his close friend, Edmund Gosse, the influential editor and critic, and a frequent guest at Belvoir. 'War is the sovereign disinfectant and its red stream of blood is the Condy's Fluid that cleans out the stagnant pools and clotted channels of the intellect,' Gosse wrote in a much discussed essay published in the *Edinburgh Review:* 'Our late past years of luxury and peace have been founded on a misconception of our aims as a nation, of our right to possess a leading place in the sunlighted spaces of the world. We have awakened from an opium-dream of comfort, of ease, of that miserable poltroonery of the "sheltered life". Our wish for indulgence of every sort, our laxity of manners, our wretched sensitiveness to personal inconvenience, these are suddenly lifted before us in their true guise as the spectres of national decay; and we have risen from the lethargy of our dilettantism to lay them, before it is too late, by the flashing of the unsheathed sword.'

Other leading cultural figures took up Gosse's theme, among them H. G. Wells, whose jingoistic articles were appearing in the *Daily Chronicle:* 'One talks and reads of the heroic age and how the world has degenerated. But indeed this is the heroic age, suddenly come again. No legendary feats of the past, no battle with dragons or monstrous beasts, no quest or feat that man has hitherto attempted can compare with this adventure, in terror, danger and splendour.'

The notion that there was something wrong with England, that, like some Edwardian glutton, it must take the cure, was held across the political spectrum. 'Diagnoses of that disease varied,' the historian Samuel Hynes wrote, 'depending on what guilts, resentments, private quarrels and self-interests the diagnostician brought to the case. But most Englishmen who confronted the question agreed that whatever the disease was, it had deflected the nation from its proper course. The war had been sent to put England right.'

The years before the war had been the most divisive that anyone could remember. Trades unions, the Suffragettes, and the situation in Ireland were all exerting pressures against established society and its mores. In 1912, the government had once again tried — and failed — to get a Home Rule bill for Ireland through Parliament; in the same year, the miners went on strike for seven weeks, and the Suffragettes began their attacks against London property. By the spring of 1914, the sense of threat had greatly increased. Ireland was in a state close to civil war and British troops at the Curragh were threatening to mutiny. In London, the suffragettes' campaign accelerated to new levels of violence as houses, churches and public galleries were smashed and women rioted in front of Buckingham Palace. Class conflict was also rife: for the first time, in a bid to secure higher wages and workers' rights, the trades unions were proposing to call a General Strike.

'I do not suppose any country was more actively engaged in quarrelling amongst itself than was England at the very time war was being sprung upon us,' Henry told his estate workers at a recruitment meeting in late August: 'Now we must put those quarrels behind us and pull together to defeat the worst menace the world has ever faced. I have stood on this platform on a good many occasions before now, but never on an occasion when I felt more ready to do what little I can to try and help the country.'

His motives were not entirely altruistic. The Edwardian era, with its eight years of radical Liberal government, had eroded his authority both locally and nationally. Lloyd George's vicious attacks against Britain's dukes had called into question his very existence: 'A fully equipped Duke costs as much to keep up as two dreadnoughts, and Dukes are just as great a terror, and they last longer,' the Chancellor of the Exchequer famously remarked in his ground-breaking speech at Limehouse. The taxes he had introduced — coming as they did on top of the agricultural depression — were crippling Henry, reducing his capacity to hold sway in his locality through the distribution of jobs and largesse. Simultaneously, the government's Parliament bill had dramatically clipped his political power. Passed on 10 August 1911, it removed the aristocracy's right of veto over financial legislation and restricted their veto over ordinary legislation to two years. A diehard Conservative, Henry had resisted the bill to the last. The war, he hoped, would reassert his moral authority. It demanded discipline, obedience and endurance — values that turned on deference and a unity of purpose.

But though he welcomed the war, he doubted that it would be won easily. 'There is one point I particularly want to press on

420

you today,' he urged his audience: 'Some people seem to think that by one great strategical coup, or one great victory, the war might come to a premature or rapid end. But it will not. It is going to be a very long war, a war which will tax to the utmost the energies and resources of every country involved in it. It is undoubtedly a war that will be a record war. Though not one that we will be proud of possessing. It has now come out officially that Germany has been preparing for it for a great number of years past. The German nation has been breeding men solely for the purpose of becoming soldiers, and they have evolved one of the most tremendous wars ever thrown upon an astonished and horrified world. It has been manufactured in a most careful way, by the most skilful of men who care not a rap for what it might mean to country, whether that country be big or small. This is the engine against which we have to fight, and it is a machine that cannot easily be put out of action.' He ended his speech with the same impassioned plea that he made at every speech he gave that summer: 'Come forward. The more of you who go, the quicker the war will be over. This is what I want. And what England wants. And I am confident that what England wants, you will not forget to give her.'

So convinced was Henry that the war would last for many years, on 21 August, a day when a partial eclipse of the sun shrouded the country in semi-darkness, he instructed his kennelmen to destroy all but four of the Belvoir Hunt's twenty-four couples of foxhounds. The army had already commandeered fifteen thousand hunters and most lawn meets had been cancelled. 'I am unwilling to pay for the upkeep of the kennels, when it is unlikely that the hounds will be hunted for many a year,' he told Violet.

Violet was not at Luton Hoo to see the King's review. She had turned down General Stuart Wortley's invitation. She chose instead to spend the day at Belvoir. Four weeks into her bid to keep John back from the war, she wanted to collect her thoughts.

39

It was harvest time and the wide, sloping fields below the castle were full of pensioners, women and children. The farmhands and horsemen had left for the war. The sounds of voices, shouting and trees being felled drifted from the woods that bordered the fields. Detachments of soldiers from the Army Service Corps were at work; out in Flanders, timber was urgently needed for duckboards and trench props, and for the miles of railway track hurriedly being constructed to rush troops to the Front.

The clover had been cut and stored but rain had delayed the harvesting of the hay. As the old men struggled to wield their scythes through the corn, the women and children worked in groups, tying bands for the sheaves they had yet to gather. High on the hill, the castle loomed above them. There was no sign of life; the blinds had been tightly drawn to screen its treasures from the sun. But at some point that day, somewhere inside the gloom,

Violet took out a piece of paper and wrote down a series of questions to herself:

Should I write to Lord Grenfell?

Or should I go and see him again?

Should I write the pros and cons and what he must take in of the possible?

Should I ask how he, Lord G, is going to get over the 'difficulty'?

Time was running out and she was making little headway in her bid to stop John from going to the Front. The 'difficulty', as she quickly realized, was his patriotic sense of duty. Her first thought was to find him a job on the staff of a general responsible for home defence; but she had abandoned this plan as it was obvious John would never agree to leave his division. Her next move — calculated on the basis that every division left a skeleton staff in England — was to try to persuade Stuart Wortley to leave him behind. 'Spare him honourably,' she had pleaded. Her callous reasoning — that John was the 'last in his family' and 'Henry's only heir' — infuriated the general. 'A son is precious regardless of titles or possessions,' he replied sharply: 'I have no possessions and my son is the last in my family and he is as treasured to me as my wife. Every one of the soldiers in my division is precious to someone: your son's situation does not render him any more exceptional than any of the other boys.'

Recognizing that the one chance she had of prising John from his division was if his transfer were to come as an order, Violet decided to go above the general's head. Her sights were set high: Lord Kitchener, the Secretary of State for War, was her best hope. It was a plan she confided to Harry Cust, her former lover and closest friend. 'Beloved, in these always terrible days I know a little how you must be suffering for others and fearing for your dear self,' he replied from the War Office, where he was in charge of government propaganda:

> Of course Kitchener of Khartoum is <u>absolute</u> and could put John on his own Staff — or anywhere. Or on Sir John French's Staff, which they say is safe. But I know you will be brave, my sweet, and understand that John's own future has to be considered. That's the awful <u>difficulty</u> of it, the two reasons of State.

The words 'King and country' had no resonance for Violet: John's obligation to his family — specifically, the preservation of its rank and prestige — outweighed any obligation to the state. Nor did she have any consideration for what John would feel were

425

he to be denied the chance of going to war — or what he might feel in the years to come, having failed to play a part in it. Ignoring Cust's advice, Violet was determined to find a route to Lord Kitchener. She knew him personally: he had stayed at Belvoir in the summer of 1911. Yet she dared not approach him herself. The stories she had heard from her friend Lady Wantage had warned her off.

A maverick bachelor and a man of 'arctic loneliness', Kitchener disliked women. Preoccupied solely with forming the 500,000-strong army that he believed represented Britain's only hope of defeating the Germans, he discouraged callers at his office in Whitehall. 'Apart from soldiers, visitors to the Secretary of State's room were only welcome if on important business affecting the war, and a rigid rule excluded ladies,' Sir George Arthur, his private secretary, recalled: 'One social aventurière was said to have wagered twenty pounds that she would obtain the desired access, but the bet was lost. Lord Haldane pleaded a special feminine case, and Kitchener told us to say that if he were to break his rule for anyone, it would be for Lord Haldane, but that he was obliged to be inflexible on this point.'

Nor did Violet expect to run into the Secretary of State for War socially. As Sir George Arthur described, he shunned society: 'Kitchener almost invariably dined at home, occasional exception only being made in favour of the Duke of Norfolk, whom he held in very high esteem. Men friends whom he knew well — his colleagues, soldiers home on leave — came occasionally to dinner, ladies very rarely. He shrank from being entertained and never entered a club or theatre except when invited by a Cabinet Minister — an invitation he thought it bad manners to refuse.'

Kitchener's dislike of women stemmed from his loathing of 'their tittle tattle'. He was notoriously secretive and distrustful of politicians, and his Cabinet colleagues resented him for failing to keep them informed of his decisions. 'If they will only divorce their wives,' he complained to Sir George Arthur, 'I will tell them everything.'

The problem confronting Violet was to find someone who was prepared to lobby the Secretary of State for War on her behalf. Four of the six men on the list she drew up at Stanton Woodhouse on 27 August were close to him. Sir George Arthur was his private secretary; Sir John Cowans served under him as Quartermaster General to the Armed Forces; Field Marshal Lord Grenfell had promoted him after his famous victory at the Battle of Omdurman, and Sir Ian Hamilton, ADC to the King, was one of his oldest friends.

Early in September, Violet wrote to each of

them requesting an urgent — and private — meeting.

Sir Ian Hamilton, one of the first to reply, gave her short shrift:

9 September 1914

Dear Duchess
Just got back. Received yours of yesterday. Alas I am off at cock crow tomorrow for three days' hard inspection work in Norfolk and Suffolk.

Yrs always sincerely
Sir Ian Hamilton

Sir John Cowans, the Quartermaster General, also replied by return. He too claimed he was too busy to see her, suggesting they meet in mid-October. Sir George Arthur did not reply at all: 'How odd "men" are about not answering!!!' she complained to Charlie.

Only Lord Grenfell agreed to see her immediately. On 3 September they met for lunch at the Ritz. A minute's walk from Violet's house in Arlington Street, it was a favourite dining venue of hers — one that she described as 'cosy'. A kindly man, well into his seventies, Grenfell was an important contact. He was a veteran of the Kaffir wars and the Nile Campaign; in advancing Kitchener's career, he had become a mentor to him. He was one of the few men the Secretary of

State for War trusted and to whom he turned for advice.

Violet was calculating in her approach to the lunch. Anticipating a second meeting, she concealed her true objective: she did not ask Grenfell to persuade Kitchener to appoint John to his staff. Instead, her tactic was to elicit his sympathy. Telling him of her grief at losing Haddon, she confided her terror of losing her second and only son. 'He was sympathetic to the "last of his family line"!!' she reported back to Charlie after the lunch.

Grenfell parted from Violet with a promise that he would think hard about what he could do for her and that they would meet again soon. But their meeting was postponed. On 14 September, his nephew, Riversdale Grenfell, to whom he was guardian, was killed in action in France.

Four days later, as the King was reviewing the North Midlands at Luton, Violet was in a state of nervous anxiety. 'Believe me,' she told Harry Cust, 'Lord G is my only hope.' Alone at Belvoir and anxious for guidance, she put to Cust the questions which she asked herself repeatedly, and which, throughout that morning, she committed to numerous scraps of paper as she tried to work out what to do. Could she afford to wait for Grenfell to come back to her? Should she write to him outlining exactly what she wanted from him? Or should she simply take the bull by the horns and see the Secretary of State for War herself?

'Beloved,' Cust replied: 'Lord Grenfell sounds much the best way if he understands and can get Kitchener of Khartoum to put John on his personal staff. I should try that. If John must go to the Front, a big Staff — i.e. Field Marshal Sir John French's — is much the safest, and Eddy Stuart Wortley (though I shouldn't mind him much anyway) couldn't possibly object to the appointment, which would be orders. At the worst, I should make Grenfell insist on Kitchener doing this. Bless, bless, my poor sweet sweet. I will go on thinking and thinking.'

Harry Cust and Charlie were Violet's only confidants. At home, she was careful to conceal her scheming from those around her. In the presence of her immediate family, the castle's servants, and the workers and tenants on the Belvoir estate, she was at pains to project the image of a declared patriot.

Her days were crowded with civic duties, and fundraising events which had been hastily organized in the villages to raise money for the dependants of servicemen fighting abroad. There were garden fêtes to open and harvest festivals to attend; there was the Leicestershire Patriotic Fighting Fund, of which she was a patron; and there were hospital visits to Leicester and to Melton Mowbray, where casualties from the first battles on the Western Front had been sent. At each of her appearances, local functionaries — thrilled to have a Duchess in their midst — had roundly applauded her and thanked her for her commitment to the war effort.

In the evenings, she accompanied the Duke to recruitment meetings, convened in packed church halls, where he gave speech after speech to drum up volunteers for the war. Invariably, he spoke of John's imminent departure for the Front: 'My boy is on the path and he will do whatever he can when he gets there. I am proud of him.' Sitting on the platform behind him, Violet had joined in the loud applause.

While her husband was working assiduously to raise armies of volunteers, her daughters were also doing what they could for the war effort. At Belvoir, Diana was spending her mornings in the fields below the castle helping to bring in the harvest. Her afternoons were spent in the servants' quarters, where, in pursuit of her ambition to become a Red Cross nurse, she watched the cook 'taking out hares' insides' to acclimatize herself to the sight of blood. Marjorie was in constant touch from Beaudesert, her husband's estate in Staffordshire. Keen to compete with her father, who had written to boast of the high numbers of Belvoir volunteers, she replied with the tally from Beaudesert: 'Pups Darling, I am glad to hear of your recruits. We have hardly anyone left here now. My 2 footmen, odd man, 4 more gardeners, the estate chauffeur and the agent's coachman all go off this morning, which totals in all about 17 or 18 recruits accepted from the people on the gardens, stables, house etc. Quite good I call it. I'm giving my footman my 1st pair of socks, knitted at Rowsley!'

Anxious not to give grounds for suspicion, and keen to give the impression that she was as enthusiastic at the prospect of John's departure for the Front as the rest of her family, Violet took it upon herself to find him a horse for the war.

As John was known to loathe riding, his appointment as 'galloper' to General Stuart Wortley amused his father and his elder sister. 'You will, after all, have to make the personal acquaintance of your enemy the horse,' the Duke teased him. Marjorie, who was a keen hunts-woman, wrote to offer him riding tips: 'J Old Boy, If you are going to ride, for goodness sake begin at once and very gradually — 10 minutes a day and get the most comfortable saddle you can get. It's nonsense people who say cheerfully "get on and gallop away." The agonies I go through when I start hunting every year are immense. Yesterday, we chased a fox up and down a pit head!!! The most curious thing imaginable. The foxes lie on the great heaps of thrown away mess by the pit heads and men go up and wake them up!! The hounds were quite black — no trace of white and tan left by the end of the day! What a lark!!'

For the most part, good horses were in short supply. In the first few weeks of the war, the government had requisitioned some nine million. Early in August, Violet's favourite pony had been taken from Rowsley and, at Belvoir one Saturday, villagers were infuriated to find they had to walk the eight or nine miles back from Grantham market after army officials commandeered the horses that had taken them there.

The search for a horse for John was ostensibly Violet's chief preoccupation for some weeks. Disingenuously, in tandem with doing her utmost to ensure that he would never ride into battle, she wrote to her friends to ask if they had one to spare. 'Violet darling — I wish I cd help you about a horse for J,' Winnie, Duchess of Portland, replied: 'We have none left except our personal hacks and a few hunters out at grass. Drape (the dealer) wd be the best person to find you one — he has such nice horses. It's a disgusting war but I do hope the Germans will be forever eliminated some day. Your devoted W.'

It was Tommy Bouche, the Master of the Hounds at Belvoir, who finally supplied the horse — a handsome bay gelding called Xenophon. His heartfelt reply to Violet, written from Tidworth Barracks in Wiltshire where he was training with the 11th Cavalry Reserve, illustrates the mendacity of her request:

My Dear Duchess

I wired my secretary at Woolsthorpe today and told him to send Lord Granby the horse I think would suit him best. I know him to be a nice ride, as I very nearly selected him to be my own charger, but came to the conclusion he was up to more weight than I required. I think you will consider him good looking and he is a fine hunter. There is some drawback to every horse in the world, and this one may be a little bit wide in the ribs for anyone who has not ridden much. I expect Lord Granby will feel fearfully stiff at first after riding him, but that will soon wear off. Anyhow, I hope he will like him.

I have been posted to a Reserve Regiment with a lot of old brother officers, and it is nice being with them again. I have always hated soldiering, and am the last person in the world to think of 'trying for glory', as you call it! Killing other people has never seemed to be particularly glorious work in any case. But, of course, there is such a thing as duty to one's country — duty of any sort is invariably unpleasant! — and it would obviously be inconceivable for me to remain behind in comfort and warmth and plenty, whilst other men (my friends) were fighting for me.

It is an extraordinarily dull spot — miles and miles of barracks on Salisbury Plain. The most interesting things are the aeroplanes, which keep circling about over our heads. The arrangements are uncomfortable — no carpets in our bedrooms, and (until I got them from Woolsthorpe) no sheets or blankets on our beds. We have to keep expenses down for the sake of the poorer officers, and as we mess for 3/6 a day, you can imagine the fare is homely. I can hear you say 'how good for you,' but I always object to being done good to — it is invariably an uncomfortable proceeding.

None of us have the least idea how long we shall be here — a week or six months. I personally am making preparations to stay for ever!

Xenophon, Violet assured John, was 'Bouche's best'. Having found him the horse, she bombarded him with letters asking him if there was anything else he needed for the Front: 'Darling, I wish you would give me commissions to do for you. Tell me anything, anything you need. Please, darling, do your men want anything? I am still buying blankets and socks and shirts for the 20,000 army at Grantham. Bless you beloved. Give me

<u>something</u> to do for you. Mother.'

Violet was not equipping the '20,000 army at Grantham' out of the kindness of her heart. General Hammersley, their commander, was one of the generals in charge of training troops for the Front. Stationed in England for the foreseeable future, there was a chance that at some point he could be prevailed upon to give her son a job. While she kept her true motive hidden in the letter she wrote to John, she revealed it in a letter written coincidentally to her brother: 'I bought 2260 blankets for General Hammersley's army at Belton yesterday! I curry favour with him,' she informed him bluntly.

There was one further piece of information Violet concealed from John. She had finally heard back from Lord Grenfell. He was suggesting they meet in London in the first week of October. To her relief, as she confided to Charlie, it would be possible to see him on a day when Henry was not expecting her to attend a recruitment meeting:

Lord G spends Tuesday, Wednesday and Thursday in London, so <u>Wednesday</u> is my day. I shall go to London <u>Monday</u> evening from Melton Mowbray probably, if Henry's meeting is in the afternoon. He wants me to be at Loughborough on <u>Thursday</u> evening for a meeting — so I can fit it in. I feel full of hope in Grenfell, so let's keep up our spirits.

Keep strong.
Yr loving VR

At Luton, unaware of his mother's manoeuvrings — and his uncle's complicity — John's thoughts were focused on the items of clothing and pieces of kit he would need in the trenches. Having no time to go to London to get them himself, he preferred to rely on Charlie, rather than Violet, to supply them.

Top of his list was a warm winter coat. In a telegram to his uncle, he described exactly the sort he wanted: 'Of thickest black Harris tweed, like my old coat, but khaki-coloured with leather lining and camel hair lining inside that, and a tall well-fitting collar to allow a thick muffler within. Can you also buy the warmest possible gloves, but not fur. Also have 2nd Lt badges on my coat. It must be of a military exterior, more or less.'

That same day, he wired Charlie again:

No time to write. Could you buy me the very best compass you can find with the poles marked by luminous points?

A few days later — on 14 October, the day the North Midlands were put on standby to embark for the Front at twenty-four hours' notice — came a flurry of requests:

Old Boy

Would you try and get me the following:

> 6 prs thickest Jaeger vests and draw-
> ers (long drawers).
> 1 air pillow.
> 6 prs of <u>thickest</u> woollen socks with
> nice long legs to them and a wool-
> len sleeping cap.
> An electric torch in a leather case for
> hanging on my belt.

I think you can get all these at Army &
Navy Stores and put them down to Father
— Acc. No. 15956.

Very many thanks indeed old boy if you
will do this.

That evening, he added another item to the
list:

Old Boy

What a damned nuisance you must think
me. There is yet one more thing I should
love you to do. I saw today a very handy
little leather medicine chest about the size
of this piece of paper, but not quite so
tall. It was like a leather cigar case, with
lots of little long glass bottles with tablets
etc in them — aspirin, quinine, chloro-
dine, and other useful things — scissors,

needles, gauze, etc. I wonder if you could find me one.

So sorry to trouble you.

First thing the following morning, having evidently spent the night thinking about the things he had forgotten, he wrote again:

Old Boy

One or two more things I should be very glad if you would get me. A Field Service Pocket Book and a good leather belt with rings on it for attaching things to, and also a pocket in it if possible. Also would you ask Savory & Moore to send me a hypodermic syringe and some serum for Tetanus. Also if you could get me a good serviceable knife with tin opener, things to take stones out of horses' hoofs, button hook etc.

So sorry to give you all this trouble — also one dozen indelible pencils.

Hope you don't mind doing this for me. A & N stores the best place.

Yr loving J

40

Charlie's house in Chelsea was a fifteen-minute walk from the Army and Navy Stores in Victoria Street. Established in 1882 for the families of serving officers, the shop was the first point of call for residents of Chelsea and Westminster with sons at the Front. Charlie had made a list of the things John wanted. Anxious to avoid the long queues, he left the house early.

On his way there, he passed Victoria station. The concourse outside was packed with troops waiting to board trains for the Channel ports, and convoys of ambulance wagons that had come to collect the wounded from the Front. The wagons, which were long and grey, and painted with red crosses, were open at the back. Crowds of onlookers, two to three deep, lined the pavement beside them. It was a scene that was replicated every day; the sight of the stretcher-loads of wounded was the one visceral experience of the war available to Londoners.

Inside the station, the platforms where the hospital trains came in were cordoned off. 'The public weren't allowed in the station,' one stretcher bearer recalled: 'It was always very quiet in there, with just the long lines of ambulance drivers and VADS and detachments of stretcher bearers waiting. The trains came in at all hours of the day and night. You saw some terrible sights. The worst case I saw — and it still haunts me — was of a man being carried past us. It was night, and in the dim light I thought that his face was covered with a black cloth. But as he came nearer, I was horrified to realize that the whole lower half of his face had been completely blown off and what had appeared to be a black cloth was a huge gaping hole. It was the most frightful sight, because he couldn't be covered up at all. There wasn't very much we could do for the boys. We just had to get them to hospital as quickly as possible.'

The ambulance wagons and the long, snaking lines of troops were a reminder to Charlie of what was in store for John. He was missing his nephew terribly. It was the first time since the summer of 1909 — when John had returned to London from Rome — that they had been parted for more than a few weeks. Charlie had seen him twice since 4 August, on both occasions for only a few hours. When he was a boy, writing from school, it was always John who had wanted to see him. Now

441

the tables were turned. Charlie had written him numerous letters, hoping for a meeting: 'I wish I could see you. I suppose there isn't a chance at present?'; 'I miss you badly. Any chance of seeing you?'; 'I don't suppose you know whether you can get a day's leave yet? I long to see you.'

In an effort to cheer himself up, and to escape the emptiness of the long evenings alone at the house he and John had shared in Cadogan Gardens, Charlie had resorted to spending one or two days a week at the Metropole, a fashionable hotel in Brighton. But this too he found gloomy. The main attractions — the two piers and the Royal Pavilion — were closed, and at night a blackout was in force. With fears of an invasion high, there were few other guests in the usually crammed hotel. Even the view from his room depressed him. Facing out to sea, it overlooked the West Pier, where engineers were working around the clock to cut out large sections of the pier in order to prevent it being used as a landing stage by the Germans.

Along Victoria Street, newspaper vendors were shouting the headlines of the day. 'Deadlock at Nantes'; 'Hospital Ship Sunk in the Channel'; 'The Enemy Reports Victory at Amiens'. Charlie's views on the duration of the war had altered. A former captain in the Blues, at the outset he had predicted 'three months of explosion and then stoppage by general consent'. But the entrenchment of both the German and British armies along the hundred-mile Front in France and Flanders had convinced him that it would go on for much longer.

His cousin, Lawrence Drummond, an officer in the Scots Guards, had given him a first-hand report of the Battle of Mons. 'His experiences are remarkable,' he wrote to John:

He was first in command of a Brigade on the extreme left, and had 5 days and nights' incessant fighting of a most terrible kind. His praise of English men's fighting is enormous, the first true opinion I have heard which can't have a suspicion of exaggeration. In many cases the men were dead beat and were asleep the moment they touched the ground, but never a difficulty in rousing them at a moment's notice when a move was necessary. The German rifle shooting was as bad as our own was good, but their shell fire is described as the most wonderful they have ever seen. Absolutely incessant all those days and nights and the air literally ablaze with shells the whole time. He said a good deal about the perfectly indescribable noise and concussion of 4 or 5 Army Corps firing at the same moment. The enormous and fearful shellfire is what seems to have surprised him most and also the very perfect behaviour of our men under really bad circumstances.

In recent weeks, long lists of casualties had begun to appear in the newspapers. Already, the sons of people he knew were being killed or wounded: 'You were quite right about Aubrey Herbert,'* he wrote to John on 17 September: 'I am told he is in a French hospital not much the worse, but I see Percy Wyndham† is killed — hard luck. I fear poor little John Manners‡ is a washout. He has been described as dead (also Lord Cecil's boy).§ Albemarle's boy¶ is wounded and a prisoner but supposed to be going on well.'

The thought that John might soon be fighting on the Western Front was one that Charlie was struggling to come to terms with. For almost two months now, he had known exactly what Violet was up to: she had kept

* Aubrey Herbert, second son of the 4th Earl of Carnarvon.
† Percy Wyndham, grandson of the 1st Baron Leconfield.
‡ John Manners, eldest son of the 2nd Baron Manners.
§ George Edward Gascoyne-Cecil, son of Lord Edward, fourth son of the 3rd Marquis of Salisbury.
¶ Captain Hon. Rupert Keppel, third son of the 8th Earl of Albemarle.

him informed of her every move. Yet he had said nothing to John. It was the first time he had withheld information of material importance to him. The problem was, he wanted his sister to succeed in her bid to keep him back from the war. John was his mainstay; for twenty years, Charlie's life had revolved around his nephew. He couldn't face the prospect of losing him.

The news from Violet was encouraging. John had told him that the North Midlands were on standby to leave at any moment; yet her intelligence suggested that it would be a while before they left England. Further, when they did, it would not be for the Western Front, but to replace regular army troops manning garrisons in the outposts of the empire.

Violet's intelligence had come from Lord Grenfell. Nine days earlier, on 7 October, she had finally managed to see him. 'Darling C, nothing definite,' she reported back after the meeting: 'Only that he is sure they will not be going to the Front for a year! I did feel comforted talking to him. And he also says the Territorials will go to <u>replace</u> — places like India, Malta etc.'

Violet had sought to corroborate Grenfell's information. That morning, she had forwarded Charlie a copy of a note that had come from Dr Donald Hood. 'Send me this back and phone, darling. Rather a comfort, isn't it?' Hood's note contained classified information, which his brother had passed him: 'I heard last night that under present regulations no Territorials will leave for another 3 months, and then the first lots will go to various garrison duties such as Malta, Egypt and Gibraltar.'

Hood's brother was a senior civil servant at the War Office. 'Don't ever give his name, or his informant away,' Violet cautioned Charlie: 'Fearfully Private.'

Later that afternoon, when Charlie got home from the Army and Navy Stores, he wrote to John. He did not report the important news that Violet had conveyed that morning:

Dear Jacko,

Army & Navy are sending you (and you should get them tomorrow) 3 pairs of their thickest vests and drawers. Not Jaeger, as they don't keep them, and say there are others far better in every way.

I'm not sure I was very pleased with them but they are the best they have got. Also 5 pairs of thick woollen socks. They, of course, will take them back if you don't like them, and on hearing from you I will at once go to Jaeger or elsewhere and enquire. Soft thick socks are of course useless as they don't wear for a day.

The air pillow from A & N is the one

mostly used, they say. I told them also to send you 2 sleeping caps. The knitted one, though hardish, is what has been proved to be far better than the soft things that are now made because it clings tight to the head. The torch was not to be had at the Stores. They say they had 50 of them last week but sold them all in 2 hours. But I found out that they came from Ian Steward in the Strand, and though he had none left, he has sworn to send you one tonight. I saw his sample one. You will have to understand — for instantaneous light you press one button, for prolonged light you press the smaller button and twist it a little round. If you want a light not to show up, you keep the leather top of the case closed.

I am going to Brighton again tonight. So if you wire, wire both places. No other news that I know of. Brighton is like martial law — no lights at night etc. I don't suppose I shall go on long with this going down there for the night, as it is rather a bother coming up early in the morning, but I get gloomy alone in London in the evenings. Hope to see you again v soon.

John replied straightaway:

My dear Old Boy

I am glad to hear you have gone to Brighton for the night as I can't bear to think of you being depressed in the evenings at 97 — although 97 has quite the most undepressing effect on me, I can quite understand its effect on you nowadays.

I should no doubt feel the same but, old boy, do not let it get the better of you, will you. We will have jolly times yet at 97 with all our old ideas of perfect interest and comfort in full force and tiles* running wild all over the place.

I hope you don't mind my giving you all these commissions but you are the only person who is sure to get the right things.

No news of any importance. If little Ariel is of any comfort to you, mind you collar hold of him.

Take care of yourself old boy, won't you — you will promise this, won't you.

The next day — on 17 October — John wired Charlie to tell him that the North Midlands had received orders to embark for the Front. They were leaving on the 30th.

Violet's intelligence, it appeared, was wrong.

* John and Charlie collected medieval tiles. Their collection included a number of whole pavements from Halesowen Abbey and Rievaulx.

Violet was at 16 Arlington Street, her London home in Piccadilly, when Charlie's telegram arrived. He had sent it as soon as he had heard from John. It was almost three o'clock. Outside, in the cobbled courtyard, which was screened from the street by an imposing set of arched gates, her chauffeur waited to take her to King's Cross, where she was to catch the train to Belvoir.

The minute Violet received the telegram she telephoned Dr Hood. It was his brother, Basil, who had told her that the North Midlands would not be going to France for 'at least 3 months'. Before calculating her next move, she wanted to establish whether Charlie's information was correct. 'Go straight to the War Office,' Hood advised her: 'I'll tell Basil to expect you.'

Some minutes later, a footman opened the front door in the pillared hall and Violet hurried past him. She was dressed in the clothes she habitually wore for an outing to London:

a long tweed suit — 'greenish-greyish-bluish-fawnish with tabs and smoky flat pearl buttons', as Diana described it — high-heeled pointed shoes with buckles, and a three-cornered hat with panaches of cocks' feathers. Clattering down the short flight of stone steps that led up to the front door, she crossed the courtyard to the waiting car.

The War Office was in Whitehall. On the approach to it, crowds of men spilled from the pavement on to the road. They were queuing to volunteer for the war. To accommodate the flood of recruits, the authorities had opened a second office in Trafalgar Square. The clothes, and the hats the men wore — bowlers, trilbys, flat caps and boaters — showed them to be of all classes. So great was the crush, they were pressed up against the car. Drawn by the Duke's peacock crest, which was painted on the outside of it, they peered in curiously at Violet, looking to see who was inside it.

Valuable minutes were lost as her chauffeur was forced to inch his way through the crowd. Violet did not have much time; she was in London on a pretext. On leaving Belvoir at 'cockcrow' that morning, she had told Henry that she had an appointment to see the senior matron at Guy's Hospital, where Diana was hoping to work as a nurse. She had promised to be back by teatime.

The true purpose of her visit to London,

which Charlie alone knew, was to see Lord Curzon, the former Viceroy of India. Safe in the belief that the North Midland Division would not be going to the Front for some time, Violet had not attached any great urgency to the meeting. However, mindful that he might be of use at some point in the future, she was anxious to establish whether he would be prepared to help her. The meeting, which had taken place at midday in the privacy of her drawing room at Arlington Street, had not gone well. 'I asked him private and loving advice, telling him not to preach at me,' she wrote to Charlie after seeing him: 'He wonders why I did not earlier in the day manage a Motor Ambulance thing for John for service in France. He gives me Lord Norreys's address, St John's Gate, as the person to apply to for Volunteer Motor Service. But he adds I daresay this may be too late if by going on ESW's Staff he already looks upon himself, or is looked upon by others, as a full-blown soldier!!'

The War Office stood opposite Horse Guards Parade. A long, seven-storey building constructed of Portland stone in the Edwardian Baroque style, it was built as a symbol of Britain's imperial power. It had four domed corner towers; along the roof were placed sculptured figures, representing Peace, War, Justice, Truth, Fame and Victory.

It was with a 'heavy heart' that Violet

stepped from her car outside the main entrance to the building. She had failed to find a means of keeping John out of the war. Now, if the news contained in Charlie's telegram was true, there was very little time left.

Entering the Grand Hall, she was met with a scene of chaos.

'One of the greatest worries to which War Office officials were exposed during those anxious times,' remembered Sir Charles Callwell, Director of Military Operations, 'was a bent on the part of individuals, who they had not the slightest wish to see, for demanding — and obtaining — interviews.'

On that Saturday afternoon in mid-October, the Grand Hall was as crowded as the streets outside. The thousand-room building, with its 'furlongs' of corridors, was the engine room of the war. Its 2,500 staff — rising rapidly to 22,500 as the numbers joining Britain's armed forces swelled — were in charge of all matters connected to the British Army. Effectively, they were responsible for five armies: the army fighting on the battlefields abroad; the army of men under training at home; the armies guarding garrisons in outposts of the empire; the army of sick and wounded; and the armies of soldiers' dependants to whom the Ministry of War paid allowances and pensions.

'A mere recital of official events would fail

to convey a true impression of the life lived at that time in the War Office,' Hampden Gordon, an assistant secretary at the War Office recalled: 'The atmosphere of those crowded months is difficult to recapture now. Some personal impressions alone can be given; the thronged hall, the hurrying escorts, the countless enquirers, the sudden arrival of news — at last — flashed from the Front in secret cipher, the dispatch to Sir John French of the bag by means of which urgent and secret letters were carried by hand to headquarters in France, the painfulness of the casualty lists and the constant enquiries from relatives and friends, the comings and goings of Cabinet Ministers and emissaries from all parties, the procession of princes, over-age peers, politicians, journalists, cinematographers.'

To marshal unwanted visitors, the ministry employed a brigade of boy scouts. 'They helped to keep such people at bay,' Sir Charles Callwell recalled: 'They took *lasciate ogni speranza, voi ch'entrate** for their motto, and adopted the method of herding the intruders into an unattractive apartment on the ground floor, as tube attendants herd subterranean travellers into the lifts, and of

* 'Abandon all hope, ye who enter here' — the supposed inscription at the entrance to Hell from Dante's *Divine Comedy*.

keeping the intruders there until they verged on a condition of mutiny. They then enlarged them in big parties, each of which was taken control of by a scout, who led his charges round and round and in and out along the corridors, and up and down between floors, carefully avoiding the elevators, until the victims were in a state of physical and mental collapse. If one of the party quitted the ranks while on the trek, to read the name marked up on some door that he was passing, the scout called a halt — it would never have done to permit that sort of thing because the visitor might conceivably have noticed the name of the very official whom he had come to see.'

Violet had not been kept 'at bay' by the scouts. The word 'Duchess', printed on her calling card, ensured that she did not have to wait long to see Basil Hood. No sooner had she handed it to a scout than he escorted her up to his office on the first floor.

Hood, a bachelor in his mid-fifties, was Private Secretary to General Edward Bethune, the Director of Territorial Forces. At the general's invitation, he had joined the ministry a few days after war was declared. He did not fit the mould of a War Office official: a former captain in the Green Howards, he had retired from the army to become a librettist and lyricist. Best known for his long-

454

running hit show, *Gentleman Joe,* he wrote musical comedies and Savoy Operas. He had also collaborated with the composer Arthur Sullivan, famous for his work with Sir William Gilbert, to adapt continental operettas — notably *The Merry Widow* and *The Dollar Princess.*

It was General Bethune's love of musical comedy and opera that led him to employ Hood as his private secretary. They had met in the 1890s when they were serving in India and had remained friends ever since. Born in 1865, Bethune — the second son of a Scottish laird — joined the Gordon Highlanders when he was twenty. A hugely popular officer, famous, as a contemporary noted, for his 'fondness of theatricals and all other forms of social amusement', he achieved notoriety following the accident that resulted in the loss of his right hand. 'During a performance of *The Sorcerer,* in which he was playing a leading part,' *The Times* reported, 'he placed too large a quantity of explosive in the magic teapot, which thereupon blew up, inflicting such injuries on his right hand that it was amputated at the wrist.' To the amazement and admiration of his contemporaries, he continued 'to ride uncommonly well', commanding a troop of mounted infantry — known as Bethune's Horse — in the Boer War. In 1901, his bravery in action was rewarded with the command of a cavalry brigade. Thereafter, he rose rapidly to the rank of Lieutenant-General, largely thanks to his close friendship with Sir Ian Hamilton, then Chief of Staff to Lord Kitchener.

Hood's office was in an anteroom next to Bethune's. The moment Violet arrived — and to her surprise — he ushered her in to see the general.

The chance meeting gave her the breakthrough she had been waiting for. As soon as it was over she wrote to Charlie in a state of breathless excitement:

I went straight to see Hood's brother on receipt of your telegram and he made me see General Bethune — a divine man. Divine! (Ought to have got to him at the start. You and I would have been happier.) For he is going to take the matter in his own hands. He understands!

I mentioned you as a professional soldier who could see no way out, and that you and you only had my confidence. I told him John could neither wield a sword or shoot anything (but partridges or grouse)! Nor ride well enough and had had no teaching whatever like real soldiers have, as he had never been one — and had only been out 1 month all told with the Territorials, so he was utterly ignorant of warfare. But was a good chauffeur — and practical — otherwise no soldier!!

He heard my case and is going to 'see to it'!! 'Trust me,' he said. It would be in the sense of John not being a soldier! And having no experience. 'We shall do a lot of weeding. Leave it to me!'

Oh, Charlie, I nearly died. Thank God for Hood and for his brother, and thank God that I got your telegram when I did. Bethune considers ESW★ a 'blustering empty ass'.

Your wire came through just as I was starting for the train. I now go by the 6.30.

Yr loving VR

The following day — a damp, grey Sunday throughout the entirety of which the low cloud shrouding the castle failed to lift above its turrets and towers — Violet did not emerge from her bedroom until after lunch.

The elation she had felt after seeing General Bethune had faded. On waking, she had a splitting headache, and when Tritton, her maid, brought in her breakfast tray, the news from the servants' quarters was upsetting. Few of the castle's indoor and outdoor servants had clocked in for work that morning. They had stayed at home to spend the last precious hours with soldiers from the North Midlands who had been given leave to

★ Edward Stuart Wortley, the commanding officer of the North Midlands.

return to their villages to say goodbye to their families.

A telegram from Lord Kitchener, with whom she sought every opportunity to ingratiate herself, had also irritated her. A guest of Lord Brownlow's at the nearby Belton House, he had declined her invitation to tea: 'Kitchener lunching at Belton today — no time to come <u>here</u>,' she wrote crossly to Charlie.

Uppermost in her mind, though, was John. In the cold light of day — and with just a fortnight to go before the North Midlands' departure for the Front — she doubted whether Bethune would be able to do anything. Lying fretting in bed, she confided her thoughts to her brother: 'Of course all my high hopes for things to get better for me seem to dwindle in face of "thinking it out",' she told him: 'Bethune said something about untrained men (which he calls John) — "I shall do a lot of weeding." But what can he do? I have sent him by train a long letter putting the details of John's case before him — so that he <u>knows</u> details of how and when and where. <u>Now I must be silent to everyone but you.</u> He comforted me amazingly in the moment. But a fortnight is short, my dear, and can John be considered as untrained!!? I feel lots of hope at times and cold sweat at others. I wish I could see you. <u>Write</u> a lot. Nothing can make me worse than I am.'

That same day — 18 October — a hundred miles away, General Bethune was at his desk at the War Office in Whitehall. He had been there since dawn.

Though it was a Sunday, lights blazed throughout the building. Out on the Western Front, a major offensive was in progress. Everywhere, everyone was in a high state of alert; along the corridors, military aides and attachés hurried to and fro delivering memoranda between departments; in the principal rooms overlooking Horse Guards Parade, the Chief of the Imperial General Staff, the Permanent Under-Secretary, the Adjutant-General, and their senior advisers stood scrutinizing maps of the battleground, which hung on the walls suspended from giant rollers. Two floors below, in the most closely guarded section of the building, armies of specially trained cipher clerks were working at full stretch to decrypt the reams of coded communiqués coming in from General Headquarters at St Omer.

Thirty miles to the east of GHQ, along a 25-mile line that stretched from La Bassée in the south to Ypres in the north, the British Expeditionary Force was poised to attack. Massed on either side of it were the French and Belgian armies.

The offensive, planned by Marshal Foch, Assistant Commander-in-Chief of the French Army, and Field Marshal Sir John French, the Commander-in-Chief of the British Expeditionary Force, was designed to win the war. For five weeks now, in the southern sector of the line, the Germans had failed to gain ground. After halting their advance on the Marne, the Allied armies had pushed them back to the Aisne. The chance had come at last to outflank the Kaiser's army. If the attack, centred on Ypres, succeeded, they could liberate Belgium and force the Germans out of France. The stakes, however, were high; if the attack failed, and the French and British armies were overrun, there was nothing to stop the Germans from reaching the Channel ports, where they could launch a strike against England.

So confident was Sir John in the success of the offensive, he was willing to risk his entire army. At the battles that had preceded it — Mons, Le Cateau, the Marne and the Aisne — British losses had been unexpectedly heavy: 31,709 men had been killed or wounded — far in excess of the figure that actuaries at the War Office had estimated at the outset of the fighting. To bring the BEF back to strength, four new divisions — a force of upwards of fifty thousand men — had been rushed to the Front from England, as had every last available reservist. Until the territorial divisions arrived — of which the North Midland was to be the first — Sir John had no other reserves to fall back on.

Two days earlier, General Smith-Dorrien, the Commander of II Corps, had questioned the field marshal's strategy. 'He was sad and depressed at the condition of his two divisions,' Sir John noted in his diary: 'He says they have never got over the shock of Le Cateau — that the officers he has been sent to replace his tremendous losses are untrained and ignorant and that there is no great fighting spirit throughout the Corps.'

It was true of half the British Army. Of the 154,000 soldiers massed along the 25-mile Front, 50,000 had been fighting almost continuously since the third week in August. Still reeling from their experiences, the men were exhausted and demoralized and their stocks of supplies and ammunition were low.

Prior to the offensive, Smith-Dorrien's was the only voice of dissent. At the War Office in London, Britain's senior military commanders shared Sir John's conviction that with one more push the war could be won. Yet that

461

Sunday morning, as they stood gathered in front of maps of the battleground, no sooner had the offensive begun than their carefully drawn plans began to go awry.

At 7.10 the previous evening, General Rawlinson, the commanding officer of IV Corps, had been given what the chiefs at the War Office considered to be a relatively simple task: at first light, he was to attack Menin, a small, strategically important town to the east of Ypres. No opposition was expected; the few German units defending the town were isolated outposts, lightly manned.

By noon it was evident from the communiqués flying between GHQ and IV Corps HQ at the Front that Rawlinson had failed to carry out the order. Initially, after a liaison officer was dispatched to IV Corps HQ to investigate the reason for the delay, a mix-up over the wording of the order was blamed, and at 13.45 hours new orders were telephoned through to him. But still, Rawlinson held back. He had received intelligence to suggest that large numbers of German units were concentrated at Courtrai, twelve miles to the east of Menin. Until he could verify the report, he was not prepared to risk his troops in the attack.

The report was one of a number that had trickled through that week. They had come from spies in the occupied zone who, besides telling of German troops concentrated at Courtrai, had reported a large force congregating from the north. Yet the heavy cloud that had shrouded the Flanders plain throughout the week had made it impossible for the Royal Flying Corps to send up their spotter planes to verify the reports.

The following morning, the cloud lifted, proving that Rawlinson was right to be cautious. At 10.30 a.m., when the grounded reconnaissance planes were at last able to take to the skies, the pilots spotted a vast army on the move. Flying high above the designated battleground, they could see German soldiers converging in their thousands. The long lines of guns and troops were coming up fast on the roads across the plain. And they were making for the British lines in front of Ypres.

They were the troops of the Fourth Army. Unbeknown to Sir John French and the High Command at the War Office, in the break since the fighting on the Aisne, the Germans had also been planning an offensive. Their intention was to encircle the BEF. Stealthily, under cover of darkness, they had moved their soldiers into position. Commanded by Albrecht, Duke of Württemberg, the Fourth Army had 130 infantry and rifle battalions and 20 cavalry squadrons. Standing facing the BEF, separated by a distance of just a few hundred yards in places, they outnumbered the British by two to one.

Extraordinarily, though the evidence of a large concentration of enemy troops was incontrovertible, when confronted with it, Sir John French refused to believe it. 'How the devil do you expect me to conduct my business, when you keep bringing up these new corps?' he thundered at Colonel George MacDonogh, his chief of intelligence. When MacDonogh, knowing the truth of the reports, threatened to resign, French still refused to believe him. Dismissing his intelligence out of hand, he accused MacDonogh of conjuring 'celestial' divisions and ordered his corps commanders — and particularly the recalcitrant Rawlinson — to press ahead with the attack.

His decision would cost him what remained of the original British Expeditionary Force. Numbering 84,000 in August 1914, at the close of the battle* the BEF had sustained losses of 82,060. The greater part of this loss fell on the infantry battalions that had landed in France in August. By mid-November, on average, only one officer and thirty-one other ranks remained in these battalions — a casualty rate of 97 per cent.

But this was to come.

On that fateful Sunday, around the time

* The First Battle of Ypres, 19 October–22 November 1914.

that Sir John French sent his adjutant to IV Corps HQ to investigate why Rawlinson had failed to attack, Violet's letter arrived at the War Office.

Addressed to General Bethune, it contained the 'details of John's case' — the 'how and when and where', as she had cryptically mentioned to Charlie.

The letter has not survived; the general probably destroyed it as soon as he had read it. But at some point later that afternoon, he set aside his war work to compose a reply to her.

'My Dear Duchess,' he wrote:

I received your letter this afternoon. No one shall ever know that I have been in communication with you over this matter.

I have started on one project — which may or may not succeed. If it does not then I must try something else. One thing and one only will be an insuperable block, and that will only occur if your son insists on going with the Division. We could do nothing against that, but I must try and devise some means of getting round that.

Even as a professional soldier I cannot see that there is any good reason for his going on the continent untrained.

I will do all I can to help and no one

shall trace your influence in the matter.

                                    Believe me,
                         Yours very sincerely,
                              Edward Bethune

The 'project' he had 'started on' had necessitated writing another letter. It was to
General Edward Stuart Wortley, the commanding officer of the North Midland Division. Acting on information that Violet had
given him, he told the general that John was
concealing a serious heart condition. Until
he could supply the War Office with a certificate of good health, he was not to embark for
France with the division.

While there was a grain of truth in the story
Violet span to General Bethune, she had lied
to him. She knew there was nothing seriously
wrong with John's heart. Some years before,
it was Dr Hood who had first detected that
his heartbeat was arrhythmic. But, as he had
assured Violet, it did not point to a serious
condition. John smoked upwards of sixty
cigarettes a day: Hood's view was that the action of his heart was being overstimulated by
excessive amounts of nicotine.

Six weeks before the meeting with General
Bethune, Violet had forced John to seek a
second opinion. In the hope that he did in
fact have a more serious condition — one
that would keep him out of the war — she

had sent him to see Dr Colman, a leading heart specialist. He had concurred with Dr Hood:

My Dear Duchess,
I am glad to say there is nothing more serious than cigarettes.

His heart is perfectly sound. There is a little irritability due entirely to tobacco. I gave him something to quiet his cough, but have told him knocking off cigarettes for three weeks is the only thing that will be of use. I do not think, in any case, you need be especially anxious about him.

Events moved quickly after General Stuart Wortley received General Bethune's letter.

At four o'clock on the afternoon of 19 October, a telegram boy appeared over the brow of the hill at the top of the drive leading up to the castle. Hot and breathless after the long cycle from the post office in Woolsthorpe, he propped his bicycle against the battlements and crossed the terrace to the small priest's door that was set into the corner of the portico. There, he handed the telegram to the hall porter.

The telegram — addressed to Her Grace the Duchess of Rutland — was from Henry, who was at Boodles, his club in London. He had just had lunch with General Stuart Wortley:

Have seen ESW. He takes Division abroad. He has had letter from War Office which utterly perplexes me. Am writing to you but fear you must come London tomorrow as position is very difficult and unpleasant and I cannot explain by wire. Rutland.

Straightaway, Violet forwarded the telegram on to Charlie. Knowing there was nothing wrong with John's heart, and dreading the 'interview' with her husband, she scrawled a note on the back of it: 'This means Bethune has done something!! Oh I am frightened!! If I come up tomorrow, I must see you before Henry.'

No record exists of what was said when Violet and Henry met. But it is clear from the fragments of evidence that remain at Belvoir that it was Charlie, not Violet, who orchestrated what happened over the course of the next twenty-four hours.

The details are sketchy. Almost immediately, to suit his own objectives, and for reasons of realpolitik, Charlie swore the principal players to secrecy. But, at a few minutes to three o'clock the day after Stuart Wortley received General Bethune's letter, John emerged through the arch that led from the courtyard outside his parents' house. Looking fit and tanned after the long hours spent training with the North Midlands at Luton, he was wearing his service uniform. Turning left, he headed up Arlington Street towards Piccadilly.

He had come up to London for the afternoon to obtain the medical certificate the authorities at the War Office were demanding. It was a crisp fine day and he was enjoying the break from the routine at Luton. After his appointment with the doctor, he planned to go to Maggs, the antiquarian bookseller. Then he was hoping to have tea with Charlie. Exactly how the War Office had got wind of his heart condition puzzled him. But he was not anticipating a problem; only the previous month, Dr Colman had pronounced his heart 'sound'.

After passing Gordon Selfridge's house, and the Marquis of Salisbury's, he crossed the road and rang the doorbell at number 7 Arlington Street. A tall narrow Georgian house, it was the home of Dr Vernon-Jones, an eminent GP.

What John did not know as he stood on the doorstep waiting for the doctor's servant to answer the bell was that the outcome of the medical examination that was to follow had been predetermined.

That morning, after catching an early train from Belvoir, Violet saw Dr Hood at Arlington Street. At Charlie's instigation, she asked him to persuade Vernon-Jones to deliver the diagnosis they required: 'Hood absolutely alive to all our wishes,' she reported back to her brother: 'says he can easily tell him in confidence exactly the importance of the delay etc and can vouch for its coming out as we wish.'

Whether — fortuitously for Violet and Charlie — Dr Colman was unavailable that afternoon, or whether they persuaded John that it was Vernon-Jones and not Colman that he should see, is not clear. What is clear, however, is that the doctor did exactly as

Hood asked him.

Shortly after the appointment, Vernon-Jones's servant retraced John's route along Arlington Street. At the gatehouse to number 16, he handed a letter to Mrs Seed, the Rutlands' elderly gatekeeper.

The letter, which was addressed to the Duke, contained a short summary of the results of John's medical examination:

7 Arlington St
London, S.W.

My Dear Sir
I am sorry to say that I found Lord Granby's heart very rapid in action and intermittent and dilated.
I should hardly think that the War Office knowing this would let him go on Active Service.
Believe me, My Lord Duke
Yours faithfully
L. Vernon-Jones

In the twenty-four hours that had intervened since Henry's lunch with General Stuart Wortley, it seems that Violet had talked her husband round; when he showed John the contents of the letter, he forbade him from getting a second opinion.
The row that ensued has to be imagined.

The cross words exchanged between John and his parents on that 'uncomfortable afternoon' — as Charlie would later refer to it — were not recorded. But the fact that there was a blazing row, one in which John accused his mother of influencing Vernon-Jones's decision, a decision which, before leaving that evening for Luton, he told her he intended to challenge, becomes apparent on reading the letter that Charlie sent him the following morning:

Jacko,
It struck me that the whole of that uncomfortable afternoon of yesterday should be a complete washout in the minds of the three people besides yourself who took part in it. Consequently your mother has not breathed one word (nor ever will) about it to a soul on earth. Your father I will see before he sees anyone else. I don't, of course, know what decision has been arrived at — but should there be any difficulty about your getting out, I not only wish to shield your mother from any suspicion of having meddled with it, even amongst her most intimate friends, but also to save you from having to accuse her of anything of the kind. This is I believe sound.

As to your mother, she assures me that nothing she has ever said to anyone could possibly explain what has happened.

Forgive me for writing in this way.

Remember that no one has any suspicion of what occurred yesterday.

His letter was as cruel as it was deceitful. The one hope John had of contesting the doctor's verdict was to accuse his mother of having influenced it. Knowing that he was desperate to get out to France, Charlie was seeking to stall the only means he had of getting there. His message was clear: he was not to risk his mother's reputation: his loyalty to her must take precedence over his duty to his country.

Intentionally, he had forced John into a corner. There was a further subtext to the carefully calculated wording of his letter. By assuring him that no one had 'any suspicion of what occurred', he was trying to convince him that, if he were to accept the doctor's diagnosis, the story would never get out. Knowing John mistrusted his parents' discretion, in swearing Violet and Henry to secrecy, Charlie was hoping to persuade John that it was safe for him to duck out of the war.

John's reply to Charlie's letter is missing from the Muniment Rooms at Belvoir. But shortly after receiving it, showing great courage and in defiance of Charlie's ensnarement, he confided in General Stuart Wortley.

It was then that the general decided to take

the matter into his own hands.

Early the next morning — Thursday 22 October — the general's chauffeur-driven Rolls-Royce turned off Piccadilly into Arlington Street. Progressing at a stately pace, it drew up outside number 7.

Stuart Wortley was there to see Dr Vernon-Jones. He had not made an appointment.

Stepping smartly from the car, he cut an impressive figure. Six feet four, and of a slim, muscular frame, he had startlingly blue eyes and was strikingly handsome; the rank badge of a major-general — a crossed sword and baton with a star above — was woven on the epaulettes of his uniform and a double band of twisted gold braid adorned the peak of his cap. 'A darling of the Gods,' as *Vanity Fair* gushingly described him, and a hero of the Battle of Omdurman, he was descended from John Stuart, 3rd Earl of Bute. Following a difficult childhood, when he was forced to leave Eton because his alcoholic father could not pay the bills, his army career had been far from conventional. After failing the exams for Sandhurst, he had worked his way up through the ranks. Famous for his short temper, he was known to be a strict disciplinarian. Controversially, in 1899, he ordered the Italian crew of a ship carrying a cargo of mules to the Boer War to be flogged. The men had treated the mules so badly during the voyage that most of the animals had died. It was after corporal punishment had been abolished in the British Army, and he had only narrowly escaped being court-martialled.

As he mounted the steps to the doctor's house, the general was not in a good humour. The unscheduled visit to London necessitated losing precious hours out of his morning; with just a week to go before his division embarked for the Front, he had innumerable details to attend to.

The conversation that followed was brief; there was just one question he wanted to ask the doctor. Infuriated by his response, Stuart Wortley left in a hurry, instructing his chauffeur to drive him straight back to Luton. As soon as he got there, he wrote a stern letter to the Duke:

My dear Henry,
I happened to have to go to London today for an hour and saw Dr Vernon-Jones. I put him the question straight — whether he considered Granby was in any real danger owing to his heart, to which he replied 'No'.

As he was passed fit for active service at Leicester, I see no reason to go against the doctor's opinion on that occasion.

I am stopping his excessive smoking.

I should be sorry to see a nice smart

boy like him ruined by staying at home, eating his heart out, which he would do.

I do not, therefore, intend to take any further steps in the matter.

My medical officers here support my action and do not consider that any grave risks are being run.

Yours very sincerely,
Edward Stuart Wortley

The general's obduracy wrecked Bethune's plot. After writing to the Duke, Stuart Wortley told the War Office that John was fit for active service and that he could vouch for his health.

Two days later, John drove up to Belvoir to say goodbye to his mother. Despite the embarrassment she had caused him, after returning to Luton he wrote her a touching letter in which he did his best to console her:

Mother My Dear

I did not say much to you at Belvoir on purpose as everything one says is always more likely to depress one. You must not be depressed as everything will turn out well in the end — and even if I had been in Kitchener's army I should have had to go out in the end. In fact every more or less able-bodied man will have to go before the war is finished.

I do hope you do not feel too miserable

as I hate to think of you having any form of worry — so try to forget all about it, won't you.

Yet even as John was writing this letter, Violet and General Bethune were already hatching a second plot.

44

'I have started on one project — which may or may not succeed. If it does not then I must try something else.'

This was the promise Bethune gave Violet when he launched his first attempt to stop John from going out to the Front. 'One thing and one only will be an insuperable block,' the general continued, 'and that will only occur if your son insists on going with the Division. We could do nothing against that, but I must try and devise some means of getting round that.'

In those last weeks in October, Bethune was privy to secret discussions in progress at the War Office. He knew that while the North Midlands were under orders to embark for France, behind the scenes in Whitehall, the army chiefs were still debating whether or not to send them.

It was part of a wider debate regarding the territorial divisions. Despite the urgent need for reinforcements, a question mark hung over the territorials' readiness for battle. The problem confronting the military commanders was that the standard of training within the individual divisions was inconsistent. While some brigades were ready, others required further preparation. The talk, therefore, was of breaking up the divisions. Those brigades that were up to standard would go out to France; the remainder would be held back in England.

General Bethune played a central part in these discussions. As the commander in charge of Britain's 280,000-strong territorial army, it was his job to assess the divisions and to advise the Secretary of State which of them — or which brigades — were ready to go out to the Front.

At the eleventh hour, five days before the North Midlands were due to embark for France, Lord Kitchener decided to delay their departure by a few weeks. While he held the division in high regard, he was of the view that some of the brigades needed further training.

The reprieve gave Bethune the opportunity to launch his second 'project'. Far more audacious than his first, it turned on an extravagant abuse of his position.

John, as he had feared, *had* become the 'insuperable block'; he *was* insisting on 'going with his Division'. There was nothing Bethune could do to stop him wanting to go, but he could stop the North Midlands from going. Regardless of their actual readiness — and they were almost ready, which is why they had been selected as the first of the territorial divisions to be deployed on active service — and solely for the sake of the 28-year-old Marquis, he advised Lord Kitchener to break up the division. Just one of the brigades was of fighting standard, he argued: the other two, including John's, should be held in reserve in England. Further, as John was ADC to General Stuart Wortley, to make doubly certain there was no question of him getting out to the Front with his general, Bethune urged Kitchener to appoint Stuart Wortley as the commander-in-chief of the reserve brigades.

Kitchener, however, refused to agree to Bethune's proposal. Violet gave her own rendition of the conversations that took place between them. 'The interview wasn't <u>very happy</u>,' she wrote to Charlie after a meeting with Bethune: 'K of K <u>so</u> difficult whenever B tries to take things away from ESW — like bits. K of K says <u>no</u> — no — I can't tell you why, but NO — I want to keep it intact. B argues but <u>some</u> bits are SO ready, why not take them and send them out — but NO. His — B's — idea was to so pull the Division to pieces that Eddy SW would only be left to look after the <u>Reserve</u> portions.'

Early in November, Bethune — whom

480

Violet was beginning to think a 'buffoon' —
admitted defeat. In desperation, he suggested
that Henry ask Lord Kitchener to spare the
North Midlands. Even Violet, as she confided
to Charlie, thought it a ludicrous suggestion:

> B says K of K is fond of Dukes! But I
> said how can Henry ask K of K to keep a
> Division back to please him and me!! B
> agreed.

In the interim, Violet had in fact been in
touch with Lord Kitchener herself. Whether
she told Bethune that she had written to the
Secretary of State for War, or whether she
concealed it from him, is not clear. But — as
it turned out — it was Kitchener's reply to
her letter, rather than Bethune's manoeuvrings, that determined her course of action
in the coming weeks.

Her letter was a last resort, sent in a moment of desperation. Her friends and infor-
mants, wary of Kitchener's dislike for women,
had told her that on no account must she approach him herself. But secretly — somewhere alone in the castle — she had written
it the weekend that John had come to Belvoir
to say goodbye to her.

Violet's letter has not survived; but Kitchener's reply was among the gold-dusted letters
that she kept separately from the rest of her
papers.

At the time the Secretary of State for War was writing, he was grappling with the loss of almost a third of his army in the First Battle of Ypres. It was his arm that pointed on the poster 'Your Country Needs You'. Yet even he showed signs of falling for Violet's charms. His letter, which was handwritten, hinted that he was willing to make an exception for John:

War Office,
Whitehall, S.W.

My dear Duchess
General Wortley's Division is not going abroad yet.

If you feel nervous about your boy would it not be better for him to be ADC to a General on the home defence?

I am afraid Wortley's Division is the first to go when territorial divisions are sent unless some other Division is better trained, but there is no intention at present of sending territorial divisions as they are not sufficiently trained.

I am rather busy so excuse this scrawl.

Despite its less than bellicose tone, it was not the reply Violet was hoping for. She knew the North Midlands would not be going to the Front for a while. Bethune had told her. *Force majeure* — in the form of an order — was all that could stop John from going out to France. The Secretary of State for War had merely suggested he join the staff of a general on home defence; evidently, he was not going to help her. He had not offered to find him a position; nor, as she was expecting, had he offered to appoint John to his staff.

Violet, however, was not going to give up. After seeing Kitchener's letter, she decided to alter her focus. She had exhausted all means of keeping John back in England but, if he must go, the safest place on the Western Front was General Headquarters. Her goal now was to persuade Field Marshal Sir John French, the Commander-in-Chief of the British Army in France, to appoint John to the General Staff.

Violet did not know the field marshal personally. But this time — unlike with Lord Kitchener — she had a direct entrée to French. His closest friend — a 'sinister' American called George Gordon Moore — was in love with her daughter Diana.

Moore — as Violet knew — was a controversial figure. Aged thirty-five, he was reputedly worth $5 million.* His fortune, made quickly and at a young age, had come from railroad construction. But where he came from, and why he had moved to England, no one could say. His appearance fuelled the ru-

* The equivalent of almost $1 billion at today's values.

mours about him. Squat and muscular, he had the face of a gangster. His olive skin, and his eyes, which were a dark shade of brown — almost black — pointed, so people said, to his 'Red Indian' origins.

But it was Moore's hold over the 62-year-old field marshal that was the subject of constant speculation. Their friendship went back to the autumn of 1912, when they met, sailing from America on the cruise ship *Mauretania*. On their return to London, Moore invited Sir John, who was then ADC to King George V and Chief of the Imperial General Staff, to share a house with him. Ever since, they had been inseparable.

The house they shared — number 94 Lancaster Gate — was in Bayswater. An elegant six-storey stuccoed house, it overlooked Hyde Park and was staffed by twelve servants.

'Dined with Johnnie French at 94 Lancaster Gate,' Sir Henry Wilson, the field marshal's deputy, noted in his diary in March 1914: 'An enormous house and what he is doing there, I cannot think.'

Wilson was being ironic. Over the years, Sir John, who was married with three children, had had numerous beautiful and well-connected mistresses, and had been cited as co-respondent in at least one divorce action. Before he met Moore, the large sums he lavished on women and other pleasures had kept him deeply in debt. Moore, who idolized him, put up the capital for the house; he also insisted on paying its running expenses. The arrangement suited Sir John perfectly: it saved him from further financial embarrassment and reduced the risk of scandal. Behind closed doors at number 94, and away from his family, who were living in the modest house he rented in Hertfordshire, he was free to pursue his amorous liaisons, and — entirely at Moore's expense — to enjoy an extravagant lifestyle.

Before the war, the goings-on at number 94 had been the talk of London. Moore, who was also married, had left his wife and children in America. Night after night, the two men entertained a succession of actresses and glamorous widows, some of whom became their mistresses. They also hosted dinner parties and dances to which they invited the most powerful, most fashionable figures of the day. Winston Churchill, Lord Haldane, the Duke of Bedford, the Earl of Warwick and the painter Sir John Lavery were regular guests. So was Herbert Asquith. Unabashed, they included their 'feminine friends' — as Moore referred to them — on the guest list.

In Moore's eyes, by far the most prized was Lady Diana Manners. He had been in love with her since the summer of 1913. His interest had appalled Violet: 'Married!! And black

485

blood!!!' she exclaimed to Charlie in May 1914.

Now — five months later — his infatuation offered an invaluable entrée to the field marshal.

Violet had heard the gossip. War had not loosened Moore's hold over Sir John. To the irritation — and the bemusement — of the field marshal's colleagues, shortly after he was made Commander-in-Chief of the BEF, he had appointed Moore as his personal adviser. A room was reserved for him at General Headquarters. Whenever he visited, Sir John insisted that he sit in on meetings and battle conferences. He had also placed one of his two Rolls-Royces at the American's disposal, with a driver on standby to ferry him to and fro from the nearest railway station, or to take him to the military headquarters and establishments that French had asked him to inspect on his behalf.

Frequently, Moore cut short his visits to the Front to return to London in the hope of seeing Diana; on the face of it, there could be no better candidate to lobby the commander-in-chief.

But Diana was not in love with him; moreover, she was barely speaking to her mother.

These were the dual obstacles confronting Violet after she read Lord Kitchener's letter. As she pondered how to surmount them, outside in the courtyard of her house in Arlington Street, a footman was loading Diana's suitcase into the Duke's peacock-crested Rolls-Royce.

Diana was leaving home to join the nursing staff at Guy's Hospital.

Swallowing her pride, and at the very last minute, Violet decided to go with her.

45

The Duke's chauffeur drove them to the hospital. The day was cold and grey. Cradled in the back of the car, wrapped in travelling blankets, they said very little. They had been arguing about whether or not Diana should accept the job at Guy's for weeks. Violet sat 'sorrowing and silent', Diana remembered: 'I felt ashamed of having triumphed, but not in the least apprehensive. I do not think my mother was at all proud of me; she just hated the sordid, unvirginal aspect of it all and the loss of authority and protection.'

The car was travelling eastwards. Anxious to avoid eye contact, both women concentrated fixedly on the scenes around them. Familiar places glided past: St James's Park; Admiralty Arch; the Savoy Hotel; the Inns of Court along the Embankment; and the dome of St Paul's. Then, suddenly, after crossing Southwark Bridge, they were in a different world. Turning off Tooley Street into the maze of streets behind the hospital, the car slowed to a crawl. Inside it, the tension increased.

They had entered Shad Thames. Half a century earlier, Dickens had described it as 'the filthiest, the strangest, the most extraordinary of the many localities that are hidden in London'. A vast complex of Victorian warehouses, mills and factories, Shad Thames was situated behind St Saviour's Dock. To Dickens, it was riddled with 'every lineament of poverty, every loathsome indication of filth, rot and garbage'. One of the poorest districts in London, it was a place of 'dirt-besmeared walls and decaying foundations', where the windows, broken and patched, had poles thrust out 'on which to dry the linen that is never there'.

Violet and Diana were seeing what Dickens saw. Shad Thames had changed little since he had written about it. The buildings were black with the grime of industry; the cobbled streets, close and narrow. Stevedores wheeling trolleys and gangs of dockhands spilled out of the dingy alleyways that led off to the left and to the right. Craning their heads, they could see the prows of steamers projecting from the piers at the end of the streets.

Their progress was slow. Huge wooden crates were lined up against the walls of the warehouses; as the chauffeur inched the Rolls through the narrow streets, he had to stop and wait while the dock-hands winched the crates up to the gantries above. 'They swung them right over us. I thought they were going to fall on top of us!!' Diana reported excitedly to her sister. The noise — the shouts and whistles from the cast-iron walkways that linked the warehouses high above, the sound of metal banging against metal, the clank of winching chains and the rumble of barrels being rolled across the cobbles — was deafening. Large signs were painted on the outside of the warehouses, which were named after the spices stored inside them. Cayenne Court; Cumin Wharf; the Cardamom Building: there was a warehouse for each variety. Centuries of spices had infused the brickwork of the buildings; the smell of the spices, and the stink from the mud and slime on the banks of the river, was overpowering.

This was the catchment area of Guy's Hospital. The patients Diana would be nursing lived here in Shad Thames, and in the slums of Rotherhithe and Deptford that stretched to the east.

Diana had set her heart on becoming a nurse almost as soon as war was declared. 'How can I best serve my country in its crisis?' she asked her friends. She had no experience or training in first aid, but nursing, she quickly decided, was the solution.

Her first intention was to go out to France to nurse soldiers wounded at the Front. Her close friend Rosemary Leveson-Gower was already there, working in an ambulance unit which her mother, the Duchess of Sutherland, had taken out to Belgium. But Violet refused to allow Diana to go. Unable to broach intimate subjects with her daughter, she called on Lady Dudley, who was running a hospital for officers at Le Touquet, to explain to Diana that for an attractive girl to tend libidinous soldiers 'long starved of women' and 'inflamed with battle' could lead only to 'Rape'. 'I thought her ridiculous, and my mother ridiculous too,' Diana remarked.

The hospitals and ambulance units run by Violet's friends offered a means of leapfrogging the Voluntary Aid Detachment system; they enabled debutantes to go out to the Front without first completing their VAD training at hospitals in England. Violet's opposition blocked this route for Diana. None of the grand society women would employ her without her mother's permission.

Determined to succeed in her ambition, Diana applied for the job at Guy's. It was a poor substitute for the romance and excitement of the hospitals at the Front, but once she had completed her training she could apply for a position in France independently of her mother.

Violet had put up every obstacle. First, she had tried reasoning with Diana: work of any sort did not befit a Duke's daughter, least of all work that involved tending the sick at a hospital whose patients came from slums in the East End. Then she had tried to put her off; the hours were long, the work exhausting, the dormitories where the nurses slept cold and uncomfortable. When this failed, she had tried to frighten her. 'You'll have to see operations!' she told her. As Diana recalled, she even roped in Dr Hood, who had trained at Guy's in the 1860s, to try and dissuade her: 'Old Dr Hood, in my family's pay, would pull out stories of the Guy's of fifty years earlier — his Guy's, when the doctors kept their old coats for operations. These coats lived in the theatre and were so stiff with old blood that they stood up like armour. The students were always fainting, he told me. Neither student nor nurse ever saw their first op. without passing out.'

There was nothing romantic or glamorous about the work Diana was going to do. Unlike other London hospitals, Guy's did not admit wounded soldiers. She would be working on ordinary surgical wards, tending patients of both sexes. The thought that she would have to physically handle men — and working-class men at that — appalled Violet.

It took courage — and a 'stiff fight', Diana recalled — to defy her. Her decision to go to Guy's was courageous in other ways too. Although she was twenty-two, she had led a sheltered, pampered life. Cosseted and indulged, she was used to deferential servants. These — and the tenants on the Belvoir estate — had been her sole contact with men and women who came from a different class. She had never been on a hospital ward before and, as she admitted, 'knew no more about nursing than Nanny's plasters and doses'. Now she was to find herself in a world where she was a nobody, and where her superiors expected her to speak only when spoken to. She would have to be up by six, and in bed by ten; she was to be entrusted with only the most menial tasks and kept on her feet for nine hours with only brief breaks.

The hospital, a grand eighteenth-century building with quadrangles and cloisters, stood out amidst the squalor of Shad Thames. Situated a few streets back from the river, its entrance was marked by a pair of stone pillars, topped by sculpted globes. Founded in 1721 as a hospital for 'incurables', it was through these gates, beneath a crest of two angels, that the dying patients had been brought on stretchers. And it was through these gates, an hour or so before Diana's first shift was due to start, that the chauffeur — with just inches to spare between the roof of the car and the crest of the angels — manoeuvred the Duke's Rolls-Royce.

'Guy's looked very Dickensian that afternoon beneath its dark drizzle,' Diana remembered: 'A few shivering nurses in cotton dresses were being blown about the wide courtyard and open arcaded passages. We rang the bell at a side entrance. The door was opened by an old housekeeper in black with a hospital cap. She was as dry and grey as cinders. She led us to an upper bedroom giving on to the courtyard. Here I unpacked my modest little trunk — some underclothes, some books, concealed cosmetics, clock, pencils and paper, and a pampering hot water bottle. Every movement was watched by the old house-Gestapo.'

After unpacking her suitcase, the moment came for Diana to put on her uniform. 'My mother writhed,' she recalled: 'There was no long glass, but I later saw what was making my mother so appalled, for indeed I did look horrible. The dress was just off the floor and gathered at the back only. The print was of a minute and colourless mauve-and-white pinstripe. The apron was cut to deform the figure. There were the universal black stockings and flat black shoes. I was led away from my mother who left disconsolate.'

Diana, for reasons that had nothing to do with the job that lay ahead of her, was feeling equally disconsolate. A conversation had taken place in the car on the way to the hospital that she did not record in her account of their arrival there. But later that evening, after finishing her first shift, she mentioned it briefly in a letter to her sister

Marjorie: 'Mother was in a despairing blue all the way here. We hardly spoke. As she was leaving, she said I must make nice to GM. If I won't, J [John] will die.'

It is clear from what was to occur in the coming months that in telling Diana to 'make nice' to George Gordon Moore, Violet was asking her to seduce him.

It was a remarkable request, coming from a mother who kept her 22-year-old daughter on a very tight rein. There was hardly a moment when Violet did not have her under some form of surveillance. 'I was still forbidden to be alone with a man, except by chance in the country, or to go out anywhere on my own,' Diana recalled. During the day, whether walking, shopping or visiting a friend, Violet insisted that she was chaperoned. In the evenings, if she went to a dance, a married woman had to take her and bring her home. Even then, she was unable to slip in unobserved. At night, Violet kept the door to her bedroom open so that she could listen out for her return: regardless of the hour, she demanded that Diana call in on her to recount details of the guests and her dancing partners. There were other rules too; she was not allowed to drink cocktails; she could go to the Ritz but no other London hotel; if, by chance, she should find herself alone with a man, even 'hand-holding' was banned ('my mother felt strongly on this score'); and if she was invited to a house party in the country, to discourage her suitors from corridor-creeping, Violet instructed her to be sure to say at teatime on the day of her arrival — and in a very loud voice — that her maid always slept with her.

This regimen was designed for one purpose: to preserve Diana's virginity for the royal prince, or wealthy aristocrat, Violet intended her to marry. Most eligible was the Prince of Wales. The future Edward VIII was three years younger than Diana, but Violet was in no doubt that her daughter was eminently well qualified to be Queen and that this should be her ambition. It was one that the Duke of Connaught, Queen Victoria's son, had encouraged. Shaken by the class conflict that had dogged the country in the years leading up to the war, he was of the view that Diana, already popular with the press, was the only woman who would keep the prince on the throne. If this plan failed, Violet had a list of other candidates. Before the war, Prince Adalbert, the son of Kaiser Wilhelm, was a favourite, along with Prince Paul of Yugoslavia and numerous Russian princes. Further down her list, among the ordinary English marquises and earls, there was the fabulously wealthy Lord Rocksavage — thought to be the most handsome man of his generation — and Bobbety Cranborne, the

Marquis of Salisbury's eldest son. Violet updated her list constantly; if any of her 'eligibles' were inconsiderate enough to marry elsewhere, she drew a skull and cross-bones by their names.

Diana rejected her mother's 'chronic eligibles', as she called them. She did not want to marry someone with 'coronets on their fingers and coronets on their toes'. She wanted to marry an 'Unknown'. Lord Rock-savage bored her; his conversation, she reported to a friend, consisted of 'three words, adaptable to any remark: "Oh," "Really," "Right-ho!" ' Bobbety Cranborne, 'with his loose gaping mouth', was unattrac-tive; and she 'despised' the Prince of Yugosla-via, describing him as 'a shiny little black thing'.

But she had never imagined that Violet would force George Gordon Moore on her. Moore, despite his many millions, was not eligible. He was married and thought to be of 'Red Indian' descent. In private, her parents referred to him as Little Big Head.

In asking Diana to encourage his interest, Violet was sweeping aside her principles; not only that, she was breaking every one of her own strict rules. She knew Moore to be of dubious moral character. In the spring of 1914 she had attended a dance at 94 Lancas-ter Gate. The numbers of single unchaper-oned women had shocked her: 'GM and Sir J are running a bordello!!!' she told Charlie the morning after.

Violet was also riding roughshod over her daughter's feelings. Diana loathed George Gordon Moore — or George Gordon Ghastly, as she called him. He was the very last person she wanted to encourage.

They had met at a house party in the summer of 1913. The house, Stanway, a beautiful Jacobean manor in Gloucestershire, belonged to the Earl of Wemyss, the head of the Charteris family. The director of a merchant bank, Lord Wemyss had put up the development capital for Moore's railway company; after making a large sum of money from his investment, he had introduced the American to his friends. His imprimatur, as Diana recalled, meant that the rumours circulating about Moore were ignored. 'His riches were evident but maybe an optical illusion, so his countrymen said. Harsh things they whispered — "Kicked out of the States", "Just a crook", but we all believed in him, especially the Charteris family, whose protégé and patron he was.'

The moment he saw Diana, Moore was captivated by her — as most men were. She was recognized as a great beauty. At dances before the war, Winston Churchill and Eddie Marsh played a game based on Marlowe's line: 'Was this the face that launched a thousand ships?' Standing together at the edge of the dance floor, they would allocate the debutantes a tally of ships. Only two faces earned the full thousand — those of Diana Manners and Clementine Hozier, Churchill's future wife.

Diana was not just beautiful, she had a presence, an ethereal quality about her, which drove both men and women to startling raptures as they struggled to capture it. Enid Bagnold remembered seeing her for the first time coming down the stairs like a 'muslin swan': 'her blind blue stare swept over me. I was shocked — in the sense of electricity. Born in the city I wanted to storm, the Queen of Jericho swept past me.' Others wrote of 'her hair, pale gold and with the delicate texture of ancient Chinese silk' and her 'love-in-the-mist eyes'. To her admirers, part of her magnetism was that she was brilliantly exotic. Raymond Asquith, the eldest son of the prime minister, described her presence at a house party at Lord Manners's home, Avon Tyrrell, as being like an 'orchid among cowslips, a black tulip in a garden of cucumbers, night-shade in the nursery'. Her beauty, Cynthia Asquith recalled, had 'that festal quality which made every occasion she graced a gala. "Lights Up" was the stage direction at her entry, and when she left the room "bright-ness fell from the air." '

After the party at Stanway, Moore, who was

sixteen years older than Diana, pursued her relentlessly: 'I understood very little of what he said, but I caught his unclear accents of admiration,' she remembered, 'and he courted me in his own exaggerated way, although he had a wife and children. He gave me to understand that these hindrances could be liquidated and that his every living hour and his vast fortune would be dedicated to me — to me and Sir John French.'

Describing Moore as a 'most unusual man, Red Indian in appearance with straight black hair, flattened face and atomic energy', Diana found his attentions suffocating. Everything about him repelled her — his accent, his stocky physique, his lack of sensibility and education. He had no knowledge of the works of poetry and literature that enthralled her, and to which she and her circle of friends constantly alluded. Diana was fey and naively romantic; Moore's passion, particularly his sexual longing, terrified her. In a letter to Raymond Asquith, she likened his attentions to a 'vile torrent of gravy and steaming putrefying blood'. To her horror, he was prone to pounce; 'O Raymond, it was so sullying, almost mutilating and scarring,' she wrote after he had tried to kiss her.

Among Diana's circle, the war was already loosening social conventions. At 8 Fitzroy Square in Bloomsbury, two of her closest friends, Iris Tree and Nancy Cunard, hosted parties that were notorious for their debauchery. Convened at the last minute for officer friends home on leave from the Front, they turned into orgies. Diana always declined invitations to attend the parties. She disapproved of sexual licentiousness. The morning after one party, she went round to Fitzroy Square to help clear up. The squalor disgusted her. Everywhere, there were 'champagne bottles broken at the neck to save the trouble of drawing the cork', 'pools of blood and vomit', and 'frowsty unmade beds'.

Diana's reticence about sex added to her allure. 'She was probably the only virgin there,' Duff Cooper commented ruefully after attending a gallery opening with her. Patrick Shaw Stewart, another of her admirers, was constantly trying to persuade her to marry him or, failing that, at least to go to bed with him. 'You, you see, always want to keep (1) me (2) your old virginity. Whereas I always want to get (1) your heart and soul (2) your worshipful body.'

The thought of having to 'make nice' to the lascivious George Moore was abhorrent to Diana. Yet, as she realized, she had no choice but to go along with her mother's diktat: 'My brother John was the last male issue of our noble house and the trenches were certain death,' she remarked grimly, looking back on the episode: 'To get my brother to GHQ was

501

her obsessing hope. She thought that only I could coax this boon out of Moore.'

Diana saw Moore at every opportunity
throughout that winter. To do so necessitated
leading a schizophrenic existence. At her
mother's insistence, her time was split between Shad Thames and Mayfair. If Diana
was assigned to a morning shift, Violet would
arrange tea parties at Arlington Street so that
she could see Moore for a few hours before
returning to Guy's for the evening shift. On
her days off, Violet forced her to go to the
theatre and to the opera with him.

Encouraged by her apparent interest,
Moore showered her with gifts. Among them,
as Diana recalled, was 'an ermine coat to the
ankle (my mother chose it from Jay's), a
monstrous little monkey called Armide with
a diamond waistbelt and chain, Maupassant's
works in full morocco, countless *éditions de
luxe,* and a cream poodle called Fido cut en
papillon with pom poms and bracelets of fluff
and a heliotrope bow'. Twice weekly, he sent
her a box, 'the size of a coffin', full of Ma-

donna lilies; and he gave her jewels too: one, a gigantic sapphire, was said to have belonged to Catherine the Great. 'All this had to be accepted,' Diana wrote to her son many years later. 'Not difficult to accept, you'll say, but I really did hate him.'

It was bad enough having to accept an embarrassment of gifts from a man who repelled her, but it was the dances that Moore held in her honour that Diana found unbearable. 'I was very young and couldn't cope at all,' she remembered.

They took place at 94 Lancaster Gate. Nicknamed the Dances of Death, because no one knew which men would be alive when the next dance was held, the parties were bacchanalian. Moore spared no expense. Interior decorators were summoned to create a theme for each occasion. One evening, Bakst's vibrant set designs would adorn the ballroom; on another, erotic drawings by Aubrey Beardsley. At every dance, hundreds of purple orchids and pink camellias, grown in hothouses and specially shipped in, festooned the tables.

Moore left it to Diana and her friends to choose the guests. Held behind 'barred doors', and limited to an exclusive fifty people, the dances quickly earned a reputation for excess. 'Parents were excluded. We dined at any time,' Diana recalled: 'The long waits for the last-comers were enlivened by exciting, unusual drinks such as vodka or absinthe. The menu was composed of far-fetched American delicacies — avocados, terrapin and soft-shell crabs . . . The dancing, sometimes to two bands, negro and white (and once to the first Hawaiian), so that there might be no pause, started immediately after dinner. We kept whirling to the music till the orchids were swept away in favour of wild flowers.'

During dinner, Moore insisted that Diana sit next to him. When it was over, he would become jealous if she danced with anyone else. 'The parties were the delight of my friends but I, who could not like him because of his passion for me, found the position acutely painful,' she remembered. Her friends steered a wide berth. While they had no qualms in accepting the American's hospitality, they did not like him either.

Cosseted alone with Moore, Diana was forced to keep up the pretence of flirtation for hour after hour. Mindful that her brother's life might depend on how well she performed this charade, she had to put up with endless turns around the ballroom, letting him 'murmur love or Chich-techicher-chich-chich hotly in my ear as we shuffled and bunny-hugged around'. Escape, unless she wanted to spoil her friends' enjoyment, was impossible. 'I wanted to leave at a reasonable hour, drive twice around Regent's Park with a

505

swain and be dropped home at an hour compatible with hospital duties the next morning.' But the minute she left, Moore would turn down the lights and dismiss the band. 'When you leave, the place is a morgue,' he told her.

Frequently, Diana went straight from the dances to morning prayers in the chapel at Guy's. The thirty-minute service began at six thirty and was followed by a breakfast of tinned eggs and 'stalish fish'. As she described it, an eagle-eyed sister, sitting on a rostrum, watched over the nurses while they ate. 'My trouble was wanting not to eat. Often I would be called with several other miscreants after the meal and reproved severely. Did I know that nurses were different from other people? Their lives were dedicated to the sick, maybe dying, and they must keep up their strength by a sensible diet in order not to be found wanting.'

At 8 a.m. came the start of her ten-hour shift. Despite the strict discipline, Diana was enjoying the job at Guy's. After a difficult beginning, she had overcome the doubts of her superiors. Nurses were not expected to feature in the newspapers, or to have the prime minister enquire about their welfare; suspicious of her glamour and her privileged background, the senior matron had thrown her in at the deep end.

The first weeks on Charity, a women's

surgical ward, had not been a success. No one told Diana how to perform the menial tasks allocated to her — or where the things she needed to perform them were kept. 'I was given a very unattractive little boy of two or three as my own patient,' she remembered: 'He was recovering from appendicitis. I clung to him and tried to ingratiate myself. I was told to give the boy a bath and dress him cleanly. This meant a spate of agonizing questions. What bath? Where are the clean clothes? What soap? I had no idea how to wash a child (half-invalid) of two. I seemed to have done nothing practical in all my twenty years. The child yelled as though I'd put it on the rack.'

But, to her immense pride, it was not long before Diana was accepted as a competent member of the nursing staff. Her conduct sheet was immaculate and she was popular with the patients and the other nurses. She had not fainted at her first operation and, as she recorded proudly, she was soon allowed to administer injections, cut abscesses and prepare patients for the operating theatre. In recognition of her capabilities, she was given one of the toughest nursing jobs at Guy's. 'I was moved after a few months from my dear Charity Ward down to Ashley Cooper Men's Accident Ward — very different — a high, gaunt, sunless ward, busier and much sadder.' For the most part, the patients were dock-hands who had suffered horrific accidents at work — 'paralytics and spinal cases that in minutes had lost their powers utterly', as she described them. Every one of them had to be washed and fed. Some were so badly injured they died within a few hours of being admitted.

The satisfaction that Diana gained from the challenges she faced at work compensated for the evenings she was forced to endure with Moore. Nonetheless, it was a period of intense unhappiness for her. 'I had earned the hard name of a "scalp-collector",' she recalled. Her flirtation with the American angered her many admirers, some of whom were her closest male friends. 'On the whole my own impression is that her beauty is increasing and her humanity dwindling,' Raymond Asquith wrote to Edward Horner, a friend and rival for Diana's attentions: 'I am training myself to admire her as a natural object — the Alpine sunset, the Pink Terrace in New Zealand — instead of the damned unnatural and extremely provocative one she really is.' In an agony of jealousy, Horner wrote to Diana herself: 'I can't understand your form of loving people. I can't constitutionally believe in your loving me, and a couple more.' George Vernon, another of her admirers, also accused her of distributing her 'favours to all with impartiality mixed with a curious caprice'. Diana was aware that her very public flirtation with George Moore served only to reinforce her reputation for capriciousness. It also cast her as a fortune hunter. Very obviously, money was all Moore had in his favour. As he whirled her around the dance floor, she found it intensely hurtful that she was unable to explain to her friends why she appeared to be in his thrall.

On the rare occasions when Sir John French was in London, he attended the Dances of Death. 'The Commander-in-Chief himself looked in on the revels,' Diana remembered. 'He would not stay long.'

Whether, in the course of one of their brief meetings, Diana spoke to Sir John about her brother, or whether George Moore had interceded on her behalf, she does not record. But a cryptic note to her mother, written in the second week of January 1915, suggests the favour had already been asked: 'No word from GM or guest,' she told her.

The 'guest' was a reference to Sir John.

French was in London to attend meetings at the War Office. He and Sir Douglas Haig, the Commander of the First Army, were planning a spring offensive. Neither man doubted that the German Army could be beaten. 'Given an improvement in the weather, and adequate supplies of ammunition,' Haig told *The Times* that January, 'we could walk through the German lines at several places.'

They had been waiting for the opportunity to attack for some time. Out in France, it had rained incessantly. There had been just eleven dry days since October. In the sodden plain between Ypres and Cuinchy — the northern and southern points of the British line — the trenches had become little more than culverts. In these conditions any serious forward movement would be suicidal.

Along whole stretches of the line, the water in the trenches was waist high. For the British troops massed there, it had meant weeks of enduring extremes of physical privation. Lieutenant Charles Tennant was with the Seaforth Highlanders outside Armentières. 'Water is the great and pressing problem,' he wrote: 'The weather has been almost unprecedentedly wet and the whole countryside is soaked in mud and like a sponge. Owing to its flatness it is generally impossible to drain the trenches, and every day of rain has made them more and more unpleasant until now the chief question is how to keep the men more or less out of the water. In a summer campaign it would not matter, but when a hard frost sets in at night, and we have had several, frostbite sets in at once and the man is done for so far as his feet and legs are concerned.'

At the War Office, and at General Headquarters, getting the men out of the water and on to higher ground was the priority. By mid-February, after weeks of discussion, the battle plans were in place. But French had to wait. He could not launch his offensive until the country had dried out.

It was at the eleventh hour that Violet received the 'word' she had been waiting for. Six days before John was due to embark for the Front, a note arrived from the commander-in-chief. 'My Dear,' French addressed her:

Please don't worry yourself or be un-happy. Trust me to see that he is all right so far as anyone can be so in this kind of war. Of course, I needn't say how neces-sary it is for you to keep our correspon-dence on such a subject absolutely secret. If he once knows of it nothing can be done. But I have a good plan which our mutual friend will explain to you.

Indeed, I understand and feel most deeply for you but I hope this assurance will make you happier. I am not one of those who believe in a very long struggle — it will go on some time longer, of course, but you will probably have him back much sooner than you think.

The 'mutual friend' was, of course, George Moore.

Violet forwarded a copy of the letter to Charlie. Attached to it was a note:

Darling,
This I got this morning and at 3am I get up and see G Moore in Diana's bedroom next door. Oh dear.

Yr loving VR

For understandable reasons, Diana never wrote about what occurred in the early hours of that morning. Whether, as a reward for securing her brother's safety, Moore forced her to submit to his advances, she does not record. But he had evidently extracted some sort of price. For a married man to be found in a debutante's bedroom at that hour broke every convention.

Nor can we know Diana's feelings towards her mother. Violet had effectively prostituted her daughter to save her son; she had forced Diana to seduce a man she loathed. Yet Diana does not write of the contempt she must have felt.

'If he once knows of it nothing can be done.' The need for secrecy prevented Sir John from committing his 'good plan' to paper. Moreover, he told Violet, he would not address it for a while. First, he had important business to attend to out in France.

Unaware of his mother's intriguing, John finally left for the Western Front on 26 February. That morning, he went to Arlington Street to say goodbye to her. Disingenuous

512

to the last, Violet wrote to him afterwards: 'Remember darling, never do anything foolish or foolhardy. Be clever. Charlie and I don't know how to bear it all. 6 months of waiting makes it doubly worse. But I didn't seem to mind a bit, did I? Were you proud of me? I was — but you wouldn't be now!! Oh, do your best for me, I beseech. How I worship you.'

■ ■ ■ ■

PART VII

■ ■ ■ ■

It was 9 March — the eve of the Battle of
Neuve Chapelle — and Sir John French was
dining with his old friend Lord Esher at 20
Rue St Bertin, an elegant eighteenth-century
house behind the cathedral at St Omer. A
short distance from General Headquarters,
the town's leading notary had placed the
house at the commander-in-chief's disposal.

The two men were dining alone. A fire
blazed in the grate; outside, the temperature
had plummeted and it was threatening to
snow.

'The spider in his web,' as one contemporary described him, Lord Esher shunned
public office, but through his friendship with
the royal family and Britain's senior politicians wielded great influence. He had been
instrumental in ensuring that French was
given the post as Commander-in-Chief of the
BEF. As early as 1903, he had reported to
the King that he believed French to be the
outstanding general of his generation, not

only a brilliant commander in the field, but also a man who cared deeply for the troops who served under him.

The evening was marked by a flurry of signals and telegrams as the final preparations for the battle were put into train. From time to time, there came the clatter of hooves on the cobbled street outside — a single horse ridden at an urgent trot delivering last-minute messages from GHQ. Other sounds filtered into the dining room; the ringing of distant telephones, the brisk steps of staff adjutants in the hallway — and on the stone stairs that led up to the commander-in-chief's private office.

French was delighted that Lord Esher could be with him on such an important occasion. His mood was euphoric; at 07.30 hours the next day he was to launch the first systematic British attack since the commencement of trench warfare. He had waited for this moment for months. 'Winter in the trenches,' he acknowledged, had been 'trying and enervating'. The attack, he believed, would raise the troops' morale.

Nowhere had their experience been more 'trying and enervating' than in the sodden meadowland at the southern end of the British line. It was here, in the valley of the Lys and the Layes, some fifteen miles west of Lille, that Sir John proposed to launch his offensive.

Earlier in the day, at General Headquarters, he had shown Lord Esher a map of the battlefield. The front along which he proposed to attack lay beneath Aubers Ridge. It was not much of a ridge; approached by a gentle slope, it rose to a height of just fifty feet. Yet if the ridge could be captured, the British troops would be out of the boggy ground and in position to push on, over the plain, to Lille.

Other considerations — besides the ridge's strategic importance — had played a part in his calculations. Using spotter planes, and information gleaned from German prisoners of war, the Intelligence Corps had identified this sector as the weakest point in the enemy's line. In advance of a major offensive against the Russians, the German High Command had pulled every available man, gun and shell out of France. At Aubers, they had denuded their front more extravagantly than elsewhere. Just six companies, with only twelve machine-guns between them, had been left to defend the ridge. As 1st Intelligence Corps had observed, their trench system was shoddily constructed. The firing trench — a single line of sandbag breastwork — could be easily breached; the wire in front of it was little more than two rows of *chevaux-de-frise* — portable trestle-like structures that two men could lift to one side.

Against this flimsy barrier, French proposed

to use his troops as a battering ram. The attack was to be narrow and deep. No fewer than forty-eight battalions were to be hurled at the enemy along a front that was just two thousand yards long.

Everything, French explained to Lord Esher, depended on speed. If Neuve Chapelle — the village at the foot of the ridge — could be quickly captured, his troops would be on top of it before the Germans had time to bring up reinforcements. With this objective in mind, he planned to begin the offensive with the 'biggest bombardment in the history of the world'. For a full thirty minutes, 180 British guns, configured deep behind the lines in a horseshoe opposite the village, would pound the German trenches, blowing open a path for his troops to advance.

Sir John had spent the previous week inspecting artillery positions. The very fact of the coming attack, let alone the proposed date, or details of the weaponry to be used, were top secret. But while letters home from officers and other ranks were strictly censored, no one censored the commander-in-chief's letters. Regardless of the security risk, he could not resist confiding the details to Winifred Bennett, his mistress.

'I've just come back from a long day at the Front,' he wrote on 6 March, four days before the battle. 'More rain. Rain! It seems to do nothing else! I was on a horse for most of the morning and got a soaking! I've been looking at one of our big guns being put into position. It is what we call a 15 inch and throws a shell of 1400lbs weight — double the size of the biggest guns the Germans have used against us. All our preparations are complete for the <u>Great Event</u>. Every man is in splendid heart and spirit and only anxious to be "doing". The mail has just arrived and brought me a letter from you. I will answer it in a day or two — before we "begin". I know you won't tell a soul!'

Sir John's self-belief was boundless. He saw the assault at Neuve Chapelle as the prelude to a larger battle, one that would see the German Army driven out of France. On the morning of 9 March — the day before it began — he wrote to Winifred again: 'I don't expect to write more than one long letter for 2 or 3 weeks!' he told her. 'But be sure I shall write something every 2 or 3 days to tell you how we get on. I am always thinking of you my beautiful Beloved Lady, my beautiful Guiding Star! You are the mainspring of it all, my inspiration. Victory, when it comes, will be yours!'

That evening, shortly after nine o'clock, the low rumble of an approaching motorbike disturbed the sleeping residents of St Omer. It turned into the main square, the beam of its headlights sweeping across the shuttered windows; as the rider dropped down through the gears, the noise of the revving engine boomed off the walls of the houses and echoed around the square.

A few minutes later, an adjutant stepped into the dining room at 20 Rue St Bertin. He handed Sir John a copy of the Special Order which, minutes earlier, had been issued to the fifty thousand British soldiers massed beneath Aubers Ridge. It was a rallying message to the troops from Sir Douglas Haig, French's second-in-command:

We are now about to attack with about 48 battalions a locality which is held by some three German Battalions.

Quickness of movement is of first importance to enable us to forestall the enemy and thereby gain success without severe loss. At no time in this war has there been a more favourable moment for us, and I feel confident of success. The extent of that success must depend on the rapidity and determination with which we advance.

Zero hour — the scheduled time for the start of the battle — was set for 07.30 hours. Momentarily overawed by his own omnipotence, French turned to Lord Esher: 'It is a solemn thought,' he said, 'that at my signal all these fine young fellows go to their death.'

There was one 'fine young fellow' he did not need to worry about.

'Trust me to see that he is all right so far as anyone can be so in this kind of a war.'

French had not forgotten his promise to the Duchess. The preparations for the offensive prevented him from putting his 'plan' into train, but he knew that for the time being at least, 'Young Granby', as he referred to John, was not in danger.

The previous week, French had placed the North Midland Division under his immediate command. They were now assigned to General Reserve. His intention was to keep these troops back until the main body of his army broke through the German lines. Only then would he deploy them to sweep up pockets of resistance and to press forward the attack.

That day, to make certain there was no confusion over the position of the General Reserve troops, he summoned General Allenby — their commanding officer — to headquarters: 'I explained to him clearly,' he noted in his diary, 'that his forward units of the General Reserve were not to engage in any action until he received distinct orders from me.'

Later, after dining with Lord Esher, French wrote one last pre-battle letter to Winifred:

Darling, I must finish this quickly. We are very active and busy tonight for the big thing happens at daybreak tomorrow. The infantry fight won't develop till well on in the day, but the guns start early. I am looking for great things from the 15 inch — known throughout the 1st Army as 'Grandmama!'

'Tomorrow,' he added, I shall go forward with my war cry of "Winifred"!'

Then, with a confident flourish, he signed the letter 'Peter Pan'.

Thirty miles away, the night was just beginning for the forty-eight thousand troops massed beneath Aubers Ridge. Stealthily, moving in single file through the narrow communication trenches, they were making their way up to the firing trench. To avoid the risk of being spotted by observers in the enemy's trenches, they had waited for the cover of darkness.

The temperature hovered at freezing and a bitter north wind blew down the valley, turning the rain into gusts of wet snow. It had been a long day already. The forty-eight battalions had assembled behind the lines at dawn. There, bivouacked in the wide, flat fields, and along the banks of roads choked with the machinery of battle — supply wagons, artillery carriages and, more sinisterly, the SADS, the Supplementary Advanced Dressing Stations, spotlessly clean and, as yet, empty — they had waited for the order to move forward. The rain fell steadily; by nightfall, their greatcoats were wet through.

The operation to move the troops into position presented a logistical nightmare. The Front along which the commander-in-chief had chosen to position his forty-eight battalions was a mere two thousand yards wide. During the hours of darkness, twenty-four thousand men were to be crammed into the firing trench at the tip of the phalanx, and the remainder, lined up in the reserve trenches, ready to follow on. Just three communication trenches led up to the front line; it would be close to dawn before all the battalions were in position.

Charles Tennant was in charge of a company of Seaforth Highlanders: 'I turned in at 10.30pm leaving orders that I was to be woken at one o'clock. Breakfast for the men was punctually at 2am and the Battalion was to be ready, formed up in the road, by 2.55. We took nothing with us but rations, coats, a spare pair of socks and twenty rounds per man.'

At the entrances to the communications trenches, bottlenecks formed as battalion after battalion waited to file up the line. The water table, following the deluge of continuous rain, had been rising all day. Further along, where the narrow roadways began their descent towards the front line, it was wet and muddy underfoot; by midnight, the water was lapping over the carefully laid duckboards, making progress slow.

The order to move forward had been issued at 18.30 hours — thirteen hours before zero hour. For those troops unlucky enough to be among the first to be ordered up to the firing line, it was a long wait.

'Snow swept down on us as we waited in the flooded trenches,' William Andrews, a corporal in the Black Watch, remembered: 'We grew colder and colder — so cold that I never thought I could be so chilled and still live. It was sheer biting torture. At five in the morning my platoon was routed out again to move to a reserve trench. We shambled over ground hardened by frost. It was colder than ever. We called it a trench, but it was more of a breastwork, like a stockade, strengthened with sandbags of earth. My pals Nicholson and Joe Lee and myself huddled together close to each other with our backs to the stockade.'

Despite the cold, and the long, sleepless night, morale in the platoon, as Andrews recalled, was high: 'We were Territorials and we were going into action for the first time. Our commanding officers told us we were facing the enemy with a numerical superiority of thirty-five to one. We felt honoured to think we'd been chosen to serve in the battle. We were eager to fight, smarting to avenge the things that had been said about the Territorials. We might be raw but we were keen men, intelligent men, and every one a volunteer. We meant to do our best and we were convinced that this was the battle that might end the war! In those days we thought you only had to break through the German front and the enemy would crumple up and we would be done with the trenches because, once we had thrust through the trench system, the line would be rolled up. That was a favourite phrase then, rolled up! Of course battle plans were not revealed to a humble Lance-Corporal like myself, but at Neuve Chapelle we had a good idea of what we were after . . . the ground slowly rose towards the village of Aubers and we knew that about nine miles beyond was the city of Lille. We were hopeful enough to believe that there would be cosy billets for us in Lille on the night of the battle.'

To the right of the Black Watch, further along the firing trench, Lance-Corporal Hall was with the 2nd Battalion, Cameronians (Scottish Rifles). 'We put up climbing ladders for jumping over the parapet. We were on tiptoe with excitement because we were fed up with trenches and living in a sea of mud and we just wanted to get the Germans out in the open. We'd seen them off at Messines Ridge when they attacked in November, but *this* was *our* offensive, the first our army had made since the trench warfare began.'

After the long, cold night, the sun rose at 6.30 a.m. Crammed shoulder to shoulder in the firing trench, the twenty-four thousand troops — the first wave to go over the parapet — were just a few hundred yards from the enemy. 'When dawn came we peered across at the German lines, wondering if Jerry knew we were coming,' Corporal Andrews remembered.

For the next hour, they waited for the bombardment to begin. Behind them was the strongest concentration of guns per yard ever before assembled: sixty-two batteries of eighteen-pounders; forty 4.5-inch howitzers and eighty-two siege and heavy artillery pieces.

'At 7.30 punctually the whole sky was rent by noise — about four hundred British guns all opening fire at once in concerted bombardment of two hundred yards of German trenches,' Tennant described. 'We had a battery of — I think — 4.7s only forty yards behind us and the din was terrific. The whole air and the solid earth itself became one quivering jelly. Funnily enough, I normally have a fanatical dislike for mere noise of any kind, but I was conscious of nothing except the extraordinary sense of security the infantry man gets from hearing artillery fire from his own side.'

'The bombardment started like all the furies of hell,' Andrews remembered: 'The noise almost split our wits. The shells from the field guns were whizzing right over our heads and we got more and more excited. We couldn't hear ourselves speak. *Now* we could make out the German trenches. They were like long clouds of smoke and dust, flashing with shell bursts, and we could see enormous masses of trench material and even bodies thrown up above the smoke clouds. We thought the bombardment was winning the war before our eyes and soon *we* would be pouring through the gap.'

Looking up at the sky, blackened by the clouds of earth hurled by the falling shells, one image would remain in Tennant's mind until he was killed, seven weeks later, at the Battle of Festubert: 'Through all the bombardment,' he wrote to his wife, 'the larks mounted carolling up to the sky with shells screaming all round them, as though all that devil's din was only some insane nightmare and as though all that was really true was the coming of spring.'

At precisely 8.05 a.m. the guns fell silent. Before the echo of the last boom had re-sounded across the valley, the air was filled with the shrill sound of hundreds of whistles as, in unison, company officers gave the signal to advance.

The offensive was destined to fail. Sir John French had made a catastrophic error of judgement. So keen was he to press the attack, he had decided to overlook a serious problem on his left flank.

In the run-up to it, two siege batteries, promised by the War Office and equipped with four 6-inch howitzers each, had failed to arrive from England. Since mid-February, they had been anxiously expected. Their targets had been allocated: they were to pulverize the German trenches around Mauquissart, a tiny hamlet on the extreme left of the battle front, where 23rd Brigade would attack.

As the weeks passed and there was no sign of the missing batteries, a series of telegrams — which grew more and more heated — flew between London and St Omer. On 26 February, the War Office informed GHQ that the batteries would leave England on 1 March. GHQ wired back requesting their immediate embarkation but they were not shipped until 5 March.

It was only on the evening of the ninth — less than twelve hours before zero hour — that the batteries were moved into position in the field. The destruction of the breastwork along four hundred yards of the enemy's front depended on the firepower their eight guns delivered. But they had no time to range on their targets, much less fire a single shot.

Inconceivable as it seems, Sir John and his staff at GHQ had made no arrangements to cover the gap. For the soldiers in 23rd Brigade, the error was catastrophic; as they advanced across no-man's-land, they were advancing against German trenches that were pristinely intact.

The 2nd Middlesex led the assault. They attacked in three successive waves, climbing over the parapet into a storm of point-blank fire. Some measure of their bravery is to be found in one sentence in the Official History: 'It was thought at first that the attack succeeded in reaching the German trenches as none behind could see and not a man returned.' In fact, every man, and there had been nearly a thousand, was killed.

While the troops to their right were able to advance quickly, capturing the village of Neuve Chapelle and gaining a thousand yards of ground in the space of forty-five minutes, by the second day of the battle, the Germans had reinforced Aubers Ridge and were able to counter-attack. After another day, with ammunition running low, the battle was called off. A post-mortem revealed that at the crucial moment after the capture of Neuve Chapelle, the troops had failed to exploit their gains. They had not pushed forward quickly enough. Part of their failure to do so originated in the chaos that had ensued on the left flank as the advancing battalions came under heavy fire from German defences that had survived the initial bombardment — the four hundred yards of enemy trenches that should have been destroyed by the inoperative batteries.

At the close of the battle, British losses amounted to 583 officers and 12,309 other ranks.

48

John handed his permit to the sentry at the checkpoint, who waved his car on. He was driving the Rolls-Royce his father had lent him for the duration of the war. Next to him, in the passenger seat, was Rothesay Stuart Wortley,* the general's 23-year-old son. A second car followed behind them; inside it were four other staff officers from the North Midlands Headquarters. It was the 14 March — two days after the battle of Neuve Chapelle — and they were at the foot of Sharpenburg Ridge.

The ridge, eight miles to the west of Ypres, overlooked the Flanders plain; on a clear night, it was possible to see the frontline trenches — fifteen miles of them, stretching from Hooge to Messines.

The fog that usually shrouded it had lifted, and the smell of cordite hung in the air. It was seven o'clock in the evening and the noise of the distant firing was incessant.

* ADC to General Stuart Wortley.

Strobing flashes of orange and white lit up the sky to the east. As the two cars wound their way up the narrow track to the top of the ridge, there were three further checkpoints. Sharpenburg was closely guarded; as one of the few high points held by the British in the otherwise flat landscape, it was an important piece of ground.

A few hours earlier, the Germans had launched a surprise attack at St Eloi, a quiet sector four miles to the south of Ypres. John and his fellow officers had come to watch the attack from the ridge.

In the two weeks since he had been out at the Front, this was John's first sight of the battlefield. 'The life here is almost identical to Bishops Stortford,' he complained to Charlie: 'spend most of the morning doing sham fights just the same as in England, except in England one got to London most Saturday to Mondays, which we don't get here.'

To his frustration, the North Midlands had not taken part in the fighting at Neuve Chapelle. For three days, the division had waited, camped in a frozen field three miles behind the lines at Sailly-sur-la-Lys. They were under orders to move forward at an hour's notice. But the order to advance had not come through. A few shells had fallen close to one of the brigades' headquarters, but this had been the only excitement.

It did not seem to John that he would ever see action. 'Here we are, and likely to be for some many weeks,' he wrote to Charlie after the battle: 'My Division is what is called General Reserve, which means we are not to go into trenches, but to be kept fresh for a dash through once the German lines have been broken. But as the breakthrough looks to be an impossibility, I fear we shall be where we are for a very long time.'

If and when the North Midlands were drafted into action, his job as galloper to General Stuart Wortley was to act as a liaison between division headquarters and the brigades' battle headquarters close to the Front. On occasion, when the lines of communication were down, he would have to go into the trenches to relay messages to individual battalions. But as long as his division remained out of the line, he was consigned to the life of an ordinary staff officer. 'I suppose people would say it's a bloody sight better than being in the trenches. But I hate it,' he confided to his sister, Marjorie. 'It's awful sitting here doing nothing when men are being killed and wounded. We've had 12000 casualties in this last fight. What it's like to be in the midst of that shelling, I can't imagine. The worst part of the waiting is the fear of being frightened — not knowing whether one would stand up to it.'

And yet despite the tense wait to go into the line, John knew his position was enviable. 'The way the Staff Officers live is very agreeable, but the way the men are expected to live — even out of the trenches — is dreadful,' he told his sister. 'How they put up with it, I don't know.'

A strict pecking order, based on rank and class, governed all aspects of life behind the front line. Officers and other ranks were segregated; they lived and ate their meals separately; they used separate bathhouses and latrines; they were treated in separate hospitals. Under army regulations, they were not even allowed to use the same brothels: a blue light denoted those for officers, a red light, those for the troops under their command. Class distinctions also applied if a soldier was killed in action or died of his wounds: in some cemeteries, there were burial plots for officers, and separate plots for NCOs and other ranks.

At the top of the pecking order came the generals and their staff. Twenty-one divisions were stationed on the Western Front in the spring of 1915. Including those in command at corps and division level, some two hundred generals were responsible for running the British Army. Each had a large personal staff, predominantly recruited from the ranks of the upper classes. The troops referred to them as 'Red Tabs' — a contemptuous term derived from the red insignia the staff officers wore on the lapels of their uniforms.

The divisions rotated through the trenches: they were not in the line all the time. While other ranks were billeted in vast tented camps, or in farm buildings and labourers' cottages, the staff officers invariably commandeered the best accommodation for themselves. Beautiful châteaux, surrounded by grounds still immaculately laid with rose gardens and topiary, were converted into staff headquarters, where the officers lived and worked. Inside, the interiors were as their owners had left them. Paintings, *objets d'art* and fine pieces of furniture adorned the rooms. When the officers dined, they used the china and crystal belonging to the house. Unlike the bulk of the British Army, the officers slept in proper beds and had servants and batmen to look after them.

In the two weeks that John had been out at the Front, he had moved from château to château. As aide-de-camp, his job was to accompany General Stuart Wortley to other headquarters along the Front. They had dined with General Smith-Dorrien, the commander of the Second Army, in the sumptuous surroundings of his château at Hazebrouck; at Bailleul, with General Pulteney, the commander of III Corps; and at Château de Nieppe, with General Wilson, the commander of 4th Division. They had also 'paid their respects' to General Foch at his palatial HQ at Cassel, and visited General Plumer — who was in charge of V Corps — 'for tea' at his base, a fine seventeenth-century mansion at Poperinghe.

The châteaux John slept in at night were not on the scale of those he visited during the day; but with the exception of the Château du Jardin in Cassel — 'a bloody place, unlived in, damp and frightfully cold', he noted — they were 'comfortable'. His empathy with the living conditions other ranks had to 'put up with' did not prevent him from stocking up with the luxuries he was accustomed to in civilian life.

'You might get Fortnum & Mason to send me a box of provisions once a fortnight — including potted meat, chocolate, pates, etc,' he wrote to his father the week after he arrived on the Front: 'You might also ask the Cook to send me out once a week a good pie.' A few days later, he had asked Charlie to arrange a weekly order of 'square chocolate from Charbonnel and Walker'.

Such luxuries were commonplace at staff headquarters. Fortnum & Mason, the store's records reveal, was doing a roaring trade with well-heeled officers. From the autumn of 1914, they were able to order provisions from a special catalogue. Fortnum's offered a range of hampers. 'Parcels Post Box No. 7' — at £2 10sh — included '25 Partagás Coronas Cigars, 100 Grand Format Cigarettes, 1 *F & M* Plum Pudding, 1 Tin *F & M* Pressed Caviare, 1 Tin *F & M* Galantine Game (truffled), and 1 Air Cushion.' Officers could order more or less anything they wanted — from crystallized and glacé fruits, tins of sardines, best Dorset butter, potted meats (various), Oxford sausages and pâté de foie gras to Tunis dates, Elvas plums, and muscatels and dessert almonds.

The contents of the hampers were a far cry from the rations issued to the troops. Army regulations stipulated a soldier's daily allowance down to the last ounce. While monotonous, for many the diet was healthier — and the food in more generous supply — than the meals they were used to at home:

1 1/4 pounds fresh meat (or 1 pound preserved meat)
1 1/4 pounds bread
4 ounces bacon
3 ounces cheese
1/2 pound fresh veg (or 2 ounces dried)
1/4 oz coffee
2 ozs sugar
4 ozs jam
1/2 oz salt
5/16 oz tea
1/6 lb butter

1/8 part tin of milk

In the trenches, fresh meat was seldom available and was substituted with bully beef or maconochie, a tinned meat and vegetable stew named after its manufacturer. Bread was also difficult to get hold of and was replaced with pearl biscuits — likened to dog biscuits by the troops.

'I am very comfortable,' John wrote to Marjorie after lunching with General Pulteney at his château at Bailleul, 'but it is a quiet life. Dull and most boring.' He was also finding it frustrating. He hated the 'rulebook mentality' of the generals he met on his trips to Corps HQ, and at the headquarters of other divisions. 'Oh how I wish I could express all my feelings about this life,' he wrote to Charlie: 'The pomposity, unnecessary rudeness, red tape, and the universal habit of believing that "youth is a crime" is increased tenfold. They [the generals] no doubt know their jobs fairly well, but they all behave like prehistoric men clothed in khaki. They laugh and joke and dance when the smallest, most trivial thing goes right — but lose completely all self-control when anything goes wrong. 'There certainly will have to be a large publicly supported asylum for the millions of old decrepit and deformed generals after the War. I should also suggest for the future that all the military should go through a class of commonsense for their benefit. They sorely need it.'

The outing to Sharpenburg to watch the attack at St Eloi came as a welcome distraction from the round of château visits, but even there John found the behaviour of his fellow officers offensive. To his disgust, after an hour or so, the others unloaded picnic hampers from their car. Seated on a rug, they continued watching the attack while eating, and drinking claret. 'They might as well have been at the bloody races!' he wrote to his sister afterwards. 'Rothesay and I told them we didn't want anything. We moved further up the ridge and watched the battle on our own.'

Beneath the strobing sky ahead, almost a thousand British soldiers were being killed and wounded. John could not know the scale of the losses; if he had, his response to the other officers might have been stronger. Nor could he know that the attack he was watching had a direct bearing on him.

Twenty miles away, George Moore was at General Headquarters. He had spent the day with Sir John French.

Moore was on a flying visit to the Front. The previous evening — when he arrived at St Omer — Sir John, who was still at his Advance Headquarters at Hazebrouck, was too tired, and too depressed to see him. He had just received the casualty figures for the Battle of Neuve Chapelle. 'I am very sad tonight for our losses are terrible,' he wrote to Winifred: 'However there are many thousands of dead Germans lying on our front, and I believe their losses in this 3 day battle to have been nearer 20,000 than anything else. On both sides some 150,000 have been engaged in 3 days — the losses are 30,000 between them! Equal to 20%! Such is war of today! The casualty lists always make me sad. There is comfort in the fact that the Doctors report many more <u>slight</u> wounds than usual. We will now "go easy" for 2 or 3 days and then have another go. The German prisoners say "This isn't War but Carnage." I agree with them!'

The next morning, Moore drove up to Hazebrouck to see the commander-in-chief. The purpose of his visit was to discuss their 'plan' for John. After spending 'two quiet hours' together, they drove back to St Omer; on their way, they made a detour to Helfaut, a small village, some four miles due south of the town.

There, they saw Major Charles Foulkes.

Foulkes was integral to their plan. Some months earlier, Sir John had charged Moore with setting up a weapons research station at Helfaut. Its remit was to experiment with new devices: rocket bombs, mortars, gas, and flame projectiles. The project, which was top secret, was still in its infancy, but in the years to come, 'Special Brigade', as it was to be called, would spearhead the development of chemical weaponry, enabling the British to wrest the initiative from the Germans.

Foulkes, a charismatic, highly decorated officer in the Royal Engineers, was the man they had chosen to command the brigade. In the run-up to establishing it, chemists, meteorologists and other scientific and engineering experts were being sought — both in the BEF and at universities in England.

Moore wanted John to join the brigade; the fact that he had no knowledge of chemistry, or weaponry, was immaterial: what mattered was that it was based a safe twenty-five miles from the front line.

In mid-February, Moore persuaded the

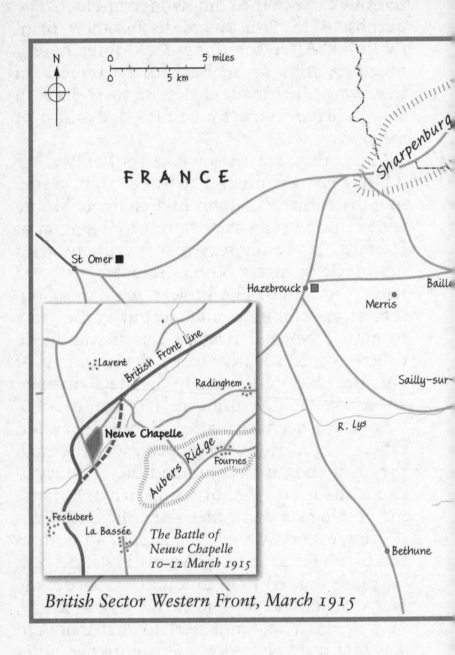

N

0   5 miles
0   5 km

FRANCE

Sharpenburg

St Omer ■

Hazebrouck ●■

Baille

Merris ●

British Front Line

Lavent

Radinghem

Sailly-sur-

Neuve Chapelle

Aubers Ridge

Fournes

R. Lys

Festubert

La Bassée

The Battle of
Neuve Chapelle
10–12 March 1915

Bethune ●

British Sector Western Front, March 1915

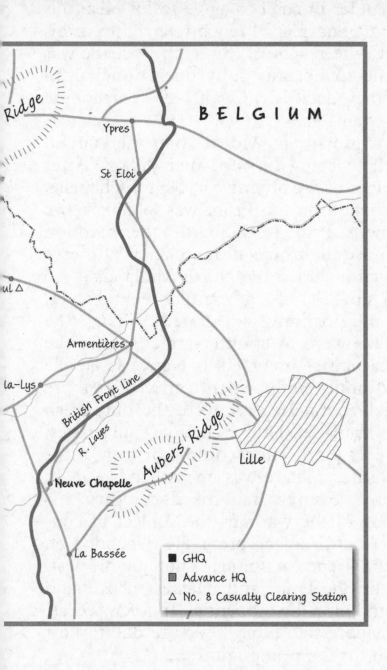

commander-in-chief to agree to his idea: this was the 'good plan' French referred to in his letter to the Duchess. But as the brigade was not due to become fully operational until June, they decided to wait before arranging John's transfer.

That morning, Moore had persuaded French to bring forward their 'plan'. After the failure of the offensive at Neuve Chapelle, the situation on the Front was looking more precarious. Prior to the battle, the intention was to use the troops of the General Reserve — which included the North Midlands — to sweep up after a successful breakthrough. Now, the position had altered. What if the Germans were to counter-attack? After the high casualties incurred at Neuve Chapelle — and until reinforcements arrived — those of the General Reserve were the only fresh troops available. Under such circumstances, Moore argued, they could not guarantee John's safety. There was one other factor. In England, French had his detractors: his handling of the war was the subject of constant criticism in the press. He depended on powerful friends at home to shore up his position, and the Duke and Duchess of Rutland were undoubtedly influential. In a few weeks' time, Moore told him, they were due to host a lunch for the prime minister.

These were the arguments that convinced French to make the detour to Helfaut. There, he told Foulkes that John would be joining the brigade.

The last thing he expected, however, was that he would have to spring him from the front line within hours.

In his diary, French gave a short account of the events of that afternoon:

I went in to St Omer to take GM back there and had a talk with him (about casualties and reinforcements), and to Foulkes (about rocket bombs and <u>Granby</u>). On my way back here, I heard a fierce and unceasing cannonade coming from the direction of Ypres.

The commander-in-chief was not prone to underlining; it was evidence of his anxiety. He was writing his diary in the early hours of the following morning after a sleepless night. The Germans, he feared, were about to break through the British lines.

It was the attack at St Eloi that he'd heard as he was driving back to Hazebrouck. Following the Battle of Neuve Chapelle, he was expecting to ' "go easy" for 2 or 3 days'; the counter-attack caught him completely by surprise.

He'd said little in his diary for that day, but in a letter to Winifred, written the next afternoon, he described what happened after he dropped Moore back at GHQ:

I motored GM back to my headquarters at St Omer and left him. On my return, I heard a most violent and prolonged cannonade suddenly break out in the northern part of the line just south of Ypres. That is where the 2nd Army are. I've seldom heard a hotter fire during the war. A little later, I got a message saying that 27th Division of the 5 Corps had been drawn out of their trenches and that the enemy had captured St Eloi. You may imagine that I didn't have a v tranquil evening or night. However, a strong counter-attack was arranged by 2 o'clock this morning, and after severe fighting the enemy was drawn out and the positions retaken by one o'clock today. This was absolutely unexpected for the Germans had reduced their troops on that front to reinforce their lines opposite to us on the 10th and 11th [the Battle of Neuve Chapelle]. This has cost us a good many more men I fear, and it shows how suddenly the situation changes — all in a moment.

So shaken was French by the attack that the minute he was told that his troops had retaken St Eloi, he ordered his ADC, Lieutenant-Colonel Fitzgerald Watt, to deliver a letter to the North Midlands headquarters at Sailly-sur-la-Lys.

Uppermost in his mind at this critical time was 'Granby'. At the point he ordered Watt to drive the eight miles to Sailly, he had no way of knowing whether the situation at St Eloi was stable. Yet, extraordinarily, he was releasing his close aide, a senior officer, to honour his promise to the Duchess.

On roads that were clogged with lines of troops and military transport, it was a round trip of several hours.

At Sailly, John and General Stuart Wortley were packed up, ready to go. It was clear some confusion reigned at General Headquarters. The division had been under orders 'to move at 2 hours' notice' since 7.30 on the thirteenth. For two days they waited for confirmation to proceed to their new headquarters, until, at 09.30 hours, GHQ wired instructions 'to stand fast in the present area'. Now that order had been countermanded, and the North Midlands were about to march to Merris, a small village some ten miles to the east.

A number of the battalions had already started out. It was a relief to be leaving Sailly. For seventy-two tense hours, dressed in full battle kit and camped in the freezing cold in a field on the edge of the village, they had waited for the order to go into action at Neuve Chapelle. They were three miles from the battlefield; the shells, fired from the Royal Horse Artillery's howitzers on the hill behind them, had screeched over their heads. After the battle ended, the scenes in the village, where numerous hospitals were located, had been depressing. Fleets of ambulance wagons had ferried in the casualties; open at the back, the wounded soldiers, their uniforms caked in blood and mud, were all too visible.

Outside the North Midlands headquarters the walking wounded still crowded the narrow cobbled street. John and General Stuart Wortley were waiting at the entrance to the building. It was mid-afternoon and they had been kicking their heels for several hours. Having completed the final arrangements for the move to Merris, yet another message had come through from General Headquarters. Colonel Watt was on his way; he had an important letter for General Stuart Wortley which the commander-in-chief had instructed him to deliver personally. The general was not to leave until Watt arrived.

It was shortly after four o'clock when the staff car carrying Watt drove through the wrought-iron gates and pulled up on the gravel forecourt. Stepping briskly out of the car, he saluted the general and handed him the commander-in-chief's letter. His instructions were to wait, he explained. The commander-in-chief was expecting a reply by return.

Stuart Wortley read the letter and passed it to John. 'He wants you to go to GHQ,' he said, looking at him quizzically: 'He tells me you're a famous inventor and that you know all about bomb-making. What do you want to do?'

An awkward silence followed while John read the letter. As Watt knew — and Stuart Wortley suspected — this was shady business. It was made the more uncomfortable by the backdrop against which it was taking place. The three men, immaculately turned out in their staff officer uniforms, were standing on the steps of the North Midlands headquarters. Through the railings that framed the forecourt, they could see the wounded going past. These were men who had fought bravely for King and country. Watt, the commander-in-chief's trusted confidant, had been privy to his 'plan' from the beginning. He knew it was the location of the Inventions Department★ rather than John's 'inventiveness' that lay behind his offer: the reference to 'bomb-making' was no more than a sop to mask his intention of removing the young marquis from the firing line.

John had barely skimmed the contents of the letter before he answered the general's question. 'The commander-in-chief must have confused me with someone else,' he replied: 'I'm not an inventor and I don't

★ The name then for Foulkes's Special Brigade.

know anything about bombs.'

Relieved to hear that he was not about to lose his ADC to General Headquarters, Stuart Wortley went in search of a piece of paper to write a note to Sir John.

A few minutes later, he returned and handed the note to Colonel Watt to take back to St Omer.

As Watt left, he saluted the general. Then he shook John's hand and wished him luck.

While John had no idea that his mother was behind the commander-in-chief's offer, his reply to General Stuart Wortley was disingenuous. It was not the first he'd heard of the job at GHQ.

'After tea, Lt-Col. Watt came over with a letter from the C-in-C for our General. I knew what it was about,' he noted in his diary later that evening.

A month or so earlier — before he left England — Moore had invited him to one of the 'Dances of Death'.

The commander-in-chief was not at Lancaster Gate that evening; he was in France, finalizing the preparations for the Battle of Neuve Chapelle. Following the customary dinner of exotic delicacies, Moore had sidled up to John and told him about the secret weapons project he was setting up at St Omer. He asked if John would be interested in joining

553

the brigade.

John shared his father's opinion of 'Little Big Head'. He thought him a swaggering, oleaginous figure, and his intimacy with the commander-in-chief — and the inside knowledge it conferred — grated. He was too polite to cut his host; as they chatted at the edge of the dance floor, he feigned interest in what Moore had to say. But he had no intention of following up the offer, or — were it to come to anything, which he doubted — of accepting it. Knowing the American's infatuation with his sister, he assumed he was bragging because he wanted to ingratiate himself.

The next morning, John called in at his uncle's house in Chelsea. A row ensued after he mentioned the conversation. Firmly, Charlie told him he ought to follow up the offer. John thought it a preposterous idea. How could he? He had no knowledge of weaponry; besides, he wanted to fight with the North Midlands. Charlie retaliated with the familiar and depressing facts: his father's estates were saddled with mortgages, which, if they were ever to be repaid, depended on his survival. If he was killed in action, his sisters and his mother would be left penniless: under the rules of entail, when Henry died, the estate, together with the dukedom and the heirlooms, would pass to his half-brother, Cecil. And what then? Cecil was a confirmed bachelor: he was never going to marry and produce an heir. Next — and the last — in line was Robert: he had a daughter, but no son. If John was killed, the line would die out. His family, Charlie reminded him, had been at Belvoir since the eleventh century; he could trace his lineage back to Robert de Todeni, a standard-bearer to William the Conqueror at the Battle of Hastings. Could he really be so selfish as to risk the ruination of his entire family?

While John pointed out that his duty was not to the Manners family, but to his country, the row ended with Charlie begging him to think about the offer. They left it at that. In the weeks that elapsed, there had been no further mention of the matter: John inferred that it had been dropped.

At Merris, on the evening of 15 March, it was with a heavy heart that John sat down to write to Charlie to tell him that he had declined the commander-in-chief's offer. He was adamant that it was his duty to serve with the North Midlands, but still he felt emotionally torn.

Since John's arrival at the Front, neither his parents nor Charlie had made it easy for him. Far from putting a brave face on things, their letters were a constant reminder of the hurt he was inflicting on them.

Violet, as the Duke reported, had taken to her bed with an illness brought on by the strain of his departure: 'Mummy has been very seedy indeed since you left, and Hood says she must take great care as she is so weak and has got neuralgic pains all over.' A few days later, Violet herself had written to tell him of her collapse: 'Darling, Very bad stupid unkind flu came and stifled my misery. I wish it had come 4 days sooner for you to be knocked down by it!! You are never out of my thoughts. <u>Please be careful</u>.'

But it was Charlie's letters that John found painful. He was missing his uncle, and being the cause of anxiety was upsetting. 'I got your letter from Folkestone,' Charlie wrote the morning after seeing him off at Victoria station: 'It was like a glass of champagne. Don't worry about me, my Colonel. When you left I think I touched the highest point of mind-misery yet reached. I fear I showed it — though I tried not to. Anyhow, now it is to be all philosophy and making the best of it.'

Charlie had not made the best of it; a few days later came another letter: 'Old boy, I do hope you are all right and that you take <u>great care</u>. Think of me sometimes after 5 o'clock, a lonely creature in my room who never has his thoughts away from you. But who looks forward always to happier times.'

'Yes, Old Boy, I have often thought of you in your room and I wished I was there for two reasons,' John replied from Sailly. 'One to cheer you up, and one to be back myself, but we must both be very cheerful and hope for better times. We are in the same place. Today a tremendous lot of gun firing and as it was a fine sunny day and good for observations and patrolling, our aeroplanes were very active. It really was a very pretty sight. There were five or six up in the air the whole time — some guarding our big gun, and others just letting the Germans know they had better not brave the ground with theirs. Yes, I take great care. I expect now we shall be in this village for some time, as we don't seem to be able to push any further ahead. Will write again tomorrow.'

He reassured Charlie again in his next letter: 'You still seem very worried about me out here. Don't be. I will let you know before you need be. I don't want you ill when I get back because we shall both have to be extra energetic to make up for lost antiquarian time.'

But only that morning, John had received yet another anxious letter:

Dear Jacko,
Your letters are wonderful. I have just got yours of Mar 12 — but you've no idea how terrified I feel at your being so forward. Don't extra risk things, my Colonel, for God Almighty's sake.
A small black kitten has suddenly taken up its abode in my tree opposite the din-

557

ing room here, which you can never see the beauty of. I was going to chase it away but Mrs Leeds says it is the luckiest thing in the world so today I bought some cats-meat and put some milk down and it jumped into my room, where it has remained. I hope it will bring both of us luck. Nothing of this kind must be laughed at now.

As John agonized over his letter to Charlie, he did not have the heart to tell him that he had flatly declined the job at St Omer; instead, he opted to break the blow gently. 'Old Boy,' he began:

The question of changing my job was started today by the General receiving by the hand of Sir John's ADC a letter from the C-in-C on that subject. I read the letter in front of the two and was asked what I should do. I had your feelings and my family well in the foreground but it was not possible to do anything but say that I had no experience in bombs or that I was a famous inventor, both of which I was accredited with in the letter. The letter was not couched in any way of a request or order but merely suggesting that as he had heard of the two attributes to my name I should be a useful person if it was true. I hope you will believe me when I say it was out of the question to do anything else.

Unwitting of his mother's role in the affair, he was also anxious to spare her feelings: 'You may use your own discretion about telling this to Mother. Perhaps it is unnecessary to tell her.

'There have been tremendous losses on both sides these last three days,' he continued: '12000 casualties at Neuve Chapelle. Awful. We move tomorrow — a little way back — what a bore not being able to tell you where. Am very well. Give my love to the cat.'

John need not have agonized over his letter. Charlie would know his decision before he received it.

At General Headquarters, Sir John had sealed the note General Stuart Wortley had sent him inside an envelope, and handed it to a King's messenger. He was to take it to George Moore at Lancaster Gate.

Even as John was writing, the messenger was halfway across the English Channel. By midnight, Charlie and Violet knew the commander-in-chief's 'good plan' had failed.

51

Early the next morning — 16 March —
George Moore summoned Charlie to see him
at Lancaster Gate. A footman ushered him
into the spacious drawing room. Moore was
in an ill humour; gruffly, he invited Charlie
to sit down.

'Your boy's failed me,' he growled, handing
him General Stuart Wortley's letter: 'I don't
understand it. He as good as promised me he
would go.'

The drawing room was on the first floor.
Overlooking Hyde Park, it was furnished with
antiques and paintings of the St Leger. The
former 'property of a gentleman', they had
been bought by Moore in a job lot at auction.

John's refusal, he went on to tell Charlie,
had placed him in an embarrassing position.
His 'Great Friend' (Sir John French) had
entrusted him to execute his plan. He had
given his word to the Duchess that he could
do something for her son. In declining the

job, John had humiliated him: he had been made to look a fool in front of both the Duchess and the field marshal.

A means *had* to be found to save face all round. But, before proceeding any further, he wanted to know why John had turned the job down. Had his general forced him to decline the offer? Or had he refused it on principle?

Charlie could only reply that while he was unable to explain what lay behind his nephew's decision, he was equally determined to secure a satisfactory outcome.

'Find out why he turned it down,' Moore instructed him. 'And find out where Stuart Wortley stands.'

Depending on the answers, he continued, they had just two options. Either pressure would have to be brought to bear on John to reverse his decision, or, if it turned out that the general was behind his refusal, he must be made to see that John should be allowed to join Foulkes's brigade.

They agreed to do nothing for the time being. It was Tuesday; they would reconvene at the Duke's house at Arlington Street on Thursday. By then, Charlie ought to have heard from John.

When Charlie got home, he was hoping to find a letter from his nephew. But there was nothing in the post. In a state of despair, he spent the rest of the day composing a long letter to him:

Dear Old Jacko
You can hardly realise the miserable broken-down old man who writes to you. Old boy, I had built all my hopes on one event and I don't think I ever really believed you would fail.

Through Moore, I have heard that you have decided not to go and all doubt removed by being shown Wortley's letter to Sir John declining it on your behalf. A letter worthy of the man, short and ungrateful and implying that you were no other use than a chauffeur and would be quite out of place on the C-in-C's Staff — 'Granby has no inventive genius', which is a damned lie. The letter was enclosed by Sir John with a note from himself showing surprise and distress. He had thought you would be sure to come to him. I don't know why I go on writing like this, old boy, except that tonight I really don't care what happens or what you think of me — utterly miserable — and an utter failure with everything I wish for, or everybody I care for.

M says he can't understand as you as good as promised him about it and thinks it's not you but a cursed pressure on you.

Do me at least the kindness, my Colonel, to let me know what happened and whether anything further can be done. I don't dare talk to your mother, even on the telephone. She is utterly broken-hearted, as so am I.

Dear, dear Colonel, forgive me for writing like this, you don't know what one feels like in England for one's friends in this ghastly war. Don't tell me not to worry because it does me no good, and it is rot into the bargain, but take this letter kindly, you won't get another one like it again.

Charlie was of course being duplicitous. He omitted to tell John that he was in league with Moore, and that — together with Violet — they were about to take steps to corral him into going to St Omer.

Two days later — on the evening of 18 March — Charlie went round to Arlington Street to see Violet. John's letter from Merris had failed to arrive. In the absence of any answer from John, and as instructed by Moore, it was important to establish where Stuart Wortley stood in the affair. Their best tactic, they decided after talking it over, was for the Duke to write to the general. It was not, they concurred, a letter that Henry was capable of writing himself. Slow-witted, and prone to ill-considered, angry reactions, he lacked the guile. Charlie would have to draft the letter for him. Violet assured him that Henry would sign it: he was as anxious for John to go to St Omer as they were.

The lights burnt late into the night at Arlington Street. It was a difficult letter to compose. Beyond eliciting a response from Stuart Wortley, its purpose was twofold. First, the general was to be left in no doubt that John's move to GHQ had the Duke's blessing. Second, in a bid to ensure his complicity, he was to be flattered into thinking that the Duke was relying on him to provide John with guidance.

Charlie's masterstroke was the lie around which the letter turned. It did not admit to the fact that the Duke already knew that John had refused the commander-in-chief's offer.

After drafting the letter, Charlie showed it to Violet:

'My dear Eddy,' it read:

I have just heard that John is about to be or has been offered by Sir John French an employment at Headquarters.

I think that John will doubtless turn to you for advice and direction as to what he should do. I would ask you, even at the risk of temporary inconvenience to yourself, to encourage him as far as you can, not to decline an offer of so great importance to himself, which from a natural feeling of loyalty to you, he may not see his way to accept.

I understand the opportunity would bring him into touch with engineering work of an inventive kind, in which I think his capabilities in that direction should ensure his being of use.

I think you will agree with me that for his own sake such a chance should not be lightly discarded.

Yours etc
Rutland

Before handing the letter to a footman, who was to take it to the Duke so that he might copy it out in his own hand, Violet inserted a note below the last paragraph. Ever the consummate flatterer, she knew it was important to make her husband feel that he had at least made a contribution:

'Then add something like, "I hope you don't mind me writing," ' she wrote: 'And something of the great praise you have heard of the Division, and its quick moving etc. Your loving VR.'

A week later, on Thursday 25 March, 16 Arlington Street was once again the setting for another clandestine meeting.

Shortly before 7.30 p.m., Mrs Seed, the elderly lodge keeper, opened the black wooden gate that screened the house from prying eyes. It was a wet, blustery evening. Above her, the wind rattled the octagonal glass mantle which hung from the keystone of the arch that led into the cobbled court-yard. The light inside it was off. A blackout — a precaution against Zeppelin air raids — was in force and the street was in darkness. There, as instructed by Violet, she waited.

Big Ben's quarter bells chimed in the distance. It was the quiet hour. On the park side of the street, looking up towards the Ritz Hotel, the forecourts in front of the houses were empty. Their occupants were changing for dinner. In half an hour's time, fleets of cars would fill the street, bringing their guests. But for now it was deserted.

Well into her eighties, Old Mother Seed, as the family called her, had served the Rut-lands since she was a child. Her position was an important one. The lodge was the only route in and out of the house. As Violet's letters reveal, she depended on Mrs Seed to spy on her children's movements: she also depended on her when she had visitors she wanted to sequester.

Earlier that day, Violet had called in on the lodge keeper. She was on her way back from Dorchester House, Lady Holford's palatial mansion in Park Lane. The house, which was now a hospital for wounded officers, was unrecognizable to her. The famous Velasquez, together with other valuable treasures, had been packed away in the cellar. On the first floor, the ballroom where she had danced as a debutante had been transformed into a sitting room for convalescents. Beds, screens, medicine cabinets and operating tables filled the other reception rooms.

Lady Holford had opened her hospital in honour of the forty wounded officers that had arrived from the Front. Among them were the first casualties from the Battle of Neuve Chapelle. It was Violet's second visit in a week — the previous Wednesday, she had spent the afternoon there with the King and Queen. After a traumatic afternoon sitting at the soldiers' bedsides, she left after tea.

As Violet hurried home, her priority was to see Mrs Seed. She had explicit instructions for her. At half past seven she was expecting an important visitor. Would she please close

the gate after his arrival: no one, she empha-
sized, must see his car in the courtyard.

At the appointed hour, the cream Silver
Ghost she had warned her lodge keeper to
look out for turned into Arlington Street. It
belonged to George Gordon Moore.

Stepping aside, Mrs Seed stood in the lee
of the arch as the car passed. Then — as
instructed — she closed the gates firmly
behind her.

An hour later, the Duke, Violet, Charlie and
Moore were closeted alone in the dining
room. To ensure their conversation went no
further, the footmen were told to leave the
room after serving them. The soft light of the
candelabra, the rich tones of the Old Master
paintings, the glint of gold and crystal, accentuated the grim expressions on their faces.

A small pile of letters lay on the table in
front of them. One was from General Stuart
Wortley: it was clear from his reply to the
Duke's letter — the one Charlie had drafted
for him — that he had not influenced John's
decision to turn down the job at GHQ.

'My dear Henry,' the general had replied:

Some days ago Sir John French wrote to
me saying that he had been told John was
an inventive genius; and asked me if I
would spare him to go to St Omer to

consult with the CRE* there on the manufacture of bombs and grenades. I told John immediately of Sir John's letter, but he said that he knew nothing of the making of such articles and could not be of any assistance in that respect.

I saw Sir John and told him this but I said that of course if he wished John to go to St Omer, I should certainly not stand in his way. Since then I have heard nothing more of the subject.

We have again relapsed into a condition of inactivity chiefly from want of gun ammunition. I do not see how we are going to supply two armies in the field at opposite ends of Europe — it is difficult enough to supply one.

The Division is getting on very well. I have a Brigade and several guns in the trenches.

Yours, Edward Stuart Wortley

The other letters were from John. Short of being ordered to go to St Omer, he was insisting on staying put with the North Midlands. He was not going to be a party to string pulling: 'my temperament will not allow of it,' he told Charlie.

While Violet had convened the crisis meeting, it was Moore who was chairing it. The

* Commander, Royal Engineers.

problem, as he explained, was that the commander-in-chief could not *order* John to go to St Omer. In recent weeks, the press had accused him of cronyism; he had appointed too many aristocratic officers to his staff. Further, John had spurned his offer: he could hardly be expected to reissue it. First, they had to find a means of keeping the offer open without compromising the commander-in-chief. How they were going to force John to back down was a separate issue — one they would address in due course.

In tackling the first problem, it was Moore who came up with a simple solution. Why not claim that Sir John's letter to General Stuart Wortley had contained a clerical error? The word 'bombs' should have read 'catapults'. Besides working on explosives, Foulkes's brigade would be developing missile projectiles. Its remit was to design weapons that could shoot long jets of flame, and hurl canisters of gas, and other chemicals, into the enemy's lines. John had turned down the job on the basis that he had no experience in 'bomb making', but his interest in medieval history was undeniable. The fact that he had no scientific understanding of the dynamics of projectiles, and that his knowledge of catapults was both cursory and incidental to his interest in the medieval period, was irrelevant. The crucial point was that if Sir John could claim that he had meant to say 'catapults', and it was John's historical expertise that he was interested in, he could reissue his offer.

On this basis, General Stuart Wortley was easily dealt with. If he was subtly made aware of the clerical error, and if it was hinted that he would incur the displeasure of both the Duke and the commander-in-chief were he to dissuade John from joining the brigade, he ought not to put up any obstacle.

Then and there, they drafted a letter to the general:

My dear Eddy,
Many thanks for your letter. I can't help thinking it was a pity John should have been so modest and diffident about himself.

His friends, at any rate, have always given him the credit for a good deal of ability and intelligence in the direction of inventions and contrivances, such as might conceivably have been of some value in these times.

In any case, his interest in such things as bomb-throwers and catapults, and the time he has spent, or wasted, over them is undeniable.

But what troubles me most is that I understand Sir John, who, as you say, had heard of John's interest in these things, is rather surprised at his decision, and naturally ascribes it to a disinclination to help him.

I have just heard this from one of Sir John's intimate friends here. I think, if you can spare him, John ought to go to see Sir John, if only to make it clear that it was a want of confidence in himself, and not a want of willingness, that induced what may have been rather a hasty decision.

Yours ever, Rutland

John was last on the agenda. After much discussion, the four of them decided their only option was to tell him that he must do as he was told.

It was left to Charlie to issue his nephew with firm — and elaborate — instructions.

In the letter he wrote to John later that evening, Charlie did not tell him that the strategy he was proposing had been devised over the course of a long, conspiratorial dinner with George Moore — *and his parents:*

Dear Jacko

I have got — again — to write to you upon the subject which I know bothers you very much, but it is simply out of the question that I should shirk it.

I have had <u>another</u> interview with Mr Moore whom I believe will be in France within a day or two. It is his wish that I say what I do in this letter, and as it is upon him that all rests in this matter, there is no use in weighing our own opinions against his as to what is best and what is not. You must use your own judgement and do what you think is right.

Your father is writing to your General by this post. In this letter, he says he thinks it was a pity you were so modest about yourself, that your friends, at any rate, have always credited you with keenness and interest in inventions, contrivances, catapults etc. He also says that he hears Sir John ascribes your decision to your unwillingness to come and is a bit sad, as he has been told that you take interest in these things. Your father suggests that if you can be spared, you should go over and see Sir John, if only to make it clear that it was really from want of confidence in yourself that you declined.

It is expected that your General will now suggest to you to go over there, and you are not to throw any obstacle in the way. In fact you are to add that you also have heard of Sir John's feelings in the matter, and that you think as a matter of fact that you ought to go and make peace. As a fact, what I have said of Sir John is true — he is a bit sad and surprised at the failure of his little effort.

In the unlikely event of your General

suppressing the whole matter, you are to try and revive it by saying you have heard a good deal from England, or from Mr Moore (who does not mind being mentioned) about Sir John's sadness. If by ill fortune you read this letter after your General has spoken to you, you are to revive the matter as explained. When your General shows you, or reads you, your father's letter, you are to say — "oh yes, it's those catapults, I understand it all now" — and then say something about your having worked at them, or interested yourself in them, and talked about them [with Sir John].

If you go back to see Sir John you are to take the line that you are far from being an expert, though always interested, and that you are willing to make yourself useful and do all you can with suggestions etc, however little confidence you have in being of use.

Mr M says that that part is the least to be feared of all. He is convinced that without any real knowledge at all, you are certain to be of use, and I am absolutely certain of it myself. Remember nothing is expected of you.

This is what I was to tell you, and this is the way Mr M wants it done if possible. If it can be done without Sir John having to give deliberate orders, it is far best.

John evidently thought the notion that he should join a top-secret weapons establishment as a leading expert in projectiles was as laughable — and as unethical — as it was. To mollify Charlie, he wrote back to tell him that he would make an appointment to see the commander-in-chief. In truth, though, he had no intention of doing so.

What he did not know was that, at 16 Arlington Street, his family were monitoring his every move.

53

'Darling C, I am in pieces!!! Can't you send a telegram to say he <u>must</u> see Sir J??'

Violet was writing to her brother from Belvoir. A week had passed since Charlie had instructed John to make an appointment with the field marshal and word had come from George Moore that he had not yet done so. 'Why is he so stubborn???' she fulminated: 'Look at the sons of other <u>Dukes</u>!!'

There was some truth in her remark. In March 1915, the heirs to seventeen of Britain's thirty dukedoms were of military age. But only ten — the eldest sons of the Dukes of Argyll, Atholl, Devonshire, Grafton, Leinster, Marlborough, Portland, Roxburghe, St Albans and Somerset — were serving in the trenches. The remainder were attached to Home Forces, or assigned to staff positions behind the lines.

Yet as Violet recognized, there was very little she could do. She dared not intervene for fear that John would get wind of the fact that she had engineered the job at St Omer. She decided to remain silent and to pretend that she was sanguine about his decision to remain with the North Midlands. The face she intended to present to him was of a loving, anxious mother who had only his interests at heart. This way, she could exert the maximum amount of emotional blackmail.

'Darling, How I wish you were here, here, and not there,' she wrote the morning after she and Charlie had sat up late into the night composing the letter from the Duke to General Stuart Wortley:

It's very hard to bear — and I have to be quite sensible with Charlie.

I wish I had more to do for you, shopping etc. Do you want warm underclothing of Father's, which are so lovely and warm? Are the socks right? We long to know your days and do take stupid extra care of yourself — some people are too silly.

I think of sending you a spoon for making a cup of tea — and some Grey's mixture tea. If ever you are chilled to the bone it is supposed that a large boiling cup of tea is the best of all things. Do you like compressed soups — and the compressed tea and Bovril I sent you? And the 'sweeties'?

Tell me this — do any of your men, officers, Doctor, want any <u>gloves</u> or <u>socks</u>? People ask a lot after you at Belvoir and they want your photographs perpetually, and Shannon is in despair that you never got painted. How I love you, my dear, my dear.

Yr most loving VR

Violet deluged John with provisions. With Easter coming, she commissioned Charbonnel and Walker to make him some special chocolate eggs. From the outside, they looked like real eggs:

My darling,
I have sent you some Easter eggs! (I thought them a novelty — Diana says rubbish!) Anyhow, I thought you might like to play a practical joke and place them for breakfast in egg cups to 'take on' the 'greedy for boiled eggs' lot on your Staff.

I sent some of our best <u>tea</u> from another shop! And some eatables in case any are divine and you want to order more.

Except for those poor ships torpedoed, London seems pleased with the war. Isn't it funny that Neuve Chapelle is considered a <u>gt victory</u> (and as the Germans admitted, surely it was?) We heard through Lady Essex spreading it — she heard it at the prime minister's Saturday to Monday

— that 5 Generals were sent home and that 500 of our men were killed by our own guns.

It is wicked — <u>wicked</u> — for any in authority to give such things into the hands of Lady Essex — to rumour abroad <u>on</u> good authority. <u>So cruel</u> for those in trouble, a thing forever to be hushed up and if 'bad luck' and 'bad judgement' should have come their way — why a soothing veil or good excuse of health or Breakdown could have been used to hide up mistakes.

<u>Now</u> I hear everything is smooth — no one sent home — and <u>only</u> *15* wounded by our guns instead of 500 killed!!

Private

Oh, keep way <u>west</u> in your motoring with R* — go see Bouch† west of Haze-brouck.

John's sightseeing trips to Ypres and to other places of historical interest terrified Violet. Her bedroom at Arlington Street resembled a military headquarters: pinned to the walls of the room were maps of Belgium and northern France. As soon as the morning's newspapers came, she would scour them for reports of fighting in John's sector. After

* Rothesay Stuart Wortley, the general's son.
† Tommy Bouche, Master of the Belvoir Hounds.

checking to see there were no battles in his area, she marked up the fighting in other parts of the front line. Then, enclosing sketches, she bombarded John with instructions on the places he should avoid:

Don't go to Armentière for fun and such near the-edge-of-battle places when you have joy rides. Go <u>west</u> I implore — there are lovely things to be seen surely. <u>Maresquel</u>, between Montreuil and Hesdin and visit <u>L'Abbaye de Valloires</u>.

John replied to just one of Violet's letters. She could see he was keeping her at arm's length:

Mother dear
All well — and really don't want anything at all — I will write when I do.
    Yes — I know of your Generals who have been sent home over that failure — and a certain quantity of our men were killed by our guns, but that is inevitable.
                                    Goodnight, John

Two weeks passed and Violet heard nothing from him. Then, on 12 April, she received a letter that threatened to sever all communication between them.

Mother dear

My General saw George Curzon today. Curzon said that you had asked him to try to get me back to near St Omer, but he said he would not interfere. I tell you this so that you may know what your confidants say. I personally would not trust Curzon one inch. He may have a wonderful brain but certainly no common sense. I don't mind one little damn what you do to gain whatever object you have — but I do not like people whom you confide in to tell everyone — and laugh at you at the same time. This is what Curzon has done.

I should give him 10 minutes of Hell for laughing at you — damned piece of machinery.

John held back from directing his fury at his mother. Her inveigling had humiliated him: 'people' were laughing at him too. But the mores of his time, and his class, dictated that he confine his attack to Lord Curzon.

Curzon was of course referring to his meeting with Violet the previous autumn, but John thought he was referring to the move to get him to go to St Omer.

His letter was proof to Violet that he suspected her of being behind the commander-in-chief's offer. In replying to John, she went through hoops to exonerate herself:

Darling Boy

Your letter just received (written Sunday) worries me — re G Curzon. Someone must have got it all wrong. Either you have misunderstood your General, or your General misunderstood G Curzon.

The last time I saw G Curzon was <u>end of Sept</u>. The last time he has written to me, or I to him, on the subject of anything but <u>Belgian soldiers</u> was <u>end of September</u>.

The rest of her letter was a complete fabrication. The previous October, she had expressly asked Curzon to meet her at Arlington Street; prior to the meeting, she had been pestering him to see her for weeks. But when it came to putting her side of the story, she denied it.

'This is how it was,' she continued: 'I have been looking through a bundle of letters and found one from him [Curzon]. It said':

'I was passing by your Bottesford yesterday — saw your castle on the heights and wondered how things are going with you and yours — do write to me.' So in writing, I remember saying, 'Oh you lucky man to have no son — this is the day for sonless parents!' Then he arranged to give me dinner that same week. Was very interested in <u>you</u> — and said, 'Why don't you get him under the Red Cross — the very thing for him with his good driving etc. Or why don't you get him on French's staff — that's what I should have done had I had a son!' I told him it was out of the question. I had never thought of it — for I was no friend of his — and that it was not likely at that distance from the beginning of the war that there was any room on his staff, and that I was happier your being <u>at home</u> with a chance of never going out at all!! And from that day to this I have not seen him! Or written to him on the subject of <u>you</u>. So, dear, someone has made a mistake!!! Haven't they?

It was not the only lie she told her son. At the end of her letter, in a veiled reference to Bethune's efforts to keep him back from the Front, she claimed she'd had nothing to do with it:

I know you suspected the fuss from the W.O. about your health came from me — I knew it didn't — and wrote a letter to your General which <u>I did not send</u> to tell him that I could only think it might come through Lady Wantage speaking to Lord Grenfell — but that I could not investigate it as she would most surely <u>deny</u> it!! Now, I begin to suspect Lord Curzon, and yet I don't believe he would have had time to think of me and mine!! He was so busy.

If he did say what you say he did, I really think he must have muddled me up with another mother. I should never let my heart out to G Curzon!! He does not possess sympathy and one should never ask for it or expect it.

As Violet was lying to John to conceal the moves she had made behind his back, she was in the midst of manoeuvring behind her daughter's back.

Diana, after completing her training at Guy's, was looking for a nursing job out on the Front. Violet was no less opposed to her going than she had been the previous summer. Determined to stop her, the plan she had come up with was to ask the Duke to turn Arlington Street into a hospital for wounded officers. If he agreed, she could convince Diana that her first duty lay at home.

Other dukes had loaned their London residences for wartime use: the Devonshires' house in Piccadilly was the headquarters of the Red Cross; Harcourt House, the Duke of Portland's house in Cavendish Square, was a hospital; Grosvenor House in Park Lane, the home of the Duke of Westminster, was being used by the government. But Henry was resistant to the idea of giving up his house.

He thought it would be 'knocked about' and that it would cost him too much money.

Recognizing that she was unlikely to convince her husband, Violet asked his former mistress, the actress Maxine Elliot, to persuade him. Since their affair had ended, Maxine and Henry had remained close friends. Violet, who had had several lovers of her own, had turned a blind eye to the affair, and was also friendly with Maxine.

Maxine negotiated a compromise: only half the house would be converted into a hospital and Henry's part of it would be reserved for his use.

Mindful of Henry's capriciousness, Violet wrote to thank him and to reiterate the case that Maxine had pressed on her behalf. Whether she felt guilty about sacrificing Diana to George Moore, or whether she simply wanted to tighten the reins she had loosened, she did not say. But Diana's probity was evidently uppermost in her mind:

Darling
This is a very sweet kind thing of you to do — and a surprise to me.

Since I discovered that you minded it so, I have hunted <u>high</u> and <u>low</u> for some other house. But for all my 'running about' looking, I have found nothing suitable.

My <u>extreme</u> anxiety is first of all for Diana. In a week or so, I may lose her forever, and the expense to you of more illnesses she may get, and the <u>over</u> freedom she will have, will cause you much more expense and anxiety! I do look ahead over this and tremble — most genuinely. You don't think I am doing it out of philanthropy, do you? But in the world's eyes it is good for <u>her</u>, and for <u>you, Dear</u> too — to give up a beautiful healthy house.

I wouldn't suggest it unless I knew it would not get hurt — the house I mean. I have seen your architect to talk it over. With his advice, there will be <u>nothing structural</u>, only the bath put into my bedroom, and where the bath is now, an active emptying sink.

My full intuition is that I should be able to make your expenses less in this house than usual. In fact similar to what they usually are during our <u>entire</u> absence from London. Housemaids and Mrs Seed are there. I will pay for every other servant.

But my dear don't, I pray you, be turned out. Try it first and see how perfectly it can be made comfortable for you. I would never have designed it unless I had known for sure that you could have lived in the house as usual, and in <u>perfect comfort</u>. <u>Better than usual</u>. Dear, promise me that you will anyhow <u>try</u> it. Please do. For you know I am if anything <u>practical</u>.

I will take down the curtains in Diana's bedroom and in mine. Those in the Ballroom are so common they can be left. And I will <u>cover up</u> the walls everywhere — 7 or 8 feet high. I shall have a writing-table in the dining-room. Diana will have my sitting-room, and I shall have the bedroom next yours. That is our <u>only</u> change.

About electric light. It will be used on this floor — very carefully — as patients don't want a blaze ever — like <u>we</u> have.

Would it be possible that if the house is a hospital the taxes can be less from June 1?

Don't forget, Dear, in this you <u>ease</u> me greatly about Diana and lift a heavy load off my heart and brain. She would doubtless infinitely prefer going out on her own to something bigger, but this would break my heart completely.

I shall put my bathroom and bedroom back to its original state after the hospital is over, and <u>nothing</u> will have been injured, I promise you.

I look forward to your taking a great interest in it, dear — and if you don't, it will be of a very great unhappiness to me.

<u>My thanks are huge</u> for the Diana trouble has been, <u>without her knowledge</u>,

very 'killing' to me for months.

Your loving wife VR

Violet had succeeded in stopping Diana from going to the Front. But John was still there and showing every sign of staying put.

Two weeks had elapsed since she had written to him about the meeting with Lord Curzon. He had not replied to her letter. Anxious to discover whether he believed her, she wrote to try to elicit some sort of response:

Darling, I want news! I always forget to say Esteeming, London, is <u>my telegram</u> registration name.

We have been making respirators — hateful — but War Office says they have enough! Is this possible, or is it that they are no good?

I see in last night's evening papers fighting in <u>your</u> region and nothing of it in morning papers — Armentière region and even Epinette? Your 'plug street' region?

Bless you, my darling, of course you know I never stop for 1 minute thinking of you.

Ten days later, she was still waiting for a reply to her letter.

Henry was faring no better. As Violet was floundering, he weighed in to exert his own form of pressure.

A few days after John received the field marshal's offer, he had written to tell his father that he had turned it down: 'Father dear, I expect you have heard by now how the Sir John affair ended — but I beg you to believe that I could not do otherwise.'

'Jack, my dear,' he replied, 'I understand, but do not miss your chance.'

In the same breath, he went on to mention his financial difficulties:

Not much to tell you here. Having got through the winter all right till a week ago, I contrived to catch a smart attack of 'flu' which kept me in bed for three days and has left me a wreck. But I am picking up and am able to entertain the Prime Minister at lunch today! A sort of friendly truce for the duration of the war. Whether I shall live till that event takes place I know not, but I don't feel like it at present.

I'm afraid that when you return you will find financial matters greatly altered for the worse. Even should matters go well for England, I can see no hope financially for anyone here. A report is being prepared as to what is recommended to be done about the whole position — for both estates, and 16 Arlington Street. I am afraid it will recommend a complete clos-

ing of Belvoir for some years; and the sale — if possible — of this house.* £113,000†
of mortgages have been called in, and to get the money the rate of interest will be at least 1% more.

Henry's focus on his financial difficulties was a heavy-handed way of reminding his son of his future responsibilities towards the Belvoir estate. While he stopped short of spelling it out, his message was clear: John was not in a position to take a moral stance over the Sir John affair. To risk his life was a luxury that he could ill afford. At the time Henry was writing, a complex set of insurance policies underpinned the mortgages on the estate. The slim prospect of keeping up the house of cards that Henry had constructed depended on John's survival. If he died, the policies would become void.

Nor had Henry any qualms regarding his own moral position. With one hand he was raising thousands of men for the war; with the other, he was pushing his son to accept a position thirty miles behind the front line, one that would guarantee his safe return.

'I hope you will see the commander-in-chief before you have gone much further,' he reminded John in the first week of April.

* 16 Arlington Street.
† Approximately £7 million at today's values.

'Recruiting is very brisk,' he added breezily: 'I am starting a bantam or another Service Battalion. I'm not sure which it will be.'

Later that day, Henry watched from a crossroads outside one of the villages on his estate as thousands of soldiers — the troops of the 11th (Northern) Division — marched past him. He was with Marjorie, his eldest daughter, and General Hammersley, the commanding officer of the division. The troops were on their way from Belton to a military camp near Farnborough, where they were to complete their training before going out to France.

The soldiers saluted the Duke and the general as they passed. The scene was one that Marjorie described to John:

Kitchener's 1st army from Belton marched through Knipton and by stages to Rugby this week, from where they go to some new camp or other. Father and I watched them from a crossroads with General Hammersley. Rather a wonderful sight — miles of them — Notts and Derby, East and West Yorkshire, South Staffs, Borderers, York and Lancs, Royal Engineers, Fusiliers, baggage wagons, pontoons, mules, ambulances etc. all the paraphernalia of war down the peaceful lanes and roads. I wonder when last England saw the like — miles of volunteer citizens on the march. Cromwell's time? 1715–45? When? They billeted 3 officers on the Knox's* (and they with no cook!) — and Knipton thrilled with billeted military and sentries for 2 nights.

Will you tell me where these new thousands are going to be put in the present line of fighting? As it is we have troops stationed almost 50 miles thick behind our firing line, haven't we? The men and horses all looked like <u>real</u> soldiers, I must say — all a match as to colour and shape — the only apparent difference being the great disparity of ages — young boys and grey-haired men marching shoulder to shoulder. I felt I'd have willingly shouldered my pack and marched off with them. I hate the feeling of standing idle with those poor dears — most of them breadwinners — doing all the dirty work.

In taking their salute, Henry, unlike his daughter, had felt no discomfort.

John treated his father's promptings to see the 'commander-in-chief' with the contempt they deserved: he refused even to acknowledge them.

The one person he was in regular touch with was Charlie. They were writing to each

---

* The Revd Knox, private chaplain to the Duke.

other two or three times a week. But he also ignored Charlie's pleas to make an appointment to see Sir John. He hadn't even written to Charlie to tell him what he thought about Moore's 'catapults' suggestion. His letters barely referred to the 'business' — as he called it.

On 12 April, almost a month after Sir John had first made his offer, and fed up with tiptoeing around the subject, Charlie's temper snapped:

Dear Jacko
I haven't time to write to you properly at this moment, as there is a pressing chance of sending this off at once, but I am told to let you have knowledge of the following extract which comes in a letter just received by Mr M from his Great Friend:
'Young Granby has never shown any sign of coming in to see me yet.'
You are urged very strongly to write to Brooke* to send for you the moment the Great Friend has time to see you. I feel sure you will understand this and act on it.

Yours C

John ignored this letter too. When he did

* Guy Brooke, later 6th Earl of Warwick, ADC to Sir John French.

write — a week later — it was to tell Charlie about the Battle of Hill 60 at Ypres.

54

North Midland Headquarters
France
20 April 1915

Old Boy,
Things are quite exciting here now.

On the 17th the English opposite Ypres had a large battle. I witnessed the fight from the top of Sharpenburg Hill. The attack was started by the exploding of six mines — laid by us under the German lines — each mine having 1 ton of explosives. We got up to the top of Sharpenburg at about 6.45pm. The mines were timed to go off at 7 o'clock. It was a most lovely evening with the sun setting behind us, thus showing up the ground in front of Ypres, and just to the north-west of St Eloi, where the attack was to take place.

The object was to capture a short line of the enemy's trench on the ridge of a hill called Hill 60 — about 300 yards in front of our own trenches. Punctually at seven, off went the mines, a most wonderful, but really awful sight. The explosion was a success, blowing up the whole of the German trench. Then, instantaneously, a terrific bombardment started. I never saw such an extraordinary sight. It was getting darkish and the hundreds and hundreds of shells bursting all the time, without intermission, made the country all around the attack look as if it was on fire, spotted with red flashes. At the same time the Germans began blazing off as hard as they could go. It was one continuous deafening roar. The Germans kept sending up hundreds of their rockets, which is a sign of wanting help when used in daylight.

In the attack, which was not altogether successful, we lost 600 men and 15 officers.

The Germans counter-attacked all that night (17th) and the following day. The impression it gave from a distance was that it was impossible to believe that anyone could live at all in such a fearful hell. The situation at 1am after the attack was this:

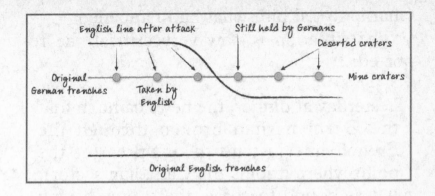

English line after attack

Still held by Germans

Deserted craters

Original German trenches

Taken by English

Mine craters

Original English trenches

So you see, even after using 6 tons of explosive, blowing up every German in the trench and knowing the exact moment when to dash forward to the attack, we were only able to occupy three out of the six craters up to the following morning (18th). Since then we have attacked again, and occupied the other three (but bringing the casualties up to 1500 men and 40 officers), and there is much doubt as to whether we shall be able to hold it, or will be obliged to fall back on our original lines.

John spent the next three days monitoring the progress of the battle from Sharpenburg Ridge. The position altered dramatically on the evening of 22 April when, six miles to the north-west of Hill 60, the Germans attacked the French and Canadian positions, firing poison gas. It was the first time it had been used in the war.

Late the following night, John wrote to

Charlie to tell him what had happened.

'The situation is now very critical,' he reported:

Yesterday at dinner, the news came in that the Germans had broken through the French line just north of Ypres (at the point where it joins the Canadian sector). It was bound to come, the enemy having been aggravated at Hill 60. Well they began their attack about 6pm yesterday with an historic bombardment not only along that bit of the line, but also all around Ypres. Ypres is now a total wreck — half the town burnt out and all the inhabitants fled. The Germans fired asphyxiating gas, which has the effect of sending one to sleep. It is a sweet-smelling stuff, which, when one smells it from a distance makes one's eyes run like anything, and makes one's mouth dry and hot. This was more than the French could stand and they fled like rabbits.

The battle is going on still something terrific. The Canadians, who had just as much gas, have behaved perfectly wonderfully. Up to now they have saved the situation by not moving at all. The French are sending up thousands of men — about fifty thousand. We have sent as many as we can — or at least are in the middle of doing so. To my mind, if the

Canadians hold out, it will be one of the finest things of this war. If they don't, well, it will be bad for our Divisions. A tremendous counter-attack will take place tomorrow morning.

The whole country along the affected line is on fire, at least everything that can catch fire. The shelling is practically as bad as at Neuve Chapelle, plus this new terror, 'gas'. I don't know what it is, but from my limited knowledge of chemistry, I should say it has a good quantity of Picric Acid in it. They fire it in cylinders — also, shells — which burst and emit fumes, some of them red fumes, others light green. Not dark green as with Lydite. Anyhow, it is a new terror, and the casualties will be awful.

As John was writing, the true deadliness of the gas began to filter through to the North Midlands headquarters. Six thousand French troops had died within ten minutes at Ypres; the Canadians had suffered a further six thousand casualties in the forty-eight hours that followed. Reports were also coming in from the North Midlands brigades in the reserve trenches at Messines. They were eight miles from Gravenstafel, where the Germans had fired the gas, but they were also feeling its effects.

'My God,' John continued after hearing the

reports, 'someone ought to be punished for this war. But England says she must play the game while her own men are being asphyxiated. If you kill, what does it matter <u>how</u>? If this gas job does not change the damned straight-laced gentlemanish habit of behaving properly, God help her. I suppose this will come out in the papers as a glorious victory. But the Germans have had a jolly good success, and it will cost us very dearly to retrieve this.'

John's anger increased after visiting the division's brigades at Messines. The authorities had failed to equip the army with any protection against poison gas. Until the respirators, now hurriedly being made in homes and factories up and down Britain, arrived at the Front, cotton mouth pads were the only form of protection available. But with the rush to supply the troops in the front-line trenches, the pads had not been issued to the divisions in reserve. Anxious to protect the North Midlands against the possibility of another gas attack, John spent the week driving to and from Boulogne, where he bought thousands of mouth pads. The authorities had not covered their cost: he had paid for them out of his own pocket.

Then, on 2 May, he visited No. 8 Casualty Clearing Station at Bailleul. What he saw there had a profound impact on him. The press censorship in force meant that journalists were banned from the front line, and from the casualty clearing stations in the rear, with the consequence that British newspapers had not carried first-hand reports of the horrific effects of the gas. Seeing the victims, John realized he was witness to sights that few outside the military had seen. When he got back to division headquarters, he wrote to his father:

Today I went with my General to see some of the men in hospital at Bailleul who were gassed at Hill 60. I am now going to put down on paper what I saw as the whole of England and the civilized world ought to have the truth fairly brought before them in vivid detail.

When we got to the Hospital, we had no difficulty in finding out in which ward the gassed men were, as the noise of the poor devils trying to get breath was sufficient to direct us. We were met by Colonel Beevor, a doctor belonging to our Division (N. Midland Div.), who took us into the ward. There were about twenty men in there, lying on mattresses, and all more or less in a sitting position propped up against the walls. Their faces, arms, hands were of a shiny grey-black colour, with mouths open and lead-glazed eyes, swaying slightly backwards and forwards, trying to breathe. I have seen some very

601

bad sights in my life but nothing compared with this. It was the most appalling sight all these poor black faces struggling, struggling for life — what with the groaning, and the noise of the efforts for breath.

Col. Beevor, who has had as wide an experience as anyone all over the savage parts of Africa etc., told me today that he had never been so sickened in all his life. There is practically nothing to be done for them except to try and make them vomit by giving them saline. The effect the gas has is to fill the lungs with a watery, frothy matter, causing gradual suffocation. In fact it is an awful form of torture — slow drowning — taking one, two and three days. Of course, only a certain percentage die, but what a death. The others may recover, but will be crippled for life. A good many already have died. Eight died this evening of the twenty fine strong men in the ward. Not one of the men I saw had a single scratch or a wound.

The nurses and doctors were all working heaven and earth against this appalling death with their usual calmness, but one could see what they were thinking and the tension of their nerves. I spoke to some and asked what they thought of it. I cannot repeat what the doctors or nurses said: the doctors because of the words they used, the nurses because it was written in their eyes.

The gas, I am told gives out a reddish-coloured vapour. It is in cylinders which, when they send it out, is propelled a distance of 100 yds. It then spreads. An officer who was in the trenches just when they let loose the gas had a piece of sponge in his jacket. He pissed on it and put it in his mouth. It saved his life, so perhaps ammonia is a good preventative. The Germans have given out that it is a rapid, painless death — the buggers and liars. I thought I would torture the next German I came across by old medieval tortures — but no, no torture could be worse than to give them a dose of their own gas.

I want you, if you will, to arrange for this to be put into journalistic language (in correct grammar etc), and published in all the papers in England, mentioning my General by name and as coming from me. Let the truth be known to every man and woman in England, and not hidden under the usual newspaper clouds.

That letter went on 2 May. The very next day he wrote another one, sent to his mother. What he had to say in the last paragraph was surprising:

Mother dear

I got your letter by Brooke and had a talk with him about things.

I quite understand your feelings and how nervous you must be feeling.

I have written a description to Father of the gassed men — quite the most appalling sights I have ever seen. I fear I have not been able to convey accurately what the effects are — as I cannot find words for my feelings. I want him to publish it abroad over the whole of England so that every man, woman and child knows what the enemy are doing to their sons, relations, etc.

Now about St Omer. I am ready to do what you want simply for your sake, though I expect I should not like it as much, as I have got more or less into this job. I know the people, etc. Do what you yourself want. But remember it must be an order.

It was almost two months since the commander-in-chief had first made his offer. John had finally caved in.

I found his capitulation utterly baffling. All along, he had refused to be a party to string-pulling: 'my temperament will not allow of it,' he'd told Charlie. Yet here he was telling his mother that he was 'ready' to do what she wanted.

My first thought was that the sight of the gassed soldiers had frightened him. But then just twenty-four hours earlier, in the letter he wrote to his father, he was angry, not fearful. It wasn't the letter of a man who wanted to run away; on the contrary, he seemed anxious to exact his own revenge on the Germans.

Violet's behaviour was also confusing. From the outset, she had been at pains to conceal the moves she had made behind John's back. Now, out of the blue, it seemed that she had admitted to him that she had engineered the job at General Headquarters. Why choose this moment to come clean when, just a few weeks earlier, she had lied to John to hide the fact that she had asked Lord Curzon to find him a job at St Omer?

And why wasn't John furious with her? He had been furious with her then: now he appeared relaxed, even sanguine, at the prospect of her intervention. 'Do what you yourself want,' he had said.

So what had she said to him? It must have been something dramatic to cause his change of heart.

Violet's letter was not in the Muniment Rooms at Belvoir. But there were three other potential sources of information: John's diary, Sir John's papers, and those of Guy Brooke.

It was Brooke, the commander-in-chief's ADC, who delivered Violet's letter; as John mentioned, they had 'had a talk about things'. I was hoping that one of them had made a note of their conversation. Since the move to St Omer came at Sir John's behest, Brooke might also have recorded it in an official report to French.

I looked at John's diary first. His reply to Violet was dated 3 May. It was more than likely that on such an important issue he was replying by return. This would mean that Brooke had delivered Violet's letter that day, or the day before. The entries for 2 and 3 May were minimal: John had not referred to Brooke — or his decision to accept the job at General Headquarters. But two words stood out:

May 2, Sunday: . . . Harry left . . . Went to see gassed men . . . Something awfull . . .

May 3, Monday: . . . Saw gassed men again . . .

Harry was John's cousin — Harry Lindsay; the 'gassed men', obviously the victims at the hospital at Bailleul. But what was *something awfull*? Was he referring to the condition of the men? Or was this a deliberately veiled reference to his decision to accept the job at

St Omer? John's punctuation and spelling were unreliable. But even he, surely, would have written, 'Went to see gassed men — something awfull.' He would not have entered the two words after a full stop, and on a separate line.

The following day, 4 May, John *had* seen Brooke. 'Saw Guy Brooke and Sonny Somerset on Sharpenburg. They came to tea,' he recorded.

Possibly, this was when Brooke delivered Violet's letter. In which case, John had misdated his reply. But, thinking about it, the date was immaterial. The main thing was that at some point during these three days a conversation had taken place between John and Brooke — one that had a vital bearing on John's future, which he had omitted to mention. If 'something awfull' *had* happened — was there a connection?

I checked Sir John's papers. I could find no record of the conversation, or any mention of John's move to St Omer. Nor could I find Guy Brooke's papers to see if they would shed light on it. In 1922, he had succeeded his father to become the Earl of Warwick. Yet his wartime correspondence was missing from the substantial collection of Brooke family papers at Warwickshire County Record Office.

It was only many months later — at Plas Newydd, the Marquis of Anglesey's home, near Bangor — that I discovered what John meant by 'something awfull'. And it was truly awful.

There, in the Angleseys' archives, was the letter Violet sent her daughter Marjorie on 3 May. She had just seen John's account of his visit to the hospital at Bailleul. 'Darling, this came from J today. Terrifying, isn't it?' Most of her letter was devoted to John's account — she had copied it out. But at the end of it, she had added a note. 'Brooke was here yesterday. He told me all about the gas. Darling, I couldn't bear it any longer. I made him take a letter back for J. I told him he must take the job at St Omer. "Don't do it for my sake. Do it for Haddon!!!" '
It was Violet's trump card and she had played it.

Guilt, it seemed, had caused John to capitulate. *But then why hadn't he joined Foulkes's brigade?*
Violet was writing on 3 May. In the weeks that followed, John, of course, was not transferred to St Omer. Instead, on 9 July, he was invalided home to England — a detail that he had spent a good part of his life excising from the record.
So what had happened between these two dates?
The suggestion — from the content of an

608

article that appeared later that summer in *The New York Times* — is that John's capitulation was in fact a feint. Whatever guilt he may have felt over the death of his brother, he was not going to let it stand in the way of his duty to King and country.

'Remember, it must be an order,' John warned his mother when he told her he would accept the job at St Omer.

As the events of the spring of 1915 reveal, his caveat proved to be the sticking point. At General Headquarters, Sir John French's position as commander-in-chief was becoming increasingly precarious. By the end of May, his fondness for members of the aristocracy was the subject of unwelcome attention. Under the circumstances — as John knew full well — it was impossible for the C-in-C to order him to St Omer.

'I have more trouble with the War Office than I do with the Germans,' French complained to Winifred on 21 May: 'While they are fiddling Rome is burning. What we want is more and more High Explosive ammunition and they do nothing but squabble amongst themselves. I devoutly wish we could get rid of Kitchener at the War Office. I'm sure nothing will go right whilst he is there.

It is hard to have enemies *in front* and *behind*.'

At the time French was writing he was embroiled in a political crisis — one that would result in the fall of Herbert Asquith's Liberal government.

On 9 May, after the failure of the Battle of Aubers Ridge, French had spoken to Charles Repington, the *Times* war correspondent. 'We had not sufficient high explosives to lower the enemy's parapets to the ground,' he told him: 'The want of unlimited supply of high explosives was a fatal bar to our success.' His admission caused a sensation: British soldiers were being needlessly killed as a result of the government's failure to supply adequate quantities of ammunition.

The finger of blame was pointed at Lord Kitchener, under whom responsibility for munitions production fell. Whipped up by Chancellor Lloyd George, who wanted to sideline the Secretary for War, the *Daily Mail* ran the story under the headline 'Lord K's Tragic Blunder' and called for his resignation.

To French's irritation, Kitchener had not resigned. Recognizing his own popularity with the British public, he had refused to go. Yet while he remained Secretary for War, 'The Great Shell Shortage' split the Cabinet, with the consequence that Asquith's government was dissolved and a coalition government formed. Within the new government, a new department was created — the Ministry of Munitions — and its responsibility handed to Lloyd George.

The scandal served to increase the enmity between the Secretary for War and his commander-in-chief. Furious at the assault on his authority, Kitchener's defenders retaliated by launching a whispering campaign against French. Besides accusing him of using the shortage of ammunition to cloak his own failure, they cast doubt over his moral integrity. For reasons of patriotism and discretion their accusations were kept out of the British press. But *The New York Times* published them in full.

'The impression has gained ground that he has lost his grip,' the newspaper reported, 'and that his removal from the chief of command of the troops in France has become a matter of urgent necessity. Little else is talked of in London and in Paris, and in spite of the very strict censorship exercised over the press on both sides of the Channel, the newspapers have been alluding to the matter in a sort of guarded way.

'The absence of any military censorship in the United States,' the 'veteran correspondent' continued, 'enables me to write more freely about this condition of affairs in *The New York Times* than in England or France, though much must necessarily be left unsaid.'

In fact, he left little unsaid. In great detail, he proceeded to outline the whispering campaign against French — a campaign that centred on his relationship with George Moore, and their proximity to members of the aristocracy, both male and female. As the report shows, the very issues that placed a question mark over French's continued command of the British Army prevented him from ordering John to go to St Omer:

The fact of the matter is that 'Jackie' French, as the British Generalissimo is known in the service, has not been altogether himself for the past three years. Son of a country parson, he developed after the Boer war, when he had reached a General's command, that predilection for the aristocracy which is the besetting weakness of the British 'bourgeoisie', and which in his case found its expression in his invariably selecting the members of his staff with a greater regard for their social rank than for their cleverness or military capacity . . . Formerly a family man, in the best sense of the word, with domestic tastes, and with a charming and devoted wife, and particularly nice children, French became entangled about four years ago in the toils of one of the fastest crowds of titled people in London, of whom a certain Irish peeress was the bright particular star. For a time he was said to have been completely dominated by her influence, which was a matter of common gossip, and then, two years ago, he developed that much-discussed intimacy with his great American crony and friend, George Gordon Moore of Detroit, Mich., and of England . . .

According to the printed admissions of this Michigander financier and promoter, his friendship with the FM is so close that Sir John has for the past two years made his home under his, that is to say, GGM's roof, in London, instead of with his family. On the occasion of French's periodical visits to London, since the beginning of the war, he has always stayed at Moore's house, and during the intervals Moore has been an almost constant guest of the Field Marshal at British Headquarters in France.

There Moore has been accorded privileges and prerogatives denied to all British visitors, even to members of the Government administration, and to peers of the realm, as well as to distinguished Frenchmen of official rank. In fact, he has been treated by the British Generalissimo, at this headquarters, as if he had no secrets whatsoever from him, official, military, or otherwise.

This naturally has excited all sorts of unfavourable comment and invidious criticisms; the more so as GGM has been charged, not only in the American press but even in London newspapers, notably in the *London World,* with being associated with a naturalized German of the name of Lowenfeld, in a London concern known as the Investment Registry Company.

Quite naturally this association of the British Generalissimo in France with an American promoter known for his German business affiliations, and the extraordinary privileges accorded to him at British Headquarters, has given rise to much unfavourable comment and criticism in English as well as in French circles. It has served to estrange Sir John from many of his former English and French friends and admirers, who find it difficult to understand why he should select in this time of danger to British Empire, as his principal confidant, a Michigander promoter.

At General Headquarters, Sir John's staff knew that Moore was behind the move to have John transferred to Foulkes's brigade. In the public eye, Moore was closely associated with the Manners family — his infatuation with Diana was well known. Under the circumstances, French dared not risk ordering John to St Omer unless he supplied him with proof that he had the necessary credentials to join the top-secret brigade. On his part, John refused to claim the expertise in 'catapults' or missile projectiles that French would need.

For six weeks, John dug in his heels. Yet despite his holding firm, in the last weeks of June the flat tone of his diary indicates that the pressure was beginning to take its toll.

On 19 June, John learned that his division was being drafted into the Ypres Salient. There, for the first time, they were to take part in an attack. 'Damn,' he wrote in his diary in response to the news. From that moment on, as I'd discovered, he had withdrawn from the dramatic events going on around him — as if something was preoccupying him.

Whatever it was, John had not confided it to his diary. However, a letter from Sir John French suggests that in the days immediately after the North Midlands received the order to move into the Ypres Salient, John was forced to reconsider the commander-in-chief's offer. Before the order came through, the North Midlands were attached to the General Reserve: John knew that as long as they remained in reserve, his job as ADC to General Stuart Wortley did not expose him to danger.

The move to Ypres changed the position drastically. For the first time, with the risk of his being killed far higher, he really did have to decide whether his first duty was to his family or to his country. It would explain why he wrote 'Damn' when he heard he was going to the Ypres Salient, and why, in the days that followed, he seemed so preoccupied.

John had ten days to reach a decision: his division was not going into action until 29 June.

But — around about 21 June — Violet forced his hand. After Charlie told her of the move to Ypres, she sent a telegram to the commander-in-chief.

It is evident from his reply that she had begged him to remove John from the firing line:

23 June 1915
General Headquarters, St Omer

Dear Violet
On receipt of your wire I told them to ask the Division to let Granby join my Staff for a few days temporarily during his General's absence.

I send you the reply which came from them by return.

This must presume that he himself wishes to remain with his Division and I feel even they would have sent him to Headquarters if he had wanted to go. I can quite understand his desire to remain with his own Staff.

I am afraid in such circumstances there is nothing more to be done.

Please write when you think I can be of use.

Yours etc, John French

It was John's last chance to escape the fighting. He had turned it down. Whatever guilt he felt over the death of his brother, he hadn't allowed it to sway his decision. His first duty was to his country.

This was the situation on 23 June, as the commander-in-chief relayed it to Violet.

Sixteen days later — on 9 July — John was invalided home from the Front on a hospital ship. He never returned.

His departure coincides with the start of the last and the most mysterious of the gaps in the family letters at Belvoir.

Years later, when John came to look back on this episode, he had wanted to wipe the record entirely. He had done all that he could to make certain that no one would ever discover that he had been invalided home from the Front.

It was his War Office file that had revealed the details of the event he'd spent a good part of his life — and his final hours — trying to conceal. Among the documents inside it was a report, written by an army surgeon, which detailed the circumstances of his departure:

The above-named officer [Lt. J. H. M. Marquis of Granby] was sent back from France on 9 July suffering from diarrhoea, the effect of old malarial poison contracted some time ago in Rome; of a very obstinate character, with abdominal pain and symptoms of dyspepsia. It is surmised that the abdominal discomfort may indicate a condition of chronic appendicitis.

The putative cause of John's illness, as I'd discovered, was nonsense. The 'old malarial poison' was alleged to have stemmed from his time at the British Embassy in Rome in 1909. Yet there was no evidence whatsoever to support the claim that he'd ever had malaria.

If the cause of his illness was specious, it cast doubt over whether he was in fact ill when he left France. Certainly, from what I knew of his activities at Belvoir after 9 July — fishing, shooting, a round of house parties — he appears to have been fit and well.

But, at the same time, I could not believe that John would have faked illness to escape the Front. From September 1914, he had resisted every one of his mother's efforts to keep him out of the war — the last, just sixteen days before he was sent home. The impression I was left with was of a brave man with a strong sense of integrity. It wasn't of a man who was contemplating, or who would have countenanced, running away.

There was something else. Among Violet's gold-dusted letters, I'd found a note which suggested that she had fixed the outcome of the medical board John attended in September, two months after he left France. Even Violet realized that she had behaved appallingly. 'Darling — I must fight! Don't be cross with me,' she begged Charlie. 'Other mothers do <u>nothing</u>. What do they get for their bravery? <u>The worst</u>.'

It appeared John didn't fail the board because he was feigning illness: it would seem he failed it because Violet told the War Office to fail him. The morning after, clearly ignorant of his mother's manoeuvrings, he'd sent a telegram to his sister Marjorie: 'Six weeks more leave STOP Damnation STOP Bitterly disappointed STOP.'

But then, if he was innocent, why had he wanted to destroy the records for this period?

And if he hadn't been faking illness, why had he left the Front?

The obvious assumption was that, somehow, Violet had been behind his escape.

For once, however, it seems Violet was innocent. As far as I was able to, I checked her movements over the course of the week before John left for France. I couldn't see anything untoward. From 28 June to 3 July she was at Arlington Street. Judging from the letters that remain at Belvoir, far from plotting to spring John from the Front, she was preoccupied in hosting a lunch party for the Aga Khan. She seemed caught up in the arrangements — and, afterwards, as she reported to John, in the gossip she had learned from her guests:

Violet Asquith, I hear, is going to marry that ugly man Bonham-Carter (nickname 'Bongy') — a long and ancient wish on his part. Her father's secretary!

Then Sonny Titchfield!!!* Marries a girl of 30!! (he is 22!). An old maid like that!! She is stuck up and narrow-minded so dear Sonnie hasn't a chance of getting out of a groove.

Miss Venetia Stanley who has only just stopped a very very serious flirtation with the Prime Minister — some say they loved each other so much he was meditating eloping!!! (hence no care for his high office and High Explosives!) — well, she is going to marry Mr Edwin Montagu. To do it she has to change her religion and be a Jewess!!

Then — after 4 July — it was Diana who monopolized Violet's attention. In the early hours of that morning, Diana broke her leg

* The Marquis of Titchfield, heir to the Duke of Portland.

falling down some steps on Brighton beach. She was with Duff Cooper. It was a bad break and Violet took charge of the search to find a top surgeon to operate. 'Your mother is nearly off her chump just now with trouble upon trouble,' Charlie wrote to John: 'Diana, poor dear, has had a baddish smash. Both leg bones broken, the smaller in two diagonally, and part of the knob at the base of the larger one. She goes to hospital tomorrow or the next day. Sir A. Lane does the op: rather a serious one.'

Charlie was writing on 6 July. As was evident from his last paragraph, neither he nor Violet were anticipating John's immediate return: they knew that his division was in action in the Ypres Salient: 'Your mother almost demented with one thing and another,' Charlie reiterated: 'dreadfully nervous about you — longing to get you over here again. I suppose there's no chance, but don't miss one if there is. The family are badly in need of you. Your father looked worried to death, poor man, but is behaving well.'

Charlie's letter pointed to one conclusion: if neither he nor Violet were expecting John back from the Front, they couldn't have played a part in his departure.

More puzzling, however, was the letter I found to John from Rothesay Stuart Wortley. He was John's fellow ADC. Oddly, though his letter was dated 10 July — the day after

John was invalided home — both he and the division's commanding officers were expecting him back at headquarters at any moment. Further, Rothesay's letter intimated that John *had* in fact been ill.

So what had actually happened?

It was only when I read the war diary of Colonel Beevor — the North Midlands Chief Medical Officer — that the blurred events of that week came into focus.

It seems John *did* leave the Front for medical reasons. They were not the ones stipulated in his War Office file, but it looks very much as if they were genuine.

According to Colonel Beevor's diary, around the time John left, a virulent stomach bug was circulating through the North Midlands in early July. Whether it was viral, or caused by contaminated water, is unclear, but a large percentage of the troops went down with it. By mid-July, Colonel Beevor was describing it as an 'epidemic'. As his entry on the nineteenth reveals, the bug claimed its victims quickly:

19 July
7.30 am. Went to Ouderdom to examine 140 sick reported as left behind by the 5th Leicesters when they went into trenches last night. There were 4 cases suspicion of paratyphoid and over 50 with diarrhoea. This latter disease is so prevalent just now. Inquiries confirm that

the men generally are most careful about the water they drink. I consider it due chiefly to catarrh of the intestine brought about by the recent cold winds and rain. The 5th South Staffords had 120 cases of it yesterday.

The illness hit the North Midlands just as the division's brigades were completing their first tour of duty in the Ypres Salient. Captain Hills was with the 5th Leicesters, the night they left the trenches. It was 5 July, and they had been in the line for six days:

We marched back to Ouderdom, feeling that we had escaped from our first tour in the ill-famed salient fairly cheaply. Even so, we had lost two officers and 24 Other Ranks wounded, and seven killed, a rate which, if kept up, would soon very seriously deplete our ranks. On reaching Ouderdom, we found that some huts had now been allotted us instead of our bivouac field, and as on the following day it rained hard, we were not sorry. Our satisfaction, however, was short-lived, for the hut roofs were of wood only, and leaked in so many places that many were absolutely uninhabitable and had to be abandoned. At the same time some short lengths of shelter trench which we had dug in case of shelling were completely filled with water, so that anyone desiring shelter must needs have a bath as well. This wet weather, coupled with a previous shortage of water in the trenches, and the generally unhealthy state of the salient, brought a considerable amount of sickness and slight dysentery, and although we did not send many to Hospital, the health of the Battalion on the whole was bad, and we seemed to have lost for a time our energy. Probably a fortnight in good surroundings would have cured us completely, and even after eight days at rest we were in a better state, but on the 13th we were once more ordered into the line and the good work was undone, for the sickness returned with increased vigour.

As Hills described, by the end of their fourth day in the trenches, a fifth of the battalion was suffering from the illness:

The weather throughout the tour was bad, but on night of 17th/18th, when we were relieved at midnight by the Sherwood Foresters, it became appalling. We were not yet due for a rest, having been only four days in the line, and our orders were to spend the night in bivouacs at Kruisstraat and return to the trenches the following evening. Weakened with sickness and soaked to the skin, we stumbled through black darkness along the track to Kruisstraat — three miles of slippery mud and water-logged shell holes — only to find that our bivouac was flooded, and we must march back to Ouderdom and spend the night in the huts, five miles further west. We reached home as dawn was breaking, tired out and wet through, and lay down at once to snatch what sleep we could before moving off again at 6.30pm. But for many it was too much, and 150 men reported sick and were in such weak condition that they were left behind at the huts, where later they were joined by some 40 more who had tried hard to reach the trenches but had had to give up and fall out on the way.

These were the troops Colonel Beevor saw on the morning of 19 July. 'Four officers were sent to hospital,' he noted in his diary: 'one so ill he had to be sent to the Base.' Other ranks were left to recover in their water-sodden billets. 'I hear the 120 cases of diarrhoea in the 5th South Staffords all recovered in 2 or 3 days after resting in huts,' Beevor reported a few days later.

It was Colonel Beevor who sent John home to England. But, as a jocular letter from Rothesay Stuart Wortley reveals, the doctor had only sent him home for a few days.

Rothesay was writing to John on 10 July — the day after he left France:

I am actually pulling myself together to

write you a letter. You have no idea what the effort is costing me. The primary reason is to send you a pass, without which it seems you cannot return to this country. What with the difficulties the authorities put in the way they would appear to think one wanted to come back!

He went on to ask John to bring back some song sheets: 'Chattanooga'; 'Un Peu d'Amour'; 'Teach Me How to Foxtrot'. Then he filled him in on bits of gossip: 'Kitchener, Asquith, Joffre, French and Millerand all had a meeting at Calais. It was arranged for 8am. French turned up in time but nobody else arrived till 2 hours later. Fury of Sir John! Asquith — when told the meeting was at 8 o'clock — said, "Oh, but I don't get up till 8.30!" And so we continue to beat the Boche!'

Only casually at the very end of his letter did Rothesay mention John's illness. 'How is your inside?' he asked. 'Well, I hope, and on the high road to recovery.' Rothesay obviously didn't think it serious. And neither, evidently, did Colonel Beevor.

The most likely scenario is that John had caught the bug that was circulating through the division. Beevor knew that it lasted '2 or 3 days' at most: it was why he sent him home for such a short period of time.

Nonetheless, it was surprising that he opted to send John back to England in the first place. He hadn't sent any other officers home; they went to a nearby hospital to recuperate. Even the worst case — 'one so ill' — went to one of the Base hospitals at Boulogne. As for other ranks, they were left to recover without treatment.

But, on closer scrutiny, Beevor's caution is understandable. Twice in the previous nine months the Duke and Duchess had questioned John's fitness for active service. On both occasions, he and General Stuart Wortley had overruled them.

The first time, as I'd discovered, was in October 1914, when Violet and Henry — in league with General Bethune — claimed John had a serious heart condition. After establishing the claim was untrue, Stuart Wortley had written to the Duke: 'I should be sorry to see a nice smart boy like him ruined by staying at home,' he told him: 'I do not, therefore, intend to take any further steps in the matter. My medical officers here support my action and do not consider that any grave risks are being run.'

Four months later — and just ten days before the North Midlands embarked for the Front — Beevor was personally involved when, for the second time, Violet and Henry questioned John's fitness on the grounds of his 'heart condition'. On this occasion, Beevor had called on the Duke at Arlington Street. He took with him a letter of introduction from Stuart Wortley: 'My dear Henry,' the general wrote. 'The bearer of this note is my Principal Medical Officer — Colonel Beevor — who will tell you his opinion about John.'

The previous day, Beevor had examined John. Having given the Duke his opinion, he gave him an official record of the examination:

I have carefully examined Lieut. The Marquis of Granby and find he has no apparent organic disease. The heart is somewhat irritable but at present no intermission of its rhythm exists and with ordinary care this officer should be medically fit to perform the duties of an ADC at home and abroad.

By standing up to the Duke, Beevor and Stuart Wortley had assumed personal responsibility for John's health. They had also promised to keep a careful eye on him. It was why, a month after Beevor saw the Duke at Arlington Street, he wrote to reassure him:

Your Grace
I feel sure you will be glad to hear from me that your son is weathering the storm of active service well — he has had a little sore throat last week, but soon got over it and now looks better than when in England. Everybody has had sore throats

and hundreds suffered from influenza, but on the whole the Division is the healthiest in the country.

There has been a great improvement in the weather lately and I trust your son will continue to benefit by the improved conditions.

Will you convey kindest regards to Her Grace and, believe me,

Yours sincerely
Beevor.

I could see why, when John fell ill in July 1915, Beevor opted to send him home for a few days' leave. He was erring on the safe side.

Yet, in sending him home, Beevor unwittingly played straight into Violet's hands.

Even as John's ship docked at Folkestone, Dr Hood was waiting to examine him.

Again among Violet's gold-dusted letters, I found a copy of the letter Dr Hood wrote to the Director General of the Army Medical Service shortly after examining John. His diagnosis was in dramatic contrast to Colonel Beevor's:

July 9 1915

Sir

I have this morning seen and carefully

examined, at 16 Arlington Street, the Marquis of Granby who has been sent home on sick leave by his regimental doctor, Dr Beevor.

I find Lord Granby suffering from gastro-hepatitic symptoms of the same character as those he has had on former occasions, following a rather severe attack of dysentery in combination with malaria, contracted at Rome some four or five years ago.

The action of his heart is unsatisfactory.

In my opinion he requires at least a month's absence from official duty, and I think it would be wise if you would kindly appoint a board to adjudicate his condition.

I am faithfully yours
Donald W. Hood CVO
Foreign Office Physician in charge of
Hospital for Wounded Officers
47 Roland Gardens

At Violet's instigation, Hood had come up with a spurious diagnosis to extend John's leave from a few days to 'at least a month'. Intentionally, he had triggered a whole set of official procedures: John could not return to the Front until he passed a medical board.

A brief entry in Duff Cooper's diary confirms that John was nowhere near as seriously ill as Hood was suggesting.

That very evening — 9 July — Duff, who was working at the War Office, went to a dinner party at John's sister's house in Belgravia. John was one of the guests. 'I dined with Marjorie Anglesey at Eaton Square,' Duff recorded: 'John Granby, Willie de Grunne, Phyllis and Jacqueline de Portalès. They were all looking very beautiful . . .'

John had evidently recovered from the bug that he had caught in France. More importantly, however, the diary entry suggests that he was not complicit in Hood's diagnosis. If he had been feigning a serious illness in order to escape the Front, he would hardly have gone to a dinner party the night he was invalided home. He would have lain low.

Hood's lie was believed. Very quickly, as the report of the army medical board John attended on 23 July reveals, it was officially sanctioned. Beevor had sent him home with a common stomach bug, yet it was Hood's version of events that the board surgeon recorded in the report:

The above-named officer [Lt J. H. M. Marquis of Granby] was sent back from France on 9 July suffering from diarrhoea, the effect of old malarial poison contracted some time ago in Rome; of a very obstinate character, with abdominal pain and symptoms of dyspepsia. It is surmised that the abdominal discomfort may indicate a condition of chronic appendicitis.

Hood was a doctor of considerable standing; he was the senior physician at the Foreign Office; the patients he treated at his general practice in Mayfair were among the wealthiest, most influential men and women in Britain. The army surgeon had no reason to disbelieve him; it was understandable that he had deferred to his opinion.

Out in France, even Colonel Beevor believed Hood's diagnosis. Early in August, John's father wrote to relay the details — and to send his commiserations to the North Midlands. On the night of 31 July, the Notts and Derby Brigade — the troops of which predominantly came from towns and villages on the Duke's Derbyshire estate — had suffered 380 casualties when the Germans attacked their trenches at Hooge. Just the week before, the Lincoln and Leicester Brigade — recruited from the Duke's Leicestershire estates — had lost seventy-five men after a mine exploded under their trenches.

Beevor had not replied to the Duke immediately; he was too busy attending the wounded:

10 August 1915

Your Grace

It was extremely kind of you to write and send your sympathy to us in this second great blow of the War — a kindly thought for which I am deeply grateful.

I am sorry to hear Lord Granby is still troubled with his digestion and am more than ever leaning to the theory of his gastric mucous membrane and liver cells having been damaged during service in the Roman Campagna. If so, all the more need for baths, massages and special foods.

You would be proud to hear your Notts & Derby Brigade saved the situation when a Brigade of the new Army was driven back in front of Hooge — not only that, but they stuck it out under unfavourable conditions for a further 5 days. They were as steady as veterans. I hope soon to get 7 days' leave and if you are in London to have the pleasure of giving you details and map demonstration of the fight. There can be no objection to my telling you by letter how gallant they were in fetching water for the New Army wounded, and on one occasion, when 30 wounded were left in a small wood on our immediate left, their stretcher bearers and Doctor went out, dressed them and fetched them in, under a perfect tornado of shellfire.

We are glad to hear of your continued good work in raising new units and wish you all the satisfaction your splendid patriotism richly deserves.

With my kindest regard to Her Grace and Lord Granby.

The one person who didn't believe Dr Hood was John.

At the medical board he attended on 23 July, the army surgeons gave him two months' leave and told him 'to apply for a Board before its expiration should he feel fit to return to France'.

The scraps of evidence left in the Muniment Rooms suggest that almost immediately John had tried to get back to the Front. Among them was a letter, dated 10 August, from his aunt, Lady Mildred Manners. John's next medical board was due on 22 September, when his two months' leave expired. Evidently an almighty row had erupted when Violet and Henry learned that he was intending to apply for an early board — as the army surgeons had suggested. Lady Mildred, whom John was fond of, had been roped in to dissuade him:

'For heaven's sake, <u>don't</u> go out before you need,' she wrote:

Sept 22nd is near enough, and <u>I</u> think it

636

rotten you should go back at all — after all there are plenty of things that your brain could apply itself to at home and be of far more service to the country than being ADC to ESW! All the twaddle that is talked about by people saying that everyone <u>must</u> go out makes me sick. Why send anyone that could do good work elsewhere to risk his life out there — and after all, you <u>have been</u>. As to going out <u>sooner</u>. That is of course merely madness on your part!

John did not apply for an early board; he waited until 22 September. But as a panicked note from Violet to Charlie reveals, he was determined to return to France. 'Darling C,' she wrote on 10 September, 'I fussed myself to arrange an "entrevue" uninterrupted with "him" and only yesterday afternoon did I get it and in an empty resounding room and I blurted on a little.'

The 'resounding room' was in the Muniment Rooms, on which John had begun work.

'He said he was sorry for Father and me,' Violet continued. 'All was quite gentle and no loud voices. I make out I have a little breathing time still, as his "board" won't be till after he has come here again on Sunday. I should like him to have another bit of long leave — and he to go to Harrogate where he is not seen by "estate people" — and then to come to London to have a job, like Rex Benson's Intelligence Dept.'

Two days later, after another talk with John, Violet wrote to Charlie again: 'He distinctly said to me, if they don't pass me, of course, this is another matter — but I did not go on. He did not snub me — but I felt I better not say anymore for fear he might think I would do <u>something</u>.'

As the date of the board approached, Violet worked herself into a spin. Her next letter to Charlie suggests that John realized that Hood was in league with her, and that he was trying to obtain a medical certificate from another doctor. His return to France was contingent on it: without it, the board would not pass him fit for active service. At the time, Colonel Beevor was home on leave in London; Violet suspected that John had asked him to supply the certificate:

Charlie dear
Is it possible that he has got a 'letter' from Beevor to say he '<u>is fit</u>' that will pass him at once? I have only just thought of that possibility.

Can you find out if he <u>did</u> get Beevor to do anything for him?

For you see Beevor told Hood he considered John quite fit to go back.

Do get at the Beevor thing!

Violet did not wait for Charlie's answer. Unwilling to run the risk that Beevor had given John the requisite certificate, she wrote to her friend, Lieutenant-Colonel Oswald FitzGerald. He was Lord Kitchener's private secretary and she had been cultivating him ever since she had first met him earlier in the spring.

'Now, I have written to FitzGerald!!' she confessed to Charlie:

I have said — from a sense of duty only — I believe my son, when he goes up to his board, will 'forget' to bring the letters from the doctor who has been attending him, so as to circumvent things by saying he is now fully well and able to leave the 22nd Sept. I asked FitzGerald to warn the board that they should see the doctor's report — as I know he considered him not yet fit to go. You know, he, FitzGerald, told me he could do this, if John was trying to get out before he was well enough.

In fact, John did not produce a certificate from Beevor when he appeared before the board. But as the surgeon's report shows — and as Violet suspected — he had 'forgotten' to take Hood's certificate with him.

The report also shows that John told the army surgeons that he was '*distinctly* better'.

639

Yet no matter what he told them, it was immaterial. Primed by Lieutenant-Colonel FitzGerald, they gave him a further two months' leave on the grounds that the intemperate conditions in the trenches would 'aggravate' his illness.

This was on 22 September 1915. Six weeks later, at his next board in November, he was passed fit for active service. But he didn't return to the Western Front. On 4 December, he'd failed the emergency medical board that the army council convened at the War Office.

On this occasion Hood *had* supplied the medical certificate. It was document that I'd found in John's War Office file:

December 2 1915

I have this day seen and examined the Marquis of Granby who has been well known to me since his birth.

He is naturally of a delicate susceptible constitution and some seven years ago suffered from a rather severe attack of dysentery contracted in Rome, since which he has been constantly affected with gastro-intestinal disturbances.

Lord Granby was invalided home from the Front by Colonel Beevor on July 9th 1915 as suffering from gastric irritation. Since that date he has had several similar attacks, so much so that I have questioned whether he may not have chronic appendicitis trouble. His heart action is far from satisfactory and he is in my opinion unfit for active military service.

John knew that Hood was lying. The fact that he'd allowed him to supply the board with a fabricated medical certificate was proof that he had colluded in the lie. Between 5 December 1915 and 16 October 1918, John failed a further thirteen medical boards. He *had* used Hood's medical certificates to escape the war. It explains why the gap in the correspondence at Belvoir begins as soon as he is invalided home from the Front. It is then that Hood — in his letter to the Director General of the Army Medical Service — first lies about the cause, and the seriousness, of his illness.

But the question of course is why had John finally colluded in the lie?

From the beginning of the war he had resisted his mother's threats and blandishments. He hadn't been feigning illness when he was invalided home in July; throughout that summer he had wanted to return to the Front. Something had happened to him towards the end of 1915 that had made him change his mind.

Later in his life, his shame had come back to haunt him. He had spent a good part of it

— and his final hours — removing the evidence that would incriminate him.

I knew what John had wanted to hide. But I still didn't know why this man, whose moral integrity and whose sense of duty to his country struck me as hitherto unimpeachable, had opted to use a fabricated medical condition to escape the war. While he had been abetted by some of the highest-ranking men in the British Army, he had effectively deserted — a crime for which 306 men were executed by firing squad in the years between 1914 and 1918.

Whatever the answer to this question, it was the source of his shame. It was what had caused him to spend the last hours of his life in the Muniment Rooms.

57

I focused on the period between 4 November 1915 — the date John was passed fit at his third medical board — and the emergency medical board convened at the War Office on 4 December 1915.

Between these two dates, just three letters remained in the Muniment Rooms at Belvoir. I found them in an obscure file labelled 'General Correspondence'. They were all from soldiers in the North Midlands. What they had to say was revealing: I was able to pinpoint the moment when John decided that he wasn't going back to the Front.

The first two indicated that he was expected back in the third week of November.

'My dear Granby,' Lieutenant-Colonel Septimus Legge, the North Midlands DAQM* wrote on 22 November: 'We were all very sorry that you did not turn up with the GOC last week. However, it's as well not to come out here unless you are quite fit. You can

* Deputy Assistant Quartermaster.

always do your "bit" at home. I can quite understand how sick you are about it. Thanks very much for your present of waders, they will come in quite useful.'

The second letter was from John's batman, Robert Maclean:

My Lord,
In answer to your letter of 18th inst . . . I had everything ready for you coming back with the General, and now I've packed up everything — your French boots and water bottle that was under the seat of the Rolls. I have also packed your knee boots.

I see Rigsby has got Pegsy* clipped, and I told him the instructions you wanted him to carry out. If I should receive any instructions about your kit, I will carry them out immediately. I have the honour, my Lord, to be your obedient and faithful servant.

The third was a colourful letter from Rothesay Stuart Wortley:

20 November 1915

My dear John
I am most awfully sorry you failed to pass

* John's horse.

the vet (horse expression) but still, the winter out here is pretty bloody and it is just as well to be in England where one can find a fire, a doe and a glass of wine.

I don't know exactly how long I am going to stay here, but anyhow I hope to come over on leave before the end of the month. I will let you know when it will be, somewhere about Nov 25th I expect. We must certainly arrange an evening of the sort you describe. It would give me extreme pleasure, yes, I think so! I want to get a day or two fox hunting and also loose off my bundook* at a fat pheasant. We might arrange a party at Highcliffe if you can think of any suitable does.

I dined with Eddie[†] last Saturday and got a teeny bit tight. Capital fun, as I live with some rather sad sods here, especially the GSO3 — who sits at the next table, has a snub nose, hair that stands on end, a raucous voice, no sense of humour, and a manner subservient to those above him and officiously offensive to those below him. He makes me damned angry and I see a row brewing for the near future! He is one of those "I-am-not-quite-sure-Sir, but-I'll-go-look-it-up-and-make-certain-we-must-get-these-things-right" kind of a

* Slang for a service-issue rifle.
† Eddie Grant, a fellow staff officer.

bugger for whom I have no use!

We seem to be losing the war, worse than usual just now, don't we? But I am still awfully brave. I went up to the ditches with Uncle Wilson and nearly got drowned so I haven't been again.

Eddie went to Paris and rogered so much that he broke a blood vessel in his head. Heated argument as to who should pay for the washing.

Eddie maintained the pillows would have to be washed in a month or so anyway. Opposition claimed that the stains would never come out — result — Eddie billed.

Love to all nice girls.

For all the talk of does and burst blood vessels, the significance of Rothesay's letter was that John had lied to his best friend. He'd told Rothesay he'd failed the medical board on 4 November, when, of course, his War Office file shows that he was passed fit for active service.

Rothesay had written in answer to John on 20 November and Legge on the 22nd. Maclean was replying to a letter that John had sent on the 18th. The postal service to France was famously efficient. The suggestion, therefore, is that by 17 November at the latest, John had already decided not to return to the Front. This could only mean that whatever had triggered his decision had occurred at some point in the previous two weeks.

It was a letter from Violet — another of her gold-dusted letters — that cracked the mystery open.

It was undated and I assumed that it related to one of John's earlier medical boards. But, in fact, Violet was writing about the emergency board on 4 December.

I was able to date the letter by a reference to Egypt. On 2 December, the North Midland Division was ordered to Cairo. Following the failure of the Gallipoli offensive, the evacuation of the Dardanelles was in progress. Fearing that the Turks would attack Egypt if the evacuation failed, Kitchener was withdrawing troops from the Western Front to defend his positions in the east.

Initially, Violet's letter confused the picture. It seemed John had had yet another change of heart:

Private

Darling C — I fear we are beaten — John means to go out to Egypt! If his General can find room for him!

He has asked Diana to prevent my trying any further at the WO. And today I have obeyed as it seems to be his determination! He longs to go back with his General. His General will wire to him to come — but not till after Xmas will he go.

I don't know how he will get round the '3 months leave'. He may have been settling that today — I never dare ask him a thing as you know.

You can imagine the bad state I am in.

For a moment, Violet's letter made me think that John's emergency board was Violet's high-water mark, her grand victory. It made me question whether John had in fact colluded in the lie that he was seriously ill. Once again, he seemed bent on overturning the findings of the board.

But then it dawned on me that whatever had caused John to abandon going back to the Front in mid-November had also caused him to abandon going out to Egypt 'after Xmas'. It looked as if he had had a crisis of conscience after the emergency board. Yet, ultimately, his desire to remain in England held sway.

The correspondence at Belvoir resumed on 5 December. Potentially, Violet's letter was an important clue in unmasking John's last secret. The traces of whatever it was that had kept him in England ought to be there.

58

On the drive up through the woods to the castle, the rhododendrons were out — huge clusters, bordering the drive, a haze of purple, crimson and pink. It was spring — almost a year since my last visit. As I followed the winding road up to the battlements, it was ironic to think I was returning to look at John's official version of events. Odder still was the thought that, possibly, the key to the mystery had been there in the Muniment Rooms all along.

I had looked at the notes that I had made when I first discovered the gap in the records. While the correspondence resumed on 5 December, until the end of January 1916, it focused on one subject — John's engagement to Kathleen Tennant. He had removed the rest of the letters for that month — presumably because they contained information relating to his sudden decision to fall in with his mother's plans. I'd had a cursory look through the correspondence. The letters between John and Kathleen were touching: John had even kept a journal of their courtship. But I hadn't thought them to be of any great significance: after all, this was nothing to do with the war.

I parked by the entrance to the Grand Portico, and entered the castle through the small priest's door. As I crossed the Guard Room, past the stands of muskets, the suits of armour and the tattered remnants of regimental flags, captured in battle, the bellicosity of it all jarred with what I'd discovered.

Inside the Muniment Rooms, it was gloomy and cold; the sun was shining on this side of the castle, but the thick stone walls held the winter chill. I gathered together the relevant files and sat down at the table next to the sofa where John had died.

I began with the file labelled 'Letters from Kathleen, 9th Duchess 1915/1916'. It didn't take me long to realize that I had found the missing piece in the puzzle — a piece which, without the medical reports in John's War Office file and Violet's gold-dusted letters, would have been impossible to slot into place.

On the face of it, the file offered a touching record of one of the happiest moments in John's life. But what it actually contained was the resolution to the last and most mysterious of the gaps that he had created in his family's records.

At the end of 1915, John had fallen in love. Kathleen — or Kakoo as he called her — was the reason why he had not returned to the Western Front. It was his love for her that had caused him to abandon his duty to King and country.

Aged nineteen in December 1915, Kakoo was beautiful. Tall, with a slim figure, and a pale ivory complexion, her elfin face was framed by long dark hair, which she wore, piled high, in a chignon. She had 'golden-brown eyes', her friend Cynthia Asquith recalled — 'eyes that seemed to claim happiness, to see all things in their brightest aspect'.

Ten years younger than John, Kakoo was the daughter of Frank Tennant, the second son of the first Lord Glenconner, whose grandfather invented bleaching powder. Lord Glenconner had made a large fortune from railways, banking and his father's chemical plants. Though Kakoo lacked a title, her family was rich and well connected. Her aunt, Margot, was married to Herbert Asquith.

On Saturday 11 December, a few days after John told Violet that he would join the North Midlands in Egypt, and that on no account was she to meddle via her contacts at the War Office, he wrote: 'I am very much looking forward to Wednesday — and there is no doubt that I love Kakoo very much.'

This was in the journal he kept of their courtship. Four days later, on the Wednesday he had referred to, he went to tea with Kakoo at the house she shared with her brothers at 57 Seymour Street, near Marble Arch:

I found all her brothers [Mark, Francis and John] in the room and they never left. So I asked her if, when I next came, the room would be full of people or not — because I said I would not come unless she would be alone. So she sent me this dear little note — which meant to me she would be alone:

"Dear John — come to tea tomorrow will you? I will be in about 5."

John's journal resumed the day after:

16th December

I went to tea of course yesterday with my K., and I pulled my self enough to the scratch as to ask my darling if she would come to Belvoir on Saturday next — and she said she would love to, but would have to ask her mother.

Just before I left her sitting room I kissed her hand — which nearly sent me mad with delight — as she did not mind. I thought perhaps I might get a rebuff.

They were the words of a man whose heart

had been broken. Before he met Kakoo, John had lost in love. It is only in the context of his previous relationship that the sacrifice he was about to make for her becomes understandable.

'I don't think I'll ever fall in love again,' John wrote to his sister Marjorie on 28 May 1914. The week before, he had broken off his engagement to Rosemary Leveson-Gower, the striking-looking and captivating daughter of the Duke of Sutherland. Twice, in the eighteen months since he had proposed, she had called it off. Their affair was finally over. John had not wanted to end it, but her mother, Millicent, Duchess of Sutherland, had given him an ultimatum:

7 May 1914

My dear John
Rosemary tells me she has wired you to come here next Thursday to lunch and motor with her and I hope stay the night?
    If you come it must surely mean you want to see her, be with her?
    Now will you forgive me for this letter, dear John. The thing that keeps you two apart is a sort of independent spirit — of not wanting to knuckle under!! Either of you!! Don't think it impertinent of me to write this — you have had a lot to put up

with. Your love was wounded: your pride hurt — and you've behaved like a brick.

But Rosemary is a tough proposition — darling as she is — and if you want to win her right out you've got to use <u>tough</u> means! It's no good being gloomy and distrait and silent with her. She wants someone to carry her off her feet. You in your sweet sensitiveness are shy in putting yourself in a false position again.

Rosemary has that gay glorious nature that takes pleasure in all life — but no man has meant anything to her but <u>you</u> — and it's up to you to play the game that will win her into your arms. Dear John, my real affection for you prompts me to write this. You can't kill Rosemary's critical, independent spirit — but you can grab her heart. Grabbing and deliberate overwhelming is the only way — not waiting on her pleasures! Women are queer! You don't know this perhaps! They yearn to be dominated rather than be worshipped. They like the 'Damn you, I'll die, or get you' attitude best!

Engagements are difficult things. Once Rosemary is yours, and you can teach her love, you'll be the happiest in the world — her mocking spirit is surely a pose. She yearns for things inwardly that she confesses not at all outwardly.

Every word of this I mean, John dear. I

know exactly what <u>you</u> are struggling with — but if you want her there are no half measures. If you <u>don't</u> want her, stay away. Bless you always, my feeling of affection for you has never wavered. You may be taking on a difficult task, but you'd never find your foundations if you didn't dig, would you?!! Marriage is a hard hunt. Rosemary has a heart of gold and the simplest and overwhelming sincerity for <u>natural</u> happiness, which makes her difficult to understand for some.

Your true friend MS

Tear this up.

John, however, knew Rosemary's 'mocking spirit' was not 'a pose'. The truth was he loved her far more than she loved him. He broke off the engagement because he knew he could never make her happy.

Throughout their eighteen-month affair, as Rosemary refused to commit to a wedding date, John's agony was compounded by Violet's loathing of her. He had tried to conceal the tempestuous passage of his relationship from his mother, but she had gleaned the details through her 'spy system'. In Violet's eyes, Rosemary — whose striking masculine looks were unfashionable — was neither rich enough nor beautiful enough: lacking any discretion, Violet made her views well known.

By February 1914, the deferred wedding —
and John's humiliation — was the talk of
London. Even Daisy, Countess of Warwick, a
notorious gossip, had become involved. She
wrote to Violet to commiserate, and to tell
her she thought it unlikely that even were the
couple to agree to a wedding date, the two
dukes — Henry, and Strath Sutherland —
would never agree to the terms of Rosemary's
marriage settlement:

Darling
I fear I cannot manage <u>this</u> week as
governess and tutor are away, and I have
the children <u>quite</u> alone with me.
   I should have <u>loved</u> a quiet day with you
— to talk — and try to be <u>some</u> sort of
comfort to you. For, my dear, I know just
what you are feeling, with all my heart I
understand and sympathise. First — I
don't think Henry will see any charm —
he will think her ugly — and all the
daughters of your house are beautiful, and
those that married into the house also,
judging by the pictures! The money is a
great obstacle.

The countess had made discreet enquiries
through Millicent, Duchess of Sutherland, to
establish the exact financial position. In the
unlikely event the marriage were to go ahead,
she told Violet to hold out for as much as she

could get:

If I might advise be <u>firm</u>. Unless more is given, the engagement can't be. Strath is a 'pincher' but I don't think he could risk making Rosemary unhappy.

It is really too bad, because <u>Geordie</u>* has his own independent income, so there are only two children to provide for. I know that Alistair[†] threatened to leave the Army unless he also was given enough — and it <u>was</u> given. Rosemary can do <u>anything</u> with Strath.

He has an hallucination that he is 'broke'. What he <u>has</u> is a million[‡] invested in Canada, and he has a million <u>here</u> to invest — so, on the pretext of poverty is having an Empire gamble — being sick of England. He keeps his yacht, costing £20,000 a year, for <u>himself</u> and uses her 2 months! Sometimes he lets her a few months, other times not. His villa at Menton [on the Côte d'Azur] is of use to <u>no one</u> but himself! He keeps it all going there and lives there 6 weeks! He has Dunrobin, and Tongue, and Hook Hill all 'going', besides London — so it is all ridiculous. He ought to give Rosemary

* The Duke's eldest son.
† The Duke's second son.
† Approximately £75 million at today's values.

£3000‡ a year at least and leave her £100,000.§ One thing is, his health is <u>precarious</u> so it would be as well to know what he has 'left her'? This is how I feel about it, and I repeat to you exactly what Millie said when I spoke to her of finance. You, darling Violet, I wish I could come to you, but you do know how I am thinking of you, don't you?

Post going so abrupt stop!

Loving Daisy

Determined to prevent the marriage from going ahead, Violet tried to lure John away from Rosemary with other candidates — even those she had previously rejected. One — as a letter to Charlie reveals — was American heiress Mary Hoyt Wiborg, the daughter of a Cincinnati ink manufacturer. Violet called her 'Hoity':

<u>Listen</u> — I never thoroughly wanted Hoity. I hated the idea all through the summer and was very worried at the time of the 'House boat' party for fear of J proposing! I should be pleased if it happened <u>only</u> if it was to keep Rosemary out. But if <u>she</u> was not on the horizon, then <u>not</u> because I hate the American ac-

‡ Approximately £225,000 at today's values.
§ Approximately £7.5 million at today's values.

cent — and could never, were I a man, kiss her mouth! Then came the big fear of Rosemary — and then I said — oh, better better far — Hoity! What a pity she isn't here now.

About this other fine healthy lovely girl* with a little money and education ('beautifully brought up' and in 'the best society', as a Paris informant tells me) and a fine breeder of tall healthy sons!! Well, I have an instinct. I have only myself had it once before about a wife for John — that was Margaretta — who has proved perfection! (and now again in slim, perfect looks — and brave sons!) Yes! The instinct that this might be the saving of us all! I will get her to Belvoir hoping John will not avoid her!!

I would give anything to stop R — gt danger. So, dear, don't go against me and don't think I am ramming Jacqueline down his throat — John would not be influenced against his wishes and what does it matter if I show her to him while he is there. I don't want him to avoid her or else it will be like in the Dresel [sic] case — mother and daughter then thought he cared nothing for her — and so quickly married someone else. And I wouldn't

---

* Jacqueline de Portalès, granddaughter of the Comte de Portalis.

like this one to be lost — snapped up — before he is sure he doesn't want to <u>attract</u> her!!

Violet had even gone so far as to tell John that Rosemary was barren — information that she claimed to have gleaned from a 'doctor friend' who knew Dr Fripp, Rosemary's GP. When, in early 1914, she heard the engagement was back on, she was forced to back-pedal furiously. 'I thought it only fair to see Fripp myself,' she told her niece, Ruby Peto:

<u>I did it well</u> (as I know him rather well) put him in no difficult position — gave him NO questions to answer — but went to him saying that as a mother longing for her son to marry would he advise <u>me</u> to help those 2 [John and Rosemary] to meet — or <u>not</u> unnecessarily to bring them together.

If he had said — as I expected — 'leave it alone' I should have begged you to put before John the misery of childlessness as a deterrent from answering a call from Milly. But instead Fripp clearly told me he believed that physically <u>she could at once have children and as many as she was given the chance of having</u>.

I know you will think, as I did, what an odd thing that this should be the same man who had told the opposite to his friend a few months ago!

It was with relief that, in the spring of 1914, Violet learned that John was not going to marry Rosemary after all. 'Darling — John says "all is off" and is hiding unhappily in Charlie's rooms,' she wrote to Diana. 'Little brute is not caring 2 straws! I may hear why tomorrow, but perhaps not — anyhow we can say if asked there is no engagement at all.'

John, of course, was 'caring 2 straws'. As his war diary shows, he hadn't been able to get over Rosemary. Throughout 1915, she haunted him; he was clearly still in love with her. 'Spent all the evening trying to instil a little organization into the HQ staff servants,' he wrote from Cassel on 4 March 1915: 'Then to bed. Picture papers arrived with a photo of Rosemary with R — how I hate to see her with anyone . . . Rothesay says I talked in my sleep last night mentioning "that she is in London": I wonder who I was dreaming of — I expect I can guess.'

A month later, he drove General Stuart Wortley to Dunkirk, where they had tea with Rosemary and her mother at their hospital for wounded officers. 'My God I know what misery is when I see Rosemary,' John wrote: 'The appalling strain of holding oneself in instead of opening my arms and squeezing her, but why should I be so sorely tried —

the darling, God bless her — she was looking jolly, but I think she was thinking just a little about me. The depression I get after seeing her is something dreadful, enough to destroy myself, but I must to bed, hoping to get to sleep. I wonder if she ever thinks kindly of me.'

John, as he told Marjorie, was convinced that he would never fall in love again. He knew when he invited Kakoo to stay at Belvoir in December 1915 that he wanted to marry her. From the moment she arrived, he was on tenterhooks.

In the record John kept of Kakoo's four-day stay, the cynicism, the brittleness — and the depression — so often present in his writing, melted away. He seemed happier than he had ever been in his life. There was hardly a minute of her visit that he had left out:

My K. arrived on Dec 18th in the evening in time for tea. I was so excited, and unfortunately Father took me into his study just before she arrived so that when I came into the drawing room there she was.

I did feel funny all over — there was Marjorie, Mother, Bridget Colebrooke,* and Charlie in the Castle. We had a very nice evening. I sat opposite to K — feeling aglow — she looked too lovely. We just did nothing much after dinner. I hardly said anything to K. Then to bed.

* Bridget Colebrooke, eldest daughter of first and last Baron Colebrooke, later married to Lord Victor Paget.

The next morning, the 19th, Sunday, we met at late breakfast. Oh, how delicious she looked. I asked her to come out for a walk, which she did. We — at least I — had a wonderful morning, and the same after lunch. We went for another walk all round Frog Hollow and back through the pasture. I did not see K. much from after then till dinner, except for a short while in Marjorie's bedroom. I sat next to K. at dinner. Oh, I was feeling happy.

I had made up my mind not to propose to her till Monday, as I wanted everyone to have left the Castle. I knew that Father, Mother, and Bridget, were leaving early Monday morning. After dinner, I managed to get a little talk alone with K. just before everyone was going to bed. So I walked her to her bedroom. It was as much as ever I could do not to propose to her then. She was too lovely. Just as we started for bed, I kissed her hand again, and I can't remember quite what K. said, but something to the effect that 'I did not mean anything' and I was quite miserable. I went to bed feeling that even if I did propose, she would say 'No' and — as she has since told me — she was dreadfully unhappy too that night. When she shook hands with Mother just before getting into bed, her dear little hand was shaking all over, so Mother told me afterwards.

My darling had come to Belvoir against all the

wishes of her family. Her family did not like me, and they had told K. that I was a flirt — and that I would never propose — but K. had come against them all, and then when I did not look like proposing, she felt that her family would be right after all, and she felt, so she told me, that she had made a mistake in coming, but that her love for me had made her come — so we both went to bed quite miserable. She thinking that I did not really love her — I thinking that she did not like me.

Dec 20 — next morning. Father, Mother and Bridget left for London about 10. Then I got K. to come for a walk. We walked down to the lakes across the large open field straight to the middle of the lower lake. Then the wonderful moment came. I asked my darling and she said 'Yes'. My God, I was happy. I kissed her dear little face all over — we walked slowly back to the Castle in time for lunch. We had made up our minds we would not tell Charlie and Marjorie till after tea. We spent a glorious afternoon and evening in my sitting room. Then — about half an hour before dressing for dinner — I went down to the Nursery and told Marjorie. She was utterly taken by surprise. K. then went and talked to Marjorie, and I went and told Charlie. Soon after that, K. and I telephoned to my Mother, and she wired to her Mother in Scotland. We sat up very late — what a perfectly wonderful evening.

The next morning — Dec 21 — and all day, we just did I do not know what — except send telegrams to say she was not going away today, as she was supposed to before, but would stay till tomorrow.

Then Dec 22nd was a sad day. K. had to go to Xmas at Hyndford, as she had promised to. I took my darling to Grantham and saw her to Scotland, and I took the train to London. I was far too wildly happy to be sad at leaving her.

The day after, John received a worried letter from Kakoo. 'My happiness is so complete that I am in a state of nerves lest anything should happen to destroy it,' she wrote. 'But you musn't let it will you John? To see you, all such thoughts would vanish. It won't be long now. Be very nice to Mother. She is rather miserable.'

When Kakoo got home, she found her parents were horrified at her engagement. During a long talk they explained to her that — with the exception of wealthy heiresses — it was virtually unheard of for the heir to a dukedom to marry a commoner. Their branch of the Tennant family was rich, but not rich enough. Annie, Kakoo's mother, doubted whether John was serious; and, even if he was, she was convinced his parents would oppose the marriage.

A letter from Annie was waiting for John

when he arrived back in London. It was the first he had heard from her. She had not written to congratulate him after he and Kakoo had wired from Belvoir to tell her of their engagement:

My dear John
You and Kathleen must forgive me for not replying at once. Her telegram knocked me flat! Frank and I could not feel happy unless your <u>parents approved</u>. It would be so dreadful if they didn't.

Kakoo's just what you see and know. I always think of her as the most transparent — perhaps too transparent creation on earth. I have been thoroughly selfish and only thought of myself and so I could not write before. I have been completely shattered since Frances* left and now this seems the end of all things for me and the beginning of what I hope will be a glorious life for you two. But I don't feel that this <u>can</u> be without your parents' approval. You would not be happy and if <u>you</u> were not happy Kakoo would be wretched.

Frank breaks down when he thinks of Kakoo leaving as they have made home

* Frances married Hon. Captain Guy Charteris, the second son of Hugo, 11th Earl of Wemyss, on 23 July 1912.

so wonderfully happy and all the best of the sunshine will go with her.

Now for what I call the horrible part. Kakoo won't have more than £2000[†] a year to start with, but she's so simple in her tastes and not extravagant. But I can't write any more about her — it's too upsetting.

I hope you are as happy as Kathleen is — I can see by her letter — Bless you and I will love you.

Annie S. Tennant

I do <u>hope it's alright</u> with your parents.

John was due to meet Annie, who had come down to London, the next morning. The meeting did not go well. 'It was a funny morning,' he wrote in his journal, 'Mrs Tennant not really liking the thought of K. leaving her by marrying, and also not much liking me.'

Later that day, Annie wrote to John to explain her apparent ambivalence:

Darling John
I fear I was very inarticulate this morning, but I was feeling very deeply all sorts of things. I felt that I wanted to give you everything I possessed! You were so kind to me, and I see that you really do love

† Approximately £125,000 at today's values.

Kakoo. If only I could make myself believe that your parents were pleased. I can't help thinking that they are not quite — you see, you are their precious only son and they would want <u>everything</u> for you. But after seeing Kathleen's face, and now yours, I feel as if the whole thing had been planned by the Almighty, and as if things of the Earth become mundane and dropped away! I wish your father would write to Frank — or, who breaks the ice first!? Frank will be easy enough — <u>all</u> he wishes is that people should be happy and that he needn't be in London but allowed to remain in the North of Scotland where he can shoot, fish and golf! He adores his daughters and gives in to them in everything.

Annie needn't have worried. Violet and Henry were thrilled. They wanted to keep John in England; the fact that Kakoo didn't have a title or a large fortune didn't matter. They knew that if John married her in January, as he planned to, he would not go out to Egypt to join his division. They were also keenly aware that if John and Kakoo married early in the New Year, the heir they longed for might be conceived. If so, even if John insisted on going back to the Front, the future of the family would be guaranteed.

Unlike Annie, Violet had replied to the

telegram the couple sent her from Belvoir by return:

20 December 1915
16 Arlington Street

Darling John
I am all smiles as if nothing mattered in the whole world to me — <u>because you</u> are so happy!
It was <u>wonderful news</u> — and war and victory fade because I know you are happy — and your little new world is my world too for pleasure thinking of it.
Bless you both

First thing the next day, she sent them a telegram:

Good morning darlings. Mother

Then came an effusive letter to her future daughter-in-law:

My dearest little Kakoo
John is so happy and it makes us all jubilant. He is such a darling — as you know, and will know . . . How I long to see you. Meanwhile, I want you never never to feel me the ordering 'Mother-in-law', but just a second edition of your Mother and a very loving one.

670

The sun is shining and I am having a divine spell of joy — and freedom from anxiety — with John 'on sick leave' and John so absolutely happy.

À bientôt little Kakoo

Your loving VR

Henry had responded to the news equally quickly. As Violet was writing her 'all smiles' letter, he was writing his own:

December 20
16 Arlington Street

Dear Boy
From what your mother tells me I gather you have made up your minds to get into double harness — my sincerest congratulations and I trust you will be very happy.

May I venture to send my affectionate greetings to the future Lady Granby?

And I am

Your affectionate father

Rutland

All that remained was for the Duke and Duchess to sort out the terms of the engagement with Mr and Mrs Tennant.

It was Henry who 'broke the ice' by writing a letter to Kakoo's father. He replied straight-away:

My dear Duke — I am delighted that you are pleased with dear Kakoo and I feel convinced that John will be a most considerate loving companion. I will do everything in my power to further their happiness.

This terrible war haunts me daily as my eldest boy is in the Flying Corps who is now in France and being shot at every day. I marvel at our apparent cheerfulness.

I am so glad you play golf and hope to have many a match with you.

Yours ever
Frank Tennant

Henry wrote back to suggest a meeting to discuss the details of Kakoo's marriage settlement:

'My dear Duke,' Frank replied:

Thanks for your delightful letter. I will let you know when I am in London, which I dislike very much at present.

I intend to settle on dear little Kakoo £10,000* in good securities also give an allowance of £1500† per ann. My English solicitors are Stow Preston and Bob Lyttleton, 35 Lincolns Inn Fields . . .

* £625,000 at today's values.
† £94,000 at today's values.

With every good wish and prosperity
for the New Year

Yours ever
Frank Tennant

Annie Tennant had also written. Evidently,
she was still mystified as to why the Duke
and Duchess had so readily agreed to the
marriage:

27 December 1915

My dear Duke — thank you <u>so</u> much for
your very kind note. I feel very bewildered
— it all seems so sudden. Kakoo is my
child and I love John too and I could not
have been happy if you and his mother
had disapproved and this seems to sum
up everything.

As John is your precious only son and
so adorable, I thought you might not be
pleased somehow as my darling Kakoo
has not all the things that are sometimes
valued most in the world — like great
wealth etc. but she has the qualities that
make for enduring happiness, utter self-
lessness, and great joyousness and a high
sense of honour. John's name and fame
will be in safekeeping for ever. They are
somehow a wonderful couple in their
amazing happiness. Frank adores her and
I know how he will love John and how he

will help them and how generous he will be to them.

I dare not think of Home without her. John was so good to me and I have taken him into my heart forever.

Yours very truly

On 28 December, John went to stay with his future in-laws at Innes House, a remote Scottish castle near Elgin, which Frank Tennant used for shooting. His visit was a great success. Soon after he arrived, he wrote to his father:

Father dear
Just a line to say we are both well and very happy. How very nice you were to Kakoo and me at Belvoir — I did appreciate it so much.

Just going out shooting — blowing a gale — and they have sent me Charlie's guns instead of mine, so I shall have some difficulty in impressing my future papa-in-law with my power of killing birds.

Love, your affectionate Son

The absence of enmity was striking. It was the first time in his adult life that he had ended a letter to his father with love.

A month later, on the afternoon of Thursday 27 January 1916, John and Kakoo were married at St Margaret's Church, Westminster.

'It really was the most movingly lovely sight,' Cynthia Asquith, Kakoo's close friend, noted in her diary. 'It made one cry to think they would ever be old or dead. John looked a like a glamorous knightly figure with perfect technique: he held her hand and everything in the most inspired way. She looked divine in the best wedding dress ever seen.'

The wedding was organized by Violet and Margot Asquith, the prime minister's wife. They had not allowed the war to overshadow it. The one concession to the events taking place across the Channel was that John was dressed in his service uniform. In every other respect, it was a glittering social occasion. The following day, a full-page report appeared in the news section of *The Times:*

The bride, who was given away by her father, wore a Venetian gown of white satin with a gold brocade train four yards long and a short mantlet of old Venetian family lace; the sleeves were long and close-fitting, and she had a long white net veil with a wreath of orange blossoms. Lady Diana Manners, who was one of the bridesmaids, designed the bridesmaids' gowns in the medieval manner; they were of white chiffon belted in silver worn with flowing veils of blue tulle held by silver bands. Each of the bridesmaids carried a tall branch of almond blossom. The Hon. Stephen Tennant, who wore a Romeo suit with a jewelled belt, was the page.

Some of the Gowns
The Duke of Rutland was among the first to come to the church, and most of the guests were there early. The Prime Minister arrived with Mr and Mrs Bonham-Carter, and Mr Balfour [Prime Minister 1902–1905]. The Duchess of Rutland wore gold charmeuse with gold tissue in her hat and rose pink velvet cloak bordered with fur. The Marchioness of Anglesey, in white box-cloth, brought her little daughter, Lady Caroline Paget [aged 2] in a little ermine coat and hat. Mrs Asquith wore a black charmeuse gown made with a ruched cape and trimmed with chinchilla; her hat was black with emerald feathers.

Mrs Tennant wore black and white embroidered taffetas; Lady Robert Manners had a long mauve coat trimmed with skunk; and the Countess of Wemyss was in black and white. Lady Tree had a pervenche panne long coat made tight-fitting and a plain black sailor hat. The Countess of Drogheda wore black and gold, Lady D'Abernon grey chinchilla furs with a black coat and skirt, and Lady Arthur Paget a musquash coat bordered with skunk. Mrs Hwfa Williams and

Lady Randolph Churchill (who was with Mrs Churchill) both wore black velvet.

The Guests
Among those present were:-
The Italian Ambassador, the Spanish Ambassador, the Duchess of Buccleuch, Countess Nadia Torby, Prince Bibesco, the Marquis de Soveral, the Marchioness of Bristol and Lady Augustus Hervey, the Earl and Countess of Chesterfield, the Dowager Countess of Arran and Lady Winifred Gore, the Countess of Lanesborough, the Earl and Countess of Albemarle, the Countess of Dundonald, and Lady Marjorie Cochrane, the Earl of Wemyss, the Countess of Lytton, with Viscount Knebworth, the Countess of Essex, the Dowager Countess of Clarendon, Viscount Valentia, Viscount and Viscountess Gladstone, Baroness d'Erlanger, Lady Nunburnholme, Lord and Lady Knaresborough, Lord and Lady Glenconner, Lady Wantage, Lord and Lady Manners and Lady Islington.

The newspaper also listed the main wedding presents:

Bridegroom to bride, large aquamarine chained with diamonds; Duke and Duchess of Rutland, jewels of diamonds and aquamarine-diamond ring, lace veil, canteen of silver and cutlery, travelling suitcase, and cheque; Mr and Mrs Frank Tennant, rope of pearls and diamond star, diamond and emerald brooch, old Japanese lacquer and four silver candlesticks; Lady Diana Manners, diamond watch; Marchioness of Anglesey, cheque; Lord Robert Manners, early silver salts; Mr Asquith, books; Mrs Asquith, black lacquer chairs; Captain Charles Lindsay, old manuscript; Lady Wantage, yellow lacquer sidetable; servants at Belvoir Castle and 16, Arlington Street, George III silver salver; employees at Belvoir, silver gilt Ambassador's inkstand; villagers of Rowsley, Queen Anne walnut and gold mirror; Derbyshire tenants, William III dressing table silver.

Following the wedding, a reception was held at Lord Glenconner's house at Queen Anne's Gate in Westminster. After an hour, John and Kakoo left to catch the train to Belvoir, where they were to spend their honeymoon.

'It was all too wonderful — travelling down with my Kakoo and feeling her to really belong to me,' John wrote in his journal. 'Mrs Tennant had told me that my darling had started her monthly two or three days before and that she was in the middle of it — so I knew what to expect which I was very thankful for, so that I should not bother my darling when I got into bed with her for the first time. But the following night it was all right — so we did things together. I did my best to hurt my darling as little as possible. We had the most glorious 3 1/2 weeks at Belvoir that could ever be. Then we went to London — to 28 Eaton Terrace.

'My darling felt a little sick on Feb 1st and I knew that she had started a baby — but I did not tell her. She only knew when the time for her monthly in Feb. was passed. Then she knew — and we were so happy about it.'

■ ■ ■ ■

PART VIII

■ ■ ■ ■

60

We are now back in the Muniment Rooms in the early hours of the morning of 21 April 1940. John lies, shrouded under an oxygen tent, on the sofa in Room 1. A fire burns in the grate, the light from the flames reflecting on the tall glass cases that surround him. For two years, he has barely left these rooms. His days and nights have been spent sifting through his mother's papers. They are almost in order, but not quite. He can do no more. He is dying.

One last letter from Violet, which was in the trunk of correspondence that John was working on before he died, explains what happened after his wedding in January 1916.

Two weeks after he married Kakoo at St Margaret's, Westminster, dressed, for all the world to see, in his service uniform, he asked his mother to write to Field Marshal Lord French, the new Commander-in-Chief, Home Forces.

It was not an easy letter to write — as Violet's draft reveals. She was having to go cap in hand to the man whose offers John had repeatedly spurned:

Dear Lord French

I am again in great anxiety about my boy/ son. If I didn't think this alone would excuse me in your eyes, I don't know how I would dare to write/appeal to you again for help after all your very great kindness to me and to him last year, which indeed neither of us are likely to forget.

He goes before a Medical Board about March 2. I can only say how greatly/wildly relieved and happy I should be if something could be found for him by that time. Something, however humble/subordinate, but that would be under your own particular wing and protection.

I know quite well it is where he has wished to be, always, even when over loyalty to his General made him throw away so great a chance/opportunity.

You will think it 'Mother's talk' but it is this very loyalty and faithfulness to those he serves which is so strong a trait in his character and upon which you, of all others, could absolutely and for ever depend. I fear his Staff experience has been too short to tell much in his favour, though he did very well, his General always praising him and relying upon him.

My great fear now, is that after the Medical Board (which is very unlikely to pass him for anything but light duty) the state of unrest and uncertainty in which he has been for some months, may drive him into taking some unwise and hasty course, which I shall not be able to prevent.

I do hope you will forgive me. It is indeed a very poor way of showing you how really grateful I am for all you have already done for me.

Early in March, John was appointed ADC to the field marshal — a post he held for the rest of the war.

John's position as one of the most privileged young men in England gave him a choice and he took it. From the perspective of the twenty-first century, his reasons for doing so are compelling: he wanted to be with the woman he loved and to see his unborn child. But in the context of his time, his decision was unforgivable. The four million British men who served in the Great War, 673,375 of whom were killed, had no choice but to fight.

One last mystery remains. John has left nothing to tell us when he came to regret his decision. After March 1916, the war lasted for another two and a half years. He could have gone back to the Front at any time. But he didn't. Whether the conflict between desire and obligation tormented him while he was in London, we cannot know. If he had confided in Kakoo, these letters are also missing from the Muniment Rooms.

The tragic irony is that, but for his brother's death, he would not have been faced with a dilemma.

Haddon was the dagger in his back. Had he lived, John's life would have followed a different trajectory. He would not have become Duke: the choice he made in the winter of 1916 would not have been open to him. Some 1,500 members of the aristocracy served in the war. Two hundred and seventy were killed in action, or died from their wounds. The heirs to Britain's dukedoms were the exception; of those eligible to fight, more than a third had escaped the trenches. But their younger brothers had fought with distinction. Had John been a second son, I was sure he would have been among them.

Throughout the first year of the war, this gentle, sensitive man had tried, in the face of all temptation, to do the right thing. He had resisted every one of his mother's efforts to keep him back from the Front. When he made his choice, he knew he was in the wrong. It was why he had held out against his mother for so long. Yet what he could not have known was the extent to which his decision would come to haunt him.

When that moment came, we don't know. But after 1918, the source of his shame was all around him. Two hundred and forty-nine men from the Belvoir estate were killed in action. For the remainder of his life, John had had to look the families of these men in the eye. Every year, on Armistice Day, he had marched at the head of the columns of veterans that had paraded through the village streets. On becoming Duke, his position determined that he was the first to step forward to lay a wreath of poppies on the war memorial. The congregation in the remembrance service that followed had risen to their feet when he came to take his place in the front pew. All the while, he had kept up the pretence that he had served honourably in the war. It was no wonder he died in an agony of guilt.

The names of the war dead are carved on the memorials in the villages below the castle. It was this lost generation — 'that mysterious army of ploughmen, horsemen and field workers', as the historian Ronald Blythe described them — that had brought me to Belvoir in the first place. In obliterating the records in the Muniment Rooms, John had prevented me from following their stories.

It seems fitting to end by remembering them.

George Allcroft	Belvoir
W R Allen	Scalford
Charles Allis	Bottesford*
Harry Armstrong	Goadby Marwood
Albert Asher	Bottesford
Cecil Frederick Asher	Croxton Kerrial
C Attewell	Scalford
H Attewell	Scalford
Charles Bailey	Stonesby
J T Bailey	Clawson, Harby and Hose
Sidney Bailey	Stonesby
Charles Baines	Clawson, Harby and Hose
Cyril Barrand	Bottesford
Frank Eric Barratt	Plungar
Sidney Jackson Barratt	Plungar
Joseph Thurlby Bass	Croxton Kerrial
Thomas Bass	Croxton Kerrial
Alfred Beet	Granby and Sutton
William Beet	Granby and Sutton
James Beeton	Waltham on the Wolds
Frederick Bell	Harston
Harry Bemrose	Branston
Charles A Bend	Bottesford

* Includes the war dead from the nearby hamlets of
Easthorpe and Normanton

Bertie Benham	Redmile
Charles J Bird	Eastwell
Henry Bishop	Waltham on the Wolds
W Booth	Stathern
Harry Bottrell	Goadby Marwood
V Boulton	Waltham on the Wolds
Walter Low Braithwaite	Redmile
Frederick W Branston	Stonesby
W Broom	Scalford
Henry Brown	Wycomb and Chadwell
George E Brumble	Eastwell
A G Bryett	Stathern
J Buckingham	Muston
Charles C Bullimore	Woolsthorpe
W Bullock	Muston
Thomas Burrows	Croxton Kerrial
Walter Burrows	Croxton Kerrial
Albert E Bursnall	Stonesby
Noel Butler	Knipton
G Alfred Calcraft	Bottesford
John Campbell	Eaton
Thomas Chambers	Knipton
Charles William Chettle	Redmile
Reginald Claxton	Saltby
A C Clove	Scalford

H Clover	Scalford
George Clower	Redmile
Ed Cook	Clawson, Harby and Hose
T Harold Cooper	Bottesford
Arthur Coy	Knipton
W H Coy	Muston
J E Dakin	Stathern
Frederick Darby	Bottesford
Albert Pickard Day	Redmile
Walter Day	Redmile
E Dewey	Clawson, Harby and Hose
George Henry Dewey	Croxton Kerrial
Robert Dolman	Bottesford
B Draper	Sedgebrook
B Draper	Sproxton
Percy Draper	Woolsthorpe
Walter Draper	Woolsthorpe
C J Driver	Scalford
J William Edwards	Bottesford
Gerald Edgar Ellis	Goadby Marwood
Albert Essery	Goadby Marwood
Arthur Etterley	Woolsthorpe
George Edward Etterley	Woolsthorpe
Campbell Victor Farnsworth	Croxton Kerrial

Wilfred Flake	Thorpe Arnold
Cecil Thomas Foister	Goadby Marwood
J R Furnival	Muston
Cyril Gale	Muston
Albert Gibson	Knipton
Arthur Gilding	Bottesford
George Arthur Good-acre	Granby and Sutton
Christopher Good-band	Knipton
David Goodband	Knipton
Jesse Goodband	Woolsthorpe
Reginald Goodband	Woolsthorpe
Bernard T Goods	Eastwell
B Goodson	Clawson, Harby and Hose
W Goodson	Sproxton
George Grass	Branston
W H Greaves	Clawson, Harby and Hose
G J Hall	Stathern
H Hall	Clawson, Harby and Hose
B Hand	Clawson, Harby and Hose
Walter Hardy	Bottesford
James Harper	Woolsthorpe
Cecil Harrison	Eaton
William Harrison	Eaton

H Walter S Hatton	Bottesford
W Helsdon	Stathern
E Hewitt	Scalford
F Hewitt	Scalford
W Hewitt	Scalford
J S Hickman	Sproxton
A Bernard Hickson	Bottesford
C H Hodson	Scalford
Derrick Hollis	Branston
Edwin Holloway	Branston
A B Holmes	Sproxton
E Hughes Holmes	Bottesford
Percy Alison Hopewell	Granby and Sutton
J Hoyes	Clawson, Harby and Hose
Russell Hubbard	Thorpe Arnold
W E G Humphries	Harston
Arthur John Jackson	Croxton Kerrial
Bert Jackson	Eaton
Everitt Jackson	Harston
Francis Jackson	Eaton
George Jackson	Eaton
John Jackson	Saltby
Montague J V Jackson	Bottesford
Matthew Jesson	Eaton
I Johnson	Muston
E Jones	Muston
Cecil F Kemp	Woolsthorpe

T A Kemp	Clawson, Harby and Hose
Tom Kew	Waltham on the Wolds
J Kirk	Scalford
W P Kirton	Muston
J L Kitchen	Barkestone
A Knapp	Statherne
W Lambert	Scalford
Arthur Latham	Woolsthorpe
Harold Lee	Granby and Sutton
F W Mabbott	Clawson, Harby and Hose
John Henry Mackley	Croxton Kerrial
Lord Robert Manners	Knipton
Walter Marriott	Knipton
Walter Marriott	Redmile
C H Marston	Scalford
Joseph Matthews	Bottesford
Arthur Mayfield	Bottesford
Ernest Meredith	Eaton
B Miller	Scalford
Clifford Millert	Bottesford
B F W Mogridge	Scalford
P Moore	Scalford
George Algernon Morley	Redmile
Joseph William Morris	Plungar

George Morrison	Waltham on the Wolds
James Morrison	Waltham on the Wolds
C H Moulds	Clawson, Harby and Hose
G H Moulds	Clawson, Harby and Hose
George Porter Musson	Croxton Kerrial
F Neale	Sproxton
John Charles Newell	Redmile
William Newton	Knipton
Richard Nicolls	Knipton
J Norman	Muston
J T North	Sedgebrook
F A Noyes	Clawson, Harby and Hose
Charles Pacey	Bottesford
Ernest Pacey	Woolsthorpe
Frank Pacey	Bottesford
John H Pacey	Woolsthorpe
Richard Pacey	Woolsthorpe
Thomas Pacey	Woolsthorpe
William E E Pacey	Woolsthorpe
C Page	Stathern
R Turlington Page	Bottesford
Charles Paling	Thorpe Arnold
Frank Palmer	Belvoir

F Parker	Scalford
E Parks	Stathern
George E Pearce	Woolsthorpe
James Pearce	Woolsthorpe
John William Pearson	Redmile
John Peregrine	Branston
George Pick	Eaton
J Pick	Scalford
William Henry Pizer	Goadby Marwood
William Plumb	Thorpe Arnold
John W Poyser	Eastwell
Harry Pritchett	Granby and Sutton
R C Pritchett	Muston
Edgar C Raithby	Bottesford
Frank Raithby	Bottesford
F C Randell	Scalford
G Rawlings	Stathern
T Rawlings	Clawson, Harby and Hose
Joseph William Rimmington	Croxton Kerrial
Thomas Rimmington	Croxton Kerrial
Thomas Gordon Robert	Redmile
Albert Edwards Roberts	Redmile
J Richard Robinson	Bottesford
Page Robinson	Knipton
J Rowe	Scalford

W H Rudkin	Sproxton
Herbert Scarborough	Goadby Marwood
F J Schofield	Barkestone
Francis Scott	Knipton
Robert W Scrimshaw	Eastwell
Frederick Shaw	Bottesford
Arthur Shelton	Eaton
C Shelton	Scalford
Harry Skillington	Plungar
Herbert G Skinner	Bottesford
George Slater	Granby and Sutton
Albert Smith	Granby and Sutton
Herbert Smith	Granby and Sutton
J Smith	Clawson, Harby and Hose
William Staniland	Stonesby
G W Starbuck	Stathern
C Attewell Steans	Scalford
J Stevens	Barkestone
A H Stockwell	Sproxton
A Stokes	Clawson, Harby and Hose
James Radcliffe Streeton	Croxton Kerrial
Thomas Goodwin Streeton	Croxton Kerrial
Philip Sutton	Bottesford
Ernest Swain	Redmile

W Swain	Scalford
A R Talbot	Waltham on the Wolds
Warren Taylor	Eaton
John Thornton	Branston
E Wakefield	Muston
Ernest Wakefield	Eaton
J Ward	Barkstone
William Robert Ward	Croxton Kerrial
J C Warren	Statherne
F Watson	Statherne
Harry Welsh	Plungar
F Wesson	Clawson, Harby and Hose
G Whatton	Sedgebrook
T A White	Barkestone
Frederick Wilcox	Woolsthorpe
Richard Wilcox	Woolsthorpe
Herbert Wilford	Waltham on the Wolds
Herbert Wing	Woolsthorpe
Thomas Wing	Woolsthorpe
Walter Wing	Woolsthorpe
George Winters	Knipton
Ernest Woodcock	Thorpe Arnold
Fred Woodcock	Thorpe Arnold
Thomas Woodcock	Thorpe Arnold
Frederick Francis Woodford	Granby and Sutton

L Woodford	Clawson, Harby and Hose
George Henry Worn	Croxton Kerrial
Cecil Worthington	Woolsthorpe
Fred Worthington	Plungar
F W Wright	Sproxton
W Wright	Clawson, Harby and Hose

EPILOGUE

Between 1916 and 1925, John and Kakoo had five children. To the frustration of Violet and Henry, the first two were girls. It wasn't until May 1919 that Charles, an heir, was born. A second son, John, followed, and then Roger, born three years later, in 1925.

From early on, however, the marriage proved to be an unhappy one. Two years after her wedding, Kakoo confided in Cynthia Asquith. 'Talking of Kakoo's second baby not being a boy,' Cynthia noted in her diary, 'she said she didn't think the Rutland family was one which should be perpetuated.' The letters at Belvoir show that John was frequently short-tempered with Kakoo. He was also, as we know from his affair with Hilda Lezard, unfaithful to her. By the early 1920s, John was having numerous affairs. One with the children's nanny, by whom he had a child, threatened to break up his marriage.

Hilda Lezard had taken her secret to her grave. I was unable to find out why she broke into the castle in the dead of night after John died, or what — if anything — she took with her. While her family acknowledged the affair, they had not heard of the break-in.

Of the other protagonists in this story, there are few happy endings.

In 1920, Henry's vast debts finally caught up with him. He was forced to sell a large portion of his estate — a step he had resisted since succeeding to the dukedom in 1908. Twenty-seven thousand acres in Leicestershire and Derbyshire were sold at auction for £1,100,000.* Thirteen thousand three hundred of these acres were at Belvoir, reducing the size of the estate by half.

After the sale, Henry was beset with depression. Haunted by guilt at being the first in a thousand-year-long line of custodians to break up the family's main estate, and still haunted by the loss of his favourite son, he could see no point in living. Increasingly, he sought comfort in visiting Haddon's tomb. In a symbolic gesture, on 28 September 1920, the twenty-sixth anniversary of Haddon's death, Henry laid the dark-blue velvet mantle that as a Knight of the Order of the Garter he was entitled to wear on his son's tomb. The award of the Garter, which he received in 1918, was for his work in raising volunteers for the war.

* Approximately £34,500,000 at today's values.

'Darling,' he wrote to Violet:

I have this moment placed the Gown and my bunch of leaves on the stone at the Mausoleum.

It is a glorious day, and Haddon's robin sang, as I hoped it would. It all made one very hopeful that when one is finally taken there as very soon must happen — one will at last rest in peace.

Henry died five years later at Belvoir at the age of seventy-three.

George Gordon Moore, the man John had to thank for the introduction to Field Marshal Lord French, left England under a cloud in January 1916. The rumours circulating in the foreign press had at last been published in a British newspaper. Moore, the report alleged, was an enemy agent; through his special relationship with French, he was passing secret information to the Germans, gleaned from his many visits to General Headquarters. The rumours were without foundation, and Moore sued the newspaper for libel. Though he won the case, it left him feeling bitter and vengeful. On his return to America, he claimed to have documents in his safe which, if published, would shake the foundations of the British Empire. They were never published, but the scandal brought to an end his love affair with England and the English

— and his friendship with Lord French.

In America, Moore's notoriety — based on his immense wealth and his brooding presence — continued. A celebrated breeder of polo ponies, the matches he hosted at his palatial Californian ranch were attended by Hollywood film stars and some of America's wealthiest families. When F. Scott Fitzgerald's *The Great Gatsby* was published in 1925, it was thought that Moore was the model for the novel's mysterious hero, Jay Gatsby. Four years later, Moore lost the bulk of his fortune in the stock-market crash.

His 'Great Friend', Lord French, fared little better. In 1921, after serving as Lord Lieutenant of Ireland for three years, he left the sumptuous surroundings of Vice Regal Lodge in Dublin. It was his last official posting. Without Moore's financial support, French was unable to afford a home in England. Shunned by his wife and family for his many affairs, he led an itinerant existence. Much of his time was spent in France, where he spoke at ex-servicemen's gatherings and unveiled war memorials on the battlefields of Flanders. In 1923, after he was given an earldom, Lord Beauchamp, Lord Warden of the Cinque Ports, offered French the appointment of Captain of Deal Castle, an honorary position which gave the field marshal the right of residing at the castle.

He died there in May 1925. Two weeks

later, a funeral service was held at Westminster Abbey — the first of a major war leader. Spectators stood twelve deep outside the abbey and in the nearby streets. The majority of them were veterans of the original British Expeditionary Force that had set out for France in August 1914, and which French had commanded. As his biographer wrote, 'they stood stiff and hatless as the coffin passed. Some wept unashamedly; not so much for their old chief, perhaps, as for their own youths and for a past which now seemed as remote as the long aching summer of '14.'

Charlie Lindsay also died that spring. He was sixty-three and had cancer. His last letter to John, written a few weeks before his death, is in the Muniment Rooms at Belvoir. He had entrusted John with looking after his valet, to whom he'd left a large sum of money. He was anxious that the legacy should be kept secret. At the time, homosexuality was illegal; the implication in Charlie's letter is that his valet was also his lover:

Dear Jacko
I explained to you a few days ago what I wanted done. So this is only to remind you. Alongside of this letter is my will, in which you will see that I have left Birt some money, as I mentioned to you. He has behaved well to me, and I have been selfish in keeping him in my service when

703

in my opinion, with the talents which I believe he possesses, he might have started some career which would have been more lucrative. I therefore take this opportunity of thanking him, as well as making up — to a certain extent — for my selfishness. At the same time I do not feel very happy in the way I have done it, and if I am given time, I propose to make you a trustee for this money, which I feel, though it might give you a little trouble, you would do for me as a great kindness.

The money I have left him is too much for him to have command of all of a go. What I should have wished would be that he should have had the interest only of the money for a certain number of years — say till he was about 30 years old . . . Anyhow would you do the best you can for him. I shall speak to him myself and recommend him strongly to take your advice. And Jacko, keep an eye on him, that he doesn't go to hell — he hates service I believe, and hankers after stage and dancing, the latter he is very good at, and it may be his metier — I don't know — abroad and colonies I cannot believe he would prosper in.

I am writing all this very fast, and can think of very little else to say. I don't want my will read out, if that can be avoided, and, of course, no funeral ceremonies or expenses that can possibly be avoided. And Jacko I have a pleasant fancy for that mausoleum at Belvoir — isn't it odd! — a dislike to being away from my friends perhaps, but really indeed it cannot possibly matter one little bit — so don't even suggest the thing unless it seems to you right, and quite easy.

So, to a possible future meeting, you dear old pet, what wouldn't I give to think it could be so.

Charlie

John had mourned his uncle's death deeply. It was only when he came to go through his mother's papers in the last years of his own life that he discovered that Charlie, the person he had depended on as a boy and whom he had loved and trusted more than anyone else, had betrayed him. Not a single one of Charlie's replies to the many conspiratorial questions Violet asked him in the first year of the war has survived in the Muniment Rooms. We cannot be certain of John's motives, but it seems he destroyed his uncle's letters because the evidence of his betrayal was simply too painful to him.

Nor had John kept many letters from his sister Diana. She was the one true patriot in the family; her war was spent tirelessly nursing the sick and the wounded. Many of her closest friends were killed, a loss she wrote movingly about, and which remained with her for the rest of her life. She, of course, was instrumental in John's escape from the war. Yet after it, their relationship seems to have been distant. Again, we cannot be certain, but the suggestion from the absence of letters between brother and sister is that it was the cause of some sort of rift between them.

After the war ended, Diana disappointed all of her mother's dreams by marrying Duff Cooper. 'That awful Duff,' as Violet called him, was neither a royal prince nor the heir to a great fortune: he was a career diplomat earning the paltry sum of £300 a year. His pedigree also fell far short of Violet's expectations: though Duff's maternal uncle was the Duke of Fife, his mother was a 'bolter', and his father a doctor who specialized in venereal diseases.

When Violet first learned of the engagement, she was beside herself. She told Diana that she would rather John had been killed in the war, or that Diana had cancer, than that she should marry Duff. 'Her Grace is raising tally-whack and tandem all over London,' wrote Lady Desborough, who disliked Violet intensely and was thrilled at her disappointment. The press were equally thrilled when news of the engagement leaked out. *Cassell's Saturday Journal* gleefully reported that the couple would have to live on '£300 a year and a ducal curse'.

Diana's old admirers rallied around her. George Moore offered to give her £6,000 a year from the time of her marriage. The offer was refused, but Diana allowed him to deposit £500 in her bank account and to guarantee her overdraft.

Violet retaliated by insisting that her engagement should last for at least a year. She accused Diana of wanting to marry Duff purely to spite her and, in a series of acrimonious letters, did her best to put her off:

What has always been my cry to others who have repeated it to you? That <u>I cannot believe in your love</u>, since you have always given it to others to tell me of.

I never have in my life had the feeling '<u>I don't want to be beaten</u>'. 'To win' never gives me pleasure at the expense of anyone I love 'giving in' to me — in fact I always have the feeling 'please don't'. But you have always, I think, seen in this a <u>fight</u>. Why?

God knows, I have said to you — before Letty and Kakoo — if only I could believe you loved as I understand love!

My nature is <u>not</u> snobbish. I shall always maintain that — however much you and friends may think so. If you are born in a set that without snobbish struggling <u>is</u> 'up there' — say in highest <u>worldwide interest</u> — there is no need to fling it all away as

707

you have always loved to do triumphantly <u>as against me</u>.

After raging at Diana, Violet had tried to make her feel sorry for her.

'Anyhow,' she wrote, 'your friends completely took you from me — and I have been <u>very very</u> miserable in consequence in a year and a half.'

Diana married Duff in June 1919. Soon after their wedding, she became a successful actress. By 1923, she was earning $1,500 a week touring America playing the lead role in Max Reinhardt's play, *The Miracle*. Mobbed and fêted wherever she went, her success, combined with Duff's burgeoning political career, ensured that they became one of the most glamorous, most sought after couples of their generation.

And finally to Violet.

When Henry died, she sold the contents of 16 Arlington Street, and moved into the Lodge, where Mrs Seed, her gatekeeper, had lived. Then, after the house itself was sold, she devoted the last years of her life to creating a home out of the two houses she bought in Chapel Street, Belgravia. 'With the huge nest-egg laid by Arlington Street's sale,' Diana recalled, 'my mother doubled its length, lit it with high orangery windows, joined the two houses and built a second orangery drawing-room on the opposite side which still left a large garden with a terrace, a lawn, flower-beds and a statue.'

Her days were spent finishing Haddon's tomb and filling her house with things that dated from his childhood at Cockayne Hatley. She even wore the clothes she had worn then.

'The Hatley brocade curtains, at last bleached to her desired faded blue, were hung,' Diana recalled: 'The lace drawer, the feather drawer, the one for ribbons and the one for furs found their places, as did the immovable chest for stuffs and dress-lengths and patterns, a yard square, taken on trial from furnishers and never returned. Shelves were filled with Tauchnitz books bought on journeys in the '70s, '80s and '90s, bound extravagantly enough in half-vellum and marbled paper . . . There was nothing ordinary in her house, not even the meals, which would have been unusual had they existed. She disapproved of spending money on food, and still more upon drink, so it was abandon hope the greedy and the alcoholics. She herself nibbled Marie biscuits and sipped Ovaltine, living comfortably and healthily upon nothing.'

It was in this house that Violet died, aged eighty, on 22 December 1937. In the last week of her life, after an operation for appendicitis failed, she lay delirious, singing, as Diana recalled, 'snatches of old songs like

Ophelia, and describing in some new-given idiom, the things strange and beautiful that passed before her half-blind eyes'.

John and Diana were with her at the end. And yet there is a macabre twist to Violet's passing.

Within hours of her death, John released a statement to the press. It was published in *The Times* the next morning:

> The condition of Violet, Duchess of Rutland, was stated last night to show a very slight change for the better.

For five days, John went on issuing bulletins to *The Times* and other papers, saying his mother's health was improving, when actually she lay dead at Chapel Street. 'I stayed with her,' Diana recalled, 'through this macabre holiday, warding off the inquisitive press, lying to anxious enquirers, trying to calm and silence the faithful maid and the rest of her people.'

John had not wanted his mother's death to interfere with the family Christmas at Belvoir — a gathering of more than twenty friends and relations. It was only on 28 December, six days after Violet died, that he finally allowed the announcement to be made. It appeared in the Court Circular pages of *The Times*:

We have to announce that Violet, Duchess of Rutland, died yesterday morning. The funeral will take place at Belvoir on Thursday.

Violet was buried in the mausoleum alongside Haddon and Henry.

Two months after her death, John donated his brother's tomb, which his mother had spent half her life sculpting, to the Tate Gallery.

It was only after his death in 1940 that a copy of the original was placed in the chapel at Haddon Hall — a wish that Violet had expressed from the beginning, and which John had denied.

NOTES

GENERAL NOTE

All letters/diaries are late nineteenth- and early twentieth-century papers from the Muniment Rooms at Belvoir Castle unless otherwise stated. The archives have not been catalogued, therefore it is not possible to provide citations for the individual documents.

Abbreviations

MR	Muniment Rooms
WO	War Office
PRO	Public Record Office

PART I

Chapters 1–6: General Note

The descriptions of Belvoir Castle in 1940, the manner of doing things, and the rumours, events and anecdotes referred to in these chapters have been drawn from conversations with servants working there at the time (or their relations) and members of the Manners family.

They are:

The Marquis of Anglesey, nephew of John, 9th Duke of Rutland

Gladys Brittain, the wife of Ted Brittain, the butler in 1940

Lady Ursula D'Abo, eldest daughter of John, 9th Duke of Rutland

Clarence Harper, footman

Helen King, tenant of the Duke of Rutland

Lord Roger Manners, youngest son of John, 9th Duke of Rutland

Viscount Norwich, nephew of John, 9th Duke of Rutland

Sheila Osborne, former pantry maid

Tonia Pacey, the daughter of Ted Brittain

Dorothy Plowright, the daughter of Bill Hotchin, the boiler stoker

Emma, Duchess of Rutland

George Waudby, footman

Chapter 2

Belvoir Castle had been . . . : National Archives, PRO 18 and PRO 18/1

At Chancery Lane . . . : ibid.

The oldest and most important . . . : ibid.

Ten days earlier . . . : ibid.

Appointed Physician-extraordinary . . . : Francis Watson, *Dawson of Penn,* Chatto &

Windus 1950

Chapter 4

Horse Key, Pringle . . . : Belvoir Estate
 Records, MR
These women thus being . . . : Michael Hon-
 eybone, *Wicked Practise & Sorcerye*, Devon
 2008

Chapter 6

First a pane of glass was smashed . . . :
 National Archives, PRO 18/1
'I thought I ought to let you know . . .': ibid.

Chapter 7

In 1914, the Duke of Rutland's estate . . . :
 Belvoir Estate Maps, MR
The testimony of farm worker Leonard
 Thompson . . . :' Ronald Blythe, *Akenfield*,
 Penguin 1999, pp. 31–44
'We were all delighted when war broke
 out . . .': ibid., p. 38
We arrived at the Dardanelles . . . : ibid.
Of the men who left . . . : Information
 gathered from the village war memorials
A few weeks after war was declared . . . :
 Grantham Journal, 29 August 1914
'No man in the prime of life . . .': A. J. P. Tay-

lor, *The First World War,* Penguin 1974, p. 22

In an age when the word 'nobility' . . . : Brian Masters, *The Dukes,* Blond Briggs 1977, p. 9

In 1914, there were thirty of them . . . : Includes the Royal Dukes: Albany, Connaught, Cumberland and Teviotdale, and Rothesay

Within living memory . . . : ibid., pp. 9–10

So opulent was their lifestyle at Belvoir . . . : Philip Ziegler, *Diana Cooper,* Hamish Hamilton 1981, p. 10

'It was not just that millions died . . .': Mary, Countess of Wemyss, *A Family Record,* The Curwen Press 1932, p. 235

Chapter 9

Even so, in the sixteen weeks since the division . . . : General Edward Stuart Wortley to Lord Stamfordham, Private Secretary to King George V, June 1915, Royal Archives, Windsor

On a warm summer's evening . . . : John Milne, *Footprints of the 1/4th Leicestershire Regiment,* Naval and Military Press 2006, p. 31

'It was a pleasant bivouac . . .': ibid.

'Everybody knew what a visit there . . .': ibid., p. 30

'What a track it was . . .': ibid., p. 32

At 8 p.m., General Clifford, the Commanding Officer . . . : 138th Brigade War Diary, National Archives, Kew

'The Companies marched back independently . . .': Milne, *Footprints of the 1/4th Leicestershire Regiment*, p. 34

In the autumn of 1915, at the Battle of Loos . . . : Nick Lloyd, *Loos, 1915*, Tempus 2006

Twenty of John's fellow officers . . . : Milne, *Footprints of the 1/4th Leicestershire Regiment 2006*, p. 55

'A significant proportion of the regiment's casualties . . .': *Grantham Journal*, October–November 1915

Chapter 10

Sigmund Freud had also suggested . . . : 'Some Character-Types Met with in Psycho-Analytic Work 1: "The Exceptions" ', in Freud, S. E. (1957)

Chapter 12

In the months that followed . . . : Wikipedia: 1908 Messina earthquake

Some weeks earlier, Herbert Asquith . . . : *The Times*, 12 January 1909

The King had concealed them . . . : Christopher Hibbert, *Charles I, A Life of Religion, War and Treason*, Macmillan 1968

Chapter 13

Among the documents . . . : National Archives, HS 9/921/5

I was dropped . . . : ibid.

Chapter 14

The sources in this chapter are drawn from files held at the National Archives, PRO 18 and PRO 18/1.

Chapter 16

The break with his mother . . . : In her letter to Charlie, Violet misremembered John's age. He was eight years old at the time.

Chapters 17 and 18

The newspaper sources from which the events of these chapters are drawn are:

Bedfordshire Mercury, Sept./Oct. 1894

Bedfordshire Standard, Sept./Oct. 1894

Bedfordshire Times and Independent, Sept./ Oct. 1894

Biggleswade Chronicle and Sandy Times, Sept./Oct. 1894

Grantham Journal, Sept./Oct. 1894

Grantham Times, Sept./Oct. 1894

Leicester Chronicle, Sept./Oct. 1894

Leicester Daily Express, Sept./Oct. 1894

Leicester Journal, Sept./Oct. 1894
Melton Mowbray Times, Sept./Oct. 1894

Chapter 19

The family had employed 110 servants then . . . : Belvoir Castle Household Accounts, 1894

Chapter 20

Both Henry and Violet had close links to the Queen . . . : *Burke's Peerage,* 107th edition

Chapter 23

Mary, Countess of Minto . . . : Mary, Countess of Minto, 1858–1940, married Gilbert John Elliot-Murray-Kynynmound, 4th Earl of Minto, July 1883
Mary, Countess of Wemyss . . . : Mary, Countess of Wemyss, 1862–1937, married Francis Richard Charteris, 10th Earl of Wemyss, August 1883

Chapter 26

Famous only for his handsome looks . . . : Philip Ziegler, *Diana Cooper,* Hamish Hamilton 1981
Born in 1852 . . . : *Burke's Peerage,* 107th edition

As a matter of course, whenever he entered . . . : *Leicester Journal and Midland Counties General Advertiser*, 23 July 1852

At Leicester, a few weeks after Henry was born . . . : *Leicester Chronicle*, 24 April 1852

A beautiful set piece . . . : ibid.

The picture she paints of him . . . : Lady Diana Cooper, *The Rainbow Comes and Goes*, Rupert Hart-Davis 1958

'Ruin stared us in the face . . .': ibid., p. 21

Though he 'worried and fretted' . . . : ibid., pp. 20–21

'Sadness fell from the air . . .': Diana Cooper, *Autobiography*, Faber and Faber 2008, p. 282

Chapter 27

Household Accounts . . . : All price comparison figures throughout the book are calculated using Economic History Services (http://eh.net/ hmit)

There was never an hour . . . : Lady Diana Cooper, *The Rainbow Comes and Goes*, Rupert Hart-Davis 1958

'The watermen are difficult to believe in today . . .': ibid., pp. 35–6

Joining the watermen . . . : ibid.

Throughout the night . . . : ibid., pp. 36–7

Then there was Betsy . . . : ibid.

Diana's favourite was the Duke's tailor . . . : ibid., p. 35

As the century turned . . . : ibid., p. 27

Every day, after lunch, the old Duke . . . : ibid., p. 28

Perfection — 'snow-white . . . : ibid.

On the days he chose not to ride . . . : ibid. pp. 29–30

'My grandfather would uncover his head . . .': ibid., p. 30

On Sundays, the Duke's post-lunch routine . . . : ibid., p. 31

After the stables came the kitchen garden . . . : ibid., p. 32

The inspection continued . . . : ibid.

Last came the kennels . . . : ibid.

Chapter 28

Its aim . . . : Lloyd George, House of Commons, 29 April 1909

'My father was frankly philistine . . .': Lady Diana Cooper, *The Rainbow Comes and Goes*, Rupert Hart-Davis 1958, p. 38

Chapter 29

To avoid a dilution in rank . . . : Brian Masters, *The Dukes*, Blond Briggs 1977, p. 20

In the early 1890s . . . : Ruth Brandon, *The Dollar Princesses*, Knopf 1980

'Until then,' New York heiress . . . : Daisy Goodwin, 'Cash for Titles', *The Mail*, August 2010

In 1895, the Duke of Marlborough . . . : ibid.

Her dowry was a staggering . . . : Amanda
Mackenzie Stuart, *Consuelo and Alva
Vanderbilt*, Harper Perennial 2005, p. 135

That year alone . . . : Daisy Goodwin, 'Cash
for Titles'

In 1903, after seeing off the Duke of
Manchester . . . : *The New York Times*, 11
November 1903

Alva, her socially ambitious mother . . . :
Amanda Mackenzie Stuart, *Consuelo and
Alva Vanderbilt*, p. 4

The Duke had never loved her . . . : ibid., pp.
252–4

Margaretta Drexel was the . . . : *The New
York Times, The London Times*, May–June
1909

The Drexels had arrived in style . . . : ibid.

Chapter 34

John's battalion, the 4th Leicesters . . . : John
Milne, *Footprints of the 1/4th Leicestershire
Regiment*, Naval and Military Press 2006,
p. 57

He had been one of thirty to embark . . . :
ibid.

The previous December . . . : Philip Warner,
The Battle of Loos, Kimber 1976

They had fought at Ypres and Loos . . . : 'The

Long, Long Trail', www.1914-1918.net/

Chapter 35

The Army Council was . . . : 'The Long, Long Trail', www.1914–1918.net/

We should have been guilty of one of the most . . . : *Grantham Journal,* 12 September 1914

Chapter 37

It was first light on the morning of 27 August . . . : Violet to Diana, 27 August 1914: MR

By any standards . . . : Lady Diana Cooper, *The Rainbow Comes and Goes,* Rupert Hart-Davis 1958, p. 52

Unkindly, Margot Asquith . . . : Richard Davenport-Hines, *Ettie,* Weidenfeld & Nicolson 2008, p. 47

Her daughter-in-law . . . : Cynthia Asquith, *Haply I May Remember,* James Barrie 1950, p. 86

The 'stylized scream' . . . : Lady Diana Cooper, *The Rainbow Comes and Goes,* p. 24

'My mother spent the mornings . . .': ibid.

Downstairs, Henry . . . : Violet to Diana, 27 August 1914: MR

I think you ought . . . : Henry to Violet, ibid.

In the 1890s, she had persuaded . . . : Philip

Ziegler, *Lady Diana Cooper,* Hamish Hamilton 1981, p. 8

'I had a letter . . .': Richard Davenport-Hines, *Ettie,* p. 59

By the end of it, she had drawn up a list . . . : MR

Chapter 38

Three weeks later, on an overcast morning . . . : *Luton News and Bedfordshire Chronicle,* 24 September 1914

To allow plenty of time . . . : *Luton News and Bedfordshire Chronicle,* 24 September 1914; *Bedfordshire Advertiser and Luton Times,* 25 September 1914; *Luton Reporter,* 21 September 1914

Opposite the troops . . . : ibid.

Morale among the troops . . . : ibid.

Until the King arrived . . . : ibid.

At Stockwood Park . . . : MR

The others — the sons of brewers . . . : Alan MacDonald, *A Lack of Offensive Spirit,* Iona Books 2008

'Just as His Majesty took the salute . . .': *Bedfordshire Advertiser and Luton Times,* 25 September 1914

Only a portion of the twelve thousand . . . : *Luton News and Bedfordshire Chronicle,* 24 September 1914; *Bedfordshire Advertiser and Luton Times,* 25 September 1914

In September 1914 . . . : Paul Fussell, *The Great War and Modern Memory*, Oxford 2000, p. 9

After completing his inspection . . . : *Luton News and Bedfordshire Chronicle*, 24 September 1914; *Bedfordshire Advertiser and Luton Times*, 25 September 1914; *Luton Reporter*, 21 September 1914

'War is the sovereign disinfectant . . .': Samuel Hynes, *A War Imagined*, The Bodley Head 1990, p. 12

The notion that there was something wrong . . . : ibid., p. 16

'I do not suppose any country . . .': MR

'There is one point I particularly want to press . . .': ibid.

So convinced was Henry . . . : *Grantham Journal*, 29 August 1914

Chapter 39

Detachments of soldiers from the Army Service Corps . . . : MR

Should I write to Lord Grenfell . . . : ibid.

Time was running out . . . : ibid.

'Beloved, in these always terrible days . . .': Violet's notebook, private collection

A maverick bachelor . . . : John Lee, *A Soldier's Life*, Macmillan 2000

'Apart from soldiers . . .': Sir George Arthur, *Not Worth Reading*, Longmans 1938

'Kitchener almost invariably dined . . .': ibid.

Kitchener's dislike of women . . . : ibid.

Sir John Cowans . . . : MR

Violet was calculating . . . : MR

Grenfell parted from Violet . . . : MR

Alone at Belvoir . . . : MR

'Beloved,' Cust replied . . . : Violet's notebook, private collection

Her days were crowded with civic duties . . . : *Grantham Journal,* August–October 1914

In the evenings . . . : ibid.

Her afternoons were spent . . . : Lady Diana Cooper, *The Rainbow Comes and Goes,* Rupert Hart-Davis 1958, p. 118

For the most part, good horses . . . : *Grantham Journal,* 29 August 1914

Chapter 40

On his way there . . . : Charlie to Marjorie Anglesey, private collection

The wagons, which were long and grey . . . : Lyn Macdonald, *The Roses of Picardy,* Penguin Books 1993, p. 171

'The public weren't allowed in the station . . .': ibid., pp. 172–4

Charlie had seen him twice . . . : Letters from Charlie to John, August–October 1914, MR

In an effort to cheer himself up . . . : ibid.

Along Victoria Street . . . : *The Times,* 16 October 1914

Chapter 41

Violet was at 16 Arlington Street . . . : Violet to Charlie, 17 October, MR. This is the first of the letters which Violet wrote to her brother that day — letters which enabled me to track her exact movements over the course of this important day

It was almost three o'clock . . . : ibid.

The minute Violet received . . . : ibid.

She was dressed in the clothes . . . : Lady Diana Cooper, *The Rainbow Comes and Goes*, Rupert Hart-Davis 1958, p. 51

On the approach to it . . . : Violet to Charlie, 17 October 1914, MR

On leaving Belvoir . . . : ibid.

The true purpose of her visit . . . : Violet to Charlie, 18 October 1914, MR

It was with a 'heavy heart' . . . : Violet to Charlie, 17 October 1914, MR

'One of the greatest worries . . .': C. Callwell, *Experiences of a Dug-Out 1914–1918*, Constable 1920, p. 29

The thousand-room building . . . : Hampden Gordon, *The War Office*, Putnam 1935

'A mere recital of official events . . .': ibid., p. 291

'They helped to keep such people at bay . . .': C. Callwell, *Experiences of a Dug-Out 1914–1918*, p. 29

Violet had not been kept 'at bay' . . . : Violet to Charlie, 17 October 1914, MR

Hood, a bachelor . . . : Wikipedia

It was General Bethune's love . . . : Violet to Charlie, n.d., MR

Born in 1865, Bethune . . . : *The Times*, 3 November 1930

Hood's office . . . : Violet to Charlie, 17 October 1914, MR

The elation she had felt . . . : Violet to Charlie, 18 October 1914

Chapter 42

Out on the Western Front . . . : Lyn Macdonald, *1914*, Headline 1994

Thirty miles to the east . . . : ibid.

The offensive . . . : ibid.

At the battles that had preceded it . . . : Ian F. W. Beckett, *Ypres, The First Battle*, Longman 2004

'He was sad and depressed . . .': E. G. French, *The Life of Field Marshal Sir John French*, Cassell 1931, p. 248

At 7.10 the previous evening . . . : Lyn Macdonald, *1914*

By noon . . . : Ian F. W. Beckett, *Ypres, The First Battle*

He had received . . . : Alan Palmer, *Ypres, 1914–1918*, Constable 2007, p. 60

The report was one of a number . . . : Lyn Macdonald, *1914*, p. 357

They were the troops of the Fourth Army . . . : Alan Palmer, *Ypres, 1914–1918*, p. 61

Extraordinarily, though the evidence . . . :
Ian F. W. Beckett, *Ypres, The First Battle*, p.
62

Numbering 84,000 . . . : C. R. Simpson, *The
History of the Lincolnshire Regiment, 1914–
1919*, The Medici Society, 1931, p. 74

It was to General Edward Stuart Wortley . . . :
ESW to the Duke, 22 October 1914, MR;
Vernon Jones to the Duke, 20 October,
1914, MR; telegram, Violet to the Duke, 19
October 1914, MR

Chapter 43

The details are sketchy . . . : Charlie to John,
21 October 1914, MR

'A darling of the Gods . . .': Alan Mac-
Donald, *A Lack of Offensive Spirit*, Iona
Books 2008, pp. 25–8

In those last weeks in October . . . : Lord
Grenfell to Violet, various letters, October
1914, MR; Sir John Cowans, QMG, to
Violet, various letters, September–November 1914, MR

At the eleventh hour . . . : ibid.

Regardless of their actual readiness . . . :
Violet to Charlie, n.d.

Violet, however, was not going to . . . : Letters to Charlie, various, October–December
1914, MR

His closest friend — a 'sinister' American . . . : Ziegler, *Lady Diana Cooper*,
Hamish Hamilton 1981, p. 62

Aged thirty-five, he was . . . : George Gordon Moore, unpublished memoir, private collection

His fortune . . . : ibid.

His olive skin . . . : Diana Cooper, *The Rainbow Comes and Goes,* Rupert Hart-Davis 1958, p. 96

Their friendship went back . . . : George Gordon Moore, unpublished memoir, private collection

An elegant six-storey . . . : ibid.

'Dined with Johnnie French . . .': Richard Holmes, *The Little Field Marshal,* Cassell 2005, p. 135

Over the years, Sir John . . . : George H. Cassar, *The Tragedy of Sir John French,* University of Delaware Press 1985, pp. 181–3

Before the war, the goings-on . . . : ibid.

Winston Churchill . . . : George Gordon Moore, unpublished memoir, private collection

Unabashed . . . : ibid.

Whenever he visited . . . : ibid.

Swallowing her pride . . . : Diana to Marjorie Anglesey, private collection

Chapter 45

Violet sat 'sorrowing and silent' . . . : Diana Cooper, *The Rainbow Comes and Goes,* Rupert Hart-Davis 1958, p. 119

Half a century earlier . . . : Charles Dickens, *Oliver Twist*

The buildings were black . . .: J. G. Broodbank, *History of the Port of London*, D. O'Connor 1921

Huge wooden crates . . .: Diana to her sister Marjorie, private collection

Large signs . . .: John Pudney, *London's Docks*, Thames and Hudson 1975

Diana had set her heart . . .: Philip Ziegler, *Lady Diana Cooper*, Hamish Hamilton 1981, pp. 47–8

Her first intention . . .: ibid.

Violet had put up every obstacle . . .: Diana Cooper, *The Rainbow Comes and Goes*, p. 118

First, she had tried . . .: Violet to Charlie, various letters, August–October 1914, MR

'Old Dr Hood . . .': Diana Cooper, *The Rainbow Comes and Goes*, p. 126

The thought that . . .: Violet to Charlie, various letters, August–October 1914, MR

It took courage . . .: Diana Cooper, *The Rainbow Comes and Goes*, p. 118

Although she was twenty-two . . .: Philip Ziegler, *Lady Diana Cooper*, pp. 48–50

'Guy's looked very Dickensian . . .': Diana Cooper, *The Rainbow Comes and Goes*, pp. 119–20

'My mother writhed . . .': ibid.

'Mother was in a despairing blue . . .': Diana

to her sister Marjorie, private collection

'I was still forbidden . . .': Diana Cooper, *The Rainbow Comes and Goes,* p. 76

At night . . .: ibid., p. 111

There were other rules too . . .: ibid., pp. 76–129

Most eligible was . . .: Philip Ziegler, *Lady Diana Cooper,* pp. 30–31

It was one that the Duke of Connaught . . .: ibid.

If this plan failed . . .: ibid.

Diana rejected . . .: ibid.

In private, her parents . . .: Duke of Rutland to Marjorie, n.d., MR

Diana loathed . . .: Philip Ziegler, *Lady Diana Cooper,* pp. 62–4

They had met at a house party . . .: ibid.

The director of a merchant bank . . .: George Gordon Moore, unpublished memoir, private collection

'His riches were evident . . .': Diana Cooper, *The Rainbow Comes and Goes,* p. 96

At dances before the war . . .: Philip Ziegler, *Lady Diana Cooper,* pp. 23–4

Enid Bagnold . . .: ibid.

Raymond Asquith . . .: ibid.

Her beauty, Cynthia Asquith remembered . . .: Cynthia Asquith, *Remember and Be Glad,* J. Barrie 1952, p. 90

'I understood very little of what he said . . .': Diana Cooper, *The Rainbow Comes and*

Goes, p. 96

Describing Moore as a 'most unusual man . . .': ibid.

In a letter to Raymond Asquith . . .: Philip Ziegler, *Lady Diana Cooper,* p. 62

At 8 Fitzroy Square . . .: ibid., pp. 54–6

She was probably the only virgin there . . .': ibid., p. 56

'My brother John . . .': Philip Ziegler, *Lady Diana Cooper,* p. 61

'To get my brother . . .': Diana Cooper, *The Rainbow Comes and Goes,* p. 144

Chapter 46

At her mother's insistence . . .: Violet to Diana, various letters, October 1914–January 1915, MR

Among them, as Diana recalled . . .: Diana Cooper, *The Rainbow Comes and Goes,* Rupert Hart-Davis 1958, p. 96

. . . and he gave her jewels: Philip Ziegler, *Lady Diana Cooper,* Hamish Hamilton 1981, p. 63

'I was very young . . .': ibid., p. 62

Nicknamed the Dances of Death . . .: Diana Cooper, *The Rainbow Comes and Goes,* pp. 142–4

'Parents were excluded . . .': ibid., p. 143

'The parties were the delight . . .': ibid., p. 144

Mindful that her brother's life . . .: Philip

Ziegler, *Lady Diana Cooper,* p. 63

'I wanted to leave . . .': Diana Cooper, *The Rainbow Comes and Goes,* p. 144

The thirty-minute service . . .: ibid., p. 122

Despite the strict discipline . . .: Philip Ziegler, *Lady Diana Cooper,* pp. 49–50

'I was given . . .': Diana Cooper, *The Rainbow Comes and Goes,* pp. 122–3

Her conduct sheet was immaculate . . .: Philip Ziegler, *Lady Diana Cooper,* pp. 49–50

'I was moved after a few months . . .': Diana Cooper, *The Rainbow Comes and Goes,* p. 131

'I had earned the hard name . . .': ibid., p. 95

'On the whole my own impression . . .': Philip Ziegler, *Lady Diana Cooper,* p. 64

'I can't understand . . .': ibid.

'The Commander-in-Chief . . .': Diana Cooper, *The Rainbow Comes and Goes,* p. 146

Out in France . . .: Alan Clark, *The Donkeys,* Hutchinson 1961, p. 39

'Water is the great . . .': Lyn Macdonald, *1915,* Headline 1994, p. 18

Chapter 47

A short distance . . .: Richard Holmes, *The Little Field Marshal,* Cassell 2005, p. 255

'The spider in his web . . .': ibid., p. 121

His mood was euphoric . . .: Letters to

Winifred Bennett, Imperial War Museum

'Winter in the trenches . . .': Lyn Macdonald, *1915,* Headline 1994

Nowhere had . . .: ibid.

The front along which . . .: ibid.

Using spotter planes . . .: Alan Clark, *The Donkeys,* Hutchinson 1961, pp. 48–9

Against this flimsy barrier . . .: ibid.

If Neuve Chapelle . . . : Lyn Macdonald, *1915*

Sir John had spent . . . : Letters to Winifred Bennett, Imperial War Museum

'I've just come back from . . .': ibid.

Sir John's self-belief . . . : George H. Cassar, *The Tragedy of Sir John French,* University of Delaware Press 1985

On the morning of 9 March . . . : Letters to Winifred Bennett, Imperial War Museum

We are now about to attack . . . : Lyn Macdonald, *1915,* pp. 112–13

'It is a solemn thought . . .': Esher War Journal, 9 March 1915, Churchill College, Cambridge

'Trust me to see that he is all right . . .': Sir John French to Violet, February 1915, MR

The previous week . . . : Sir John's war diary, Imperial War Museum

'I explained to him . . .': ibid.

Darling, I must finish . . . : Letters to Winifred Bennett, Imperial War Museum

To avoid the risk . . . : Lyn Macdonald, *1915,* p. 82

There, bivouacked . . . : Alan Clark, *The

Donkeys, p. 50

Charles Tennant . . . : Lyn Macdonald, *1915,* p. 91

'Snow swept down on us . . .': ibid.

'We were Territorials . . .': ibid., pp. 89–90

'We put up climbing ladders . . .': ibid., p. 102

'When dawn came . . .': ibid., p. 92

At 7.30 punctually . . . : ibid.

'The bombardment started . . .': ibid., p. 93

'Through all the bombardment . . .': ibid.

In the run-up . . . : Alan Clark, *The Donkeys,* pp. 50–51

As the weeks passed . . . : Lyn Macdonald, *1915,* pp. 84–6

It was only on . . . : ibid.

The 2nd Middlesex led . . . : Alan Clark, *The Donkeys,* p. 55

Chapter 48

He was driving . . . : John to Charlie, 15 March 1915, MR

It was seven o'clock . . . : ibid.

In the two weeks . . . : ibid.

For three days . . . : 137 Brigade war diary, National Archives, WO 95/2683

'I suppose people would say . . .': John to his sister Marjorie, 14 March 1915, private collection

'The way the Staff Officers . . .': ibid.

Officers and other ranks were segregated . . .

: Paul Fussell, *The Great War,* OUP 2000

Twenty-one divisions . . . : Roy Westlake, *British Battalions on the Western Front,* Leo Cooper, 2001

In the two weeks that John . . . : John's war diary

The châteaux John slept in . . . : ibid.

His empathy with the living conditions . . . : John to his family, various letters, February/ March 1915, MR

Fortnum's offered . . . : Fortnum & Mason Christmas Catalogue for the Expeditionary Force, 1914

1 1/4 pounds fresh meat . . . : *Derbyshire Times,* 28 August 1914

In the trenches . . . : Paul Fussell, *The Great War,* p. 49

'I am very comfortable . . .': John to his sister, Marjorie, n.d., private collection

'They might as well . . .': ibid., 14 March 1915

Chapter 49

'I am very sad . . .': Letter to Winifred Bennett, 13 March 1915, Imperial War Museum

After spending . . . : ibid., 14 March 1915

There, they saw . . . : Diary of Sir John French, Imperial War Museum

Some months earlier . . . : George Moore, unpublished memoir, private collection

The project . . . : Major-General C. H. Foulkes, 'Gas!', Naval and Military Press 2009

Foulkes, a charismatic . . . : ibid.

Moore wanted John . . . : Charlie to John, various letters, March–April 1915, MR

In mid-February . . . : Sir John French to Violet, February 1915, MR

That morning . . . : Violet to Charlie, various letters, March 1915, MR

I went in to St Omer . . . : Diary of Sir John French, Imperial War Museum

I motored GM . . . : Sir John French to Winifred Bennett, 14/15 March 1915

So shaken . . . : John's war diary

Chapter 50

The division had been . . . : 46th North Midland Battalion and Brigade war diaries, WO 95 2662/2663/2683

They were three miles . . . : Captain J. D. Hills, *The Fifth Leicestershire,* Naval and Military Press 2002

Outside the North Midlands headquarters . . . : John to Charlie, 15 March 1915, MR

It was shortly after . . . : John's war diary

Stuart Wortley read . . . : John to Charlie, 15 March 1915, MR

John had barely skimmed . . . : ibid.

A few minutes later . . . : John to Charlie, 16

March 1915, MR

John shared . . . John to Charlie, various letters, January–February 1915, MR

The next morning . . . : John to his sister, Marjorie, n.d., private collection

Since John's arrival at the Front . . . : Letters to John from Charlie, Violet and the Duke, February–March 1915, MR

Chapter 51

Early the next morning . . . : Charlie to John, 25 March 1915, MR

'Your boy's failed me . . .': ibid.

The drawing room . . . : Charlie to John, May 1914, MR

John's refusal . . . : Charlie to John, 25 March 1915, MR

But, before proceeding . . . : Charlie to John, 16 March 1915, MR

'Find out why . . .': ibid.

Depending on the answers . . . : The Duke to Edward Stuart Wortley, 18 March 1915, MR

Two days later . . . : Note, Violet to Charlie, MR

Chapter 52

Shortly before 7.30 p.m. . . . : Note, Violet to Charlie, MR

It was a wet, blustery evening . . . : *The Times,*

26 March 1915
Well into her eighties . . . : Various references,
  MR
Earlier that day . . . : Note, Violet to Charlie,
  MR, 25 March 1918; Violet to Charlie, 18
  March 1915, MR
Lady Holford had opened . . . : ibid.
At the appointed hour . . . : George Moore,
  unpublished memoir, private collection
To ensure their conversation . . . : This is not
  documented, but it is reasonable to assume
  that they would not have wanted the foot-
  men to hear the conversation that followed.
  In extremis, the practice of the day was to
  dismiss the footmen after dinner was
  served.
While Violet had convened . . . : Inferred
  from Violet's note of meeting, MR. A scrap
  of paper: '1. GHQ — too many titled officers. 2. Sir J — spurned/reissue? 3. J? How?'
In tackling . . . : Charlie to John, 25 March
  1915, MR

Chapter 53

In March 1915 . . . : G. E. Cockayne, *The
  Complete Peerage,* Vol. VIII
Her bedroom at Arlington Street . . . : Violet
  to Charlie, March 1915, MR
The previous October . . . : Violet to Charlie,
  18 October 1915
Determined to stop her . . . : At the time,

Violet and Diana were trying to set up a hospital at Hardelot in France. However, the project had run into problems. Anticipating that it would fail, the Arlington Street Hospital was Violet's fallback. But it was not until the following year that it became operational.

Other dukes . . . : Chatsworth archives; Lost Hospitals of London (website); Wikipedia

He thought it would be 'knocked about' . . . : Henry to Violet, n.d., MR

Violet, who had had several lovers . . . : Besides her long affair with Harry Cust, which began in the 1880s and continued until well into the 1900s, Violet also had an affair with Montagu Correy, Disraeli's private secretary, who was thought to be the father of her second daughter, Letty.

Later that day, Henry watched . . . : Marjorie to John, private collection

Chapter 55

At General Headquarters . . . : The full extent of Sir John's troubles that spring and early summer was reported in *The New York Times* in a long article published on 4 July 1915

'I have more trouble . . .': Sir John to Winifred Bennett, Imperial War Museum

'We had not sufficient . . .': *The Times*, 14 May 1915

The finger of blame . . . : Richard Holmes, *The Little Field Marshal,* Cassell 2005, pp. 288–91

The scandal served . . . : *The New York Times,* 4 July 1915

'The impression . . .': ibid.

'The absence of any . . .': ibid.

The fact of the matter . . . : ibid.

It was his War Office file . . . : National Archives, WO 374/28523

It was only when I read the war diary . . . : National Archives, WO 95/2670

Chapter 56

According to Colonel Beevor's . . . : National Archives, WO 95/2670

19 July, 7.30 am . . . : ibid.

We marched back . . . : Captain J. D. Hills, *The Fifth Leicestershire,* Naval and Military Press 2002, p. 45

The weather throughout . . . : ibid., p. 47

'I dined with Marjorie Anglesey . . .': Duff Cooper's diary, private collection

The above-named officer . . . : National Archives, WO 374/2852

Very quickly . . . : National Archives, WO 374/2852

Among them was a letter . . . : For reasons unknown, Lady Mildred's letter to John was included among Violet's papers in the trunk of her correspondence that John was working on when he died

'Darling C,' she wrote . . . : Again, for reasons unknown, this letter to Charlie from Violet — and the two that follow — was among her gold-dusted letters. Whether Charlie had returned them to her, or whether she had made copies, we cannot know

The 'resounding room' . . . : Violet told Charlie that the room was in the 'old offices'. This was where the Duke's land agent and his team had worked. These rooms became the Muniment Rooms.

The report also shows . . . : National Archives, WO 374/2852

I have this day seen and examined . . . : ibid.

Between 5 December 1915 and . . . : ibid.

While he had been abetted . . . : *Shot at Dawn* (website)

Chapter 58

She had 'golden-brown eyes' . . . : Cynthia Asquith, *Remember and Be Glad,* J. Barrie 1952, p. 90

'I don't think I'll ever . . .': John to Marjorie, 28 May 1914, private collection

Twice, in the eighteen months . . . : Violet's letters to Charlie and others, November 1912–May 1914, MR

He broke off the engagement . . . : Rosemary Leveson-Gower to John, various letters, November 1912–May 1914, MR

Chapter 59

The wedding was organized by Violet and . . . : Mrs Annie Tennant to John, January 1916, MR

The bride, who was given away . . . : *The Times*, 28 January 1916

The newspaper also listed . . . : ibid.

Chapter 60

Some 1,500 members of the aristocracy . . . : Gerald Gliddon, *The Aristocracy and the Great War*, Gliddon Books 2002, p. xiii

It seems fitting . . . : Information taken from the war memorials in the villages on the Belvoir estate

Epilogue

'Talking of Kakoo's second baby . . .': Cynthia Asquith, *Diaries 1915–1918*, Hutchinson 1968

One with the children's nanny . . . : *Burke's Peerage*, 107th edition

Thirteen thousand three hundred . . . : Sales catalogue, MR

George Gordon Moore . . . : *The World*, January 1916

On his return to America . . . : Letter, Rothesay Stuart Wortley to John, February 1916, MR

A celebrated breeder . . . : *Carmel* Magazine, spring issue, 2007

His 'Great Friend' . . . : Richard Holmes, *The Little Field Marshal,* Cassell 2005, pp. 362–6

He died there in May 1925 . . . : ibid.

'She was the one . . .': in the wider Manners family, Henry's half-brother, Lt.-Col. Robert Manners, also served with distinction. The Commanding Officer of the 10th Northumberland Fusiliers, he was killed in action in France in September 1917

'That awful Duff . . .': Philip Ziegler, *Lady Diana Cooper,* Hamish Hamilton 1981, p. 104

When Violet first learned . . . : ibid., pp. 102–3

Cassell's Saturday Journal . . . : ibid., p. 104

Diana's old admirers . . . : ibid., p. 105

Soon after their wedding . . . : ibid., p. 129

When Henry died . . . : Diana Cooper, *Autobiography,* Faber Finds 2008, p. 290

'With the huge nest-egg . . .': ibid., p. 346

Her days were spent . . . : ibid., pp. 346–7

'The Hatley brocade curtains . . .': ibid.

In the last week of her life . . . : ibid., p. 453

'I stayed with her . . .': ibid.

ACKNOWLEDGEMENTS

My first and greatest debt is to the Duke and
Duchess of Rutland for allowing me access
to the Muniment Rooms at Belvoir Castle,
and for their unstinting help and support. I
am also indebted to the descendants of previous generations of the family that I spoke to,
many of whom showed me letters, photographs and diaries without which it would
have been impossible to shed light on particular episodes in the book. I would especially
like to thank the Marquis of Anglesey, who
kindly allowed me to see the large collection
of private family letters at Plas Newydd; the
Earl of Wemyss, who found the long letter
Violet wrote to Mary, Countess of Wemyss,
after Haddon died; and Viscount Norwich,
whose help has been invaluable. Besides
showing me his father's unpublished diaries,
and a notebook that Violet kept in the early
years of the First World War, I would like to
thank him for his generous permission to
quote extensively from *The Rainbow Comes*

and Goes — the first volume of his mother's wonderful memoirs.

I would also like to thank Lord Roger Manners, John's youngest son, for his recollections of his childhood at Belvoir, and his memories of his father.

I am grateful to the staff of the following libraries and archives for their assistance: the British Library, the Imperial War Museum, the Royal Archives at Windsor Castle, the London Library, the National Archives, the Bodleian Library, the British Newspaper Library, Leicestershire Record Office, Churchill College Library, Derbyshire Record Office, Eton College Library, Hertfordshire Record Office, and the Liddell Hart Centre for Military Archives.

The letters in the Muniment Rooms run to many tens of thousands, and it would have been impossible to get to grips with them without the help of the Duke of Rutland's archivist, John Granger — and, more recently, Peter Foden. His work in tracking down particular documents and answering innumerable questions has been tireless, and his knowledge of the pre-twentieth-century history of the Belvoir estate indispensable. I am also grateful to Marion Wood for her help in the early stages of my research. Thanks are also due to Sallyann Jackson, the former House Coordinator at Belvoir; to Harvey Proctor, Private Secretary to the Duke of

Rutland; and to Phil O'Brien, who, throughout the writing of the book, has been my point of contact at the castle. I am grateful to him for his encouragement and forbearance.

By its very nature, so much of this book has been a collaborative effort. I would like to thank my editor, Eleo Gordon, for her unflagging support and her suggestions over the many drafts of the manuscript, and my agent, Georgina Capel, for all her wonderful support. I would also like to thank George Davies for his painstaking work in deciphering John's letters from Rome, and Dr Christian Carritt for her help in looking into the medical aspects of Haddon's accident. Undergraduates Pippa Bregazzi, Alexander Hill, Lotte Murphy Johnson and Jack Owen have been brilliant at tracking down documents at the Imperial War Museum and in other archives. Anne Carnt, William Eccles, and Lea Sellers read the manuscript in its entirety and offered invaluable suggestions. I am also grateful to Sarah Day, and Keith Taylor at Penguin, for their meticulous care during the final stages of editing.

It is impossible to reach the end of a large undertaking like this without realizing how lucky I have been in the support of my friends and family. Over the past couple of years, I have sought refuge at Combe and for that I have to thank Alexandra Henderson and her family for their hospitality — and Audrey

Grimsey for keeping an eye on me. Patrick Forbes, Jasper McMahon, and William Sieghart were a never-ending source of encouragement to me when the book appeared to stall, and suggested alternative avenues of research and different approaches to particular aspects of the story. I owe them a huge debt. I would also like to thank those who were at pains to remind me that there was life beyond the Muniment Rooms at Belvoir, and who made the difficult moments bearable: Dorothy Cory-Wright, Sarah Cole, Martin Bailey, the Farman family, Sara Tibbetts, Konrad Gabriel, Christopher Kemp, Daniel Rosen, Rupert Bondy and Martyn Johnson.

Lastly, I would like to thank my mother, Carol. Without her help in deciphering and typing out the many thousands of letters I found in the Muniment Rooms, and the many hours spent discussing them, the book would have been even longer in gestation. It is dedicated to her with love and thanks.

ABOUT THE AUTHOR

Catherine Bailey read history at Oxford University and is an award-winning television producer and director, making a range of critically acclaimed documentary films inspired by her interest in twentieth-century history. She lives in West London.